Black Voices
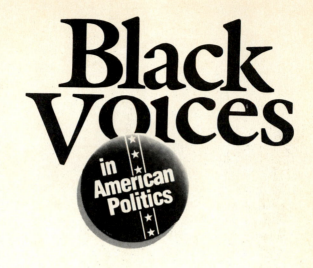
in American Politics

Black Voices

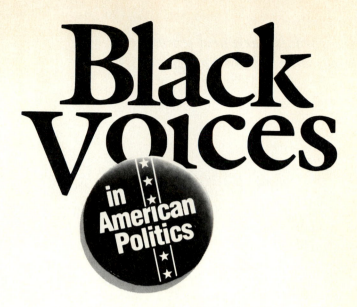

in American Politics

Jeffrey M. Elliot
North Carolina Central University

Harcourt Brace Jovanovich, Publishers

San Diego New York Chicago Atlanta Washington, D.C.
London Sydney Toronto

To My Father
For his words, spoken and unspoken,
this book, with love and gratitude.

ISBN: 0-15-505500-3

Library of Congress Catalog Card Number: 84-81485

Printed in the United States of America

Preface

You start a question, and it's like starting a stone. You sit quietly on the top of the hill; and away the stone goes, starting others.
Robert Louis Stevenson

The purpose of this collection is to explore, in their fullness and depth, the words and deeds of twenty-four prominent black political leaders—men and women who have been and continue to be at the cutting edge of the struggle for equal justice. My intent in these interviews is not to question their motivations or to discredit their actions. That approach is both absurd and inappropriate. Instead, I have chosen to ask questions that demand frank and forthright responses—questions the reader deserves to have answered. These interviews differ markedly from those published in such periodicals as the *National Enquirer* or *People* magazine. I do not view my role as that of a journalistic voyeur; for that reason, I consciously eschew such popular topics as sex, drugs, idiosyncrasies, and money. These interviews are not intended to titillate; they are intended to inform. However, no subject was viewed as taboo. The interviewees asked no quarter and received none. None of the subjects saw the questions in advance of the interview. And no interviewees made any attempt to influence the direction of the interview or to dictate the final outcome.

This volume does not pretend to include every major black political leader. No single volume could make such a claim. Instead, it brings together a wide variety of individuals—men and women of diverse points of view, ranging from elected and appointed officials, to heads of national organizations, to well-known citizen-activists. In selecting my subjects, I considered a wide range of factors: position, background, geography, philosophy, achievement, and interest. I began with a list of over 125 potential subjects. I contacted each individual and asked if he or she would be amenable to a personal interview. Advance discussions were held with many of the respondents to establish the ground rules.

Based on these responses and my subsequent conversations, I selected twenty-four individuals who, I felt, would best represent the richness and diversity of black America.

Once I had settled upon the final list, I contacted each of the subjects and set up a personal interview. At this point, my work had just begun. In preparation for each interview, I painstakingly read everything I could find about the person. I consulted numerous reference works, academic textbooks, popular publications, official documents, and other materials that could provide grist for the mill. In many cases, I scoured dozens of libraries, reading hundreds of articles, speeches, essays, biographies, autobiographies, and sundry other materials by and about the subject. I contacted the interviewee's admirers and detractors and questioned them at length about the person. Once this phase was completed, I compiled a list of approximately 150 questions that would compose the basis of the interview.

The work itself was a labor of love—a personal tribute to the triumphs of twenty-four uncommon men and women—individuals who have pledged their lives to a struggle that transcends their personal welfare. In each case, the interviewees have made a significant contribution. They have left their mark upon the political fabric of the nation. In doing so, they have left behind a solid legacy, one that observers can examine and debate.

In conclusion, I wish to express my sincere thanks to those individuals who have contributed to this book. My greatest debt is to the interviewees. Their willingness to be interviewed—often for many hours and/or days—made this work possible.

I also wish to note the support and encouragement of Joseph R. Aicher, Jr., chairperson of the political science department at North Carolina Central University, who helped to formulate many of the questions for the interviews with Richard C. Erwin, Julius L. Chambers, and Harvey B. Gantt and who actively participated in those sessions.

The book owes much to my adroit research team—Dante Noto, Marion V. McKinney, Jr., and James S. Guitard—who spent myriad hours in the library and who unearthed countless resource materials. I owe a special debt of gratitude to Dante Noto, who also proofread the manuscript, transcribed several of the interviews, and offered many helpful suggestions.

Finally, I am deeply grateful to Drake Bush, my editor at Harcourt Brace Jovanovich, who had the initial faith in the idea and encouraged me throughout the project. His counsel and assistance proved invaluable. I also wish to extend thanks to Gene Carter Lettau, my manuscript editor, and Ruth Cornell, my production editor, who had the unenviable task of maintaining editorial consistency between two covers. They did a peerless job. Kim Turner, the production manager, efficiently and expeditiously saw the book through the various stages of production. Art editor Tricia Griffith skillfully supervised the selection of the photographs. And designer Dean Reed applied his creative talent to intergrate the whole—type and graphics—into a result that captures in visual form the spirit and intent of the volume. For their efforts, I am deeply indebted and most appreciative.

JEFFREY M. ELLIOT

Contents

Foreword

Black politics, as an academic area of political science, is evolving slowly for several reasons. First, the very basis of black politics, the black electorate, was, until the 1965 Voting Rights Act, severely restricted at the polls. Second, those individuals who had been elected to represent the black community—namely, black elected officials—were few in number prior to the 1965 Voting Rights Act. Third, as Professor Emmett E. Dorsey, the late chairman of the department of political science at Howard University, often said: "Negro politics" (as it was called as late as the mid-1960s) was long considered an "offbeat field of political science," an academic graveyard for the young scholar who sought academic respectability and an opportunity to rise to the forefront of the discipline. At best, it was viewed as an occasionally interesting subject—an intellectual toy that one might tinker with from time to time. But since it, like black people, was looked down upon by society and, therefore, academia, one could not afford to devote extensive time, effort, and attention to the subject in any sustained and consistent fashion.

Sadly, Professor Dorsey's insights and observations are as profound and prophetic today as they were in 1964 when he made them. Many political scientists still dabble in black politics. They pen quick and hasty articles but basically view black politics as a sideline, one that is of peripheral personal interest. With an article or two under their academic belts, these fly-by-night experts quickly move on to their real interests, in Congress, elitist democracy, voting behavior, the judicial process, or, perhaps, crime. Black politics is not, as they view it, a subject worthy of sustained interest and reflection. Thus, with a quilt of scholarly patchwork studies, the field cannot help but proceed slowly.

In addition, many academicians eschew black politics as a serious field of study and cite the negative manner in which the news media cover the subject. Indeed, the press delights in harpooning black elected officials and their efforts and holds them up to derision, ridicule, and humor. These officials are depicted as crooks, clowns, buffoons, and pleaders—individuals who feed at the public trough and bleed the public coffers of scarce resources. All too often, black officials are portrayed as welfare seekers, social schemers, and advocates of costly government giveaway programs that inevitably lead to double-digit inflation, record budget deficits, and crippling taxation. In the end, these officials are personally responsible, according to the news media, for retarding growth, progress, and prosperity in American society.

In this atmosphere of negative press, many academicians are quick to link their prestige and credentials to words supporting and promoting this popular mood and consciousness. Other scholars quietly find some new field to probe, analyze, and write about. In either case, the net result is the same: the denigration of black politics and reduced interest in this emerging area.

In his distinctive work, *Black Voices in American Politics*, Professor Jeffrey M. Elliot defies this popular trend and strikes back at this disciplinary conformity. In doing so, Elliot has devoted Herculean effort, driving energy, unrelenting hard work, and intellectual vigor to a subject long considered off the beaten track, to a point where it confronts and challenges what I will call the "judgmental" consciousness of the discipline.

In undertaking this work, Professor Elliot interviewed—often for many hours and/or days—twenty-four prominent black political leaders, ranging from elected officials, to heads of national organizations, to civil rights activists. That was no mean feat, and the care and dedication Elliot brought to the project shine brightly on page after page. All in all, Professor Elliot's seminal work will stand to embarrass those who, in the future, simply wish to dabble and tinker in the area.

This volume is, in every sense, a ground-breaking work. It explores, with passion and force, the engines of black politics—namely, the leaders themselves—and allows them an opportunity to express themselves on the great issues of the day. Sadly, in the mid-1980s, black elected officials, who live and work in the midst of the greatest communications revolution in the history of humankind, are truly without a forum. The news media rarely, if ever, solicit their views and opinions and relegate them to the back burner of public opinion. At the same time, today's opinion makers bemoan the lack of creative solutions to society's age-old problems. With the exception of a handful of black talk shows, most of them local, and the black press, black elected officials are seldom invited to hold court on such major national programs as *Face the Nation, ABC News Nightline, 60 Minutes,* and *Freeman Reports.* No major magazine or national newspaper's Sunday supplement solicits their opinions or seeks their views.

Professor Elliot succeeds in doing what the news media have failed to do—that is, to give expression to the words and deeds of America's black political leaders. And he does so at every level of American political life. At the congressional level, Elliot permits freshmen and senior black congressmen to express their innermost thoughts, while at the executive level he brings the reader face-to-face with former and current black cabinet officers to share their viewpoints and experiences.

From there, Professor Elliot transports the reader to the judicial level, where he plumbs the thoughts and feelings of high-ranking black judges, and later to the national headquarters of major civil rights organizations, where he encourages those leaders to voice their views and opinions. In the latter case, Elliot introduces us to the young civil rights warriors, like Benjamin Chavis, as well as to the longtime gladiators like John Jacob.

But Professor Elliot does not rest there. He travels from the national level to the state and local level, where he probes the hopes and aspirations, as well as the trials and tribulations, of black statewide elected officials, black mayors of large and small cities, black officials who are out of power and those who seek power, and black state legislators.

Professor Elliot has captured—for both the present and the future—the words and deeds of two dozen of America's most celebrated black political leaders. In doing so, he has provided these leaders with a prestigious forum for the presentation of proposals and counterproposals that have all too frequently been ignored in the political marketplace of ideas. The responses he elicits from his subjects are rich in promise and opportunity; they suggest policy options that are both hopeful and humane.

This work could not have succeeded were it not for Professor Elliot's masterly interviewing skills. Professor Elliot *knows* his subject; his questions are far-ranging, incisive, designed to reveal the interviewee's thoughts and feelings. Above all, Elliot's lively mind sees black politics in a wider context of history, which can only enrich this area and the surrounding territory of American politics. These interviews will surely provide a valuable record for the future.

The diversity of ideas, the latitude of the discussion, and the lively and provocative nature of the questions and answers are impressive. Although each interview mines an important theme, each also—however different in content and tone—relates organically to the others.

This work raises a plethora of interesting themes. However, one theme looms particularly large: Reaganomics. Repeatedly, these black leaders assail Reaganomics, arguing that it is both destructive and regressive, and urge Americans to find a more humane way to achieve the same results. These Blacks remind readers that public policy must always be tempered with social justice.

Thus, the moral as well as the political content of this book speaks not only to black Americans, but to *all* Americans. It honestly and courageously raises the right issues, examines them with skill and sensitivity, and affords us all an opportunity to begin anew the quest for freedom and justice. Professor Elliot's book deserves the widest possible audience. From the man in the White House to the man on the street, this work should spark a new national dialogue.

In addition, this volume serves another salient function. It affords black elected officials and black political hopefuls an opportunity to observe firsthand the trials and tribulations of other black public servants, as well as to ponder their victories and successes. Armed with Elliot's book, these aspiring black officials can now come to their positions better prepared and with the hope of achieving greater success.

For political scientists in general and black political scientists in particular, this work is a treasure trove. Surely, today's teachers, students, and researchers will delight in mining the data. Moreover, as an historical document, this volume will be valuable even a hundred years from now. Future generations of historians may well consider Elliot's book a landmark that allowed the black voices in American politics to cry out when so many others would not or could not.

HANES WALTON, JR.
Fuller E. Calloway Professor of
    Political Science
Savannah State College

Black Voices

in American Politics

PART ONE

The Legislative Process

Gus Savage

Power for a Purpose

Gus Savage was born October 30, 1925, in Detroit, Michigan, and moved to Chicago, Illinois, at age five. Reared in abject poverty, Savage resided with four brothers, a sister, mother and father, cousin, and uncle and aunt in a three-room rear apartment at 4212 Cottage Grove, an early 1940s battleline between Blacks and hostile whites in Chicago, which was then one of the most segregated cities in the North. A street-gang leader as a youth, Savage later lived in public, low-income housing (Altgeld Gardens on the far South Side and Ogden Courts on the West Side).

Savage's bitterest taste of racial discrimination occurred in the South while he was serving in the armed services during World War II. Rebellion against this dehumanizing experience, inside and outside of the service, led to his conversion from gambling and violence to Christianity and social concerns before reaching his twenty-first birthday.

Upon discharge from the service, Savage returned to school with a determination to discover the causes of social injustice. He studied history, philosophy, and political economy with a passion. Savage received a Bachelor of Arts degree in philosophy from Roosevelt University in 1950 and pursued a Master of Arts degree in political science at Roosevelt University. He later attended Chicago-Kent College of Law, where he was selected as intercollegiate moot court champion. As his understanding broadened, his commitment deepened— and black liberation became a lifelong mission.

After completing his education, Savage became a newspaper reporter, editor, and publisher. As a journalist, he edited such diverse publications as the *American Negro Magazine*, the *Illinois Beverage Journal*, the *Woodlawn Booster*, the *Southtown Economist*, and the *Bulletin Newspaper*. At present, he writes a syndicated column, which appears in black newspapers across the country, and is a radio interviewer-commentator on a local Chicago station.

Savage was elected to the United States House of Representatives in 1980, after two previous unsuccessful attempts in 1968 and 1970. He was re-elected in 1982 (and 1984) by an overwhelming margin (though he had never held public office before) after surviving Democratic primary opposition from the party-endorsed candidates, white-owned daily newspapers, and white liberal voter organizations. No previous black or white independent candidate had won Chicago's "machine" Democratic primary without the strong endorsement of these groups.

Savage boasts a lifelong commitment to the civil rights movement. He led housing demonstrations for veterans; organized sit-in demonstrations and informational picketing to win the right of Blacks to be hired as department store clerks and to be served in restaurants in downtown Chicago; organized and demonstrated to win the right of Blacks to live in Lake Meadows (a middle income housing development); led mass demonstrations in Washington Park's open air public forum where he developed his oratorical and debating skills; organized Chicago protests against the Emmett Till lynching, including picketing of the White House by ministers; led marches for black economic and political representation and empowerment on Chicago's West Side; "Marched Against Fear" with Dr. Martin Luther King, Jr. and Stokeley Carmichael in Mississippi; sponsored and organized the Chicago contingent at the Resurrection City protests in Washington, D.C., in memory of Dr. King; was jailed for defending black contract home buyers; visited Africa where he denounced the Reagan Administration's foreign policy; and led a mass march of 200,000 demonstrators for world disarmament in Lisbon, Portugal.

Since his election to Congress in 1980, Savage has sponsored legislation to memorialize Joe Louis, the former heavyweight boxing champion; introduced a bill to provide public transportation fare to aid job-seekers; co-sponsored a measure to extend youth training and employment programs to include remedial education; co-sponsored and led the floor debate for the extension of the Voting Rights Act; sponsored legislation to curb home mortgage foreclosures in communities with high unemployment; co-sponsored a resolution to indicate opposition to President Reagan's lifting of controls on domestic oil prior to the previously set expiration date; co-sponsored a resolution to voice the sentiment of the House against the elimination of the $122 minimum for Social Security beneficiaries; co-sponsored a resolution to eliminate invitations to South African officials to visit the United States until apartheid is terminated; and co-sponsored a bill to prohibit arms sales or credits to El Salvador.

Savage's efforts on behalf of poor people and minorities have won him numerous honors and awards, including: the Award of Merit (for heroism in risking his life to help save hostages in a currency exchange robbery)—Operation PUSH; the City of Chicago Medal of Merit (highest official award)—Chicago City Council; the Merit Award for Best Columnist—National Newspaper Publishers Association; the Man of the Year Award (as freshman congressman)—Evanston, Illinois NAACP; the Freshman Congressman of the Year Award—Maryland State Conference of NAACP; the Achiever of the Year Award—Chicago South Chamber of Commerce; and *Ebony Magazine* named him one of the "One Hundred Most Influential Black Americans."

JE: As a member of Congress, do you view yourself more as a spokesman for black America or a spokesman for the voters of Chicago's Second District?

GS: First, I want to set the record straight. I don't just represent Blacks in my district. I represent *Americans*: Blacks, whites, Hispanics, and others. And I would represent their interests whether or not they lived in my district. Many whites falsely assume, for example, that because I have a black face, I can only represent black voters. That's nonsense! When Reverend Jesse Jackson ran for President in 1984, he was described as a "black candidate." However, when Senator Alan Cranston (D-Calif.) announced his candidacy, no one described him as a "white candidate." The press never describes a white candidate as "a white candidate." It's only when a Black runs that the press describes him that way. Again, it's a double standard—part and parcel of America's racist mentality.

Back to your question: Take an issue like jobs. That issue affects both Blacks and Hispanics. When I speak out on the jobs issue, I'm not only representing the interests of those Blacks and Hispanics who live in my district, but the interests of Blacks and Hispanics everywhere. The jobs issue is not limited to my district; my interests don't stop at the boundaries of my district. They encompass the entire nation. Likewise, if I speak out for world peace, it's not just peace for Blacks in the Second District—that would be ridiculous!—but peace for the entire nation and world.

My interests are not limited to Blacks. They span the peoples of the world. My primary constituency, however, is the disadvantaged, whatever their color may be. And since Blacks are the most disadvantaged group in America, my efforts appear to relate most directly to this group. But my interests go well beyond Blacks. I fight for principles that are universal. My goals are peace and freedom—for all people. When I fight for justice in the Middle East, it's not for Blacks. After all, the Palestinians are white. No, I fight for justice—I am a drum major for justice.

JE: Why did you run for Congress? What appeal did it hold?

GS: My motive for running for Congress was identical to my motive for going into journalism. I didn't go into journalism because I was interested in becoming a good journalist. I knew I would be good at whatever I did. To understand Gus Savage, you have to understand my past. Who and what I am today is the direct result of the forces which shaped me.

I grew up in Chicago in the 1930s and 1940s. We lived in a rough neighborhood—a poor neighborhood. Discrimination was a fact of life. You could see it on every street corner. Segregation defined my world. In fact, I lived in a neighborhood in which one side of the street was all black (with the exception of one white kid) and the other side was all white. I had to fight the white kids to swim in the lake. I fought every white kid who crossed my path. Back then, whites viewed Blacks as inferior. We were inherently unequal. But something in me rejected that notion. I couldn't relate to whites. In school, all of my teachers, with one exception, were white. And they taught from a white perspective— that is, everything that was European was good. Their teachings reflected that mind-set. For example, when we studied music, we studied European music. On the other hand, African music was viewed as inferior. And that bothered the hell out of me.

I started high school when I was twelve. I was a bright kid. However, I had so many fights that it took me an extra year to complete high school. The whites turned me into a little monster. But, I don't blame them; they didn't know any better. There was no way they could have known. Their mind-set really got to me. I wanted to know what the hell was wrong. Why didn't the whites treat me right? Why did those white folks treat me the way they did? So, I wanted some answers. I wanted to understand the world around me. I wanted to know why I was always dumped on. Had I even wanted to fit in, they wouldn't have let me. However, I don't think I really would have conformed even if that had been possible. I've always been different. Unlike most kids, I didn't go to college to earn a living. I didn't view college as a vocational school. I went there seeking answers to questions. Although the college required 120 credits for graduation, I took over 150 credits. I wasn't particularly anxious to graduate. I wanted to learn everything I could.

As I grew up—and traveled beyond the ghetto in which I was raised—my outlook broadened. I attended college with whites. I used to follow them home to see how they lived and what books they had on their shelves. And that made me wonder more. I wanted more answers. I was particularly intrigued by the wealthy whites. I was amazed that there were people who lived that way. I could never understand why some people seemed to have everything, while others had nothing. It had nothing to do with race. I was fascinated by the discrepancies.

My world view continued to expand in the armed services. I served in World War II. Back then, they sent Blacks from the South to the North and Blacks from the North to the South in order to acclimate us to Jim Crow. I began to think about war. Why do people kill one another? Why can't nations get along? Why is it so difficult to live in peace? I was full of questions.

When I left the service, I went back home. I couldn't help but notice the pain around me. I would see a friend—a bright kid— carted off to jail. And I would ask, Why? Why couldn't he make it? Where did life fail him? I'd spend hours questioning the world around me. I was tormented by questions. I couldn't understand what went wrong. Why couldn't Blacks and whites live together as brothers? What was so bad about being black? What had I done to cause such hatred?

My head was spinning with questions. I read everything I could get my hands on. I became quite a student. I didn't just read what the teachers assigned, but I read every book I could find on the subject. I read to find answers. And the more I read, the more questions I had. It was an unending process. After a while, I became consumed with reading. Each new book raised a new question. And each question led to another question. I was a junkie. I couldn't stop. I had to find out who I was—and why people acted as they did.

And so I became a radical. I suppose I still am. I realized that I didn't have to accept the world as it was. I could change it—or at least try. I realized that people didn't have to go to sleep hungry, that people didn't have to kill each other, that love was more powerful than hate. There had to be a way, I thought, for people to live together in peace. I was determined to change the world around me. At times, I was consumed with pain, so much so that life didn't seem worth living. But I'd always come back to the thought: It doesn't have to be this way. Maybe things can change. Maybe you can *make* them change. But I knew that one person couldn't change the world—that it would take an army of concerned people. At first, I tried to solve the world's problems myself. But I knew that wasn't enough. I knew that violence wasn't the answer. I had had plenty of fights. I had fought over the least little thing. But I wanted to change. So I started doing things that would contribute to that end.

I became involved with the school newspaper. I didn't receive any pay, but that didn't matter. I wanted to write something that might contribute to people's understanding of what I thought and felt. Later, that experience led me to try writing on a professional basis. But it was all accidental. I never set out to become a writer. I was drawn to writing for two reasons: First, it gave me a way to express myself. I thought that, based on my experiences, I could make a contribution. Second, I discovered, much later on, that writing could help to broaden my understanding of the world around me.

The more I wrote, the more I liked writing. And when I became an editor and publisher, I discovered that I could make an even greater contribution. I could use writing as a forum from which to achieve other objectives. Writing gave expression to my activism. It became a tool for self-expression. I never wrote for the sake of writing. I wrote for impact, for social change.

Later, I ran for Congress for the same reasons. I never viewed politics as a career. I never saw Congress as the crowning achievement of my life. Rather, I saw it as an opportunity—a vehicle to effect change. Had I viewed Congress as a career, I would have gone, hat in hand, to the Chicago Democratic machine and asked for their endorsement. In truth, I was the only Democratic incumbent in Congress who refused to appear before the Democratic Party and ask to be slated. They invited me, but I declined. I'm not a fool. I know what it takes to stay in Congress. I view Congress as part of an ongoing process—the same process that led me to refuse to be slated and to wage an independent fight for re-election. I value my independence. And I view struggle as desirable. I don't crave acceptance. I march to my own tune. If the machine doesn't like it, that's tough. If my colleagues don't like it, that's also tough. I don't buy Sam Rayburn's dictum: "To get along, go along." I didn't run for Congress for personal aggrandizement. I ran to help people. That's my goal.

JE: Did you come to Congress with any illusions about the institution or the process? If so, what?

GS: No. In fact, my first year in Congress I led a picket line around the White House. I was the first member since Adam Clayton Powell (D-N.Y.) to take such an action. Most members, after being elected, view themselves as part of the institution. They would never lead a protest against the institution. I went even further. I voted against my own party's budget the first year I arrived. I thought it was too lopsided in terms of defense—at the expense of domestic programs. This action cost me several friends in the House as well as the support of the Speaker. I did what I did because I thought it was right. I had nothing to lose. I didn't give a damn what the Speaker thought of me. And I still don't.

JE: Don't such actions hamper your effectiveness? Aren't they counterproductive in the long run?

GS: It depends on how you define "effectiveness." If by effectiveness you mean that it prevents me from convincing one or two white folks in Congress to support one of my bills, then I suppose you're right. But I don't give a damn. For example, I went to Europe and spoke at a radical peace conference. When I came back, the press ripped me apart, calling me a "leftist" and so forth. That didn't bother me. I expected it.

If you look at the role and duties of a congressman in the narrow sense—as basically legislative in nature—then I think you miss the opportunity that being in Congress affords. Being a legislator is only one side of the coin. But there's another side—namely, the ability to serve as an informal mass educator, a mobilizer, and, when necessary, an agitator. As I see it, my job is to galvanize people, to energize people. That's how I view my contribution. For example, I think I was better able to contribute to the Nuclear Freeze campaign outside of Congress than I was as a member. I led 200,000 people in a Nuclear Freeze demonstration in Lisbon, Portugal. That march proved far more significant than my efforts in Congress.

I don't accept the conventional tactics—logrolling, pork barrel, patronage, and so forth. If you view such actions as important, then I suppose my behavior could be described as "counterproductive." But that's not how I measure effectiveness. If those actions were signs of effectiveness, then we wouldn't be in the mess we're now in. The traditional approach has failed. For example, Senator Hubert H. Humphrey (D-Minn.) served in Congress for years. Was he effective? Everybody said he was. But, no, he wasn't effective. The country is in far worse shape today than it was when he was alive. President Johnson is always praised for his effectiveness. Was he effective? Hell, no. If so, how do you explain the Vietnam War, high unemployment, the collapse of the smokestack industries? I think I'm one of the most effective members in Congress. Why? Because I view my role in broader terms. There's far more to being a congressman than being a legislator.

JE: Doesn't your abrasive style, your sharp tongue, undermine your ability to influence the course of legislation?

GS: Look, house members come from 435 different constituencies. Suppose I court a member, take him to lunch, play golf with him, go drinking with him. But his district consists of tens of thousands of white racists in southern Indiana. Do you really think I'm going to convince him to support racial quotas or affirmative action? The problem is bigger than the member. It lies in the people he represents. If you can reach his people, then you can probably convince him. Otherwise, you stand very little chance of changing his mind. He has no reason to change.

However, there's another aspect to the answer. I don't really care what that member thinks about affirmative action or racial quotas. I'm not interested in convincing him. I'm interested in getting him to straighten out. I don't care if he likes me. I don't give a damn what white people think of me. I couldn't care less if they like me. If racial justice hinged on that, then I would have thrown in the towel long ago. No, I'm interested in getting the power to make whites do what they have the power to make me do. To make them say "yes," when they want to say "no." To make them respect me or to kick their behinds.

JE: Speaking of effectiveness, you've been criticized by the *Chicago Sun-Times* for having one of the worst attendance records in Congress. How can you be effective when you're not present?

GS: That's a good example of wrongheaded logic. According to the *Sun-Times*, I have the worst voting record of any member of the Illinois delegation, because I've voted less frequently than other members of the House. Yes, others vote more frequently, but they also more frequently vote wrong. I'm one of the hardest-working, most able, and loyal servants of the people in Washington. I believe that members should be judged more by *how* they vote than merely by the number of times they vote. Some members never miss a vote—they just sit there, like bumps on a log, nodding, and repeatedly voting against jobs, Social Security, equal rights, food programs, and peace.

During the campaign, I announced publicly that I would change my priorities temporarily so as not to become just another old-time politician. I told the voters that they never need fear that I would miss an important vote. I have countless written commendations for my work on committees. I have proposed dozens of bills, including several major ones. Perhaps that is why many Reagan Republicans, old-time machine Democrats, and some white liberals have proposed knocking me out of Congress through redistricting, since they have failed to defeat me at the polls where the people are all-powerful.

JE: If your goal is not to change your colleagues' minds or influence their votes, then what is it? Isn't political persuasion central to your role as an elected representative?

GS: I don't care whether my colleagues change their minds or not on an issue. That doesn't matter. What matters is that they act differently. I don't want them to change their views on anything; they have the right to believe whatever they want. But I want them to straighten up and act right. For example, take slavery. Why did Blacks behave? They behaved because whites had the stick. Well, if I had the stick, it wouldn't be like that. Whites would act right. And I wouldn't treat them the way they treated me. I would treat them the way they *should* have treated me. So, no, I'm not interested in convincing whites to change. That's the wrong approach. We've been trying that ever since the first

Black was elected to Congress. It didn't work then, it doesn't now, and it won't work tomorrow. The key is power. Once Blacks get the stick, they won't have to beg whites to do the right thing. Whites will do right—or else.

Let me give you another example. Suppose you want the Democratic Party to support racial quotas. You can beg party members to support quotas—citing all the right reasons. Or, you can do it another way. You can go to the party leaders and say, "Look, I want you to vote for quotas. If you don't, I will ask my people to stay home in the next election. If I do, the Democratic Party will lose." Now, you see, I didn't persuade the officials in question to support quotas per se. But I made them act on the basis of their own self-interest and respect me in the process. That's what I'm talking about.

And yet another example. I recently led a fight against toxic waste pollution in my district. Despite great protest, the protesters did not meet with much success. As a member of the Public Works and Transportation Committee, I have certain political leverage, particularly in terms of the Superfund. So, at my initiative, we went in and attempted to resolve the problem. The area in question was an all-white suburb. The residents would have a heart attack if a Black stayed there overnight. It's that kind of place.

As a result of redistricting, I became their congressman—replacing a white member. He hadn't done anything about the problem. But here came this black congressman and, while they may not have loved Blacks, they were forced to admit that he fought for their interests, while the white congressman sat back and did nothing. Then, they would read the newspaper and see that the chemical industry political action committees had contributed large sums of money to the members of the Illinois congressional delegation. Of the members of the delegation, they saw that I received the smallest contribution, whereas the previous white congressman, whom they had loved, had received a bundle of money. And they would say to themselves, "Gee, he may be black, but he cleaned up the stench. He can't be all bad."

JE: Can you discuss the workings of Congress? Is the textbook view an accurate one?

GS: I can't really answer that question. You would have to ask someone who has been here longer or someone who has penetrated the system. However, in order to penetrate the system, to master all of the nuances, many members pay a price. But I'm not willing to pay that price. So I'll never be a part of that system. Moreover, I don't think the price they must pay is in the best interests of the people. And it wouldn't benefit the people for me to be on the inside. That's why the country hasn't moved forward. If the people had benefitted from this gamesman-ship, then we would have passed the Nuclear Freeze Resolution long ago, and the Congress would not have voted vast sums of money for the Pershing missile, the cruise missile, and the B-1 bomber. If the leader-ship had any real power or scruples, they wouldn't have buckled under to the president in these areas. So, being on the inside doesn't necessarily mean you will be in a position to influence government policy or ad-vance the public interest. I could play that game. But it would be hypo-critical. And I'm not going to do it.

Still, the Congress is, in my estimation, a much better body than the press gives it credit for being. It's far more accountable than the press. The press isn't accountable to anyone. The Congress is far more representative than the press. The press is top-heavy with white liberals and Jews. It's more knowledgeable than the press. The press is woefully ignorant of Congress and the political process. In my estimation, Con-gress represents the best interests of America. Comparatively speaking, the members are brighter than any other group I've observed, including college professors. Although the members are statistically older than the general population, members of Congress are far more energetic, hard-working, and conscientious. Most members have an enormous amount of energy. Owing to the demands of political campaigning, the members are healthier, more alert, more informed, and more diligent. Look at Congressman Claude Pepper (D-Fla.); he's over eighty. And yet he travels all over the country, battling tooth and nail for the nation's senior citizens. No, I think Congress is more representative than any other body in this nation.

Now, having said that, I should add that I still hold Congress in very low regard. As a nation and as a people, we are terribly flawed. And the Congress reflects those flaws. Unfortunately, many flaws cannot be corrected by legislation. America desperately needs a new generation of leadership. A congressman must be more than a legislator. He is the political representative of over 500,000 people. The people elect him to be their spokesman, their voice, on domestic and international matters. Some members honestly attempt to give voice to this mandate. Others are more concerned with securing their position than in using their position to effect social change. For many members, if not most, the bottom line is re-election. In order to maintain their position, they frequently eschew stands—however important—which could cost them votes.

JE: For most members, their election to Congress is the culmina-tion of their political careers. As a result, they're often unwilling to take a stand which could jeopardize their re-election. What makes you differ-ent? Why are you willing to take a stand?

GS: I've been a risk-taker all my life. For example, I refused to become the second black journalist hired by a white daily in Chicago and perhaps the fourth or fifth Black to be hired by a white daily in the entire country in 1960. I declined for the same reason that I refuse to compromise in Congress. I'm not interested in the values of white people. Their values are not mine. It's hard for many whites and, for that matter, some Blacks, to understand my reasons. After all, most Blacks are trained, to some extent, by whites. Formally or informally, whites control the major media. The white press can't understand why I, as a Black, won't play their game. It's beyond their comprehension.

JE: Most black house members share your goals, but they have chosen to work within the system—that is, to make certain concessions in order to advance the interests of black America. Why haven't you?

GS: How many black members have lived in public housing? Not one. But I have. For me, the pain of living is too great to be balanced by being a member of Congress, or even the President of the United States. Life must be more than that. It's far more important for me to make a contribution, to be a selfless and courageous spokesman for my people. I don't mean to suggest that I embody those ideals. Rather, they are the ideals to which I aspire. But my goal is to contribute to the story of history. That story has long been one of human progression—of mankind mastering the elements in order to forge better human relationships. I'm not interested in recognition or acceptance. My purpose in being in Congress is to make a contribution to the struggle for peace, justice, and prosperity.

JE: Which members of Congress come closest to representing that ideal?

GS: It's difficult to say. I have very few close friends in Congress. Historically speaking, I would say that the member I most admire is Adam Clayton Powell (D-N.Y.). He was one of the greats. In addition, I greatly admired Vito Marcantonio (D-N.Y.), who served from the 1930s to 1950. He was a great congressman but not a particularly good politician. He eventually lost his seat in 1950.

JE: In the past, you've had several disagreements with other black house members. When a disagreement arises, do you confront your colleagues directly, or do you follow the prevailing folkways of the House?

GS: I've confronted members on the floor, and I've done it in private. That's no problem. I don't find it difficult to challenge a colleague, be he black or white. But I don't do it too often. I simply don't have time for one-on-one encounters. I don't try to convince people one at a time. I'm not going to live long enough to be effective that way. So, no, I don't spend much time trying to convert my colleagues. I much prefer to deal with large groups. Instead, I attempt to reach their constituents who, I hope, will influence them. For example, I write a weekly column, which is syndicated in many black newspapers. I don't write the column to win votes. Obviously, the voters in Los Angeles or Atlanta can't vote for me. I write to educate and motivate and, in the process, hope that these people will read what I've written and apply pressure on those members who refuse to speak or act in the best interests of black America.

JE: Despite the fact that you're a professional journalist, you've had a lifelong feud with the press. Why?

GS: To a large extent, the problem boils down to racism. Next to the church, the media is the most racist institution in the country. Furthermore, the problem is compounded by press ignorance and arrogance. For example, a *Chicago Sun-Times* journalist, as I stated earlier, wrote that I had the worst attendance record in Congress. The charge was ridiculous! Unfortunately, he didn't know any better. He failed to point out that many of the votes were quorum calls. It's one thing to miss the vote on a Nuclear Freeze; it's quite another to miss a quorum call. As far as he was concerned, they cancelled each other out. Now, that's ignorance! And if you attempt to chastise members of the press for their ignorance, they go after you. They adopt an extremely arrogant attitude. Their ignorance and arrogance are made possible by their lack of accountability. They're not accountable to anyone. If a television commentator can increase his ratings by calling you a dog, no one above him will give a damn. In fact, he'll be praised.

As an editor, I trained many young journalists. The first thing I'd ask a new journalist was not what he knew or where he went to school, but what he *didn't* know. I wanted to see whether he knew what he didn't know. The secret of being a good journalist is knowing what you don't know. Most of them were totally lost when I asked the question; they just couldn't understand what I was driving at.

I've been a journalist for nearly thirty years. A lot of people go into journalism because they want to express their opinions or wield influence, without ever having paid their dues. They don't want to study. They don't want to burn the midnight oil. Obviously, in order to cover Congress adequately, a journalist must be smarter and more knowledgeable than the average member. Very few journalists are willing to invest the long hours that a member puts in. Most journalists who cover Congress view the job as short-term—that is, they will cover Congress for a few years and then be assigned to the State Department or some other agency. They're constantly shifting assignments.

In addition, most journalists are racists. They're particularly resentful of a Black who doesn't respect them. The press is disproportionately represented by white liberals and Jews. Why? Part of it lies in their education. A liberal arts education tends to produce liberal thinking. Many of these people choose journalism as a profession and hope to use their skills to effect social change. Jews also wield great influence in the media. Like white liberals, their influence is partly attributable to education. The Jewish tradition holds education in high esteem. But in this evil society, the effect of a liberal education will give you a disproportionate number of positions in the professions and in the communications field. I'm *not* well liked by the white liberals or the Jews, who oppose my positions on the Middle East, racial quotas, affirmative action . . . . That adds to the problems I have with the press. Finally, the problem is compounded by an additional factor—one which I hate to admit. I'm not a nice guy. I know enough about public relations to know that if you romance the press, you'll receive good treatment. Everybody likes a rubdown. The problem is, however, that it's not easy to come out of public housing, to grow up on the streets, and to be nice. You don't survive that experience without developing psychological scars. And I have lots of scars.

As a young man, for example, I had to convince two whites who ran a wholesale drug operation that I was almost illiterate before they would give me a job as a porter. That's the only job that was open. And so I swept floors. When I decided to quit, they wanted to know why I was quitting, what they had done wrong. They said I was the best porter they had ever had. I told them that I was a law student, that we were on our Christmas break, and that it was time to return to school. Law school was so rough that I couldn't really hold down a job. And they asked: "You're a law student? How'd you get into law school?" Then they said, "You told us you never finished high school." I said, "Well, yes, I know, but the truth of the matter is that I've accumulated X number of hours toward my master's degree, and I'm deep into my second year in law school. If I had told you the truth, you wouldn't have hired me." Then they asked me why I thought that was so. And I said, "Look around here. Do you see Blacks doing anything other than sweeping the floors. I'm not dumb. That's how you view Blacks." So, yes, I have a lot of scars. Perhaps you can understand why. It's difficult to escape the streets without being maimed.

JE: How would you describe your relationship with the white press? Does it differ markedly from the black press?

GS: Given my background, I don't trust white journalists. I could cite any number of reasons. I don't cooperate with them. I don't give them interviews. I don't assist them in any way. They know how I feel, so we have minimal interaction. As for black journalists, I try to be more cooperative. I figure that a black journalist has a better understanding of me and what I'm trying to do. However, I make a distinction between those black journalists who work for black publications and those who work for white ones. As for the latter group, these journalists are judged by the same standards as whites. They're beholden to the white establishment. They have very little independence. Remember the case of Janet Cooke, the *Washington Post* reporter who won a Pulitzer Prize for a series she did, only to admit later that the story was a hoax? Well, all she did was to give the whites what they wanted—lies. She gave them the lies, and they crucified her for it. As a result, I view black reporters who work for white publications much the same as I view white reporters. The black reporter may sympathize or empathize with my objectives, but, in the end, he owes his allegiance to his white boss. As for black reporters who work for black publications, we get along fine. I have no problems with the black press. I try to be very cooperative. We're on the same wavelength.

JE: Suppose you were to be defeated for re-election. Do you think you would regret having bucked the system?

GS: That's an interesting question. Some time back, a very wealthy guy raised the same issue with me. He said, "Gus, we ought to get together and make some investments. God forbid, you may not always be in Congress. It's time to think about your future. Who knows what might happen?" I said to him: "No, if I stopped to concern myself with that, then I would not do many of the things I do." The older you get, the longer you serve here, the more likely you are to make concessions. But not me. If I ever start feeling that way, I will simply quit Congress and walk away. I will no longer be of much value to the struggle.

I have risen from public housing to membership in the most august legislative body in the world. I am rapidly approaching sixty, with perhaps twenty more years to live. Given my background, it's highly unlikely, at this point in time, that I would give thought to security, when I have never given it thought in years past. I don't want to die. But if I walked out this door today and was hit by a car, I would not die with a frown. I'm far ahead of the game. Death is inevitable. But I've done my best. If I am defeated, I can certainly live without the recognition, the perks, the ego massaging . . . . If that happens, I would be very disappointed. But on balance, I would still be far ahead of the game. I think I'm tough enough and have lived long enough to be able to handle that or anything else that fate has in store for me. Long ago, I decided how I wanted to live my life. And I've done my best to achieve my goals. I have not achieved everything I set out to achieve. And I guess I never will. But, at least, I've stayed on course. I'm satisfied in the main. And I want to die that way. I don't want to die afraid, insecure, broken. I'm willing to take a chance on the future.

JE: Do you have a thick skin? Do you take criticism well?

GS: Probably not. I don't like criticism, particularly if I've made a mistake. If I give a speech on the floor and a colleague makes an ass out of me by disproving my facts, that hurts the hell out of me. It means that I did not work hard enough or that I wasn't thorough enough. It makes me mad at myself. Why should a colleague know more about the subject than I do when I was the one who chose to speak on it? That kind of criticism always bruises my ego. It proves that I wasn't up to the challenge. I'm only sensitive to criticism that hits squarely on the mark. On the other hand, I couldn't care less if, after I gave a speech, no black congressman spoke to me. That wouldn't bother me in the slightest. That's their problem, not mine. Their failure to speak wouldn't mean that I erred. It would simply reveal their own shallowness and stupidity.

JE: Most people crave approval. Don't you?

GS: Yes, very much so. I crave approval, too. But I'm only willing to go so far to win approval. I won't do it at the expense of principle. Nothing is worth that, including my life. If you pointed a gun directly at my head and I was convinced you were going to pull the trigger unless I said "Master," then you'd have to pull the damn trigger. Life isn't that precious. I draw the line at principle. Yes, I want approval. But I will not surrender my ideals in its pursuit.

JE: Do you enjoy the political game? Does political campaigning agree with you?

GS: Yes, a great deal. And I'm one of the best, if not *the* best, in the business. I love people—ordinary people. I don't think much of important people. If you were to walk through my district with me, you would see that I can't walk down the street, or into a laundromat, or past a bar without someone saying, "Hey, Gus, how 'ya doin'?" The people know if you're one of them. They know if you're genuine. I love campaigning. I don't stay home when I'm in the district. I don't sit around the office. I stay on the streets, in the churches, at the news-stands, in the gambling joints . . . . I like to be with people. I'm concerned about people. They keep me going.

JE: Do you favor the establishment of a national black political party? If so, why?

GS: I'm not sure. You're asking about form, rather than sub-stance. I'm interested in substance. I would support any form that would promote the substance. But the form is a matter of tactics. I'm much more concerned with the substance. As for a black political party, that's putting the cart before the horse. I'm not for any particular party. I would be for the Democratic Party if it were a vehicle to advance black aims and objectives.

JE: Does the Democratic Party, as it presently exists, represent black America?

GS: That's like asking me, "Do you like wearing a tuxedo?" My answer would depend on where I'm going. It would depend on the time, place, and circumstances. The Democratic Party is a form. I don't like or dislike forms. It's the substance that concerns me. As far as substance is concerned, the record of the Democratic Party disturbs me greatly. Rather than being an independent voice, it falls all over itself trying to accommodate the Reagan agenda. And that agenda is not in the best interests of black people.

I'd like to go back to your previous question. If a black political party were the best vehicle for promoting peace, justice, and jobs, then I'd be for it. If not, then I couldn't support it. Again, it's the substance that matters. The form doesn't interest me.

In the same vein, I'm not for racial equality as other than a strategy. I think that black empowerment is essential to humanize whites. It's essential if Blacks and whites are to live together as brothers. I'm not for black empowerment simply because I want Blacks to be powerful. If we could be brothers without empowerment, I would not insist on empowerment. So, my objective is not empowerment. My objective is brotherhood. I'm for Blacks being racial, because I believe that's the only answer to racism. Race only matters when one race is excluded from the process. Chicago can't elect only whites and then argue that race doesn't matter. Obviously, it does. Race will only become irrelevant when Chicago elects both blacks and whites without regard to race. I'm for a racial-less society even more than whites. But that will only occur when people demonstrate that race doesn't matter. Until whites begin to share power with Blacks, at every level, we will have a racist society. Whites cannot insist that Blacks backpedal race as long as they have their feet on our necks.

JE: Finally, in recent years, you have been sharply critical of the Jewish community. Why?

GS: For many reasons, chief of which is its opposition to racial quotas. I support a quota system for Blacks, in order to eliminate quotas. The American Jewish Congress opposes quotas. They argue that quotas are bad. I think they're wrong. Jews supported a quota system when they were on the outside but oppose it now that they're on the inside. I favor quotas for Blacks for the same reasons that Jews favored quotas when they were on the outside. Once Blacks get their quota, we won't need a quota system. So, don't tell me that we don't need quotas, when I don't have my quota. Jews just don't understand. But that's what racism does. That's why racism is so divisive.

The advantage which Blacks presently enjoy and which Jews enjoyed earlier is that when you're oppressed, you're forced by circumstances to understand your oppressor. But the oppressor, because of his power, is never required to understand you. Blacks will save America because of this fact. In the process of oppressing people, you also humanize them. You dehumanize the oppressor, which is just the opposite of what is thought to be true. The oppressor thinks that he's the human and that his oppression has dehumanized the oppressed. But history proves just the opposite. The Fascists in Germany thought they had dehumanized the Jews. However, the opposite occurred. In the process, they dehumanized themselves and made the Jews more human. As a result, Jews began to see the cosmopolitan nature of their struggle. This enabled them to overcome the oppression. The same will be true in the case of Blacks. In the process, we will humanize whites. We will force them to confront their own inhumanity and, in the end, to repudiate it. Both groups will be more human.

My point is simple. Oppression blinds the oppressor. The oppressor has no reason to question his actions. But I do, because I'm the oppressed. And that's why, in the end, Blacks will save whites. We will force whites to confront their oppression—to see how wicked and evil racism is. And when they do, when they come to grips with their sins, we will all be free.

Parren J. Mitchell

Uncle Sam as Employer

Parren J. Mitchell was born April 29, 1922, in Baltimore, Maryland. He holds a Bachelor of Arts degree from Morgan State College (1950) and a Master of Science degree from the University of Maryland (1952). Mitchell comes from a distinguished political family. His older brother, Clarence Mitchell II, served thirty-eight years as the NAACP's Washington lobbyist and was affectionately known in Washington as the "101st U.S. Senator." Clarence Mitchell III, Parren's nephew, is a Maryland state senator, and another nephew, Michael, is a member of the Baltimore City Council. Parren's sister-in-law, Juanita Jackson Mitchell, is a former president of Maryland's NAACP state chapter and a well-known lawyer.

In 1950, Mitchell, who was then twenty-seven years old, brought suit against the University of Maryland to admit him as its first black graduate student. Upon completing his master's degree in sociology, he accepted a faculty appointment at his alma mater, Morgan State College. During the 1950s and 1960s, Mitchell became deeply involved in the anti-poverty program. As executive director of Baltimore's anti-poverty program, he frequently lobbied in Washington for the agency. In 1968, Mitchell waged an aggressive primary bid for Congress but was defeated by a mere 5,000 votes to an eighteen-year incumbent. Undaunted, Mitchell ran two years later, and won, becoming Maryland's first black congressman.

During his fourteen years in Congress, Mitchell has served with distinction as a member of the House Budget Committee, vice chairman of the Joint Committee on Defense Production, and chairman of the Congressional Black Caucus. Presently, Mitchell serves as chairman of the Small Business Committee; whip-at-large; a senior member of the House Banking, Finance, and Urban Affairs Committee; chairman of the Subcommittee on Housing, Minority Enterprise, and Economic Development of the Congressional Black Caucus; and a member of the Joint Economic Committee.

In 1976, Mitchell attached to then President Carter's $4 billion Public Works Bill an amendment that compelled state, county, and municipal governments seeking federal grants to set aside 10 percent of each grant to retain minority firms as contractors, subcontractors, or suppliers. Mitchell's single amendment resulted in more than $525 million (15 percent) being channeled into legitimate minority firms. Following numerous court challenges, "The Mitchell Amendment" was upheld as constitutional by the United States Supreme Court in July 1980.

Mitchell also introduced legislation which, in 1978, became Public Law 95-507, requiring proposals from contractors to spell out goals for awarding contracts to minority subcontractors. This law potentially provides access to billions of dollars for minority businesses. And, in 1982, Mitchell amended the $71 billion Surface Transportation Act of 1982 to provide that at least 10 percent of the funds (or $7.1 billion over a four year period) be set aside for minority businesses.

Although closely identified with minority business legislation, Mitchell has championed legislation on housing, employment, health, and education. Often described as "the conscience of the Congressional Black Caucus," he conceived the "brain trust" concept to support the work of the Caucus and has been one of its most active and effective members.

For his efforts, Mitchell has received numerous awards and citations, including eight honorary degrees (four Doctors of Humane Letters, three Doctors of Law, and one Doctor of Social Sciences), in addition to more than 400 awards from national and local consumer groups, civil rights organizations, business and economic groups, fraternities and sororities, religious organizations, and educational groups.

JE: How would you characterize the current state of black America? Have conditions improved under the Reagan Administration?

PM: No. There are 10 million counted unemployed in this nation, and hundreds of thousands if not millions of uncounted unemployed. The national black unemployment rate is a staggering 18.4 percent. Too many of our brothers and sisters are living out their lives in hopelessness, despair, and fear.

The bankruptcy rate for small businesses, for example, has increased 47 percent over the last year. Black businesses struggle to stay alive, but far too many fail each day. It is reported that unless help is forthcoming, black businesses will face extinction by 1990.

Because of savage cuts in federal funds for higher education, almost a million young men and women will not be able to enter colleges and universities this fall. Blacks will suffer disproportionately, and the source of future black leadership will be threatened.

We see assaults daily against affirmative action at all levels of government, as well as manifestations of resurgent racism and acts of violence by demented Klansmen and other degenerate hate groups.

JE: Do you also see signs of hope? If so, what?

PM: Yes. This is no time to despair, and I do not despair. We are a strong people not given to despair but given to struggle, not cowed by the circumstance but charged to meet the challenge. No, all is not grim. We must understand that the severe tests confronting Blacks come about not because we have failed, but because we have succeeded too well. Once virtually excluded from the body politic, Blacks have now mastered the political process. Once labeled uneducable, Blacks have made contributions to every segment of American society, making life richer and better for millions of people. Once treated as merchandise in the economic life of this nation, Blacks have built great businesses. We are moving toward economic parity—we are building an economic base, an economic legacy to pass on to future generations.

Yes, the conditions are grim. Yes, the odds against us are awesome. Yet, we are not strangers and afraid in a world we never made. A new and positive attitude dominates black America. We fear no man, no group, no force. We have developed strategies that have stood the test, and we shall use them again in our quest for ultimate freedom. We shall use the courts, as we have in the past. We shall use the legislative halls, as we have in the past. We shall stage protests if we must. We shall engage in selective economic boycotts if the situation demands it. We shall not be stopped. We shall not be turned around. We shall not retreat.

JE: To what extent, if any, is President Reagan responsible for the problems you've described?

PM: Blacks must face the fact that this country, without question, has either ignored us or has turned its back to us. A new philosophy of government and economics, which is being thrust upon the nation, is crushing us. To understand the serious dimensions of this crisis, we must know more precisely the exact nature of this new philosophy.

When President Reagan campaigned on the platform, "We must get government off the backs of the people," he was spelling out his philosophy with respect to the role of government. His belief, blindly followed by far too many persons in Congress, is that government should not provide safe, sanitary, decent housing—only the private sector should do this. He believes government should not provide health care, nor assistance to education, nor jobs, nor job training—only the private sector should promote these things. But nowhere in the history of America has the private sector done these things on a satisfactory basis.

No one in the administration will ever say it publicly, but the ultimate objective of this administration is to destroy all programs that meet human needs, and that includes the Social Security program. Even the opponents of the administration will not say it publicly, but I have said it, and I will continue to say it. I will say it at any time, in any forum: The Reagan Administration, the extreme right wing of the conservative Republican Party, is determined to wipe out all of the federal social programs. This is their objective.

JE: If you are correct, how does the administration intend to accomplish this objective?

PM: They have devised a diabolically clever three part game plan. Part one of that plan is to smear and discredit every major social program. For example, they have the television cameras zoom in on a child who throws away a free lunch, and immediately, cries of "waste, fraud, and abuse" were raised. It is important to note, however, that few, if any, voices were raised when a $2 billion cost overrun in the purchase of army cargo planes was revealed.

They continue to repeat the old canard about people who use food stamps to purchase crab claws and vodka. They repeat such canards over and over again so that the air resounds with cries of "waste, fraud, and abuse." However, an almost deadly silence reigned when the disclosure came about an 80 percent cost overrun in the multi-million dollar ship building program at the San Diego naval shipyard.

Part two of their plan is to chop away at these programs, again and again, and to claim that these cuts are necessary to reduce the federal budget deficit in the name of a balanced federal budget. Last year, for example, the government cut almost $2 billion from higher education and made cuts of similar amounts in 1984. The Republican budget approved last year in the House of Representatives slashed $834 million from Medicaid, $414 million from public assistance, and $837 million from food stamps. The Republican budget which prevailed in the House cut $7.4 billion in entitlements and discretionary programs and seeks a total reduction of $32.6 billion in these programs over the period from 1983 to 1985.

Consider the budget the House of Representatives passed in 1982. It was so cruel that it eliminated the free mailing of large braille print tapes for the blind. Libraries and blind people cannot afford expensive postage. This is a budget which imposed cruel pain on the handicapped, the unemployed, the aged, the small business community, and the youth, who are our future. It's no wonder that the *Washington Post*, in an editorial, stated that having no budget at all would be better than having one which treats so viciously those who most need help simply to survive.

The third part of the plan was the administration's three year tax cut, approved by the Congress. This tax cut has cost the federal government $730 billion in lost revenues. Now Reagan and his cohorts argue, "We must end these programs, because we do not have the revenues to pay for them."

This fiendish game plan is working, and the federal programs to aid black businesses, the aged, and the poor . . . have been decimated. That is why I—and other members of Congress—fought so hard against the Reagan budget. We lost. However, even in losing, I recalled the line, "It is better to fail in a cause that will some day triumph than to succeed in a cause that will some day fail." Reaganomics is failing. The desperate unemployed in black communities, the frightened senior citizens, and the disillusioned college students know that Reaganomics has failed them.

JE: What can be done, if anything, to reverse the present situation?

PM: In these grim and perilous times for black people, journalists in the black press bear a singular and sobering responsibility. They must give our people a sense of hope. They must prevent our people from wallowing in despair. We have faced far more difficult times in the past, but we have survived. They must tell our people, over and over again, that we have faced adversities of far greater magnitude but we have prevailed. They must repeat the history and legacy of our forefathers time and time again so that that history, that legacy, will provide a beacon light in this tormented period. We must retain the will to struggle, for if we do so, inevitably, we shall have the power to prevail.

Second, members of the black press must be a part of the force which nurtures our youth and encourages them to maximize their talents. They must provide opportunities for our young writers and encourage our young doctors, businesspersons, lawyers, and artists. In this struggle, we must constantly increase our forces. The new young warriors must stand beside the seasoned veterans as we struggle for our final liberation in this nation.

Third, the leaders of the black press must be part of the force to weld us into political unity. The only real weapon we have is the power of the ballot box, but we cannot harness that power as long as we remain politically factionalized, as long as we pit one set of leaders against another set of leaders, and as long as we cannibalize those who seek to provide leadership.

JE: Are you equally hopeful about the world scene? If so, why?

PM: I do not count myself among those who are totally pessimistic about the future of the world. Many pessimists argue that political systems throughout the world are disintegrating. They argue that economic conditions throughout the world will continue to deteriorate until they collapse totally. They argue that such great moral and spiritual decay exists that we are on an irreversible course to a new age of uncertainty, doubt, and retrogression.

I do not believe these things. Quite the contrary, I think that we stand poised on the brink of enormous new scientific and technological breakthroughs that will continue to revolutionize the world and that will ever increase the standard of living for all human beings who inhabit the earth. I do not believe that America must become a service economy. We have the genius, the resources and, I hope, the will to remain strong in the fields of industry and manufacturing. Telecommunications will become the multi-billion dollar industry of the future. Telecommunications, coupled with computerization, will make radical changes in our lives. Cordless telephones, computerized recall systems, idea banks—all of these—will become common usage items, perhaps within our lifetimes. We must act to guarantee that our young people receive the education required to compete in this new world. I recently read about a summer camp that was teaching four and five year old children about computer operations. We must make sure that our youngsters receive that kind of early start so that computers can compete with basketballs and baseballs as everyday playthings. This may require a significant alteration in the public school system, but so be it.

Past opportunities to employ our talents and abilities were few in number. Now that we stand at the threshold of a new society, a society dominated by automation and significant new technological breakthroughs, we would be foolish to assume that there will be a great rush to utilize the talents and abilities we possess. At the precise moment in history when vast social, technological, and economic changes are taking place—at that precise moment, there exists a fierce, unrelenting effort to destroy affirmative action. Put another way, the powers that be will attempt to exclude us rather than include us.

JE: Can anything be done to prevent this from occurring?

PM: Yes. We must fight with tenacity and skill for our inclusion. We must establish a system of information gathering on awards, grants, and contracts, and we must be able to spread the word quickly. "The fastest with the mostest" remains the operative doctrine of the day.

Second, every black professional is an expert in his or her chosen field. There's no question about that. Unfortunately, we must set even higher standards of excellence for ourselves. Historically, the black applicant has had to be super-qualified, often over-qualified, for a lower position in both the public and private sectors. We must accept the fact that competition will become increasingly intense, government dollars will become even more scarce, and public attitudes against us will continue to harden. We must make ourselves so excellent, so superior, so good that we will be regarded as indispensable in both the public and private sectors.

JE: In 1983, you introduced a landmark public works jobs bill. What was it designed to accomplish? How has it been received?

PM: The Public Works Employment Act of 1983 reauthorizes the local Public Works Capital Development and Investment Act of 1976 and represents a significant step toward the continuance of major public works programs on behalf of job creation and economic development.

Since the administration continues to half-heartedly promote the government's role in ensuring job creation, the Congress must reconfirm its responsibility in this area. Even as we approach the beginning of the congressional budget cycle, we cannot look to the president's economic package to contain anything other than a replay of the numerous tax breaks granted in the past in an attempt to encourage the private sector to respond to the continuing unemployment crisis. Consequently, we cannot sit idly by and ignore our chances to provide the needed economic stimulus to promote job creation.

This measure was proposed as part of a long-term economic revitalization program. Its provisions conform with the thrust of the Community Renewal Employment Act Congressman Augustus F. Hawkins (D-Calif.) introduced in 1983. The Hawkins Bill provides grants to local governments for labor costs associated with the repair and maintenance of roads, water systems, mass transportation systems, and educational facilities; the rehabilitation and conservation of public lands and resources such as erosion, flood, drought, and storm damage control, forestry operations and reclamation of public lands damaged by strip mining; and services such as health care, emergency food and shelter, and child care.

The President, who opposes this kind of approach, is apparently not aware that every 1 percent increase in joblessness costs the nation at least $22 billion a year. Those who label this "make-work" should look at the still enduring projects the Works Progress Administration, the Public Works Administration, and others created during the 1930s and 1940s. We in the Congress cannot procrastinate on this issue—joblessness is the number one problem in this nation, and it is now at crisis proportions and demands congressional action.

JE: How would you assess the president's record in the area of minority enterprise?

PM: Let me give you a concrete example of the attitude of the administration—in this case, the Small Business Administration (SBA).

In 1981, I requested that the Department of Justice investigate what was clearly a conspiracy against Wallace and Wallace Chemical and Oil Corporation.

In 1974, Charles Wallace sought to build an oil refinery in Macon County, Alabama. From the inception of the project, local, state, and federal entities used almost every device at their command to thwart the construction of the first black-owned oil refinery in America.

The chief culprit at the federal level was the Small Business Administration. It is my firm belief that the SBA imposed certain contractual requirements on Wallace and Wallace with the full knowledge that those requirements in and of themselves would almost guarantee that the oil refinery would not succeed.

A recent court decision, which ordered that a minority firm be reinstated to 8(a) status, demonstrates that the Small Business Administration did indeed make arbitrary and capricious demands on a minority firm. This case involved Oklahoma Aerotronics, Inc., which had been dismissed from the 8(a) program. In 1981, the U.S. Court of Appeals for the District of Columbia ordered that Oklahoma Aerotronics, Inc. be restored to 8(a) status, ruling that the SBA acted unlawfully, arbitrarily, and capriciously.

I believe that the SBA followed a similar vendetta in the case of Wallace and Wallace. We must not—and can not—permit the stifling of minority enterprise in this fashion. In 1981, Wallace and Wallace, requesting injunctive relief, filed suit against the Small Business Administration.

JE: Is this an isolated example or a symptomatic response of the Small Business Administration?

PM: It is *not* an isolated example. My office has been swamped by inquiries and protests from minority businesspersons concerning the requirements the Small Business Administration has proposed and implemented. Indeed, I wrote to Michael Cardenas, then Administrator of the Small Business Administration, about these and other problems. And they are legion in number. For instance, the SBA unjustly denied an 8(a) contract to a black contractor from Sacramento, California. In this case, J.R. Pope, president of J.R. Pope, Inc., had unsuccessfully negotiated an 8(a) contract with the Bureau of Reclamation, Department of the Interior. The contract was for excavation and construction on the Salt-Gila Aqueduct, Reach 1-A Project. Pope met all of the necessary requirements to undertake the project. However, at the instructions of Cardenas, the San Francisco Regional Office of the Small Business Administration refused to award the 8(a) contract to Pope. Indeed, they tentatively planned to offer the contract to another 8(a) contractor, El Camino Construction, located in Cardenas's hometown of Fresno, California. Again, I could cite numerous such cases.

JE: Is the Small Business Administration directly responsible for the desperate state of minority enterprise?

PM: Yes. The SBA has launched the most vicious attack on the minority community in recent memory. Its failure to adequately defend a major court challenge to the award of federal contracts to several disadvantaged firms in its 8(a) business development program is the most recent in a series of moves aimed at minority businesspersons. This latest action will affect 8(a) firms which are nearing competitive status but which have technically exceeded SBA's definition of a "small business concern." If these businesses are abruptly forced out of the 8(a) program, many may go out of business in less than six months. A recent General Accounting Office decision, which is only advisory in nature, is now being used to deny contracts to twenty-three minority 8(a) firms. These firms will have to lay off over 7,500 workers, many of whom are minorities.

The SBA Administrator, James C. Sanders, has refused to amend its regulations to redefine the term, "small business," for purposes of the 8(a) program. The inclusion of increases in employment and gross receipts to the base on which size is measured is artificial when these increases are attributable only to the performance of 8(a) contracts which are by no means permanent sources of income as this latest maneuver demonstrates.

The Small Business Administration has consistently acted to deny economic parity to minority businesses. Programs for economic advancement have been sabotaged by those very persons who, by law, are directed and charged with responsibility for their proper implementation. SBA's failure to stop these abuses is testimony enough to its lack of commitment to the economic revitalization of this nation in general and the minority business community in particular.

JE: In addition to your ongoing battles with the Small Business Administration and the General Services Administration, you have also done battle with the Social Security Administration. What is the source of the problem? Have you made significant progress?

PM: I've done battle with the Social Security Administration since I was elected to Congress in 1971—for fifteen long years. The problem is, when we win—when we really turn the screws—they make minor reforms and create additional opportunities for Blacks. Then, two months later, they slide right back. It's difficult to ride herd on the agency on a week-to-week or month-to-month basis. The Social Security Administration closely resembles other government agencies—they operate on the basis of a triangle theory when it comes to Blacks and other minorities. Most Blacks are at the base of the triangle. There are very few at the top. Even more heinous, in my opinion, is the fact that the Social Security Administration has given up its efforts to promote upward mobility. There's very little impetus today within the agency to encourage minority mobility.

JE: Recently, you proposed the establishment of a Minority Business Legal Defense and Education Fund. Why is such a fund necessary?

PM: The fund is to be an independent, nonprofit foundation, financed totally with private funds and not connected to or a part of any other organization. Organizers will seek one-half million dollars as the initial, annual operating level of this fund.

The purpose of the fund is to act as an advocate and representative of the minority business community in legal matters of a class nature which affect the growth and development of the minority business community. The fund will not represent individual minority business firms on legal matters, unless its board of directors determines that such a case has clear, national implications in terms of its impact on a major sector of the minority business community or the minority business community as a whole.

The idea for a permanent legal defense fund for the minority business community came about as a direct result of my recent, personal suit against the General Services Administration (GSA) for failure to properly implement Public Law 95-507. In this case, the GSA made millions of dollars in illegal contract awards in 1979. Public Law 95-507 requires major federal contractors to include details for subcontracting with minority firms in their bid packages. The GSA failed to do so, which is why I brought suit.

The GSA suit, the Supreme Court challenge to the 10 percent minority set-aside contained in the Local Public Works Act of 1978, and recent challenges to the Department of Transportation's minority business regulations are all clear signs that key battles for economic parity will take place in courtrooms across the nation. The same has been historically true as the minority community has sought political and social parity. The minority business community must be ready to aggressively pursue its goals and then defend its gains, if necessary, at all costs. The Minority Business Legal Defense and Education Fund will be a major weapon in this fight.

JE: What conclusions can be drawn from these examples?

PM: For the past fifteen years, as a member of Congress, I have fought to advance minority business enterprise. When I was first elected in 1971, minority entrepreneurs received less than one-half of 1 percent of all federal procurement contract dollars. Now, nearly fifteen years later, minority businesses receive only about 2 percent of all funds the federal government spends in procurement and contracting. That is a national disgrace. Yet, incredibly, there are those organizations and persons who seek to negate even those limited gains. In my own state of Maryland, the situation is much the same. Minorities are virtually excluded from participation in state contracting and purchasing.

The opponents of minority business enterprise continue to hurl feckless allegations: For example, minority business participation drives up costs; minority business regulations are burdensome; minority business regulations are inflexible; and on and on, ad nauseum. These spurious allegations have been disproved time and time again, but conservatives continue to raise them.

At a time when black unemployment is spiralling, at a time when we are witnessing the decimation of human support programs at the federal level, and at a time when resurgent racism again threatens to promote further polarization in more and more communities, we cannot and must not evade or terminate the nation's efforts on behalf of minority business entrepreneurs. To the contrary, this is precisely the moment in history when our nation should attempt to strengthen and expand its efforts on behalf of minority businesses.

JE: During the past four years, you have been extremely critical of President Reagan's "New Federalism." What are its main failings?

PM: The president's "New Federalism" has had little if any effect on the economic problems that confront this nation. Mr. Reagan has attempted to divert our attention to a discussion of a relatively esoteric issue concerning the appropriate role of the federal government in providing basic services. Meanwhile, he remains strangely silent about the continued reductions in programs designed to train and educate Americans who are not equipped to take advantage of those employment opportunities which might become available as a result of his economic recovery program. Moreover, he remains equally silent about the fact that his plan to return the responsibility for administering over 40 federal programs to the states will not include sufficient revenues to operate these programs at their current levels: The states will be unable to provide needed services without dramatically increasing state and local taxes. By 1991, the time specified within the plan for a complete shift of responsibility from the federal government to the states, Americans will be paying more taxes for less services and no safeguards for the future.

The President has also proposed an experimental program to revitalize depressed urban and rural communities by providing additional tax preferences and the relaxation of various regulations. As we know, Congress has already enacted substantial tax relief to increase business investment. Thus, the likelihood of a further dramatic increase in business investment and job creation is minimal. Small businesses provide two-thirds of the current jobs. The greatest need of small businesses is not additional tax preferences but, rather, sources of capital with which to expand or improve existing conditions. This proposal, given its costs in terms of lost revenues, may well endanger the day-to-day survival of citizens who live in these depressed areas. Clearly, we should not view this proposal as a substitute for existing targeted urban programs.

JE: Is the President correct when he states, as he has on countless occasions, that the ultimate solution to the unemployment problem rests with the private sector?

PM: No. We must face the reality that, while the private sector has shown signs of recovery, it is not capable of solving the unemployment problem. My position is very simple: If the private sector cannot solve the problem, then the public sector—the government—must attempt to solve it. In this regard, it is imperative that the Congress pass a *real* jobs bill—one that is well funded—and that enjoys the enthusiastic support of the administration. The program passed by Congress—which provides only $5 billion—is totally inadequate. Instead, we need an adequately funded jobs bill which will produce significant revenue in the form of taxes.

The Reagan Administration has turned a deaf ear on such a program. I believe that the administration reflects a philosophy based on social Darwinism—namely, the survival of the fittest. I honestly believe that that philosophy best describes its approach to government. The administration assumes, as have others before it, that if Blacks are unable to find work, then something must be wrong with them. The same comment would apply equally to Hispanics and Asians. It was very clear, in the recent presidential campaign, that President Reagan simply wrote off the minority community. He has no plans to do anything for the minority population in this country, and he has done precisely what he promised—nothing.

JE: Are you concerned that, despite all the problems you've identified, we are witnessing little if any organized protest?

PM: Yes, it does concern me. But I'm encouraged by the increasing numbers of Blacks who have registered to vote and are voting in local and state elections across this country. The enormous outpouring of black votes last year should be interpreted as a clear message to the president—to wit, we don't like you, we don't like your program, and we intend to do everything possible to oppose it. I think that makes sense. Chicago Mayor Harold Washington's election, for example, not only signified the coming of age of Blacks in that city, but also the fact that Blacks are angry at this president and his administration. Certainly, I am disturbed by the lack of active protest—demonstrations, picketing, boycotts—but voting against the president, when and wherever possible, may be the better approach.

JE: How do you view the relationship between economic parity and political access? Are the two part and parcel of the same problem?

PM: Yes. You cannot separate economic parity from political access. While it is important for Blacks to elect black mayors and black state legislators, it is equally important that we focus our efforts on the economic arena. I have always advocated economic and political parity. The two are inseparable.

To date, Blacks have yet to achieve economic parity. Remember, black civil rights gains did not come freely; they were granted begrudgingly. The gains we have made have come through sweat and blood and muscle. However, when you come down to it, the thing that runs this country is money. Too many Americans, both black and white, are blinded by the dollar. For many, that is their primary motivation in life. Despite the gains Blacks have made on the political front, whites seem to be totally unwilling to share economic power. Until Blacks achieve economic parity, we will remain at the periphery of American society. Like other groups, Blacks must share in the economic fruits of this nation. For far too many Blacks, life consists of simply trying to eke out a subsistence income. As the richest nation on earth, we have an obligation to ensure that all Americans, regardless of color, share in the nation's economic prosperity. We will not be satisfied until we can sit down together at the same table and break bread—on equal terms, with equal portions.

JE: From your perspective, is the federal government itself guilty of discriminatory hiring and personnel policies?

PM: Yes, it is. Since the election of President Reagan, we have seen a steady reduction in the number of Blacks in positions above the GS-2 to 5 levels. We still remain concentrated in those ranks. The reduction in force that the administration has implemented has hit Blacks the hardest. When you examine the hiring practices of this administration, it is clear that Blacks have fared even worse than they did under President Nixon. The facts are clear. There exists a steady erosion in the number of Blacks in top federal positions.

JE: Is the private sector less discriminatory today in its hiring and promotion policies than in earlier years?

PM: Unfortunately, what progress we have made in this area has, for all intents and purposes, come to a standstill. As a result of the Bakke case, recent court rulings, and the position of the administration, the private sector has adopted the position: "Forget it, we don't need to worry about it. We've got a friend in the White House."

I believe in political activism. In order to break some of these large corporations, we will have to seriously consider the possibility of economic boycotts. We must hit them in the pocketbook; that's where they're most vulnerable. They simply won't act on the basis of altruism.

JE: In recent months, you have pressed for improved relations between Blacks and Jews. Do you believe that the present rift can be resolved?

PM: Yes. Historically, there existed a strong alliance between Blacks and Jews. That alliance served the nation well during the tumultuous civil rights decade. Unfortunately, that alliance is less viable today although I am fully aware of the present efforts of both communities to resolve their past disagreements. At the same time, I am also aware of incidents and positions taken which, in my opinion, exert a counterproductive force, thus undermining their efforts. First, several major Jewish organizations voiced support for Alan Bakke, which served to erode the alliance. Then, some segments of the Jewish community opposed the 10 percent minority business set-aside to the Local Public Works Act of 1978, which further eroded the alliance.

Some time ago, I read a press account that four Jewish organizations had attempted to alter the Small Business Administration regulations. That alteration would have increased the difficulties Blacks confront in their quest for economic parity. Needless to say, I was greatly disturbed. As a result, I asked the four organization heads to meet with me in an effort to repair the damage as a result of this action. That meeting proved worthwhile, and hopefully we can work together to rebuild the alliance that has served both Blacks and Jews so well over the years.

JE: Recently, the Ku Klux Klan and the American Nazi Party have experienced a new resurgence. What can or should be done to curb such hate groups?

PM: Clearly, the Justice Department must increase its anti-Klan and anti-Nazi enforcement activities. I am concerned that the Justice Department is interpreting the existing definitions of "intent" and "conspiracy" within the present statutes too narrowly. These narrow definitions have resulted in few convictions of alleged offenders.

We are presently experiencing a nationwide resurgence of hate-group activity. It now appears that the strength of these organizations is as great as it has ever been in traditional southern strongholds. More ominously, many areas in both the Northeast and Midwest have begun to display covert repressive behavior toward certain minority groups.

As early as April 1981, I held hearings in my own state on the resurgence of these hate groups. Subsequent research revealed that the Justice Department has been reluctant to prosecute these groups under Title 18 of the Civil Rights Act of 1968. In order to prosecute under Title 18, victims must prove that such groups have conspired to deprive the victims of their civil rights. However, according to several federal court rulings, victims do not have to supply the details of the intent or conspiracy.

Vigilante groups who conspire to violate the Constitution have long wreaked havoc on racial and religious minorities in America. Refusing to prosecute these groups would serve to reopen wounds which have only recently begun to heal. My ultimate objective is to have the Klan and similar hate groups classified as terrorist organizations. In addition, I would like to see stronger federal legislation in this area as well as see additional class action suits brought against these groups.

JE: Do you view the Reagan Justice Department as a friend of black America?

PM: No. For the first time in recent history, the Justice Department has, in a very real sense, become the *enemy* of black people. It just has, and I don't mind saying so. I become sick inside when I compare a man like Ramsey Clark with the current Attorney General, Edwin Meese. When I consider how many top men we've had in the Justice Department, men who supported the principle of political and economic justice for black Americans, it makes me ill. No, we've taken several giant steps backwards. I only hope we can correct them before it's too late. As it stands now, the Justice Department is deaf to the plight of black America.

JE: Much has been said and written about black capitalism. How would you define black capitalism? Is it succeeding?

PM: First, I think it's imperative that we define "capitalism" itself. I don't view capitalism in the same light that most people do. Capitalism, like all other man-made institutions, is constantly evolving. So, when I speak about capitalism, I'm obviously not speaking about what people typically consider as pure capitalism. That's gone, and it will never return.

As I see it, capitalism is a tool, a mechanism, a vehicle—a means by which Blacks and other minorities can achieve economic parity in this country. That's my definition of capitalism. I think that black capitalism must be modified, changed, and made more compatible with the realities within the black community. For example, I strongly support the concept of tithing, whereby the black capitalist would tithe 10 percent of his gross profits to the black community. That's the kind of black capitalism I would like to see practiced. I see little virtue in the "ledger psychosis" approach—namely, to see how much money you can make. I think that tithing can be extremely beneficial in the area of community development.

JE: Are either of the two major parties committed to black capitalism? If not, why?

PM: No. Remember, most of the major social programs of the past twenty-five years have been instituted for political, not economic, reasons. These decisions were the result of hard political realities, based on strong political motivations. President Johnson proposed the "War on Poverty" as a means of diffusing the social unrest which existed at the time. President Nixon proposed black capitalism for purely political reasons. He needed black votes. Nixon had failed repeatedly to make inroads into the black community. As a result, he concluded that his best chance lay in the business community. I'm not particularly interested in his political motivations, but I am interested in the results. Toward the end of his term, he did propose several incremental steps which proved helpful. But, no, neither political party is committed to black economic empowerment. The commitment just isn't there.

JE: Do you support the establishment of a national black political party? Would such a party serve to make the two major parties more responsive to the interests of black Americans?

PM: Yes, I do. But I think that it must evolve the other way. I don't think that you can impose a political party at the national level. Instead, I would like to see each of the states attempt to develop a state party and then, out of that development, coalesce into a national party. I think it would be unwise to do it the other way. Developing political strength is a long-term process. I certainly don't see such a party appearing overnight. But I think a black party could prove extremely useful.

JE: How would you respond to the argument that since the Democratic Party has taken Blacks for granted, it would be politically advantageous for Blacks to join the Republican Party and attempt to exert greater influence within both political parties?

PM: If it were not for the Reagan Administration, the Ford Administration, and the Nixon Administration, I would advocate such an approach. But until such time as the extreme right wing no longer controls the Republican Party, Blacks have no chance of moving into that party in any significant numbers. If the Republicans want us, they will have to moderate their position on major issues. I very much admire Senator Charles McC. Mathias, Jr. (R-Md.), but clearly, he is in a distinct minority. I would much prefer to see men like him control the Republican Party than the corporate barons.

JE: Do you favor basic systemic changes in the capitalist system? If so, what?

PM: Yes. I think the time is ripe for another round of income redistribution in the country. We've done it before. For example, Social Security represented a redistribution of wealth. The disparities between the haves and have-nots have grown so great that the time has come to consider another major step in this direction. In addition, I think we must look for ways to modify the profit motive as the grease pin of the economic system. How do you do that in a capitalist system? I just don't know. But there must be a way, and eventually someone will figure it out. Despite recent tax reforms, we still permit corporations to get away with murder. That's endemic to the capitalist system. We must look for ways to curb the defiance of the corporations, particularly as it relates to their tax burden.

JE: Finally, what would you tell young Blacks who argue that the system is stacked against them—that nothing, including voting, will improve the situation?

PM: I would tell them that during a recent lame duck session, when few people expected much to happen, I introduced an amendment to the Surface Transportation Act of 1982, which represents a $71 billion expenditure over four years. My amendment provided a 10 percent set-aside for minority businesses—that represents $7 billion over four years. Now, that's using the system. I would also point out that, in 1975, under the Public Works Act, I introduced an amendment to create a 10 percent set-aside. From that, we received $400 million out of a $4 billion expenditure. In reality, it amounted to over $625 million that flowed into minority businesses. I would further point out that, under the Nixon Administration, I added an amendment that increased the number of summer youth jobs to 1 million. Despite Republican opposition, it passed. That resulted in 250,000 additional jobs for young people as compared to the previous year.

Obviously, it's not easy to effect change. Blacks must develop the sophistication, savvy, and intelligence to bang the system and make it work. There are no guarantees in life. But one thing is sure: If we fail to try, we are certain to lose. If we fight back, we might just win. Isn't it worth the chance? The system isn't perfect—it never has been and it never will be. But that doesn't mean that Blacks should pick up their marbles and go home. It means that we must redouble our efforts. We can't throw in the towel. The game is far from over. We can win—and we must win. But winning depends on hard work. It's easy to give up, to throw up our hands, to condemn the system. But what will that get us? We must make our presence felt at every level of government. And we must keep fighting until we're free. Whoever said that freedom came easily? It takes sustained effort. But, we can succeed—if we are smart enough to understand the system and use it to our advantage. We can do it. And we're not alone. There are many people—of every race, color, and creed—who support our cause. Like us, they recognize that they will not be free until we are free. Together, we can make it happen—if we don't give up.

Louis Stokes

The War Against Black America

Louis Stokes was born February 23, 1925, in Cleveland, Ohio. He received a Bachelor of Arts degree from Western Reserve University in 1948 and a Doctor of Jurisprudence degree from Cleveland Marshall Law School (now Cleveland State University). Prior to his election to Congress in 1968, Stokes had practiced law in Cleveland and was chief trial counsel for the law firm of Stokes, Character, Perry, Whitehead, Young, and Davidson. As a practicing attorney, he argued several cases in the United States Supreme Court—most notably the landmark "stop and frisk" case of *Terry* v. *Ohio* (1968).

In 1968, Stokes was elected to Congress from the 21st Congressional District of Ohio on his first try for public office. By virtue of his election, he became the first black member of Congress from the State of Ohio. He has since been reelected seven times and is currently the senior Democratic representative from Ohio and the dean of the Ohio Democratic Congressional delegation.

Stokes's career in the House of Representatives reflects his rising power and influence within that institution. Stokes was first elected to the House in 1968. As a first-term member, he was appointed to the Education and Labor Committee and the Un-American Activities Committee (since renamed the House Internal Security Committee).

In his second term, he was appointed the first black member ever to sit on the Appropriations Committee and, in 1972, was elected chairman of the Congressional Black Caucus. He served two consecutive terms in that capacity. In addition to his seat on the powerful Appropriations Committee, in 1975, he was elected by the Democratic Caucus to serve on the newly formed Budget Committee. He was twice reelected to the Budget Committee, serving a total of six years.

In 1976, Stokes was appointed by Speaker Carl Albert to serve on a special Select Committee to conduct an investigation and study of the circumstances surrounding the deaths of President John F.

Kennedy and Dr. Martin Luther King, Jr. One year later, House Speaker Thomas P. "Tip" O'Neill appointed him chairman of this committee. In 1978, Stokes completed these historic investigations and filed with the House of Representatives twenty-seven volumes of hearings, a final report, and recommendations for administrative and legislative reform.

In 1980, Speaker O'Neill appointed Stokes to the Committee on Standards of Official Conduct (Ethics Committee), and, in 1981, he was elected chairman of this committee. He was reelected to serve as the Ethics Committee chairman at the beginning of the 98th Congress.

In 1983, O'Neill appointed Stokes to the Permanent Select Committee on Intelligence. The committee enjoys legislative, authorization, and oversight jurisdiction over the intelligence agencies and intelligence related activities of federal agencies.

Ebony Magazine has named Stokes as one of the 100 most influential black Americans each year since 1979. In 1979, *Ebony* nominated him in three categories for the Second Annual American Black Achievement Awards. His nomination was based upon his becoming the first black to head a major congressional investigation and to preside over nationally televised hearings which unearthed several startling new facts on the assassinations of President Kennedy and Dr. King. The following year, his colleagues in the Congressional Black Caucus presented Stokes the William L. Dawson Award. He received this coveted and prestigious award in recognition of his "unique leadership in the development of legislation."

JE: How do you view the present political climate as it relates to the future of black America?

LS: My emotions are mixed, reflecting both frustration and hope. I am frustrated because we have entered a period in our nation's history when the rights of black Americans to full participation in the economic, social, and political life of this country are being challenged today as perhaps never before in this century. Not only are we being challenged through the front door by successful efforts to reduce federal funding for programs which provide a lifeline for millions of Blacks and other Americans, but we are also facing attacks through the back door to undercut fundamental civil rights laws through regulatory and other means. Today, we are witnessing a full-scale attack on school desegregation, affirmative action, tuition tax credits, and other issues of critical importance to black America.

At one time our government was committed to principles of social justice and welfare. This was true under President Lyndon Johnson, who engaged this nation in a War on Poverty. And it was true under President Franklin Roosevelt, who said: "The test of our progress is not whether we add more to the abundance of those who already have too much; it is whether we do enough for those who have too little."

As a nation, we have become less concerned about people. We have become a nation more preoccupied with arming and preparing for war against nations and no longer committed to waging a war on poverty. Today, Congress is more concerned about balancing the federal budget than it is about balancing people's lives. Now, we have an administration which thinks nothing of spending over $1.7 trillion for nuclear warheads, MX missiles, and other nuclear armaments, and sending millions of dollars to places like El Salvador, Nicaragua, and Honduras at a time when more than 11 million people are unemployed; when 22 million Americans depend upon food stamps to eat; when soup kitchens and hunger centers are besieged by more people than they can possibly feed; and when 2 million homeless sleep on grates in the streets because they have nowhere else to go.

JE: How would you assess the current priorities of the Reagan Administration? Do they reflect the goals and aspirations of black Americans?

LS: No. There is something shamefully wrong with the priorities of a nation which continues year after year to spend more and more money on military hardware and weapons for Nicaragua, Honduras, and El Salvador while sending cheese to Detroit, Chicago, Cleveland, and other major cities in the United States.

I am deeply concerned and troubled about the lack of priorities at the national level. In human terms, the consequences of the misplaced priorities of the Reagan Administration's economic policies have proved devastating. We have witnessed at the grass roots level and experienced first-hand the tragic results of this administration's policies to slam the door in the face of a major segment of the population which needs and has the right to expect assistance from its government.

JE: How would you assess the president's policies in the area of job training and equal employment opportunity? How have they affected America's black population?

LS: President Reagan talks about self-sufficiency, claiming that jobs exist for all who want to work if they would just read the want ads. He promised at the start of his administration that 3 million new jobs would be created each year as a result of his economic policies. We now know that these jobs were not created. In fact, we lost 3 million jobs and witnessed, over the past year, the highest number of persons unemployed since the Depression.

Blacks, of course, were the first to be fired after decades of struggle to get a foot in the door, not to mention get hired. With 1 out of 5 Blacks out of a job, it is the black community which has suffered the brunt of the failed policies of this administration. More and more black families have been pushed over the edge of economic despair. Instead of waging a war on poverty, this administration has created more of it. Under the Reagan Administration, more black families are now officially classified by the federal government as living in poverty. These families are desperately poor. And when we examine what poor people can now expect from their government, we see a grim picture of unfair and inequitable budget cuts that have assaulted poor people and given little hope for a better future. For example, the Aid to Families with Dependent Children program (AFDC) does little more than help to ensure that poor families are able to eke out a decent existence. Still, it is a vital lifeline to over 10 million households, 44 percent of which are black and mainly female. Since the start of the Reagan Administration, 365,000 families have been terminated from AFDC, including 1.5 million children. Many of these families lost Medicaid coverage as well. An additional 260,000 families have had their AFDC benefits reduced, from levels which were none too generous in the first place. The Reagan Administration is continuing its attack on this program, seeking $722 million in cuts for fiscal year 1984, in addition to the cuts of similar magnitude enacted in the fiscal years 1983 and 1982.

JE: The Reagan Administration has targeted several key areas in terms of budget cuts, one of which was the Food Stamp Program. How serious have these cuts proved to be?

LS: Since the enactment of the Food Stamp Program, malnutrition in America has been all but wiped out. Although the program provides only a meager benefit of 47 cents per person per meal, it enables 22 million poor Americans to obtain food and nourishment. Nearly 40 percent of all food stamp recipients are black and half are children. Yet, since the start of the Reagan Administration, the Food Stamp Program has been slashed by over $2 billion a year, 1 million beneficiaries have been terminated, and about 4 million have had their benefits reduced. The fiscal year 1984 Reagan budget would cut this program again by $756 million.

JE: Are you equally critical of the president's record in the area of health care?

LS: Yes. The president's budget proposals can only be labeled "Hazardous to the Health of Black Americans." Ironically, some of the president's health budget cuts are criticized by his own Commission for the Study of Ethical Problems in Medicine and Biomedical and Behavioral Research. Charged with ascertaining the federal government's ethical responsibilities in health care and research, the commission issued the latest indictment of health care in America on March 28, 1983. In a 220-page report called "Securing Access to Health Care," the commission concluded that the federal government *does* indeed have the ultimate responsibility to see that an adequate level of health care is available to all citizens. Moreover, this prestigious panel (with eight Reagan appointees) warned that the government is falling far short of this goal. The commission also noted that hardest hit are "working families of modest income, the very poor, members of racial and ethnic minorities, and people who live in very rural and inner-city communities."

It is no surprise that black people receive too little health care and usually too late. The statistics which reveal that Blacks suffer higher death rates than whites for 13 of the 15 leading causes of death tell us that. The statistics which document that the black infant mortality rate is twice as high as the rate for whites tell us that black mothers and children are not receiving the health care they need. Yet, the Reagan Administration would have us believe that the primary role for the federal government in health care these days is to cut costs, not to promote health—never mind the fact that in health care we save money in the long run by spending money in the short term to prevent illness and sickness.

JE: To what extent have the president's cutbacks in the Medicaid program undermined its effectiveness?

LS: In 1965, the Medicaid program was enacted because Congress felt that access to health care ought to be a right, not a privilege. Over 23 million Americans now depend upon Medicaid to help pay for checkups, medical treatment, hospitalization, and medicine. Still, one-half of America's poor are ineligible for Medicaid and thus lack the resources to pay for costly health care.

Instead of expanding the program to reach these needy individuals, the federal Medicaid budget was slashed by nearly $1 billion a year for the fiscal years 1982 through 1984. Recent budget cuts have effectively eliminated the working poor from the program, and the states have been given greater flexibility to cut back services and reduce eligibility, despite the increasing need from families with unemployed members. President Reagan has proposed cuts of $300 million in 1984 in addition to those already implemented. Medicaid recipients would be required to pay a fee before receiving any services, thereby further limiting access to health care for black Americans who already receive less than they need.

Since President Reagan assumed office, cutbacks in essential health programs, such as community health centers, maternal and child health programs, sickle cell clinics, and community mental health centers, have made it even harder for Blacks and low-income Americans to gain access to the health care they need to stay alive and well. At last count, over 100 community health centers have been terminated from federal support, thus eliminating 400,000, mostly poor persons, from services. Funding for prenatal care, immunizations, and checkups for mothers and children has been slashed by nearly 20 percent, and over 200,000 children and mothers have lost preventive and child health services. Thousands of nutritionally at risk mothers and infants are on waiting lists to receive milk and other food supplements under the Women, Infants, and Children program (WIC), which President Reagan wanted to consolidate into a block grant, and federal support for community mental health centers has been consolidated into a block grant, with overall funding cut by 30 percent.

JE: At the outset of the interview, you said that you viewed the future with both hope and frustration. What is the source of that hope?

LS: Despite this litany of budget cuts—harnessed on the backs of the poor—I have hope. I have hope because the American people are growing tired of a government that lacks human compassion, a government that refuses to see the necessity of investing in our people, a government that always places guns over butter. I have hope because the American people are beginning to be frightened by the policies that their government is proposing. People are finding it harder and harder to understand how an unending escalation of the arms race contributes to American security or improves the prospects for world peace. They recognize the importance of military preparedness, but they also understand that America cannot hope to *win* a nuclear war, and they view with horror the towering stockpile of nuclear weapons—over 1 million times the power of the Hiroshima bomb—already accumulated by the superpowers. Americans are willing to pay for a strong defense, but they are also alarmed at the ever-increasing costs of the present military build-up. They see defense spending becoming an obstacle to economic recovery, squeezing out domestic investment in capital and human resources, weakening further the United States' competitive position in world markets, and contributing to unprecedentedly high federal deficits.

I have hope because Americans are counting the costs of cutbacks in social spending. They are finding it harder and harder to understand why 3 million children were unable to receive a hot lunch last year due to cutbacks in the federal school lunch program, when we continue to subsidize "three martini lunches" for businessmen through the tax code. They find it hard to understand how the states are going to pick up funding for mental health, drug abuse services, child welfare, and runaway youth programs when many of the states are battling deficits of their own.

I have hope because the American people are beginning to realize just how important a role the federal government plays in meeting the human needs of this country. In many of the areas I've mentioned—such as mental health, child abuse, drug abuse—we know that there are critical needs, which can only be met by training a cadre of specially prepared people equipped to address these problems. There is compelling evidence that the social and economic payoff from an effective and efficient social service delivery network far outweighs the initial costs.

JE: Do you sense a growing political awareness among black Americans and a commitment to reversing this nation's present priorities?

LS: Yes. We have turned the corner. The black community is on the threshold of moving from despair to hope, from apathy to unity, from pride to power. We now have 21 black members of Congress—the highest number ever; more than 300 black state legislators, over 200 black mayors, and 5,000 elected black officials at the local level. There are 17 million blacks of voting age in this country. And, with the recent victory of Mayor Harold Washington in Chicago, black voters are demonstrating that they can no longer be taken for granted or ignored.

The late Dr. Martin Luther King, Jr., once said: "The most important step that a person can take is that short walk to the ballot box." Black voters have supplied that margin of victory in the defeat of conservative congressmen Albert Lee Smith in Alabama and John Napier in South Carolina and in gubernatorial races in New York and Texas. We came close to electing the first black governor and the first black congressman from Mississippi since Reconstruction.

Indeed, black politics is on the threshold of a new era. Who would have guessed just three years ago that we would be talking about a black presidential candidate and be taken seriously! While no one believes that this country is ready for a black president, fielding a black presidential candidate—Jesse Jackson—has served a number of important objectives. First, he served to elevate on the list of priorities issues of vital importance to Blacks, such as the need for additional jobs, education, and training. Second, he served to stimulate voter registration in the black community and give Blacks strong leverage in the selection of the Democratic presidential candidate.

JE: How would you assess the political and economic gains that Blacks have made over the last twenty years?

LS: Obviously, we made significant gains during the 1960s and

1970s. These gains were principally due to the enormous impact of the civil rights movement of the 1960s and the political, economic, and educational empowerment which came about as a result of legislation in both the 1960s and 1970s.

However, measure those gains by any standard, and two things will become apparent. One is that, while a few Blacks have moved into a status known as middle class, they have left behind a large number of black Americans who can be categorized as low and moderate income: the unemployed, the ill housed, the poor, the urban elderly, and even those who fit into a category appropriately coined the "underclass."

JE: To what extent has the Congressional Black Caucus, of which you were a founding member, succeeded in calling attention to these problems and influencing the actions of Congress?

LS: The Congressional Black Caucus remains committed to the position that government must be an active force for the enhancement of social justice and human dignity. We have had to become leaders and fight aggressively to protect constitutional freedoms and social justice for not just minorities but for all Americans.

During this session of Congress, thanks to the Reagan Administration, we have been kept very busy. Indeed, these are very serious times, and our nation has very serious problems. We are now just emerging from a deep recession where interest rates soared to the highest figures in history. Unemployment figures reveal that, despite the claims of the President, more than 11 million Americans are out of work.

All my life I have been taught that government existed for people; that there are people who simply cannot help themselves and are therefore dependent upon their government. As I view the dismantlement of government through budgetary cutbacks in human needs and social service programs, I find myself asking whatever happened to the phrase, "Government of the people, by the people, and for the people."

The Congressional Black Caucus believes that two decisions the government has made under the leadership of President Reagan are responsible for the current state of the economy. The first was the decision of the Federal Reserve Board, which had the strong backing of the administration, to fight inflation by increasing the cost of credit. The high interest rates, which are the result of tight money policies, have driven credit-sensitive small farmers, small businessmen, and homebuilders to ruin. For while people can afford the cost of housing and businessmen the cost of inventory and farmers the cost of seed and fertilizer, they cannot afford the 17–20 percent cost of money they have had to borrow to purchase those items.

A second governmental decision which has plunged the nation into deep recession was the decision of the president and the Congress to cut taxes for the well-to-do and profitable corporations by a staggering $750 billion over the next five years, while at the same time increasing defense spending to a record $1.6 trillion over the next five years. As a result, four records were established by the administration: record cuts in so-called "safety-net programs," record give-aways of tax resources, record increases in defense spending, and a record deficit.

The budget battle which the Congressional Black Caucus waged was a battle for a fair and decent America. It was a battle about whether we will continue to invest federal dollars in the young, in families, in the needy, and in working men and women or whether we will invest in the rich and in more and more arms, which will surely lead us down the path of economic and moral bankruptcy. It was a battle about whether we will invest in human capital—new generations of healthy, well-educated, productive citizens—or whether we will choose short-term profit and easy political fixes. It was a battle about who and what we Americans are as a people and as a nation.

JE: Now that President Reagan has won reelection, what will a second term mean for the future of black America?

LS: As I look down the road into the 1980s, I envision the next several years as being a difficult time for minorities. I base this not only upon the policies of the administration, but upon the conservative mood of the Congress. Fiscal and social conservatism has now become the dominant political, cultural, and social trend for the 1980s. It is characterized by an increased mood in Congress of indifference, antipathy, and hostility toward social and governmental programs on behalf of minorities, the poor, and the disadvantaged. The re-election of President Reagan has given impetus to the shift to the right in Congress, and we are now confronted with renewed efforts to oppose affirmative action programs, government spending for social welfare programs, busing, and the Equal Rights Amendment. Conservative politicians also now propose reduction of the minimum wage, tuition tax credits, and restoration of the death penalty.

JE: Would you agree with the charge that the Reagan Administration is hostile to the needs of America's Blacks?

LS: Yes. Despite President Reagan's pained denials, this administration appears to have declared war on black Americans. In area after area, black Americans have borne the brunt of this administration's policy initiatives.

This administration appears to be engaged in a systematic effort to reverse the civil rights gains of Blacks and other minorities achieved over the past three decades. This is the first time in eight administrations that vigorous attempts are now being made to turn back the clock on the individual rights guaranteed by the Constitution, Congress, and the Supreme Court.

In many important areas of civil rights enforcement, the Justice Department has all but ceased its operations. Not a single school desegregation suit has been filed since President Reagan took office. In the same period, only two new cases have been filed to enforce the voting rights laws, and only two cases have been filed under the fair housing laws. In addition, the Civil Rights Division of the Justice Department has repudiated affirmative action as an appropriate relief in employment discrimination cases and has stated that under no circumstances would it impose such a remedy.

Under the Reagan Administration, both the Justice Department and the Education Department have made a major effort to weaken the government's role in desegregating public school systems. The Justice Department, which has the primary responsibility for desegregation of public education, either has done nothing or has taken the anti-civil rights side of the case. In fact, Assistant Attorney General for Civil Rights William Bradford Reynolds proclaimed: "We are not going to compel children who don't choose to have an integrated education to have one." Moreover, the Justice Department announced that it may ask the courts to dismantle court-ordered school busing plans. The assistant attorney general has also stated that the Reagan Justice Department is opposed to mandatory busing as a means of desegregating public schools.

The Education Department has abandoned court-ordered criteria for the desegregation of higher education, even though now, thirty years after the historic *Brown* (1954) desegregation decision, much of American higher education remains substantially segregated. Education Secretary Terrel Bell has said that he refuses to enforce school desegregation laws which, in his words, are "against my own philosophy."

One of the most unconscionable acts of this administration occurred when it announced on January 8, 1982, that it would no longer challenge claims for tax-exempt status made by schools that discriminate on the basis of race. Since 1970, the Internal Revenue Service (IRS) has denied claims for tax-exempt status made by schools that exclude or otherwise discriminate against Blacks and other minorities. The administration explained that it reversed the IRS policy because it was not specifically authorized by law but, rather, was promulgated by administrative fiat.

Four days later, following a barrage of criticism by members of Congress, civil rights leaders, and others, President Reagan issued a statement defending the reversal on grounds that the IRS had no authority to deny such tax-exempt status to private schools and other institutions that practice racial discrimination.

JE: Is the Reagan record markedly better in the area of equal employment opportunity?

LS: No. The attorney general and assistant attorney general for civil rights have unilaterally adopted policies that reverse the long-standing tradition that the Justice Department should play the lead role in enforcing the mandate of equal employment opportunity. They have also abandoned the advocacy of goals and timetables to help correct pervasive discrimination in employment discrimination suits. As stated by Assistant Attorney General Reynolds, the Justice Department opposes "the use of quotas or any other numerical or statistical formula designed to provide to victims of discrimination preferential treatment based on race, sex, national origin, or religion."

JE: President Reagan first opposed, then waffled, and then supported the extension of the Voting Rights Act. How would you interpret his actions in this area?

LS: President Reagan refused to take a position on extending the Voting Rights Act for almost a year, and then opposed the extension approved overwhelmingly by the House of Representatives on October 5, 1981. He initially favored expanding the act's coverage to all the states rather than only to those states with a history of discrimination practices. This would have allowed the states to totally gut the act by making it virtually impossible for the Justice Department to enforce.

JE: The picture you paint, despite earlier statements of optimism, is extremely bleak. Do you see any signs of progress?

LS: My comments were intended to paint a real picture of the real world in which I live and work. At the same time, I can say that we will survive. We will survive because we have always known adversity, oppression, discrimination, and racism, but we have survived. Our ability to survive is deeply rooted in our history.

In 1981, I stood in the old slave quarters on Gori Island, just off the coast of Senegal. This was one of the main ports of embarkation for the slave trade from West Africa. The African guide, after showing us the cold, concrete sections of the slave quarters, took us to the rear of the old house. There, he showed us the narrow passageway through which the slaves came as they boarded the gangplank onto the ship. He explained how those who were sick or infirm as they came through the passageway were simply shoved off into the ocean. Still, we survived.

Lying chained together in the belly of ships, we survived the journey. We survived the heat, the meanness, and the degradation of plantation slavery. Historians tell us that between 1619 and 1860, of the millions of slaves who left the shores of Africa, only one-half reached America. But we survived, and any group of people who could survive slavery will also survive Reaganomics.

So, as I look at America, thirty years after *Brown*, obviously we have made a great deal of progress. Many Blacks have moved into the so-called black middle class. Some Blacks are not only driving Cadillacs, Corvettes, and Mercedes, but they are also making the payments on time. But many of our black brothers and sisters have not yet tasted of the American dream. It should be obvious that we still have a great need for our black organizations. And it should be equally obvious that we must continue fighting for our rights.

JE: In addition to political action, what else would you recommend in terms of reversing America's priorities?

LS: When you really think about it, *education* is the mechanism through which we transfer knowledge and, in the process, realize the human potential that is basic to our nation's strength. That strength lies not in nuclear warheads but in our people and their productive capacity. Our nation's wealth is derived from educated minds and trained hands. Thus, federal support for equal opportunity in higher education is no less an investment in our nation's fundamental well-being, growth, and security.

JE: How would you evaluate the Reagan Administration's commitment to equal educational opportunity?

LS: We have a tremendous pool of talented students who are not being adequately tapped and given an opportunity to receive a first-class education at every level. We have a tremendous wealth of talent and ingenuity in our young people that is being wasted. I consider this to be a tragic loss of human potential, which this nation desperately needs.

Unemployment among our black youth has reached a shocking 50 percent. One out of two black youth lacks gainful employment. Many of these youth have never had a Social Security card and, indeed, have never had a job. And yet, our national investment in these youth is declining, not increasing. Young people with basic academic competence and highly developed skills will be in high demand in the labor market of the 1980s and 1990s, while those without these skills will fall by the wayside.

The only way in which we will decrease the pool of disadvantaged students is to help them acquire the information, knowledge, and technical know-how they need to survive. This is what building for the future is all about.

I find it ironic that the Reagan Administration, despite its professed belief in promoting economic growth, seems bent on limiting the supply of the *one* ingredient essential to an economic rebirth: the supply of talented and trained people. The administration's proposals to decimate, dismantle, and downgrade higher education programs threaten our nation's very ability to produce sufficient numbers of scientists, engineers, and the whole panoply of skilled personnel necessary to improve our country's long-term productivity and stimulate economic revitalization.

Since the advent of the Reagan Administration, education programs have suffered from an attack unparalleled in the history of federal aid to education. In President Reagan's first year in office, he proposed to cancel 1 out of every 4 federal dollars slated for education. Under the guise of "refocusing federal education assistance on the 'truly needy,'" President Reagan plotted the further destruction of existing education assistance by slashing President Carter's education request of $17.7 billion by a massive $4 billion.

In Reagan's second year in office, the administration again struck out against education, since Congress had refused to support all of the budget cuts proposed earlier. President Reagan asked that Congress rescind another $1.6 billion from the enacted 1982 education budget and carve still another $3.5 billion out of the education budget for the following year. Although we had long ago eliminated all the fat and were aiming for the meat and bone of education spending, this was not enough. Nothing short of abolishing the Department of Education would satisfy this administration.

It took the Congress two long years to muster the courage to stand up to President Reagan. In the 97th Congress, members rejected the meat ax approach to education advanced by this administration. For 1983, President Reagan requested $10 billion for the Department of Education. We appropriated $15 billion, restoring all the proposed cuts and adding more for some high priority programs. We may never know, however, how many students were discouraged from pursuing a higher education during the interim. We may never know how many dreams were demolished because of this administration's demoralizing efforts to deny federal assistance to needy college students.

JE: Finally, what role has and should the black church play in the struggle for freedom and justice?

LS: Historically, the black church has been the *only* free institution in our captive community. The black preacher has been the only independent voice capable of articulating the needs of our people without fear of financial retaliation.

No other Black can say the same. Black politicians, black businessmen, black educators, and black professionals cannot claim this kind of independence. Therefore, if we as a people are to move from pride to power, from despair to hope, from apathy to unity, the black church must remain the cornerstone in our struggle for liberty and equality.

The church was a sanctuary where we not only came together to hear God's word, but we also came together to hear how we were coming on freedom's trail. From slavery until the turbulent 1960s, it was the church where we had to meet—often in the dark of night. Ours is a history in which ministers gave their lives, and churches were bombed and burned to the ground.

The struggle still goes on. And behind the pastor and behind the church has been a dedicated and committed people. Probably no people in the history of the world have been as oppressed, or enslaved, or so discriminated against. And yet, we have survived with an unfaltering faith in our God. And along with our faith in God we have had faith that one day this nation would rise up and live up to its creed—that "all men are created equal."

Throughout it all, we have never doubted that one day we shall overcome and that this nation will come to know the true meaning of its own pledge of allegiance of "one nation, under God, indivisible, with liberty and justice for all." As a people, we could not have survived without the black church. It has been more than a sanctuary—it has been the institution which carried us over; the institution which gave us the modern Moses, Dr. Martin Luther King, Jr.; the institution which through all of our struggles, remains today the strongest foundation in our community. In a real sense, the black church has been our crutch for survival.

Major R. Owens

The Predicament of Power

Major R. Owens was born June 28, 1936, in Memphis, Tennessee. He received a Bachelor of Arts degree from Morehouse College in 1956 and a Master of Science degree from Atlanta University in 1957. A librarian by profession, Owens was an adjunct professor of library science and director of the Community Media Program at Columbia University, as well as a community coordinator at the Brooklyn Public Library, one of the largest systems in the country. In 1979, he was the keynote speaker at the national White House Conference on Libraries.

Owens's career as a legislator began with his 1974 election to the New York State Senate from the Brownsville and East New York sections of Brooklyn. During New York City's "fiscal crisis" and its aftermath, the then Senator Owens proved himself an unusually effective advocate on behalf of a broad range of social programs. He chaired the Senate Day Care Task Force and served on the Senate Finance and Social Services Committees, among others.

Prior to his election to the State Senate, Owens served six years as commissioner of New York City's Community Development Agency. In this post he was in charge of all of the city's anti-poverty programs. Mayor John V. Lindsay appointed him on the basis of his record at the Brownsville Community Council in the mid-1960s where, according to Charles Morris in his book, *The Cost of Good Intentions*, Owens was "the most capable and canny" of all of New York's neighborhood-based anti-poverty program directors.

Owens boasts a long and distinguished record of community activism. He chaired the Brooklyn Congress of Racial Equality; was vice-president of the Metropolitan Council of Housing, a city-wide tenants' rights group; and was a member of the International Commission on Ways of Implementing Social Policy to Ensure Maximum Public Participation and Social Justice for Minorities, at The Hague, Netherlands, in 1972.

In 1982, Owens was elected to the United States House of Representatives from New York's 12th Congressional District, created under the Voting Rights Act in the 1982 legislative reapportionment. His district includes several of the neighborhoods formerly represented by the now-retired Congresswoman Shirley Chisholm.

A member of the House Education and Labor and Government Operations Committees, Owens also co-chairs the House Freshman Caucus Task Force on Employment. He has made a full-employment-based economic recovery policy his major legislative priority and has worked tirelessly on behalf of programs aimed at the poor and minorities.

JE: To what extent can your interest and involvement in politics be attributed to your parents' influence and early childhood experiences?

MO: My father was an avid reader of the daily newspaper. He was a day laborer in a furniture factory. Dad followed the news and discussed current events at the dinner table. He frequently expressed his views on the state of the world, as well as on the rightness or wrongness of government actions. My father idolized Franklin Roosevelt as a result of his strong leadership during the Depression and the various programs which formed his New Deal. After all, Roosevelt rescued the nation from near-disaster, a fact which Dad never failed to mention. As a result, we were treated to endless discourses on the virtues of Franklin Roosevelt and the New Deal. To a large extent, what I learned at home from the opinions of my father, who exerted a major influence on my world view, shaped my philosophy.

JE: Is your political approach a product of Franklin Roosevelt's New Deal philosophy?

MO: Yes, to a large extent. I can't remember a time when I wasn't aware of the fact that a much bigger world than my own personal universe was out there. We were very poor. We always seemed to have financial problems of one kind or another and had to struggle just to make ends meet. Still, I was also aware that we were not alone—that millions of people, both in this country and abroad, were faced with similar kinds of problems. I also realized that what happened in the larger world affected my family and its personal welfare.

My father also hero-worshipped Dwight Eisenhower. He closely monitored the events of World War II, reading *Life* magazine and the news of the war in the press. My father was a frustrated militarist. I didn't get the name "Major" by accident. He wanted to join the army in World War I but wasn't old enough to enlist. In World War II he failed to be drafted because he had too many children to support. But he would have liked very much to have gone into the army. As a result, he followed world events closely—particularly the war—and enjoyed theorizing and strategizing about battlefield tactics and maneuvers. We kept in touch with the world through his eyes. My father was keenly interested in the future of his children; he had a profound sense of destiny. He had no real sense of what would become of us, but he was confident we would accomplish great things, somehow.

My father's optimism about my future had a great impact on me. I felt there was no reason why I couldn't go out and scale life's summits. The world didn't frighten me. And the next steps have never frightened me. I've never felt inadequate. I've always felt up to life's challenges.

In retrospect, I think that my attitudes about myself—and life in general—are due to my father's positive outlook and, of course, my mother's nurturing. My mother was not as political, nor was she as involved in the day-to-day events of the larger world. She was the scholar of the family. She had a very good record in school. She was disciplined and hardworking. And she set high standards for herself and worked hard to achieve them. That attitude affected me as well, and I suppose that much of what I have achieved and hope to achieve is a direct outgrowth of what she taught me.

JE: Is your interest in politics traceable to a particular individual or event?

MO: It's difficult to say. My interest in doing well—in wanting to help my people and contribute to the struggle for freedom and justice— did not develop because I wanted to go into politics. I never perceived it that way. I wanted to be a writer. Early on, I developed an interest in writing. I don't know exactly where that was. At one point, my mother was very sickly. During that period, I listened to an endless series of soap operas, which served to fire my imagination. I got the bug and decided that I wanted to be a writer—a novelist. I enrolled in college with that objective in mind, but my parents urged me to choose a more practical career such as pre-med or engineering. I was good in math and science in high school, but I was not particularly interested in pre-med, primarily because of the long period of study involved. Moreover, I thought it would be too expensive to pursue a medical career. At the time, I didn't realize you could apply for financial aid, so I wrote off the possibility of a pre-med course of study. My goal was to attend college for four years, graduate, get a job, and raise a family. So I focused on engineering as the more practical option.

Although I still had the writing bug, I eventually majored in math and minored in education. Finally, in my last year, I decided to go into library science. At that time, there was a nationwide demand for librarians. I thought that by becoming a librarian, I could mesh my interest in writing with my desire to make a decent living.

JE: As a college student, did you participate in the civil rights movement? If so, how?

MO: Yes, to some extent I did. I was involved in a campaign to integrate the local library and movie houses. Not much ever came of it, but the seed was there. I graduated from Morehouse College in 1956 and enrolled in Atlanta University the following year. Nineteen fifty-seven marked the beginning of the Montgomery Bus Boycott. At the time, the civil rights movement was in high gear. I was involved in various student protest groups. We attempted to pressure the administration to play a more active role in combatting segregation in the Atlanta area.

But again, I viewed myself first as a writer. I was the editor of the college newspaper as well as editor of the school literary magazine. I identified closely with those students who saw the newspaper as a political instrument. But, for me, it was primarily a way to perfect my writing skills although I also saw its potential for influencing student attitudes. Unlike many politicians, I never was president of my class. Nor did I aspire to be. I always felt more comfortable in the background.

JE: What issue or issues most concerned you as a young college student?

MO: I was primarily interested in issues involving freedom of speech and academic freedom. I was also interested in strategic questions—questions related to the approach taken by traditional black leaders in the area of race. But my concerns went well beyond race. They centered on the conflict between accommodation and confrontation. The fact that many black leaders seemed too quick to compromise and that they were, as such, exerting a conservative influence on the movement, troubled me. These leaders did not realize how entrenched they were and how their actions reinforced many of the ills they sought to curb. At the time, the writings of Machiavelli, as well as Jewish capitulation in Germany during Hitler's early rise, impressed me. I started to think about sacrifice and what it meant. I started to ask myself such questions as: What does it take to be a man? When do you sacrifice your manhood? What price is survival worth? These questions were very important to me. Ultimately, I asked myself the question: What price will you pay in order to succeed? I spent considerable time studying the pre-King civil rights era and the era that followed. The great emphasis in the black community had always been on individual success. Blacks said: If you succeed, you will automatically help your race—others will benefit from your success. This inevitably required accommodation. The post-King era marked a significant change of attitude. The civil rights movement emphasized the group approach: the need to make personal sacrifices in order to achieve group goals. In addition, it stressed the importance of confronting the white power structure even if it meant risking your life and well-being. I found this new approach intoxicating. And it had an important impact on my life and work.

JE: Looking back, which individuals played the greatest role in shaping your philosophy, your approach to life, and your attitudes about government?

MO: There are very few *direct* influences. As I've said, my father was a strong influence. My college professors also played a salient role. At the time I was attending Morehouse College, the president was Dr. Benjamin Mays. Although I often disagreed with his policies and pronouncements, I had tremendous respect for him. Mays had great style and class. He had a clear perception of the mission of the black college and its relationship to the larger mission of the world. He was a fantastic speaker. When he spoke, you listened with rapt attention. I tried to emulate his style. He could really move people.

A major influence was my humanities teacher, whom I later married. She taught humanities at Morehouse College from an interdisciplinary perspective—one that emphasized music, art, literature—in a manner that would reveal the essentials of the creative process. She was a tremendously hard-driving teacher and proved to be a major force in my life. She helped me to understand my own preoccupation with problems larger than literature. I believe that life imitates art—art provides insights into the dynamics of the universe. She inspired a heightened awareness of art and how it contributes to a deeper appreciation of virtually all other aspects of life.

JE: Have you ever regretted your decision to pursue a political career as opposed to one in law or library science?

MO: No, not really. I don't regret it. Perhaps I'm a bit foolish, but I still harbor the dream that I will return to fiction writing. In the long run, the interplay of experiences I've had, combined with my feelings about those experiences, will enhance my ability to write better novels, short stories, plays . . . . I have thousands of ideas swimming in my head.

When I first went to work in the Brooklyn Public Library, I spent the first two years writing a novel, which I eventually finished. But that occurred during the early 1960s—at the height of the civil rights movement—and I grew increasingly restless. My days were spent writing—rising early and retiring late—while the outside world was moving at blitzkrieg speed. When I completed the novel, I took it to several publishers—but met with little success. At that point, I became active in the civil rights movement, which ultimately led to a political career. Still, I *did* write one novel. It's sitting on my shelf, waiting to be revised. I've since completed one play and have begun another. I still harbor dreams of writing, but that will have to wait.

In retrospect, I don't think I've wasted my time. I don't regret having pursued a career in politics. It's proven to be very satisfying. I think I've made a contribution, and I hope to make a larger one in the future. In the long run, my goal is to make an imprint on large numbers of people. I think I can have a greater impact as a writer than as a politician, but my political involvement will, I'm sure, enhance my future literary efforts.

I view politics as extremely important. I certainly don't wish to minimize the significance of my present efforts. What I'm doing, in my estimation, is extremely valuable. But my first love is writing, and it's writing that affords me the greatest satisfaction.

JE: When did you first become involved in The Congress of Racial Equality (CORE)? What did that experience teach you about politics and the political system?

MO: I first became involved in Brooklyn CORE in 1961. My involvement stemmed from a desire to invest my time and talents in something socially significant. I faced the same problem which, I suspect, many young people face today. When I was writing full-time, I had this burning desire to do something meaningful. But it's funny, when I'm doing such things, I have a burning desire to write. At the time, I had just completed my novel—which I felt good about—and wanted to become involved in the movement. As a result, I joined Brooklyn CORE, which had a very small, but active, membership. I became deeply involved in the planning phase of the March on Washington, which I viewed as extremely significant. I also became involved in voter registration and took part in several rent control strikes. In fact, I organized a number of rent strikes. Back then, I was involved in a variety of nitty-gritty issues—particularly at the local level. Local government fascinated me. My involvement in the rent control movement and, later, the housing committee gave me a first-hand understanding of the workings of local government and the way in which local government impacts on people's lives. I concluded that, in order to be effective, people have to combine the confrontational approach with the systems approach—that the best way to bring about change is to become system-wise. I attempted to convince CORE that, in the long run, this approach promised the greatest results.

At the time, Brooklyn CORE was extremely successful—particularly in the area of confrontational politics. It was less successful in terms of using the system to effect change. That process proved less glamorous. As a result, I met with considerable resistance when I proposed such an approach. After all, if you're going to bring about change, it is imperative that you understand the system. Otherwise, you have much less chance of being able to influence the political actors and the decision-making process. In the end, CORE concluded that this approach had merit—so much so, that many of us decided to run for public office.

My entry into politics came as the result of external pressure. I never aspired to elective office. However, several friends and associates urged me to run, believing that I could help to bring about social change. At the time, I was chairman of the housing committee and, later, of a city-wide rent strike committee. Shortly thereafter, I became chairman of Brooklyn CORE, a position which I held two years. It was during my second year as chairman that several people suggested that we take a stab at elective office. No one thought we would win. Our intent was to dramatize the fact that elective politics was a natural second step in the evolution of our activities. By then, we were fed up with the system. We realized that community organization, though important, had certain limitations. We also realized that you had to change the elected officials in order to change the system. The year before, the Mississippi Freedom Democratic Party had made history at the 1964 Democratic National Convention. In 1965, we decided to build on their success, calling ourselves the Brooklyn Freedom Democratic Movement. I ran for a seat on the city council and lost. The same year, John Lindsay ran for and was elected Mayor of New York. During the campaign, I had an opportunity to meet and talk with him. One thing led to another, and, two years later, I was appointed commissioner of New York City's Community Development Agency—which was the city's anti-poverty program. My appointment stemmed, I suspect, from my work for the Brownsville Community Council. Looking back, though, my experience at CORE prepared me best for my later political activities. It gave me a heightened understanding of city politics and the way in which the system works. My experience on the rent strike committee and the housing committee also proved valuable in preparing me to direct a local community action agency and, later, to serve as commissioner of the city's anti-poverty program. So, one thing led to another.

JE: In 1974, you were elected to the New York State Senate from the Brownsville and East New York sections of Brooklyn. What appeal did the State Senate hold?

MO: As a member of Brooklyn CORE and, later as chairman, I saw my mission in life as building community-based institutions so that people could better fight for their interests. The community action field proved to be a golden opportunity to earn a living by doing precisely what I wanted to do with my life. But my first priority then was to return to writing. My second priority was to become involved in community empowerment. I saw the latter as a means by which oppressed people could fight the system and win. That became my mission in life. President Lyndon Johnson's "Great Society" and John Lindsay's "War on Poverty" contributed mightily to community empowerment.

I enjoyed my work as commissioner of New York City's Community Development Agency. It gave me great personal satisfaction. Looking back, we were able to accomplish many of our objectives. But six years in that position proved enough. By that time, Lindsay himself had changed. Initially, he was a Republican, fighting a Democratic-controlled city. The people on the outside—the fringes of society—banged down the traditional doors. He was their savior. After a while, he gave up and switched to the Democratic Party and ultimately decided to run for president. He became extremely political, so much so that during the last few years I was there, he allowed the local politicians to dismantle many of the programs he had fought so hard to establish. In the end, I concluded that community empowerment ultimately depended on political power. We had no choice, I felt, but to enter the political arena. The time had come to run our own candidates. I preached this message to everyone who would listen. Then we started to look around for potential candidates. At the time, few candidates could really be trusted. So, I decided that the time had come for me to take the plunge.

I felt it was important to run in an area in which I was known—where I had a long record of public service. Clearly, my best prospects lay in the Brownsville area and in the adjacent parts of central Brooklyn. Initially, I decided to run for the city council. The city council, more than other governmental bodies, was responsible for subverting many of Mayor Lindsay's most crucial programs. Moreover, I personally disliked Sam Wright, the councilman from the Brownsville area, who was among the most vicious and backward of the politicians who were attempting to take over the anti-poverty program. So, I decided to challenge him. However, in that year, the federal government ordered the state legislature to reapportion its legislative districts. In doing so, it created a new senatorial district—one with no incumbent. At the time, it seemed the logical place from which to run, if I wanted to win elective office. So I ran for the State Senate.

Our campaign organization was staffed, for the most part, by amateurs. Still, I had considerable name recognition, owing to my long record of community involvement. At the time, the two major political clubs in central Brooklyn were at war with one another, which resulted in a three-way contest. I slid in through the middle, winning by a narrow margin. But I won.

After the election, it became clear that if I wanted to protect community institutions, I would have to develop greater clout. Otherwise, I was simply wasting my time. After all, it's fairly easy for one councilman or one assemblyman or one state senator, in a matter of months, to undo everything you've worked so hard to build, simply by applying political leverage in the right places. Therefore, it was necessary to build a political organization. So, we formed such an organization—one which would help to safeguard the gains we had made. As a result, I became a thorn in the side of not only Sam Wright, but also the Brooklyn machine, which backed Wright. The machine was determined to destroy me. They gave me two years. Their plan was to wage an aggressive campaign against me when I ran for re-election. I countered by running my own candidate for the State Assembly. By that time, we had built a strong organization, and I had learned some important political lessons. The results proved it: I was re-elected, and our candidate for the State Assembly also won. We had done it. We had beat the machine. The next year, we elected several district leaders. We were well on our way to capturing the city council, when reapportionment reared its head (1980). The machine believed that, with reapportionment, they could destroy us. They felt that the best way to defeat us was to use their power to sway the state legislature—which they controlled—to draw a reapportionment plan which would dilute our strength. This could best be accomplished, they felt, by redrawing my district to make it virtually impossible for me to win re-election. They proved successful in their efforts. But, at the same time, they created two new congressional districts, both of which were tailormade for Blacks.

Earlier, I had thought about running for Congress. That was always a distinct possibility. But there was another strong candidate, whom I was prepared to support. However, I concluded that it would be difficult, if not impossible, for me to win re-election to the State Senate. As a result, I had no choice but to run for Congress. At the same time, the other candidate decided not to run. I had to make a decision. And I decided to run for Congress.

Clearly, I was not prepared to run. I had minimal funds to run a congressional campaign. In addition, I wasn't psychologically prepared to run. Moreover, a new candidate had entered the race. He had the backing of the machine as well as the money which went with it. I felt, however, that it would be a disgrace if he won by default. So, when I finally decided to run, I knew the odds were definitely against me. But in the back of my mind I knew that if I were defeated, I could go back to writing. It certainly wouldn't be the end of the world.

JE: Do you have a personal formula when it comes to politics? What is the secret of your political success?

MO: I think it's attributable, in large part, to my faith in the underdog—to the people who most need help—and to establishing myself as their champion. They have elected me because they have believed in me—and they will only believe in a candidate if they perceive him or her as someone who really wants to help them. They're smart enough to see through politicians who try to use them for their own political gain.

However, I'm not a "successful" politician, if by successful you mean that I've been able to deliver. I've never been able to deliver large numbers of patronage jobs because I was always at war with the machine. As a result I never benefitted—nor have my supporters benefitted—as have many politicians. I've always charted my own course and relied on my own formula. Many "pundits" have prophesied that my organization would crumble because I was unable to deliver jobs to my people. And yet that has not happened. They believe in me and what I stand for. That's not to say that I haven't been able to produce—I have. I've produced programs for the poor and the oppressed—but not jobs for my supporters. For example, my running battle with the city over the drawing of city council districts failed to produce jobs for my supporters, but it did produce a more equitable redistricting plan. This contributed to a whole new era in black politics. I followed much the same pattern that Mayor Harold Washington of Chicago followed when he challenged the machine. Like Washington, I came away empty-handed—in terms of the machine—but better off, in the long run, because my actions produced many new voters. At the time, the senate district consisted of three assembly districts. The key assembly district was controlled by Sam Wright, who was elected and re-elected (as an assemblyman) with 1,500 votes. We zeroed in on that figure and went out and registered 2,000 new voters. And that's why—when he stepped down and tried to hand pick his successor—we were able to get our candidate elected. The numbers were very small, but we got people excited. And the people we registered were those who hadn't received patronage jobs or other favors. They were people who wanted to improve their community as well as challenge the power structure. My political success has always rested in my ability to inspire people to look beyond immediate benefits and to think in terms of the larger community. Don't misunderstand, I haven't always been sure it would work, but my approach has been vindicated in virtually every race I've run. I've been extremely successful in getting out the vote. This was particularly important in my race for Congress, where my opponent (Vander Beatty) outspent me 4–1 and had the backing of the machine. Despite this fact, I won—by an 8 percent margin. This proved extremely significant because later Beatty tried to have the results set aside in the courts. If I had not won by 8 percent, but by 3 percent, for example, I would have been forced to run a second time. I almost *was* forced to run a second time, as it was.

JE: What was the basis of Beatty's challenge? Was it difficult to overcome?

MO: In 1982, my principal opponent was Senator Vander Beatty, who sat two seats away from me in the State Senate. He had more seniority than I did. Beatty was well-to-do financially. He certainly had ample resources. He was closely connected with President Carter, for whom he had campaigned for President. As a result, he had close ties with many top Democrats. And he used those contacts when he ran for Congress. That gave him a big head start. He had a lot of money, as well as the support of the Brooklyn machine, which proved extremely important in the district. Their support meant that Beatty was also assured the support of several assemblymen and other local politicians. The machine could literally handpick the Democratic nominee. Once they endorsed a candidate, everyone else would fall in line. This proved to be the case in our race.

Beatty was determined not to lose. Moreover, he was afraid to lose. The thought of losing affected his mind. He did a number of very negative things. Beatty was known as someone you couldn't trust. He had that kind of reputation. Although the machine backed him, he wasn't highly regarded. He had a reputation in the community for being, if not criminally dishonest, heavy-handed in the way he dealt with people; for exploiting situations for personal advantage; and for squeezing people for a buck. Voters saw many negative qualities in him. In addition, he became so preoccupied with running for Congress that he neglected his state senate responsibilities.

While I was present, day after day, voting on bills and making speeches, he traveled around the country trying to raise money. As a result, he had an atrocious voting record. He was just never there. Also, I was a better speaker. He made the mistake of agreeing to several debates that served to finish him off. He also claimed to have been endorsed by Coretta Scott King and Martin Luther King, Sr. We caught him in this lie and exposed the fact during the closing days of the campaign. Mrs. King went public and denied ever endorsing him. These things took their toll and, when publicized, began to wear away at his credibility. Many people saw the race as one between Major Owens and a totally irresponsible clown! As a result, we won—and by an 8 percent margin.

The defeat did terrible things to his mind. He would not concede. Instead, he charged that our camp had forged signatures on 1,300 voter cards at the polls and that the election would have to be run over again. I think he masterminded the whole scheme. The machine didn't want anything to do with it, but he pressured them until they had no choice. In the end, they cast their lot with him and joined forces to have the election results set aside. His scheme was to challenge the election on grounds of fraud. He argued that our forces had forged more than 1,300 signatures on voter cards. This took place, Beatty charged, in those areas of the district which I won handily. He argued that a clear pattern existed, one which revealed blatant fraud.

Beatty manufactured a nice little scheme. He took his case to court where he argued that I had masterminded the whole thing. When the case came up, he was forced to prove his charges. The cards were thoroughly examined and, sure enough, 1,300 forgeries were discovered. He called several handwriting experts, as did we. We proved that the forgeries could *not* have been done on election day, as he had charged. There were as many as twenty false signatures in the same precinct. How could one person—or two persons—as they had charged, have voted twenty times in one district? In addition, the fraud took place at polling places throughout the district. The same forger would have had to travel from one end of the district to the other, vote twenty times, and not be discovered by the inspector. The upper part of the district is totally black, while the lower part is totally white. Poll officials would certainly have noticed the same forger, be he black or white, when he went into that part of the district where he was a minority. The handwriting experts testified that the forgers wrote distinctively so they would be discovered. They wanted to be detected. In fact, they tried hard to be discovered. There was ample evidence of this fact. For example, the forgers used the same pen over and over again in different places.

We suspected that the judge was also part of the scheme. The machine had appointed him to the bench. During the case, he accepted their claims and counterclaims, barely batting an eyelash. I kept telling myself that no one—let alone a judge—would take part in such a fraud. We proved, beyond any doubt, that the Beatty people themselves had forged the 1,300 false signatures on the cards during a post-primary visit to the Board of Elections Office. Despite the evidence, the judge dismissed our case out of hand. He ruled that forgeries and fraud had occurred and that, therefore, a second election must take place. Beatty's lawyers delayed the case until late Thursday afternoon, at which point the judge ruled that the new election had to be held the following Tuesday.

We immediately appealed the judge's ruling. We had to act quickly since we had only Friday and Monday to win an appeal. In the event the appeals court ruled against us, we also had to be prepared for Tuesday's election. It was like running a second primary but this time in four days. At the same time, we had to use the time to pursue the various legal channels necessary to win an appeal. The case was deliberately drawn out in order to pin us to the wall. We took the case to the appellate division. In New York, the appeals process is two-pronged: The Brooklyn machine controls the appellate division—which is situated in Brooklyn. Although only a borough, Brooklyn has more than 2 million people and, as such, constitutes an entire division within the state court. The appellate division upheld the lower court's ruling. However, as a result of our tenacity, the court of appeals agreed to hear the case. We succeeded for two main reasons: First, because the case was so outlandish and, second, because the *New York Times* publicized the case and exposed the chicanery involved. When the court of appeals heard the case, they threw it out. They did so based on the law—namely, that Beatty had to prove that not only did fraud take place, but that it had to be organized by the winner. In other words, he had to prove that I was behind it. He argued, in turn, that the fraud had occurred in those areas where I had won by large margins. Beatty failed to prove, however, that I had organized the scheme or that my people were involved in it. As a result, he could not tie me to the forgeries. In addition, the court of appeals said that, from all indications, the forgeries had taken place after the election. In the end, the court held that I had been duly elected—just eighteen hours before the scheduled second election.

The costs of the challenge were enormous. We spent money for campaign literature, for advertisements on radio, and for telephone banks. Nevertheless, the challenge *was* thrown out. And we were spared the trauma of a second election. As a postscript, the judge in the case—who ruled in favor of a second election—is presently under investigation. And my opponent has since been indicted by the district attorney on charges of forgery, conspiracy, and election fraud.

JE: Looking back, how did you feel when you finally took your seat? What thoughts went through your mind?

MO: As I've stated, I never gave much thought to running for Congress. It was never a personal goal. When I was sworn in, I could not help but be lost in my own thoughts—particularly the thought, "My God, here I am! It's a miracle. Here I am!" I thought about the many problems we faced, the sacrifices my family had to endure, and the financial hardships we had to bear, all of which made the moment more sweet. Financially speaking, the challenge was disastrous. Contrary to what most people assume, politics represents a major drain on your personal resources. If you're not a part of the crowd or a part of the machine, running for office requires a huge financial sacrifice.

However, one thought, more than any other, dominated the moment—namely, that in winning the election, I had not cut any corners. I was not so ambitious that I offered myself for sale to be elected or sold out along the way to advance my career. I never sold myself to the highest bidder. And here I am despite it all. It's a miracle! And, I intend to follow the same course now that I am here. I will not take any shortcuts. I will not bend over backwards as several of my freshman colleagues did. For example, during the opening weeks of the session, many of us worked very hard to get the freshman class in the 98th Congress to go on record in favor of reducing unemployment. The Speaker, Thomas P. "Tip" O'Neill, needed our support. Our twenty-six votes could determine whether the Democrats would have working control of the House of Representatives. We knew that when we arrived. I was shocked at the conservatism of my freshman colleagues. Most of them aspire to long political careers. They're determined not to rock the boat. I found it all very amusing because the last way I expected to advance my career was to come here and *not* rock the boat; it was just the opposite.

JE: Now that you are a member of Congress, how do you see your role? What would you hope to accomplish?

MO: To push the prerogatives of a congressman to the limit. Congress gives me a platform. The media attention that one receives as a state senator is far different from that of a congressman. New York is a special place because it's the media capital of the nation. In New York lower-level politicians rarely—if ever—appear on television or radio. Too many things are happening, so that local politicians never gain access to the media until they become congressmen. But then they do get local coverage. Politicians in other parts of the country find understanding this fact difficult because they have access to television. But as a state senator from New York City, I had no such access. As a congressman, I do. I now have a platform. And I intend to use that platform to offer leadership in several major areas, some of which don't directly relate to federal matters but do relate to matters important for New York. People are looking to me for leadership, and I intend to provide such leadership.

As for the legislative process, I think we must stretch it to its limits. My experience in the State Senate convinced me that passing bills is not half as important as introducing pertinent bills—focusing on the issues that count. Most new members have to dig in, serve an apprenticeship, and wait for a long time to develop the influence necessary to get their own legislation passed. In the meantime, they're permitted to introduce legislation which they deem important and to raise hell about the importance of these bills.

My principal focus is on jobs and employment. From my perspective, the Democratic-controlled House has been extremely negligent in this area. It has shown little, if any, urgency about the plight of the nation's unemployed. I think the Democrats have made a grave mistake in not focusing more on the issue of jobs. That it's the issue of today—and tomorrow—will become increasingly clear as the present recovery begins to fizzle. The Democrats should push vigorously for jobs creation programs—not only for those who are unemployed (and there are many)—but also for those people who have jobs but are afraid of losing them (of whom there are far more).

As a result, I've introduced a constitutional amendment to guarantee a job opportunity to every American who wants work. Unfortunately, I've found few members willing to co-sponsor the measure. I don't expect it to pass this year or next. But I do expect it to have an impact. When I ask my colleagues to co-sponsor my amendment, I'm met with interesting reactions, such as: "The time is not right"; or "I just can't go that far"; or "It sounds too radical"; or "It's really a good idea, but I'd like to think about it."

For too many elected officials, structural unemployment has become an accepted way of life in this country. With each succeeding economic cycle, the level of "acceptable" unemployment rises. We can all remember when 2 percent unemployment was considered to be "full employment." The "acceptable" rate has risen to 7 percent in some quarters. More than ever, we need to guarantee the right to employment opportunity with a constitutional amendment. The critical need for an employment centered economic policy is painfully obvious. Americans must face the issue and expand the debate. What the Humphrey-Hawkins Full Employment Act of 1978 began must proceed by constitutional amendment to produce an ongoing response which prevents unemployment. We must compel the government to make the survival of working Americans a priority concern. We cannot leave their well-being to the whims of administrations which come and go.

The government's responsibility must be explicitly set forth within the Constitution. In the face of such a clear mandate, Congress will have no choice but to discharge its responsibility for employment-centered planning and policy. Congress and the administration will be bound to fulfill their obligations. The unemployed will have a means of addressing indifference and hostility toward their basic need to work. Government, then, can no longer push job creation efforts off the agenda. Unemployment will remain a high priority concern which the government will have to address and resolve.

Structural unemployment exists in many industrialized countries. The form of government and the economic structure varies, but the basic cause remains the same—a failure to plan for full employment within the context of changing industrial and human needs. Pope John Paul II noted this failure in his 1981 encyclical, *Laborem exercens*. The Pope defined the role of government as an indirect employer who ". . . substantially determines one or other facet of the labor relationship, thus conditioning the conduct of the direct employer when the latter determines in concrete terms the actual work contract and labor relations." The Pope focused on the importance of work as a central factor in the establishment of human dignity and identity and on the personal, spiritual, social, and political consequences of unemployment. The goal that government must seek is not profit for some in the society, but well-being for all.

High unemployment is a disease that brings immeasurable pain to individuals and to our society. We cannot accept this as normal or necessary. To abandon a significant percentage of the working population is to accept a form of triage which violates the social contract and weakens the bonds that bind this diverse nation together.

As human society developed, people banded together in groups for the mutual benefit of all. This was a step away from the jungle where survival of self and family was the only consideration. The basic social contract was a willingness to submit to group rules and regulations in exchange for the protection of the individual by the group. Individuals made this choice voluntarily with the expectation that the resulting society would always offer a better chance for survival than the raw natural environment. The basic social contract has not changed. The need to work to meet personal needs and to contribute to the larger society remains.

At times in our history population, resources, and the level of technological development interacting freely in the marketplace might have ensured a decent living for all of our people without planning. Those times have been infrequent, and it now appears that they will never occur again. With each economic swing it becomes crystal clear that more and more people who want to work are driven to despair because they are unable to provide a living for themselves and their families.

We must change the basic frame of reference for the discussion of the unemployment problem in America. An economic policy that views full employment as its primary goal must receive the highest priority. A commitment to each working individual in our society will again result in the utilization of the energies that have made this nation a model of freedom, compassion, and common sense.

JE: In addition to unemployment, what other issues most concern you?

MO: I asked the house leadership to assign me to the Education and Labor Committee because I view education as the cornerstone of the future. Unfortunately, this country has adopted a Neanderthal approach to education. One committee report after another has underscored this fact. We've reached a critical juncture. Our educational system is both ineffective and dysfunctional. Our future depends upon a thorough reassessment of that system: its goals, methods, values, and priorities. This issue relates closely to that of jobs and employment. Today's young people must be prepared to function in a high-tech world. This demands a drastic overhaul of the educational system—one which we must make if our young people are to compete in a vastly different world.

In addition, I'm deeply concerned about the continuing problem of discrimination and its ongoing effects on the nation. Despite Congress's professed commitment to racial justice, for example, there is little evidence of affirmative action on Capitol Hill. On many committee staffs, Blacks are either unrepresented or underrepresented. The situation is even worse among the support staff—for example, the restaurant workers. Their treatment and complaints are striking evidence of Congress's unwillingness to practice what it preaches. The complexion of Congress changes when you go to the basement. When you go upstairs, it's one color (white); when you go downstairs, it darkens dramatically (black). Despite the efforts of the Congressional Black Caucus, I wonder why more has not been done. It's a shameful situation.

JE: In what sense, if any, did your expectations about Congress differ from the realities you confronted?

MO: Not very much. However, I've talked to several freshman congressmen who are experiencing a kind of culture shock. They were shattered when they arrived. But I spent eight years in the State Senate— and New York is called the second most effective legislature in the country (California is number one). As state senators, we met more often, spent more money, and drew a higher salary than most state legislators in the country. During those eight years, I was a member of the minority. In fact, the Democrats were a minority in the state senate the entire time. I had a good taste of what it was like. So, no, I've not been shocked by what I've found here. There is, of course, the psychological shock when you walk out of a 60-member State Senate into a 435-member House of Representatives. When you step onto the floor and see the hundreds of seats, something happens to you. You can't help but feel like a tiny cog in a big wheel. And it's a very big wheel—a very powerful wheel.

However, compensations become immediately apparent. You're the subject of royal treatment from many quarters. You're wined and dined, quoted and praised. Such treatment can become quite intoxicating. You're the object of great interest and attention. People make you feel important. After a while, you believe that you're important—that you deserve such treatment. And you come to like it. You begin to think that it may not be such a bad way to spend your life. In fact, it's a damn good way (for most). Unfortunately, that mentality makes it increasingly unlikely that you will say or do anything which could threaten your chances of being re-elected. And that's the danger. After a while, you begin to compromise—you begin to play it safe.

JE: How have you avoided being seduced? Have you found it difficult to maintain your integrity?

MO: Yes, much more difficult in Congress than in the state legislature: Congress is much more seductive; there's so much more bait to nibble on. And the system is structured to reward obedience. As a Democrat, I'm now part of the majority. It will definitely be more difficult for Congress than the state legislature. In my case, however, I'm sensitive to being controlled by anyone. It's a part of my constitution. I may be wrong, but I don't think I'll fall victim to the lure of power. But the minute I sense that I've changed—that I've begun to compromise— I'll recoil. I'm sure I'll make enemies of those people who thought they could be my mentors or my controllers. I won't let anyone control me.

Still, I recognize the need to work within the system. I've made a lot of compromises, and I will compromise in the future to help my district. But I'm not going to take that extra step that would place me in bondage to someone—be he the Speaker or a committee chairman. Once a person takes that step, then other entanglements are inevitable. From there, things go steadily downhill. I will cooperate. I will go so far. But I will never sell my soul to the powers that be.

JE: Do you enjoy the perquisites of power? Do they ever make you feel uncomfortable?

MO: At this point, I find my position somewhat difficult. I'm presently going through a transition. As a congressman, I receive far more attention than I did as a state senator. In the state senate, I represented 300,000 people. In Congress, I represent 500,000 people. But that doesn't mean that I only do twice as much work, or that the expectations are only twice as great. The expectations of my constituents are ten times as great. In one sense, the media exposure is a godsend. But it has also increased the demands on me. The voters expect me to work miracles. The problems are no greater than when I was a state senator, but the voters somehow expect me to be able to solve any problem that arises—and to be in a thousand places at the same time. I must learn how to set priorities—how to say "no" to people. But it's difficult. As I've said, this is a transition phase. Once I get through it, I think I'll enjoy the job more.

JE: Does political life agree with you? Are you a "born" politician?

MO: No. I don't enjoy the nitty-gritty campaign aspects of politics. I hate to attend dinners and the obligation to work the crowd. I don't like to walk around and shake hands with everyone. That's not my style. I do, however, enjoy speaking. I enjoy talking about subjects which interest me. I'm a generalist. As a librarian, I enjoyed the generalist nature of the discipline. I like to dabble in many things. That's also true of politics. As a congressman, I have an opportunity to exert leadership in many areas. This affords me an opportunity to express myself, both verbally and in writing. It's the next best thing to being a successful novelist.

JE: What does it take to be effective in Congress? Do you see it as a long-term process?

MO: There are several requirements. First, my colleagues must perceive that I enjoy the support of my constituents. That's true of all congressmen. However, freshmen are viewed differently than other members. They're not fully accepted until they have won re-election. So, being popular in your district is vital. Moreover, I must be able to demonstrate leadership ability, both in and out of Congress. Finally, effectiveness hinges on being able to get things done. In my case, it will depend on the degree to which I am perceived as a threat.

Now, what do I mean? I'm fascinated by the fact that large numbers of white members owe their elections to black voters. I want to document that fact. I want to know who these members are. I think this entails certain obligations on the part of white members. After all, a white member who won because of black support, but who proves insensitive to issues of concern to black Americans, could face serious re-election problems if that fact were exposed. I want to develop increased leverage with these members. They must know that their re-election depends, in large part, on the support they give to issues of concern to black America.

JE: Finally, which members do you most admire? What makes them unique?

MO: It's difficult to say. The giants today are vastly different from those I'd read about in earlier times. Perhaps once I get to know them, I'll find greater similarities. The person who fascinates me most is Majority Leader Jim Wright (D-Tex.). He has a reputation for being a great politician—a master when it comes to compromise, negotiation, and coalition building. When he steps onto the floor and speaks, you're proud to be a member of the House—to serve with him—because he's such an erudite speaker and thinker. He also has a very charismatic personality. I don't know him very well, but I certainly like the way he operates. I look forward to the day when he becomes Speaker. I suspect he's the annointed heir to the title. And he's an excellent choice. He's a fascinating person to watch.

As for black members, I have great respect for John Conyers, Jr. (D-Mich.). He has courage and integrity. He helped me in my campaign, but I didn't really know him at the time. That's the kind of guy he is. At times, he'll go off on some issues, and, sometimes, like Don Quixote—because it's right—he'll ride directly into the windmill. He possesses the anger, guts, and commitment necessary to effect change. However, he's not always effective, perhaps because he lacks certain other qualities—namely, the ability to work through the group process, to convince others to support him, and to put together a coalition. He seems quite impatient with such things. Still, I admire him greatly.

I also admire the way Ronald Dellums (D-Calif.) transcends his district's problems and focuses on the all-important issue of world survival. He has made a monumental contribution to the cause of peace. He has spoken out forcefully against nuclear war, as well as subjected himself to being a member of the Armed Services Committee in order to be an advocate of peace. Talk about the lamb in the lion's den. Those military guys are vicious. I admire Dellums's courage. I wish we had more like him.

Among the white members, I very much admire Barney Frank (D-Mass.). He is extremely impressive: bright, articulate, sensitive, energetic, committed. However, not too many others spring to mind. I have problems, in general, with the Democratic leadership. I don't think they're staking out the right positions on issues of critical importance. For example, the Democratic Party took no position on the MX missile. Despite what the leadership said, or how they voted, they failed to unify behind a single position. The same was true of Social Security. There was no party position, although the leadership will argue to the contrary. I know when the leadership takes a position: I receive four calls a day asking me how I'm going to vote. It means nothing when the party simply announces it has a position. The budget was the only issue on which the party took a position in my freshman term. In the case of the Nuclear Freeze Resolution, a party position wasn't required. Supporters of the resolution had done their homework. The nuclear freeze is a classic example—and I saw it up close—of legislators not voting out of conscience or personal preference, but voting out of fear of reprisals by the voters back home. The grass-roots strength of the anti-nuclear movement was so great that members dared not vote against it. Interestingly, some of the same people who voted for the nuclear freeze turned around and voted for the MX missile. The seeming contradiction baffled many people, but it did not baffle me—they voted for the nuclear freeze because they *had* to; they voted for the MX missile because they *wanted* to. It troubles me greatly that, on the most critical issue of our time— the preservation of human civilization—the Democratic Party, as a party, has remained silent.

Mervyn M. Dymally

Science and the New Orthodoxy

Mervyn M. Dymally was born May 12, 1926, in Cedros, Trinidad, West Indies. He holds a Bachelor of Arts degree in education from California State University, Los Angeles (1954); a Master of Arts degree in government from California State University, Sacramento (1969); and a Doctor of Philosophy degree in human behavior from United States International University in San Diego (1978). He is a member of Phi Kappa Phi, the National Honor Scholastic Society.

Dymally originally came to the United States as a nineteen-year-old student to attend Lincoln University in Jefferson City, Missouri. Among other jobs, he worked as a janitor, union organizer, and teacher of exceptional children before entering politics. He presently serves in the United States House of Representatives, where he represents California's 31st Congressional District, which includes several communities in the southern portion of Los Angeles County.

Dymally was first elected to the House of Representatives in 1980 following a long and controversial career in California politics. Dymally began his political career in 1962 when he was elected to the California Assembly where he served for four years. In 1966, he was elected to the California Senate. During his eight years as a state senator, Dymally served as chairman of the Senate Democratic Caucus and chairman of numerous committees, including: Social Welfare, Military and Veterans Affairs, Elections and Reapportionment, and the Subcommittee on Medical Education and Health Needs. He also headed the Senate Select Committee on Children and Youth, the Joint Committee on Legal Equality for Women, and the Joint Committee for Revision of the Election Code. As a state legislator, Dymally won top ratings from consumer, environmental, labor, women's, and civil rights groups and was the organizer of a highly successful institute to train minority youth in government and politics.

In 1975, Dymally was elected lieutenant governor of California and was defeated for reelection in 1978. As lieutenant governor, he headed the State Commission for Economic Development and the Commission of the Californias. He also served on the Board of Regents of the University of California and the Board of Trustees of the State College and University system. He was responsible for organizing the Council on Intergroup Relations, the California Advisory Commission on Youth, and the Commission on Food and Nutrition.

As a United States congressman, Dymally brings many years of experience and a deep concern for a broad range of people-oriented problems to the House of Representatives. He is presently a member of the Committees on Foreign Affairs, Education and Labor, and Post Office and Civil Service, and serves as chairman of the Subcommittee on Judiciary and Education of the District of Columbia Committee. He also serves as chairman of the Congressional Caucus for Science and Technology. His legislative interests include science and technology, immigration reform, educational opportunity, and Caribbean affairs.

JE: How would you assess the gains in black empowerment over the last twenty years?

MD: If one looks at the United States Congress, Blacks have gained significant political power over the past two decades. We now boast a number of senior black congressmen. Additional Blacks have been elected each term, and there are many black congressmen in the middle ranks as well. Senior Blacks chair or are high-ranking members of a number of important and influential committees.

Let me cite several notable examples: Augustus F. Hawkins (D-Calif.) chairs the Education and Labor Committee as well as the Employment Opportunities Subcommittee of the Education and Labor Committee and is a major voice in the area of employment training. He is also a senior member of several other prominent subcommittees.

Ronald V. Dellums (D-Calif.) chairs the District of Columbia Committee. In this capacity, he has led the fight for home rule for the District of Columbia—a city which is 80 percent black. He also chairs the Armed Services Subcommittee on Military Installations and Facilities, the authorizing committee for military installations around the world.

John Conyers, Jr. (D-Mich.) is chairman of the Judiciary Subcommittee on Criminal Justice, is a senior member of the Subcommittee on Civil and Constitutional Rights, and has worked tirelessly to safeguard the rights of black Americans in the criminal justice system.

Parren J. Mitchell (D-Md.) is chairman of the Small Business Committee and has made literally millions of dollars available to black businesses. He is also chairman of the Minority Enterprise Subcommittee, as well as a senior member of the Housing and Community Development Subcommittee of the Banking, Finance, and Urban Affairs Committee.

Cardiss Collins (D-Ill.) chairs the Government Operations Subcommittee on Government Activities and Transportation. In this capacity, she oversees the activities of several important agencies within the executive branch of government.

Walter E. Fauntroy (Delegate-D.C.) is chairman of the Domestic Monetary Policy Subcommittee of the Banking, Finance, and Urban Affairs Committee, and as such exercises great power over the monetary policy of the country.

Louis Stokes (D-Ohio) is a senior member of the Appropriations Committee. He formerly chaired the toughest and most respected committee in the House, the Committee on Standards of Official Conduct.

Other black members have also achieved influence and prominence: Julian C. Dixon (D-Calif.) is chairman of the Appropriations Subcommittee for the District of Columbia; William H. Gray III (D-Pa.) chairs the Budget Committee and serves on the Appropriations Committee; William Clay (D-Mo.) is a senior member of both the Education and Labor, and Post Office and Civil Service Committees; Harold E. Ford (D-Tenn.) is a senior member of one of the most powerful committees in the House, the Ways and Means Committee, which determines federal revenue policies; Mickey Leland (D-Tex.) chairs the Postal Personnel and Modernization Subcommittee of the Post Office and Civil Service Committee as well as the Select Committee on World Hunger; and Charles B. Rangel (D-N.Y.) is a senior member of the Ways and Means Committee and chairs its Oversight Subcommittee. He also chairs the Select Committee on Narcotics Abuse and Control.

So, Blacks are in key positions of power in committees that have strong influence over jobs, business opportunities, the courts, federal employment, civil and constitutional rights, the military, education, health, and housing. Additional Blacks continue to be elected to the House in each session. This strongly suggests that Blacks are likely to maintain significant power in the House for the forseeable future.

JE: Have Blacks achieved similar gains at the state and local level, as well as in private industry?

MD: Yes. As we survey the national political scene, it is readily apparent that blacks are at the helm of many of America's largest cities. Black mayors include Tom Bradley in Los Angeles, Harold Washington in Chicago, Coleman Young in Detroit, Wilson Goode in Philadelphia, and Andrew Young in Atlanta. And those cities span the country from west to east, from Los Angeles to Atlanta. We see similar progress in the private sector. Blacks now control a number of major businesses, among them: Johnson Publishing Company, Motown Industries, Seaway National Bank of Chicago, Fedco Foods Corporation, and North Carolina Mutual Life Insurance Company. Some black businesses now gross in the hundreds of millions of dollars annually. As early as 1977, black businesses had gross receipts of nearly $9 billion.

JE: How would you assess the overall picture? Have Blacks achieved full parity in American society?

MD: No. Clearly, Blacks have won impressive gains in industry and government. However, we must ask the more important question—namely, whether the benefits that have accrued to the black middle class will, in the future, be shared more generally by the rest of black America. We can find many reasons to believe that prospects for further near-term progress on civil rights are dismal. Several factors stand in the way of future progress: First, no Blacks whatsoever serve in the United States Senate. Second, a black governor has yet to be elected, and third, President Reagan and his administration have thwarted and will, in all likelihood, continue to thwart black aspirations.

JE: How would you assess President Reagan's record in the area of civil rights?

MD: In one word, abominable. The Reagan Administration has systematically undone much of the civil rights progress of the past twenty years. For example, the administration initially supported tax exemptions for segregationist schools and reversed its position only under intense pressure. It initially opposed portions of the Voting Rights Act when it came up for reauthorization and backed off only when a majority of both houses of Congress opposed the administration's position. The White House has politicized the Civil Rights Commission, which has long derived its respectability and effectiveness from the fact that it was an independent nonpartisan commission. It also opposed a national holiday to honor Martin Luther King, Jr. until shortly before passage of the bill which enjoyed bipartisan support.

Moreover, under President Reagan, the Justice Department has been lax in enforcing the Voting Rights Act. It has even reversed its position on a number of pending cases. The President also nominated conservative Edwin Meese as attorney general. Meese, according to newspaper accounts, has been behind the moves at the Justice Department to not enforce existing laws aimed at ensuring equal rights. The White House has attempted to eliminate the Legal Services Corporation, which has been a significant avenue for poor people to obtain equal justice.

The White House has sought to eliminate most funding for low income housing. It has also refused to strengthen the ability of the Department of Housing and Urban Development to enforce any remedy in fair housing cases. Instead, it has attempted to assign responsibility for such enforcement to the Justice Department, which has filed only six such cases in two years compared to 20–30 cases filed annually by previous administrations.

JE: Given your comments, how would you assess the prospects for future progress in the civil rights field? Where is the movement headed?

MD: Twenty years ago, coalitions formed to pass the Civil Rights Act because many citizens viewed the act as a statement of general philosophy. It was a measure around which Blacks, Hispanics, Native Americans, Asians, women, Jews, white liberals, the poor, and organized labor could unite. Once it passed, the work of implementing its provisions began. As each segment of the coalition began to work for its own interests in specific civil rights areas, inevitably cracks occurred in the coalition.

Rather than a civil rights coalition, we now have a large number of discrete groups each working for their own civil rights agenda. Often the rights of one group conflict with those of other groups. For example, Jews favor equal access but oppose quotas as a tool. Organized labor favors a balance of ethnic and racial groups in the labor force but supports seniority as the criterion for retention when there is a reduction in force. Some Blacks favor restrictions on immigration because they perceive immigrants as taking jobs from Blacks, while many Hispanics oppose restrictions on immigration because family members and friends are among the potential immigrants and because the restrictions could encourage employer discrimination against all Hispanics. Many women's groups favor the right to abortion while some black groups oppose abortion on religious grounds.

Clearly, there are also disagreements within each group. Some women favor the Equal Rights Amendment while others oppose it. Some women support the right to abortion, and some oppose it. There are black and Hispanic ultra-conservatives, as well as black and Hispanic progressives. Some unions attempt to accommodate equal opportunity in the face of great job market pressure while other unions eschew equal opportunity in favor of strict seniority. Some Jews and Blacks support each other's civil rights while other Jews and Blacks openly oppose one another. Some Hispanics support immigration restrictions, and others oppose them.

JE: If this is the case, how likely is it that concerned Americans can revive the old coalition?

MD: It's not very likely. The old coalition will never again be able to achieve unanimity of purpose. There will be inevitable areas of conflict in the future because the realization of specific rights for one group will require a sacrifice from other groups. And people will not always make these sacrifices willingly.

Civil rights groups should consider a new agenda as a means of reestablishing a working coalition. For example, these groups must develop a civil rights stance toward the job market: Technological changes will continue to eliminate certain types of jobs that minorities or women have traditionally held. In addition, civil rights groups need to develop a stance on the exporting of jobs overseas.

At some point, the leaders of the old coalition may need to hold a kind of summit meeting. This meeting ought to begin with members acknowledging their differences. However, they should then move to a frank discussion of those areas where they still have unanimity of purpose. A primary objective of all segments of the old coalition, for example, should be to prevent President Reagan from further eroding civil rights gains. Another common objective should be to restore equal educational opportunity to all groups. Likewise, all groups should have access to job training and retraining opportunities. All groups should be able to work together to stop the avalanche of people who are falling into poverty. Perhaps all groups could work to bring about a less warlike American foreign policy toward Third World countries.

Those at the summit should identify those areas which are the primary concerns of a single group and which other groups might at least not officially oppose. Which issues should be primary is open to discussion but might include: abortion rights for the poor, equal pay for comparable work, an equitable immigration policy, pragmatic school busing, and increased military aid to Israel.

Finally, the summit members should look at those areas of intense disagreement and examine compromises which would do the least damage to the important cooperative efforts that must continue in other areas. Candidates for this group might include: Palestinian autonomy, hiring quotas to achieve racial equality, racially or ethnically targeted jobs and educational programs, and racial tension generated by the displacement of "old minorities" (i.e., Blacks and Hispanics) by "new minorities" (i.e., Vietnamese, Cambodians, and Thais).

The consequence of not finding areas where the old coalition can act forcefully as a unit is that no single group will be strong enough to preserve its most prized civil rights alone. One by one we will lose these rights.

JE: During your tenure in the House of Representatives, you have developed a keen interest in science and technology. To what extent are Blacks adequately represented in the sciences?

MD: The picture of Blacks in the sciences is like a picture puzzle with many of the pieces not yet in place. A part of the border is in place, enough so that we have some idea how the finished picture might look. But we have a long way to go before we can stand back and say that the work is done. What complicates this picture puzzle even more than its own intricacy is that once a piece is put in place, there is no guarantee that someone won't come along and take the piece back out again. The progress of Blacks in the sciences is not necessarily linear. One success does not guarantee other successes. Our efforts must, therefore, be constant although we may have to change the thrust of that effort from time to time to take best advantage of the current political and social tide.

JE: What is the relationship between science and politics? Does the president's position concern you?

MD: Yes. When we talk about science and politics, we must carefully consider the science policy intentions of the Reagan Administration. The Congress will react to those policies, and the options and limitations that administration policy imposes on the sciences in the United States will determine what happens. This will most certainly be the case if the Democratic House and the Republican Senate deadlock over those aspects of science policy which each body desires to implement. When this occurs, administration policy will become the only operative policy.

JE: How would you characterize the administration's science policy? What are its major components?

MD: It includes three main components: development of new talent in science and technology; pursuit of excellence in a limited number of scientific disciplines; and development of partnerships among industry, government, and academia. Is aggressive affirmative action a component of the administration's effort to develop a new scientific talent? Not long ago, a group of science policy experts who advise the Congress met with Dr. George Keyworth, the president's science advisor. They asked him whether the administration intended to pursue an aggressive policy of affirmative action. His response was that the administration does not intend to be like a father who has neglected his child since birth and then in a fit of remorse goes out and buys his child a Corvette.

I think we can interpret that statement to mean that large sums of money and other large-scale efforts to correct inequities in the sciences will not come from this administration. In fact, we cannot expect large sums of money or other support dedicated to bringing young people in general into the sciences from the White House. The administration is convinced that its primary opportunity to develop new talent in the sciences comes through support of graduate research and not through benevolent and affirmative intervention in undergraduate, primary, or secondary education—indeed, quite the contrary. It is well known that the President considers primary and secondary education to be the responsibility solely of the states and localities. It is important that the administration has attempted to limit the scope of the requirement that educational institutions receiving federal funds be non-discriminatory in their admissions policies. If the President is successful, then this affirmative action safeguard would cover only a fraction of federal education funds. This is one of the pieces of the puzzle which the administration may take out of the picture, although it has been in place for some time.

JE: What implications do such policies have for black America?

MD: These policies have important consequences for those who wish to see more black people trained and properly employed in the sciences. They have a potential impact at every stage of training and employment. I can illustrate this best by citing the administration's policy as it relates to scientific training. This policy is to place the major intervention at the graduate level. Clearly, the process by which a black person becomes properly employed as a scientist begins long before graduate school. The process is perhaps at its midpoint or beyond at the point where a black person enters graduate school. To gain admission to graduate school, a black person would already have had to survive at least sixteen years in the educational system. According to the 1980 census, fewer than three out of every ten black high school graduates attend college. Fewer than one in ten makes it to graduate school. If the primary point of federal intervention is at the graduate level, then black people face serious difficulties. And if the administration eliminates federal protection against discrimination in educational institutions, then such action will simply compound those difficulties.

For a moment, however, let's put aside the fact that intervention at the graduate school level will not reach over 90 percent of the potential black graduate students—the ones who did not make it that far for one reason or another. Instead, consider the nature of federal intervention at the graduate level. Aid to graduate education is expected to flow out of general support for research. That is, the funds are not, for the most part, targeted to support students directly. There will be a few more scholarships and fellowships, but the major flow of aid to graduate students will be through research and teaching assistantships—which will, in turn, flow from research grants to faculty. This would be a sound way of proceeding were other factors not present.

The research assistantship, after all, draws the graduate student into a close relationship with his or her adviser. And that is good. The quality of a graduate education depends largely on the closeness of the student's working relationship with his or her adviser. I do not believe, however, that black students in many graduate departments have equal access to the graduate advisers and to the graduate education of their choice.

Unfortunately, collecting reliable statistical data on this contention is extremely difficult. One indicator that women and members of minority groups lack sufficient access to their graduate advisers presently is that more of them supplement their departmental monetary support with off-campus jobs than do other graduate students. What we are really talking about here is the contention that racial and sexual prejudice exists in graduate schools. For obvious reasons, few graduate students are free to be candid about such experiences, but I have heard enough anecdotal information that I have become convinced of its presence. And because of its presence, I have become convinced that direct monetary aid to minority graduate students will be necessary for a long time to come. I do not think that scholarships are the best way for the federal government to support graduate education because scholarships disassociate monetary support from the educational process itself. But scholarships are a necessity for minority graduate students because they make possible basic survival in an atmosphere of discrimination. As long as we have discrimination in graduate school, women and members of minority groups will not have a fair chance if they are subject to a policy which places the greatest amount of federal aid in graduate education in research and teaching assistantships.

JE: What, then, do you see as the solution?

MD: If black people are going to achieve employment in decent positions in the sciences, then the process of intervention must begin early in the future black scientist's life. The impediments that prejudice places in the path of black people have to be set aside in the first grade, second grade, and in every other step of the educational and employment process.

I know this sounds like something that might have been said in 1954 rather than 1984. And I acknowledge that great changes have taken place in the past thirty years. A black child no longer has to be accompanied to the classroom by armed policemen. The effects of waning prejudice are visible in many ways, not the least of which is that aptitude test scores of black children have risen dramatically while the scores of the general population have declined. Our people have blossomed as the oppression of overt prejudice has been lifted. But the prejudice has lessened—it has not disappeared.

JE: In your view does the administration base its science policy on the assumption that discrimination no longer exists?

MD: Yes. If you look at two of the three components of the administration's policy—namely, excellence in graduate education and excellence in selected areas of research—you will see that the goal is to create a meritocracy. Those who make it to graduate school will receive rewards. Those sciences which achieve the greatest strides will receive the most generous support. What such a policy ignores is that unnecessary and artificial barriers will prevent most black people from ever reaching the point where they will even be eligible to receive the rewards. (By the same token, rewarding only those sciences which are already making spectacular discoveries may have the effect of assuring that the other sciences will not have the means to reach their peak of productivity.)

JE: As you see it, what would be an ideal science policy for Blacks?

MD: It would begin with the recognition that excellence in graduate education does not begin with graduate education. Such excellence begins much earlier with the basic educational foundation that prepares a student for graduate school. An ideal science policy for black people would be one which begins with the premise that every child must have the opportunity to learn to the maximum extent of his or her ability, unimpeded by artificial barriers. Under such a policy, the federal government would work with state and local governments to put access to a conducive learning environment within the reach of every child.

Under a science policy ideal for black people, there would need to be a way to measure progress toward equality of opportunity. One way to do this would be to say that we assume that ability is normally distributed in the population. Therefore, the proportion of Blacks entering the sciences should be proportional to the number of whites entering the sciences. Moreover, employment levels should be proportional within each racial group. We would achieve maximum progress under this policy when actual proportions and actual distributions reached the predicted proportions and distributions in an environment free of prejudice.

A science policy that would be ideal for black people is just a dream, unfortunately, and a distant one at that. However, the efforts of Blacks in the sciences must be constant—Blacks must never relax their pressure for equality.

JE: What concrete steps would you recommend to reverse the president's policies in this area?

MD: If the long-term trend is to give the most generous funding to the sciences presently making the greatest strides, then we must ask ourselves how we might take greatest advantage of this state of affairs. Our weak point is that we will be the victims of withdrawal of aid to primary and secondary education. We must compensate for that weakness. If the president says that he is placing primary and secondary education in the hands of state and local officials, then we must organize at the grass-roots level. We must become active members of the parent-teacher associations in our school districts. We must push state boards of education to set state curriculum standards that are rigorous enough to provide some assurance that our children will be prepared for college. We must lend our support to programs which identify and stimulate those of our children who show some inclination toward the sciences. I think it is worth noting that in the 1981–1982 school year, almost 11 percent of all master's degrees awarded to minorities in the United States in the field of engineering went to students who had been identified and aided by a single such program, known by the acronym "GEM" (Graduate Degrees in Engineering for Minorities). The University of Notre Dame administers this program. Another program, "MESA" (Mathematics, Engineering, and Science Achievement), run by the University of California at Berkeley, has also attempted to assist minority students with aptitude and interest in engineering. These programs demonstrate that a lack of support from the public sector need not stop our progress. They also demonstrate how effective Blacks can be if such programs identify and stimulate those who evidence talent and interest in science or engineering.

One way to stimulate more minority youth to enter the strongest fields of science and engineering is through proper career counseling. Many college-bound Blacks have not been counseled with care to choose the institution they will attend. More often than not, Blacks choose a particular college for convenience rather than with a mind toward the kind of preparation attendance at that college will afford.

JE: The solutions you propose are, for the most part, long-term. What immediate steps would you propose to address the problem?

MD: Those who are employed in the sciences, be they black or white, should think in terms of coalition building. Many laws and regulations are on the books which, if followed, would lead to equal employment opportunity. When people's rights are violated, speaking out is often difficult. They fear that the retribution may be worse than the initial violation. Black people within a discipline, black people within the same workplace, and black people within the same town need to join forces and participate in self-help organizations. Those who would be courageous enough to stand up for what is rightfully theirs should receive support from the black community. After all, the entire community stands to benefit ultimately.

JE: How important is affirmative action in terms of eliminating inequities in the sciences?

MD: I think affirmative action is indispensable to eliminate such inequities. But I do not think that the inclination to act affirmatively is apt to come freely from the institutions that employ scientists. Black scientists must initiate affirmative action by insisting that institutions and businesses adhere to the laws, regulations, corporate policies, and procedures already on the books and those designed to foster equal opportunity.

Let me cite an example of what can happen when people band together to stand up for their rights. You may have noticed on the evening news that the threat of terrorist attacks has made security officials in the Capitol Hill area beef up their security. You have seen pictures of the new barricades around the White House. One such security measure is a new identification system for the House of Representatives. With little forewarning, all congressional staff members recently received a form on which they were asked to fill out personal information about themselves. They were asked to present this form at a certain office which would issue them new identification cards. The cards would have a computer strip which contained this personal information. The form asked each individual to identify his or her sex and racial background. The vast majority of staffers simply filled out the form and presented it. Most people were not aware that the Privacy Act forbids people having to identify their sex or race on such forms. Several members of my staff were taken aback by the request for this information. When the time came for them to present themselves for their new IDs, they instead informed the sergeant at arms that this procedure was a possible violation of law.

The upshot of their protest and refusal to supply this information is that House Speaker Thomas P. "Tip" O'Neill has begun an inquiry into the matter. A member of the Judiciary Committee is considering holding hearings on the process by which the decision to make major changes in house procedures occurs. And my staffers as well as staffers who raised a question in other offices have been told that the office will reissue their IDs without requiring them to provide any information they feel invades their privacy.

So, yes, I believe in affirmative action in the workplace whether that workplace be a scientific laboratory or the House of Representatives. But just as firmly, I also believe that affirmative action begins at home. We must insist on fair treatment before we receive it.

JE: Let's move from science education to education in general. How would you assess the progress that Blacks have made in the area of equal educational opportunity?

MD: In the past twenty-five years, the access of members of minority groups to an education of their choice has changed dramatically several times over. Prior to the 1960s, they had little choice. A minority youth could expect to attend an underfunded, poorly staffed grade school and high school and could expect only limited opportunity to pursue a college education. While 18 out of every 100 high school graduates enrolled in college in 1960, the median educational attainment for Blacks in 1960 was the eighth grade. The strength of the civil rights movement forced progress toward equality of opportunity in primary and secondary education, and it opened the doors of many universities which had previously been closed to members of minority groups. The peak of black enrollment in college occurred in 1975, when 32 of every 100 high school graduates enrolled in college. Hard won advances toward equity over the past two decades have contributed to the growth of a black middle class. Today, 13 black families in every 100 have family incomes of $30,000 or more per year. And the children of this new middle class have enjoyed access to the finest education the country has to offer. These young people will probably be able to preserve their gains even in the face of adversity. They have the wherewithal to survive (if not compete) in the educational and economic marketplace. However, today's black college graduate earns, on the average, about as much as a white high school graduate. But if the civil rights movement has taught us anything, it is that even modest progress toward equal opportunity is cyclical, not linear. The gains of one decade may be lost in the next.

JE: In what ways, if any, has today's conservative tide affected the educational fortunes of black youth?

MD: Clearly, the conservatism which has swept the nation has also affected education. One can see numerous manifestations of this fact, in proposals such as tuition tax credits, educational vouchers, attempts to abolish the Department of Education, curtailment of the school lunch program, reductions in Aid to Families with Dependent Children, restriction in the number of scholarships and grants available for those wishing to pursue higher education, support of reverse discrimination cases by the Justice Department, and a preference on the part of federal officials to negotiate rather than enforce affirmative action requirements.

The effect of these and other measures will be to reserve access to the best education to those who already have the monetary resources to purchase it.

Devastating as those measures will be to the education of minority students, they are part of an eight-year decline in access to higher education for minority youth. From the 1975 high of 32 black college enrollees per 100 black high school graduates—a rate essentially equal to the white high school ratio—the percentage has dropped to 28 per 100 today, while the white ratio has remained at 32 per 100. However, this is only part of the story. With a decline in the availability of grants in aid to support college studies, minority youth who do attend college have begun to attend local community and junior colleges, rather than leaving their hometowns for the universities they once attended. By staying close to home, these students have not only minimized the cost of their educations but may also have lost access to the social networks that help to further the careers of many who attend major universities.

JE: Given these facts, how do you view the future of minority youth?

MD: Unfortunately, the future is far from certain. Newly limited access is not the only major consideration that must figure into the educational deliberations of young people from minority backgrounds. The same twenty-five years that have seen a rise and decline in equal access to quality education have also seen a transformation of labor force requirements. I suspect it's too early to say with certainty, but probably technical advances will gradually bring about a situation in which the industries which produce the greatest profits will also require only a small number of employees who have highly developed and highly specialized technical or scientific training. This has profound implications, particularly for minority youth, since the traditional means for equalizing access to resources—namely, employment—will be an option for fewer and fewer people. If the Labor Department's projections are accurate, then the greatest need for personnel in the future is likely to be in service-oriented jobs, which may not require a high degree of skill. Many of these occupations have traditionally been at the low end of the wage spectrum. Should this continue to be the case, we can expect in future years that large numbers of people will be permanently unemployed, underemployed, or will work at jobs which are neither challenging nor intellectually stimulating.

JE: As you see it, what are the major educational decisions that confront minority youth?

MD: On the one hand, they will have to struggle much harder than their older brothers and sisters to attain even a basic education. At the same time, high educational attainment may not open the doors of economic opportunity.

Is education worth the struggle for today's minority youth? The answer is an even more resounding "Yes" than it was for their parents and grandparents. At one time, members of minority groups were grossly overrepresented in the ranks of the poor, the disadvantaged, and the powerless. Their lives were ones of victimization. Gradually, some few among those ranks climbed out of that pit. They climbed against great odds to a crest of self-fulfillment that gave hope, courage, and pride to their brothers and sisters. Their success was a legacy for all who would follow. It was a legacy of possibility—the possibility that eventually all could escape the slave pit of victimization and ascend to the heights of self-determination. That legacy is now sorely threatened.

JE: Is prejudice the principal barrier to black educational progress?

MD: No. The technological progress of the world threatens to divide humankind into those who possess the knowledge to function in the world and those who are unable to do so. Those who fall back into the slave pit will find that it has not only steep walls, but also a barred and locked door at the top. These people face the likelihood of being trapped in long-term unemployment or in low-wage, mind-numbing, lifetime underemployment.

Therefore, the challenge confronting minority youth today is broader in scope than it was for those of previous generations. Those who came before had the challenge of overcoming prejudice and assisting their brothers and sisters in achieving economic opportunity. That challenge is still strong. In fact, it has intensified in recent years. Now, however, in addition to resisting deprivation due to prejudice, it will also be necessary to overcome deprivation imposed by inadequate intellectual development.

Today's youth are citizens of a world increasingly controlled by information. Only those youngsters who develop the intellect and skills necessary to create, acquire, and manipulate information will be truly autonomous, truly self-determining.

In the fight against prejudice, our adversaries are other humans. But information is not human. It is the product of machines and processes driven by human intellect. The struggle against ignorance, against a literal lack of information, will not be directed at other humans. It will be a personal struggle, a struggle to develop one's abilities to their utmost. That is the challenge each child of the information age must face. And the resolve with which each individual meets that challenge will in large part determine the quality of choices available to that individual throughout life. For many years, we have struggled for our freedom against external foes. Those of this new age will find that when these foes are at last defeated, there will be one shackle left. Each individual will have to choose either to open that shackle and cast it off or to close it tight forever.

JE: What does the future hold for historically black colleges? Has the president kept faith with his promise to assist these institutions?

MD: No. Black institutions differ from non-black institutions not only in their patterns of funding but also in funding trends. For both black and non-black institutions, federal support for student financial aid grew steadily from 1973 until 1978 when it peaked. Federal funds for student aid have been declining ever since 1978. But at non-black institutions, *total* federal assistance has not declined along with the decline of financial aid. This is because support for certain areas, such as science, has grown sufficiently to offset the decline. This has not been the case at black institutions, however. Total federal support for black institutions has continued to decline since 1978. It shrank by 5 percent between 1978 and 1980 alone. And that was before the present administration made "conservatism" the watchword of the federal government.

I would say that black institutions have demonstrated greater vulnerability to shifts in federal policy than have non-black institutions. That is because black institutions rely disproportionately on one form of support and on a single agency within the federal government. Moreover, efforts to strike a balance between support from student aid and support from research have been less successful at black institutions than at non-black institutions.

Given this state of affairs, we should consider what actions the present administration is taking and will take on funding of higher education and also consider what black institutions must do in order to ensure the survival of their institutions.

The Reagan Administration derives many of its specific policies from the general philosophical position that there should be a gradual lessening of federal involvement in all aspects of American life. It is easy to discern the specific manifestations of this philosophy in the area of education, simply by noting the facts. The President has stated forcefully, on numerous occasions, that it is his intention to abolish the Department of Education. If he cannot accomplish that, then he prefers to reduce its status to that of a small granting institution with very limited funds. Remember, 5 out of every 10 federal dollars for black institutions come from the Department of Education.

JE: Is the pattern of withdrawal of federal involvement in education evident in other critical areas as well?

MD: Yes. The National Science Foundation, for example—which has science education as a central mandate in its charter—lost its Education Directorate in the Reagan budget cuts. Along with the abolition of the Education Directorate came White House requests for a reduction or elimination of funding for educational and research activities targeted for special groups, most notably women, minorities, the poor, and the handicapped.

Let me cite just two examples. The Minority Institutions Science Improvement Program began in the National Science Foundation and later became part of the Department of Education. Its purpose is to improve the scientific capabilities of black and other minority institutions. Last year, the program experienced a drastic 40 percent reduction in funds from $5 million to $3 million. A second example: Ninety percent of students at black universities rely on financial aid to attend college. It is expected that the tightening of eligibility requirements for Pell grants, the major source of federal aid to students, will result in 12 percent fewer students being eligible for such grants in aid.

So, overall, the administration is withdrawing federal commitment to education. More specifically, it is moving to reduce its involvement in programs that have, in the past, improved the representation of women, minorities, and the handicapped in such areas as science and technology.

But this gradual shrinking from commitment to education on the part of the White House is only half the picture for higher education. A shift in the targeting of federal dollars for research and development accompanies it. The administration's position is very simple: It believes that, on the civilian side at least, only support for basic research is properly within the role of the federal government. Applied research—that is, the "D" in R&D (Research and Development)—should be left to those industries where the promise of profits serves to pursue an idea or discovery beyond the basic research stage.

A second component is part of this shift. According to the administration, not all areas of funding, even of basic research, fall within the purview of the federal government. Government advisors will determine which areas are of sufficient importance to justify funding. Other areas should be left to survive as best they can. It seems a mark of arrogance to me that White House experts believe they can separate the important from the unimportant sciences. But, not unpredictably, they appear to have chosen the physical sciences as being more important than the social and biological sciences. The physical sciences are most closely related to national defense—possibly the primary function of the federal government as far as this administration is concerned. About one-sixteenth of research in black universities takes place in the physical sciences, while about three-fourths of research in black institutions occurs in the social and biological sciences.

JE: What are the implications of this funding shift for predominantly black colleges?

MD: They're extremely ominous. Applied research and research in the social and life sciences account for most of the research and research training at black institutions. Yet, these are precisely the areas from which the federal government is withdrawing its research focus. Coupled with the planned withdrawal of federal commitment to education, the implications are grim for black colleges and universities.

JE: What can be done to minimize the impact of this shift in federal funding priorities?

MD: Clearly, black institutions need a buffer to protect them from such drastic shifts. In this regard, non-black institutions have done rather well. Their balancing of several forms of financial support safeguards them from the worst effects of these policy changes. If one form of support dries up, they have others on which to fall back.

Black institutions must also strive to diversify their funding base. This means not only that they must begin seeking funds from a variety of agencies within the federal government, but also that they must identify possible areas of cooperation with industry. And once they have identified areas of possible cooperation, they must find a concrete way to ally key leaders in the identified industry with the university. This might mean an offer to the chief executive officer to join the university board of trustees, or it might even mean sitting down to draw up a plan of mutual support. Certainly, precedents exist for such cooperation in the area of vocational education. I see no reason why such a tradition could not be cultivated for higher education as well. Likewise, there are precedents for inter-university cooperation. American universities have long engaged in exchange programs with universities in other countries. Similar exchanges of faculty and sharing of specialized resources may allow black institutions to continue to offer learning experiences they would otherwise have to abandon or even to develop expertise they would otherwise not be able to afford.

Besides diversifying their funding base, I would recommend long-term developmental planning. When facing one crisis after another, as black institutions frequently do, making only short-term plans is natural. But stable long-term growth and development depend on the accurate assessment of future developments. There is little doubt, for example, that the future will present us with a growing need for expertise in microelectronics, biotechnology, communications, and space-related sciences. Black institutions, when seeking funding, should make their greatest efforts in those areas where there will be a growing demand for knowledge, training, and personnel. Black institutions must also employ lobbyists at the state legislative and congressional levels.

JE: Finally, would you also recommend direct political action as a means of reversing current administration priorities?

MD: Yes. I, for one, am not ready to abandon the belief that the federal government should have a strong and lasting commitment to education and, more specifically, a commitment to those who have not yet enjoyed equal access to education. Federal programs have helped black institutions in the past, and we should not give those programs up for lost simply because the White House seeks to write them out of the budget.

We must insist, with organized force, that the government restore funding for the Minority Institutions Science Improvement Program and that the National Science Foundation resurrect programs which benefit minorities. We must insist that the government maintain the Department of Education, give Blacks their fair share of defense R&D funding, and maintain the Minority Biomedical Support Program in the National Institutes of Health. In addition, black institutions must reexamine their existing curricula and institute courses which are more relevant and future-oriented. And if for our efforts government officials tell us that there is no way these things can be done, it would be well to remind these hopeless souls, as has Mayor Andrew Young on many occasions, that black people are adept at making a way out of no way.

PART TWO

The Executive Branch

Clifford L. Alexander, Jr.

Blacks and the Military

Clifford L. Alexander, Jr., was born September 21, 1933, in New York City. He received a Bachelor of Arts degree, cum laude, from Harvard University in 1955, where he was president of the Harvard Student Council and First Marshal of his class. He went on to earn a Bachelor of Laws degree from Yale University Law School in 1958.

From February 1977 until January 1981, Alexander served as secretary of the army. Appointed by President Jimmy Carter, he was responsible for all activities of the department, including the training, operation, administration, logistical support, and preparedness of the army. Each fiscal year, he coordinated the development and execution of the army's budget—which totalled $40 billion in 1981.

Alexander was chairman of the Equal Employment Opportunity Commission from 1967 to 1969 and served as special consultant to President Lyndon B. Johnson on civil rights. Upon his resignation, he became a partner in the firm of Arnold and Porter until 1975. From 1975 until February 1977, he was a member of the Washington law firm of Verner, Liipfert, Bernhard, McPherson, and Alexander.

In 1963, while in the private practice of law in New York City, Alexander was summoned to the White House by President John F. Kennedy to serve as foreign affairs officer of the National Security Council. From 1964 through 1967, President Johnson appointed him—successively—deputy special assistant to the President, associate special counsel, and deputy special counsel to the President.

From 1959 to 1961, Alexander served as assistant district attorney for New York County, resigning this office to become executive director of the Manhattanville Hamilton Grange Neighborhood Conservation Project, and then program and executive director of Harlem Youth Opportunities.

Alexander was a member of the Commission on Income Maintenance Programs, as well as the President's Commission for the Observation of Human Rights in 1968. In that same year, he also served as special representative of the President with the rank of Ambassador and as head of the United States delegation to ceremonies marking the independence of Swaziland.

Alexander is a member of the bar of New York State and the District of Columbia and has been admitted to practice before the Supreme Court of the United States. He was appointed in 1975 by the Unified Bar of the District of Columbia for a six-year term on the Judicial Nomination Commission, but resigned upon assuming his duties as secretary of the army. He was a candidate in the first election in 104 years for mayor of the District of Columbia.

Today, Alexander is president of Alexander and Associates, a private consulting firm. The company provides planning and advice in corporate responsibility and manpower development. Alexander plans, organizes, directs, and coordinates programs and policy analysis in these areas for corporate directors, executives, and managers. In addition, he also serves as president of Communications for the Eighties, through which he and his team of consultants undertake media-related projects.

Alexander is presently on the board of directors of MCI Communications Corporation, Pennsylvania Power and Light Company, Dreyfus Third Century Fund, Dreyfus General Money Market Fund, and A Better Chance, Inc. He is also a member of the board of trustees of the Bureau of Social Science Research in Washington, D.C.

JE: Can you discuss the chain of events leading to your selection as secretary of the army?

CA: It's difficult to recall the exact chain of events. I received a call from Harold Brown, the secretary of defense, who first raised the possibility. A day or two later, I met with Brown and Charles Duncan, who served as his deputy. The appointment came out of left field. It caught me totally by surprise. It was Brown who tendered the offer, and I agreed to accept it.

JE: How did you view the army at the time of your appointment? Did your views change as secretary?

CA: I had a fairly positive view of the army, having served on the White House staff and the National Security Council staff. My earlier uniform contact was too long ago to be remembered in detail. I do recall it being demanding work, challenging work.

I approached the position with a healthy skepticism, and thought that an important part of my job was to ask questions and raise the kinds of issues which a civilian leader should ask. That attitude remained with me during the years I served as secretary.

JE: Did you know President Carter well prior to your appointment? What was the nature of your relationship?

CA: I did not know President Carter. In fact, we had never met. I had not been active in his campaign. My son admired him greatly, but I doubt President Carter was aware of that fact prior to my appointment. I had no reason to believe that he would appoint me to a high-level position in his administration.

JE: Did you know him well as secretary? What was he like on a personal level? How did he impress you?

CA: I wouldn't describe it as "well." I got to know him better than previous secretaries of the army might have known presidents. There were two reasons for that. First, the Panama Canal—an issue in which he was vitally interested—was part of my responsibility. As secretary, I played a large role in the negotiations and, owing to my position, had direct line responsibility to the President. This brought us into close contact. I had to conduct a number of briefings for the President concerning the status of those negotiations. Second, again owing to my direct line relationship, I was deeply involved in the field of civil works. This too brought us into close contact. So, I did see much more of him than one might expect.

He was a considerate man, but somewhat distant. He rarely let down his guard—with one notable exception. This occurred en route from Mt. St. Helens. The Corps of Engineers played a salient role in clearing the area. On that occasion, we spoke at length. He was extremely relaxed, talking about his love of fishing. That was an unusual occurrence. Most of the time he was quite formal.

JE: Did the President take an active interest in your work as secretary?

CA: Yes, very much so. He saturated himself in detail and, as you know, was criticized heavily for paying too much attention to such matters. The criticism, from my view, was unfair. I wish we had a president today who showed such an interest. Mr. Carter knew what was going on. We had a number of budget meetings, during which he revealed a keen understanding of army-related matters. His interest was reflected in many of the decisions he made. It certainly made my job easier. I could count on his support.

JE: What do you see as his greatest failings? Did these contribute to his re-election defeat?

CA: It's easy to be a Monday morning quarterback. I don't blame him as much as I do those around him, particularly the coterie of fellow Georgians, who did him a disservice by isolating themselves from the Washington establishment. They not only isolated themselves from the

Georgetown cocktail circuit, but from government officials, the news media, and other civic figures. That proved to be counterproductive. A president needs the feedback that such contact guarantees.

The President was also hurt by the "holier-than-thou" attitude that permeated his administration. All of us have our foibles, and when the President revealed his foibles, people were quick to say, "I told you so."

Mr. Carter also made a number of political misjudgments, particularly on the Iranian crisis. He isolated himself during the crisis, blowing it out of all proportion, thus undercutting his ability to lead. This fact was clearly perceived by the country, and contributed to his defeat.

The President was also hurt by the shallowness of coverage of Ronald Reagan. This had a profound effect and an unhappy one on President Carter. Mr. Reagan was permitted to make "Howdy-Doody"-like pronouncements without being called to task. The softness of his positions was never questioned. He was never challenged for his lack of knowledge. The press focused on style as opposed to substance, which worked to his advantage.

JE: What explains this lack of solid coverage? How was Mr. Reagan able to avoid press scrutiny?

CA: The media is many things, but most of all, it is *televison*. And a facility with television is extremely important for a presidential candidate. When one spends the better part of a lifetime in front of the cameras, as did Reagan, he is in a much better position to manipulate the medium. He knows its demands and requirements. Reagan proved a master in this regard. The cameras pictured him as relaxed, sincere, poised. That gave him a distinct advantage. Television played a critical role in the election.

A contributing factor was the role that money played—and the way money was used to cultivate a particular image of Reagan. Money flowed like a river on the Republican side. This gave them tremendous access to the media. They bought countless ads on television, without assuming any responsibility for the content of those ads. The sheer weight of the ads proved overwhelming. Moreover, the negativeness of the ads tarnished President Carter's image and contributed to a lack of confidence.

In many ways, we've created a monster. Televison has a great potential for good, but it also has a great potential for evil. It has served to pervert the political process. Candidates are now being packaged like soap. Slick public relations take the place of informed judgments.

I should differentiate between the print media and the live media. I have great respect for most reporters. They have a difficult job to do.

They have their own biases, as do all human beings, but for the most part, they are highly trained and extremely professional. Most of the major newspapers are quite conservative. The Republicans like to point out that most newspapers are controlled by left-wing elements. That's simply not true. The editorial pages reveal a clear conservative bias. The problem lies not so much with reporters, but with the way that the media reports elections and covers candidates.

JE: As secretary, what were your major goals? Did these change over time?

CA: My main objective—and this was not easy to accept—was to recognize the fact that I should not attempt to institute radical change. It's just not possible to transform an institution, like the army, in the short span of four years. It is more important to make it better—to work for incremental change.

Other goals emerged, of course, as I became immersed in the job. I was strongly committed to improving army hardware. We made a number of improvements in this area. I also wanted to expand the opportunities available to army personnel, particularly to women and minorities. Unfortunately, the Reagan Administration has not followed suit. We also worked hard to improve the readiness of the army. This was a difficult task, but one at which we succeeded. We also endeavored to upgrade the entrance standards of army personnel.

In terms of the latter, I want to point out that this is not necessarily a gauge of a good soldier. Rather, it is more a gauge of whether a person is likely to complete a first term of service. But increased education does not necessarily make recruits better soldiers. However, formal schooling does contribute to other positive things.

JE: How were you accepted by the army brass? Did race ever pose a problem?

CA: Whatever one might say about the army in this regard, one can also say about any major American institution. Clearly, race would affect any group of people which perceives that their lives and fortunes are in the hands of a black person. And these attitudes existed in the army. I do feel, however, that because of the command-orientation of the army, as well as its task nature, race played a less significant role than it does in the private sector. On the other hand, I do think there was, at some point, a lack of obedience because I was black. When I confronted such bias, I was able to correct it.

So, yes, race was a factor. I suspect it was less pronounced than it would have been had I been president of General Motors. The military is, to a large extent, a conservative institution. Still, in terms of opportunity, the army is more open than any comparable institution in the private sector. This is clearly evident in the command structure of the army.

If you examine the racial composition of the general officers—those who actually make the day-to-day decisions—you will find a far greater percentage of individuals with minority backgrounds. There are few Blacks in comparable positions in the private sector. And that's an indictment of the private sector. While the army has done well in this area, it still has a long way to go.

In the enlisted ranks, the record is even better. The army is approximately 20 percent black. And it's about 25 percent black at the E-9 rank, which is the highest of the enlisted ranks. This was true as recently as a year ago. Statistics of this kind are extremely important. They dispel the myth that the army is a dead end for minorities. That's simply not true.

JE: Was race also a factor in terms of how you were viewed by the White House and senior staff?

CA: Yes, very much so. I often sensed surprise at shows of intelligence. There are, were, and unhappily always will be people who hold stereotypical views of black people. Sadly, most of these perceptions are negative. Such attitudes affect the behavior of presidents, as well as their subordinates.

Not all political leaders, however, harbor such views. For example, take the case of President Lyndon Johnson. He was far ahead of his time in this area. He had an amazing openness of mind and spirit. His attitudes were quite unique. No president has come close to matching his sense of fairness and objectivity.

President Johnson was able to see beyond race—to recognize people for their worth. He did not let race blind him to their capabilities, nor limit his view of their talents. I recall vividly when he appointed Thurgood Marshall to the Supreme Court. He called and asked me to come to the White House. When I arrived, he told me that he was going to nominate Marshall to the bench. He said that the time was right. And then he said, "He's not like you. He's not from Harvard and all that. He's like me. He's of the people. He understands people problems."

Now, Johnson was mindful of color. But he had a rare ability to see beyond race. In appointing Marshall, he stated that he liked the idea that a black man would be in a position of authority. He saw it as healthy for society.

When Blacks are appointed to top-level positions, they are often viewed differently from their white counterparts. They are seen as only capable of dealing with black issues. Blacks themselves can do much to dispel this attitude. They can sit there and smile, evidence their approval, or they can speak out and exert their influence in other areas. This is best illustrated by an incident which occurred when I was secretary. A female reporter, from *Forbes* magazine, requested an interview. At the time, I had been secretary for three years. Her questions focused exclusively on Blacks. I asked her, "Aren't you interested in my views about the army?" But that's all she wanted to talk about. I said, "You know, my interests are not limited to Blacks and black-related issues. If that's all you're interested in, the interview is over." Her attitude was representative of a certain mind-set. I think the same attitude holds true today. It's much more likely that, even in the case of Democratic politicians, they would ask my views on race issues more often than they would on defense matters. The solution to this problem really rests with society, particularly whites, who tend to view blacks in very limited terms.

JE: How did you deal with the problem of racism when it surfaced in the White House and the upper echelons of the army?

CA: I did not experience any overt displays of racism from the White House. My relations with the White House were free of racial friction. There were no racial conflicts, at least of a serious nature, that surfaced during my tenure.

There were, however, some racial incidents within the army. I made it clear that racism would not be tolerated. Army personnel were warned that racial discrimination would be punished and that those found guilty of such practices would be disciplined.

I *did* experience overt racial prejudice in a number of dealings on the Hill. One case involved Representative Robin Beard (R-Tenn.), with whom I was constantly at odds. I think race played a significant role in his attitude toward me. I tried to hit him square between the eyes. And I did it in public, particularly when he expressed such attitudes in committee.

When members of Congress demeaned army personnel—and I felt their comments were racially motivated—I tried to deal with these comments head on. Much of the problem was due to ignorance, as opposed to prejudice. The best way to deal with the problem was to confront it directly, as opposed to pretending that it didn't exist.

JE: Were there times when you found yourself in sharp disagreement with President Carter? If so, how did you express those differences?

CA: That wasn't really a problem. There were very few such disagreements. Those differences that did exist concerned the buildup of the Department of Defense. Remember, there were only two areas in which I had direct line responsibility to the president. However, we had few, if any, deep philosophical disagreements.

JE: As secretary, did you feel a direct responsibility to express what you perceived to be the views of black America to the administration?

CA: Yes. On several occasions, I did feel such a responsibility. However, I did not view it as appropriate to set myself up as an expert on race issues simply because I am black. I did not want to be seen as the spokesman for black America. That was not why I was appointed. My interests related chiefly to my department. There were numerous people who spoke out on race-related issues. I agreed with most of their views, and when I did not, I expressed my own views. What was missing, at least in the Carter White House, were whites who would speak up on such issues.

I recall one incident quite vividly. The late Moshe Dayan made a racist comment about black soldiers, charging that they undermined America's readiness. I checked the transcript carefully, not wanting to believe that such a distinguished war hero would make such comments. I tried to persuade the State Department—which should have issued a response—to act in this matter. But they were chicken. They didn't want to offend Israel, which is a valued ally. They saw that as more important than the impact that such a statement would have on the hundreds of thousands of black soldiers. So, eventually, I did say something. That was a case where I would have much preferred others to respond.

JE: What were the most difficult problems you faced as secretary?

CA: I always found it difficult to deal with base closings. Congress also presented a special challenge. I received a number of positive comments from congressmen, who complimented me on my knowledge. I conducted countless briefings and took pride in being able to respond to the most complex of questions. The issue of procurement was also difficult. Finally, improving the day-to-day conditions of the soldier and his family proved frustrating.

JE: Based on your experience, what types of Blacks are appointed to high-level government positions? Do those in positions of power feel more comfortable with certain Blacks as opposed to others?

CA: Whoever is nominated must survive the confirmation process. That itself dictates the appointment of certain types of individuals. I don't think the process is quite the same for Blacks as it is for whites. When a new administration comes into office, there is a scramble for power. Many of the people who are appointed lack the qualifications that one might expect. Even so, the agencies function because there are, within each department, a group of highly trained professionals, men and women who possess broad experience in agency affairs.

There is, however, a stereotypical view of what types of positions should go to Blacks. Most appointments reflect this mind-set. The Carter Administration, however, broke the mold in a number of instances.

Quite frankly, I don't know what the future holds. I don't see, even within the Democratic Party, the kind of imagination and vision that are required when it comes to problems of race. The solution requires that our best minds, black and white, enter into a dialogue on this question. The problem demands open discussion, the kind which is so sorely lacking in the present administration. Unfortunately, the situation is not very encouraging. And it's not much better in the private sector.

JE: How would you assess the record of the Reagan Administration in the area of civil rights? Do you sense a strong commitment, on the part of the president, to racial justice?

CA: First, I'd like to say that I'm not particularly interested in whether or not Ronald Reagan is a racist. I don't care whether he is or isn't. The answer to the question does not depend on the racial attitudes of the president. Rather, we should look to the facts. And the facts make somebody in this administration out to be a liar. The President has appointed very few Blacks to positions of power and responsibility. When the Reagan Administration was threatened with a subpoena, it revealed that 4.1 percent of the president's appointments were black. And most of those were to insignificant positions, when you look at government across the board.

The record of the Reagan Administration is an insult not just to black Americans, but to all Americans. One need only examine the performance of the administration as it relates to the U.S. Civil Rights Commission. Its conduct in this regard bespeaks its true attitude towards Blacks and other minorities. The President has consistently appointed people to his administration who are either hostile to civil rights or disinterested in the problems of black Americans. Most of these individuals have extremely callous attitudes toward their fellow Americans. Look at William Bradford Reynolds, who is in charge of the Civil Rights Division of the Department of Justice. He just doesn't understand the issues. Today, no Blacks have the ear of the President. We have a President in the White House who has little or no understanding of black Americans. He lives in a fantasy world—a world that is far removed from the lives of most Blacks. Those charged with enforcing civil rights have either subverted the law or worked to weaken it. These officials have permitted the nation to regress in ways that threaten the hard-won progress that Blacks have made over the years. They have created the myth that Blacks are somehow asking for more than they deserve—that they want something to which they are not entitled. They have no understanding or appreciation of the Constitution. The Reagan administration has turned its back on black America. It has permitted one racist after another to crawl out from under the rocks and, in many cases, given them legitimacy and power. It's a terrible thing to witness. I fear for the future of my country.

JE: Does it concern you that large numbers of young people, particularly college-age students, have become increasingly apathetic and disinterested in politics?

CA: Yes, very much so. Still, I think we focus too much on the 1960s. There were scores of people who weren't in college, my late mother included, who protested injustice, going back to the turn of the century, and who fought for what they believed was right. Their efforts have had a significant impact on American political life.

Today's young people may be apathetic, when measured by the standards of the 1960s, but they are carrying on the struggle in new and different ways. They are not marching or carrying placards. But they are asking questions. And they are challenging those in positions of authority. Unfortunately, they are not raising many of the important questions that should be raised. What we need is an honest dialogue—one which involves our best minds, white and black. Sadly, there is no evidence of that dialogue.

JE: Are you concerned about the large percentage of black soldiers in the enlisted ranks of the army?

CA: No, not at all. The services are voluntary—all of them. There are more Blacks, percentage-wise, in the army than in any other branch of the service. The all-volunteer force is approximately 16 percent black. Overall, the army is about 20 percent black. People who ask this question are missing the point. Rather, they should be asking the question: Is there career opportunity for Blacks in the army? The answer is yes.

Greater opportunities exist in the military, and in the army in particular, than in the private sector. That's one of the reasons why large numbers of Blacks join the army. These enlistees believe that there is greater opportunity in the army than in other areas of life. And they're right.

JE: Are Blacks well represented throughout the army hierarchy? What about at the highest levels?

CA: Yes, Blacks are well represented, but not as well as they should be. The army is not an ideal world. It mirrors many of the problems of the outside world. Still, there is greater opportunity for advancement in the army than in the private sector. Unfortunately, there has also been some retrogression in the army, which is quite appalling. It's something we must guard against and correct.

JE: Do Blacks face any special problems in the army? If so, what?

CA: Yes, Blacks face special problems. This is especially true in the administration of justice. There are numerous incidents that can only be explained by color. This is evident, for example, in the area of court martials. The numbers are much greater for black soldiers than for white soldiers. This is partly explained by black attitudes and behavior patterns. Many whites find it difficult to understand Blacks and why they do many of the things they do because some whites have not been exposed to certain black life-styles.

I think we must take a much closer look at the service academy, which should do considerably more to attract talented young Blacks. The problem is not one of prejudice, but one of commitment. The leadership must reach out to Blacks and make them feel that they are wanted—and needed.

JE: If a young Black were to come to you and ask for advice, would you recommend the army as a possible career?

CA: No. I would not counsel him to join the army or choose any other career. That's a personal decision. If someone were interested in the military, I would recommend the army as a possibility. There are opportunities in the army, and I would make clear to him what those opportunities are. I don't see the army, however, as ideally suited to all young people. It depends upon their interests and personalities.

The army has been, from an historical perspective, a vehicle of opportunity. President Dwight Eisenhower went to West Point, not because he aspired to be a great general but because he wanted a free education. Most people join the army for reasons having little to do with the service. They do it for the benefits which the army offers. Why they join the army has little to do with whether they will be good soldiers. That depends on many other factors. The most important point is once they are in, what is the quality of the service they render?

JE: To what extent does the army promote equal opportunity? How does the army compare to other institutions?

CA: As an institution, the army can boast a better record than any other major social institution. However, I have seen, in recent statistics, an erosion of progress. There's clear evidence of decline in the number of general officers. That's quite worrisome. I hope that decline hasn't occurred in other areas.

JE: Why do you oppose the reinstatement of the draft?

CA: There are several reasons. There is no need for it. The reason you have a draft is to fill a manpower shortage. There is *no* manpower shortage in the service. Our goals are presently served by the volunteer army. Obviously, if we were to become involved in an all-out war, we would have to reinstate the draft. But that is not the case at the present time.

By the way, very little consideration has been given to who we ought to draft. People simply assume that we ought to draft eighteen-year-olds. That may be outmoded thinking. Perhaps the skills we need are better filled by people in their thirties, forties, or fifties, with particular kinds of computer skills, organizational skills, leadership skills, and personnel skills. What is missing is a thorough analysis of the manpower needs of the services.

JE: How do you respond to critics who contend that the volunteer army is made up of a disproportionately high percentage of minorities and poor people?

CA: I can't understand how so many thoughtful people can believe such malarkey. I can only conclude that they're misinformed. Do we really want every American to serve in the armed forces? I think not. What effect would this have on society in general? Presently, the army stands at about 775,000. If we were to do what some have advocated, that is, draft every qualified man and woman in the United States, the army would grow to over 20 million.

Such an increase would pose numerous policy implications. Clearly, we would need sufficient personnel to train those 20 million. We would need to provide more than twenty times the present number of guns, tanks, ammunition, and planes. And we would have to increase the military budget twenty fold. What would that mean in terms of our domestic programs? I suspect that we would undo all of the progress that we've made over the last fifty years.

Whoever said that one must put on a uniform to be a good American? Why can't people make other kinds of contributions to their country? I would argue that all of us, in our own way, are contributing to the strength and vitality of America. The teacher, the factory worker, the doctor, the mechanic, the scientist, the truck driver—all of them are making vital contributions to the future of this nation. Why must everyone make the same contribution?

The fact is, at no time have we drafted everybody. At no time, for example, has the navy or the air force had a draft. No one criticizes these branches for not drafting people. So why criticize the army? I'm afraid that much of the support for the draft lies in misplaced patriotism and sentimentality.

JE: Do you agree with those who argue that, for most Blacks and poor people, the army is a job of last resort?

CA: No, that's utter nonsense. But I'll try to respond to that criticism less emotionally and more factually. The charge is rooted in a class bias that somehow there isn't a picturesque cross section of Americans in the service—that the children of the rich don't serve.

First of all, most eighteen-year-olds have very limited assets. They might have a record collection, or a few dollars in the bank, but that's usually the extent of their net worth. If we're concerned about not having enough millionaires in the service, let's draft some old folks in the service so they can pay their dues to society. And I'm not being facetious about that. That may worry some people, but not me.

Second, if you look at the economic makeup of the army, you might be surprised. There are a number of people from affluent families. Not everybody is from the lower end of the economic scale. Moreover, many people have the idea that the army attracts the bum on the street, the drifter, the deadbeat. That's not true. Most of those people can't pass the physical. They also can't pass the aptitude test we give. There's a very small percentage of men who join the army from the ranks of the unemployed.

I would also point out that all of the officers are volunteers. There is ample evidence to demonstrate that they are performing well. And they don't all come from rich homes. I don't know what's magical about rich homes, particularly in a democratic society. Why are we so preoccupied with the rich? What do they add to the service? Is their affluence a plus when it comes to being a good soldier? I think not. Presently, the army is a vehicle of opportunity. It attracts many people who lack similar opportunities in the private sector. Why take away those opportunities? Why force young men to join the service, when they don't want to, when there are others who see the military as a vehicle to a better life?

We hear much speculation these days about why young people enlist in the volunteer army. Some say that our soldiers are trying to escape unhappiness, poverty, bad housing, and family problems in civilian life; even that they are faced with enlisting in the army as an alternative to jail or heavy fine. Others suggest that our new soldiers are seeking "only" a job and not service to our nation. There are even charges that we are not recruiting the right quality in our soldiers.

It is instructive, I believe, to examine what motivated enlistments in the past. As an example, many officers, including several of our most famous patriots, originally sought appointments to West Point because they could not afford a college education any other way. Some soldiers who enlisted in past decades sought to escape from something in their life-style or environment. But whatever the reason for yesterday's enlistments or today's volunteers, dwelling on them misses the essential point. And that point is, once they are part of our army, how do they conduct themselves? When we focus on that relevant question, the answer is that our soldiers do well. Their attitude toward service is exhibited in their day-to-day dedication, their excellent level of performance, and the personal sacrifices they make which are traditionally associated with members of our armed forces.

JE: Is the defense budget, as many have argued, riddled with waste?

CA: Yes. Defense money is being wasted by the billions. Not long ago, the Heritage Foundation issued a report which concluded that the Pentagon could save $8.5 billion *each year* in costs involved in procuring new weapons. The cost saving methods the Heritage Foundation recommended include more cost conscious weapons designs, more standardization between services, better cost estimates, and a number of other logical reforms. Two major steps are therefore urgent. One is to streamline the procurement process in order to save over $8 billion per year, while the other is to cut the size of the increase ($40 billion or 20 percent) in the defense budget dramatically.

JE: Why is the defense budget so out of whack with economic realities?

CA: Several major factors influence the evolution of our defense posture and the monies authorized and appropriated to support our efforts. The Defense Department interacts with the four services: the army, navy, air force, and marines. The product of those skirmishes is reviewed by the Office of Management and Budget and usually people on the White House staff. Various congressional committees—Armed Services, Appropriations, and Budget—in both houses have their say.

Throughout the internal development process within the Defense Department, through the executive branch budget process prior to and during congressional hearings and into markup, powerful external forces are also at work. They include hundreds of contractors who will be the direct beneficiaries of higher defense budgets as well as service-oriented lobbying groups such as the Navy League and the Association of the United States Army. They are powerful, potent, and all too often myopic in their approach. Business and civic associations near bases make their voices heard both in the executive and legislative branches. Veterans groups and others from the retired military community know the process and exploit it to the end they deem appropriate. None of this is sinister—it is the exercise of power within a democratic form of government. Occasional excesses occur, but the real danger is when there is little or no questioning of what is presented by the services and the Department of Defense. The process breaks down when too many people declare that if you don't fund what they suggest that you don't love your country and/or that you are not interested in protecting it.

Another danger to the system, particularly present this year, is a president who declares, "If you only knew what I know, you would support my budget." Then the president says, "I can't tell you what I know, but you must support me for the good of our nation." This shell game approach is not healthy for our democracy. The major reason this year's defense budget is so at odds with economic realities is because President Reagan called for a huge increase *before* he had any idea what the impact of his actions would be on our economy. He also shows no grasp for the process of assessing what the real threats are to the nation's security.

JE: As a nation, are we reacting more to buildups than to potential threats to America's security?

CA: Yes. Endless comparisons have been made concerning American versus Soviet spending levels: manpower, naval power, missile warheads, research and development, aircraft capabilities, and capability to make global projections of power. Briefings are given to congressional committees on many items and areas where we are short when compared to the Soviets. These comparisons are given particular emphasis during the period of the formulation of the defense budget. Many of these comparisons *do* have a real bearing on our national defense. Others *do not* and are used mostly to excite lawmakers to be more generous in funding a certain service's program.

The time of our defense analysts and our elected representatives would be better spent if the perceived threats to our nation's security and economic interests were examined with thoroughness, intelligence, and care. All too often this does not take place. To properly formulate a defense budget you must comprehend potential worldwide threats and, under realistic conditions, the kinds of responses we wish to undertake. To properly formulate these potential threats is extremely difficult work, and we have men and women in and out of uniform with the intellectual discipline to do this. So far the political and, to a certain extent, uniformed leadership has fallen down on the job. It is easier to get higher budgets through bleak comparisons between the United States and the Soviet Union. As is usually the case, the easy way is not the best way.

JE: What do you see as the major flaws of the present defense budget?

CA: The present budget is basically undisciplined. It has several tragic flaws. First, it has been erected without sufficient thought being given to the possible threats we face. Second, it properly perceives the threat of the Soviet Union but imprecisely measures the nature of that threat. Third, it makes a massive contribution to our budget deficit—which our nation cannot stand. Fourth, it mortgages our future by setting in motion unjustified expenditures that will continue to escalate dramatically until the end of the twentieth century. Fifth, it has not been subjected to the internal tightening up recommended by many experts in the field.

JE: Finally, how do you view the Soviets and the threat they pose to world peace?

CA: We must realize that the Soviet strength is awesome but hardly without major deficiencies. We should watch their every move with skepticism, but we should learn to assess them realistically when they stumble as they did in Afghanistan. There are two major lessons for us in this war. When the Soviets invaded in December 1979, the Soviets made it abundantly clear for those who doubted it that they will strike beyond their borders to other than Warsaw Bloc nations. It was a raw, naked exercise of power.

It also revealed the lack of skill and preparation possessed by the Soviet forces. The ineffectiveness of the Soviet fighting force was further highlighted, as a supposedly friendly Afghan army of 100,000 has now shrunk to 25,000 and is more of a burden than much else to the Soviets. The "Bear" is dangerous and treacherous, but at the same time it can be awkward and cumbersome. The world consists of more than the Soviets and the Americans. We need to see this more clearly. We also need to set our goals and priorities internally as well as externally. If we sacrifice our economy, we hurt our national security. It is as simple and as complicated as that. We must take those steps required to preserve our economic *and* military strength. Our last clear hope is our elected officials of both parties of Congress. Let us hope they examine our national interests with more thoroughness than the executive branch.

Samuel R. Pierce, Jr.

The Republican Alternative

Samuel R. Pierce, Jr., was born on September 8, 1922, in Glen Cove, Long Island, New York. He was nominated secretary of Housing and Urban Development (HUD) by President Ronald Reagan on December 22, 1980, and was sworn in on January 23, 1981, after being confirmed by a United States Senate vote of 98–0. Pierce is the highest ranking black American in the Reagan Administration.

Prior to his nomination, Pierce was a senior partner in the New York law firm of Battle, Fowler, Jaffin, Pierce, and Kheel. His federal government experience includes service as: general counsel of the Department of the Treasury from 1970 to 1973; associate counsel and later counsel of the Subcommittee on Antitrust of the Committee on the Judiciary of the House of Representatives during 1956 and 1957; and assistant to the under secretary of the Department of Labor from 1955 to 1956. He received the Department of the Treasury's highest honor, the Alexander Hamilton Award, in 1973.

Pierce served as a judge of the New York Court of General Sessions from 1959 to 1960. He was an assistant United States attorney for the Southern District of New York from 1953 to 1955, following service as an assistant district attorney for New York County. Pierce was admitted to the New York State Bar in 1949 and was authorized to practice before the United States Supreme Court in 1956.

A 1947 Phi Beta Kappa graduate of Cornell University, Pierce also received his law degree from Cornell in 1949. He earned a Master of Laws degree in taxation in 1952 and was awarded an honorary Doctor of Laws degree in 1972 from the New York University School of Law, where he was a member of the faculty for many years. From 1957 to 1958, Pierce was a Ford Foundation Fellow at the Yale Law School. He has written many legal articles for professional journals and has contributed to several books.

Pierce's civic, educational, and corporate positions include: member of the New York City Board of Education; governor of the American Stock Exchange; adjunct professor at the New York University School of Law; and trustee of the Rand Corporation, Cornell University, Howard University, Mount Holyoke College, and Hampton Institute. He has also been a director of the Prudential Insurance Company of America, General Electric Company, International Paper Company, Public Service Electric and Gas Company, and First National Bank of Boston, among others.

JE: Why do you think President Reagan selected you as secretary of Housing and Urban Development? What special qualifications did you bring to the position?

SP: I don't like to answer such questions; they make me appear boastful. Moreover, I don't really know what factors influenced his selection of me. I know there was a nationwide search—that many people were considered. For reasons known to the president and several of his top aides, I was chosen for the position. Other than that, there's very little I can say.

JE: In reviewing your background, it seems odd that you were selected for this particular position, as opposed to others, for which you appear more qualified. Were you surprised that you were offered the job at HUD?

SP: No, I wasn't surprised. On the other hand, I think I would have been just as qualified to be attorney general, or secretary of labor, or secretary of education. I think I could have qualified for any number of positions. Why I was offered the job at HUD, I just don't know.

I suspect the President had already promised several of these posts to others. For example, the then attorney general, William French Smith, had been the president's personal lawyer for many years. Likewise, I understand that Raymond Donovan, the secretary of labor, had been promised the job during the campaign.

JE: Did you expect President Reagan to name you to his cabinet? Did you lobby for a position?

SP: No. I did not expect to be appointed, nor did I lobby for a position. At the time, I was engaged in private law practice in New York City. I was extremely busy and quite happy. I had made a number of financial contributions to the Republican Party and to the president's campaign. But that was nothing new. I had contributed to a number of Republican candidates. I was not particularly active in the president's campaign. I did not serve as a fundraiser, nor did I campaign on his behalf. My involvement was primarily of a financial nature.

I did attend several political receptions for the President and, on one occasion, had an opportunity to meet Mr. Reagan. The reception was sponsored by Donald Regan, the present White House chief of staff. I did not, however, solicit a job within the administration. It just came. It's as simple as that.

JE: Did you have any apprehensions about accepting the President's offer? If so, what?

SP: Yes, I didn't accept his offer on the spot. I had had a number of meetings, including several lengthy sessions, with Pendleton James, who was in charge of personnel. We spoke several times, both in person and over the telephone. One day he called and said that Mr. Reagan would like to meet with me. So I flew to California to meet the president-elect. We had a fairly lengthy conversation, during which we talked about a number of matters. Even at the close of the meeting, he did not ask me about the position at HUD. Instead, he felt me out on the question. We discussed the boundaries—the rules—if I were to accept a cabinet post. I told him that I was interested and went back to my hotel. Later that night he called and asked if I would accept the job at HUD. And I said yes.

JE: To what extent do you share President Reagan's conservative economic views? Would you describe yourself as a "fiscal conservative"?

SP: I am in total agreement with the president's economic philosophy. In fact, that's one of the main reasons I accepted the job. We see eye-to-eye in this area. I felt then—and still do—that it's important to reduce the size and cost of government. In my view, it's critical that we reduce the huge deficits. The strength of our economy depends, in the long run, upon our ability to curb government spending.

It's also critical that we re-examine those programs and policies that produced these high deficits. That's the only way we can revitalize our economy. If we permit them to continue, we will do severe damage to our economy. We must be able to compete with other industrialized nations. This competition is good for America, but it is also good for the rest of the world.

A strong economy is the key to domestic progress. The President is determined to achieve this objective. It is vital that we reduce the cost of government programs. It's also vital that we learn to live within our means. I don't believe in spending for the sake of spending. More is not necessarily better. In fact, we must learn to do more with less. That means we will have to place a greater emphasis on efficiency.

So, yes, our economic views parallel one another. And, I might add, my faith in the president's economic program has been well justified. His policies are working. Our nation is moving again. Americans are back to work. Interest rates are down. Inflation is down. Unemployment is down. Virtually every economic indicator points to continued success. I think President Reagan has done more to turn government around than any president since Franklin Roosevelt. His record attests to that fact. Our improved economic situation today is directly attributable to his farsighted approach to economic matters.

JE: As one who knows the President, how would you assess his abilities, both as a leader and a politician?

SP: Many impressions come to mind. He's a nice guy. He's extremely affable. He has a great sense of humor. At the same time, he's strong, very strong. It's hard to push him. Once he's made up his mind, it's hard to move him. I won't say that he's stubborn or that he won't listen, but he has deep convictions, and he's willing to fight for them. That's evident in his relations with Congress. At times he has had to back off, but he'll only do so to a point—like with the MX missile. He has great tenacity, great staying power. And he's incredibly persuasive. My God, he does miracles with the Congress, including many Democratic congressmen. His success lies, in large part, in his ability to motivate people. He has a strong inner force. He's a mover and a shaker. Many congressmen believe that he's destined to win, so they go along with him. He's a master communicator—one of the best I've seen.

JE: Asked to assess your role in the Reagan Administration, William Gould, a professor of law at Stanford University and a former law partner of yours in New York, remarked: "He (Pierce) has to be very much out of place in the Reagan Administration." Is that an accurate characterization?

SP: No, not really. I don't feel out of place in terms of the president's economic policies. As I've said, I'm a true believer. I really believe his programs are grounded on solid economic principles. If the Congress gives them a chance, I'm convinced they'll work.

The one area where I might differ—and this applies more to several top aides than to the President—is in the area of civil rights. I've spoken to the President about civil rights on several occasions. He has assured me that he's committed to racial justice. And I believe that. There may be people within the administration who some might describe as insensitive in this area, but that is not true of the President, who has a strong sense of fairness.

JE: In this regard, many Americans—both black and white—were shocked by the president's action during the battle over the extension of the Voting Rights Act. Is this an example of his commitment to civil rights?

SP: It's not my practice to talk about behind-the-scenes deliberations and discussions, and I don't intend to make a habit of doing so, but since my position was erroneously reported in the press on the basis of questionable statements from some people who were present during the meetings, I want to set the record straight.

I fully supported the original Voting Rights Act, and I supported the concept long before it became law. I still do. Since I believe in a strong voting rights law, it's important to me that my position be understood.

On November 4, 1981, after the House had passed its version of the voting rights extension bill, the President called a cabinet meeting. The purpose of the meeting was to advise the President on what position or positions he should take on the matter.

I suggested three alternative positions for the president's consideration. First, I suggested that the President could support the House-passed bill. Second, he could support an extension of the existing Voting Rights Act for a fixed number of years. This was the course I had supported prior to the time the House passed its bill. Third, the President could issue a statement in favor of a strong voting rights act with reasonable "bail-out" provisions and an "effects" test. Bail-out provisions are the means by which covered jurisdictions can be relieved of pre-clearance by the Justice Department of any changes in their voting procedures. The effects test means that local practices are judged, or can be judged, to violate the voting rights of minorities if those practices have the effect of diluting minority voting strength. An effects test does not carry the necessity of proving actual intent.

JE: If what you say is true—that is, that you favored the extension of the Voting Rights Act—then why was your position singled out for such sharp criticism in the press?

SP: I was attacked in the press for making this third recommendation. The media failed to mention that I had made the other two recommendations. And with respect to this last recommendation, they failed to point out that I favored an effects test. They merely reported that I favored bail-out provisions weaker than those contained in the house bill. In that way, they left the impression that I did not support voting rights legislation. The impression created was erroneous and misleading.

JE: Why did you make the third recommendation? Wasn't it less effective than the other two?

SP: My mental process went something like this. You will recall—

and it's a matter of public record—that after the House passed its bill, the President told the press that he thought the bill was "pretty extreme." Soon thereafter, the Attorney General, William French Smith, issued a report to the President call the the house bill too restrictive, and assailing its bail-out provisions and its effects test. In its place, the attorney general recommended that the existing Voting Rights Act be extended for a period of time of not more than five years. As an alternative to that, he suggested a modification of the house bill which would include a simplified bail-out provision and an "intent" test, but no effects test. On the basis of those facts, which were publicly known at the time, I concluded that there was an excellent chance that the President might choose the attorney general's final alternative—a modified house bill with simplified bail-out provisions and an intent test, but with no effects test.

I therefore sought to preclude that possibility by suggesting a third option. In my opinion, it was much more important to have an effects test included in the legislation than to have the house bill's bail-out provisions. I particularly felt this way because I could see how reasonable men and women might differ about the effects of the bail-out provisions. Specifically, I could understand how the President and the attorney general could feel that some parts of the house bill's bail-out provisions were pretty extreme. Therefore, I concluded that the President should support a strong voting rights act with *reasonable* bail-out provisions and that the precise definition of what constituted reasonable bail-out provisions should be left to the Congress to decide.

However, I felt that there could be no compromise whatsoever about the inclusion of an effects test in the legislation because, as any civil rights lawyer will tell you, it is extremely difficult, if not impossible, to prove voting discrimination on the basis of intent. If acts result in voting discrimination, the courts should correct that discrimination regardless of whether the people committing those acts intended them to be discriminatory or not. That's what the effects test is all about. It allows the courts to eliminate voting discrimination regardless of whether the acts causing that discrimination were intended to be discriminatory or not.

Since I could foresee a potential administration position that would have introduced an intent requirement without including an effects test, I tried to get an effects test included in that position. I felt *that* issue should be brought out, should be considered, should be debated. It was extremely important to try to get an effects test included in any position taken by the administration.

On the day following that cabinet meeting in November 1981, the President stated that he would support an extension of the existing Voting Rights Act, or a modified version of the house bill with reasonable bail-out provisions and an intent test, but with no effects test. The President's decision not to support an effects test disappointed me. However, the President reflected on that decision and eventually reversed it. Consequently, on June 29, 1982, President Reagan signed the extension of the Voting Rights Act which contained reasonable bail-out provisions and an effects test.

JE: Do you believe, in retrospect, that the press deliberately sought to misrepresent your position and the role that you played in the controversy?

SP: I don't know. I do know, however, that the press *did* misrepresent my position. Disregarding or manipulating facts is counterproductive in the long run. In the short run, the big lie may capture some headlines, but the price is the loss of credibility. In our fight for equal opportunity, credibility is one of our most potent weapons, and we must not run the risk of losing it.

I was reminded of this forcefully in 1982 when the department I head became the target of an attack by a widely circulated but anonymous document. The document charged HUD with racism and cited 22 case histories purporting to illustrate these charges.

Anonymous articles are irresponsible by definition. However, I decided to investigate the charges, because as secretary of HUD and as a black person, I feel dutybound to root out even the semblance of racism if it exists at HUD. Among other actions, I directed my executive assistant, Lance Wilson, to review each of these twenty-two cases. We found that the allegations were either false or misleading. Several of those named in the document completely disavowed its allegations and also indicated that it was prepared without their prior knowledge and consent.

JE: When you were first appointed, you studiously avoided the press. Why?

SP: The press has often focused on department matters which I've viewed as quite trivial and made a great to-do about them while at the same time ignoring many of the positive things we've attempted to do.

We've done a lot here. We've changed the department in many ways. And we've done it with less money. We're helping more families with housing assistance than ever before. We've developed a variety of new programs, most of which don't cost a lot—for example, the Joint Venture for Affordable Housing program. But the press doesn't seem particularly interested. They don't want to talk about such things. Instead, they focus on silly things, such as the time the President accidentally referred to me as "Mr. Mayor." It's ridiculous!

In this case, the press made a mountain out of a molehill. They blew it out of all proportion. Let me tell you what happened. There was a meeting which a group of mayors attended. It took place in the Roosevelt Room, which is fairly small. Everybody was standing around a table. Somebody had apparently told the president that the mayors were grouped around the table. I was in among them. The President went to the table, shook each person's hand, and said, "Hello, Mr. Mayor." He went down the line. When he came to me, he grabbed my hand and said, "Hello, Mr. Mayor." Before he could finish shaking the hands of the people around the table, he caught himself and said, "Sam, I'm sorry," and I told him, "That's all right, Mr. President, I understand."

Well, the next day the incident was plastered across the front page. I was stunned! The press described the gathering as a major White House reception, in which the President, while greeting the nation's mayors, forgot who I was, confusing me for a mayor. I said to myself, "My God, how did they come up with that? They made a big thing about it. And what the heck for?"

To be perfectly frank, when I first came here, I made it a point not to talk to the press. I wanted to learn the job before I spoke about the department and my plans for the future. It doesn't make sense to shoot your mouth off without knowing what the heck you're talking about. So, I didn't. I didn't grant interviews. I didn't hold press conferences. I didn't appear on talk shows. And the press responded by dubbing me "Silent Sam." It wasn't that I was shy or that I was afraid of the press. I wanted some time to learn my job before issuing various policy pronouncements.

After about three months, I felt confident enough to face the press. At that point, I made myself readily available to the media. But so far as they were concerned, the damage was done. I'd been silent for three months, so why the heck was I speaking out now?

Don't get me wrong. Not all the press have treated me unfairly. I've seen some good stories. Some reporters have done a conscientious job, but some have ignored the positive things we've done, in favor of personality kinds of things. They cultivate the impression that HUD's stagnating, and that the secretary's sitting around doing nothing.

Let me give you another example. The *Washington Post* ran a story in which they chided me for flying first-class to a conference. They ran two or three separate stories about the incident. A reader wrote in and said, in effect, "You'd think Pierce robbed Fort Knox. Who cares whether he flies first-class? I'm sure that all the top officials at the *Post* travel first-class." They made me look as though I was ripping off the taxpayers. Nothing could be further from the truth. What do they want me to do, take the bus? What the heck does it matter?

JE: Why do large numbers of Blacks insist that the Reagan Administration is hostile to civil rights?

SP: I think it stems from the budget cuts. When you start cutting a budget, a lot of Blacks believe that you're singling them out for punitive treatment. That's not the case. In fact, you're hitting all Americans who fall within the lower income bracket. But there's no denying it, you're also hitting Blacks to a large extent.

This raises several interesting questions. Actually, we're providing more housing assistance to more families—with less money—than ever before. This is largely attributable to increased efficiency. It is possible, despite popular thinking, to do more with less.

When Blacks read about budget cutbacks, particularly in terms of programs such as food stamps, they immediately view those cuts as affecting them most directly. This causes many to view government as their enemy. Blacks must understand that once we turn the economy around, their share of the economic pie will increase.

Once this occurs, I think we'll see more and more Blacks turn to the Republican Party. Remember, in 1932, most Blacks were Republicans. They voted for Hoover when everybody else was voting for Roosevelt. In 1936, they switched to the Democratic Party. This switch was attributable, in large part, to economic reasons.

In order to attract Blacks to the Republican Party, two things must occur: First, Blacks must get a bigger piece of the economic pie, and, second, the administration must not backslide on civil rights. It must keep the fire for civil rights. It must do so because Blacks have won too much to support a retrenchment. They're not going to vote for any party or candidate who wants to go backwards. They can't afford to do so.

As a party, we must work to improve our image with black voters, particularly in the area of civil rights. And we must do more than improve our image. We must build a solid record of accomplishment. However, part of the problem relates to our inability to tell our story. Most Blacks don't know what we've done in this area.

I recently met with William Bradford Reynolds, the assistant attorney general for civil rights, with whom I discussed this matter. He spoke at length about the record of the Reagan Administration in the area of civil rights. Since this is not my field, I have to more or less accept what he says. After he finished speaking, I said to him, "Look, why don't you tell the press those things?" He told me that he had—on numerous occasions—but that they had chosen not to print them. They prefer to focus on all sorts of negative things about the administration. This makes it extremely difficult to reach the public. How can you dispel these misconceptions if the press refuses to print the facts?

JE: Have you disagreed at times with the President? Does he accept criticism well?

SP: Yes, I've disagreed with him. Such disagreements usually surface during budget meetings. I've disagreed with the Office of Management and Budget (OMB) a number of times. On such occasions, I went to see the President to present my views.

I can recall several such instances. For example, I disagreed with OMB on the Urban Development Action Grants (UDAG). The President listened to my views and later adopted my position. I also went to the President concerning the Federal Housing Administration, specifically "Ginnie Mae" (Government National Mortgage Association). Again, the President sided with me on this issue.

So, yes, I've disagreed with the President. I haven't always won. There have been times when he has overruled me. For example, I requested more money for housing than that proposed by David Stockman. The President heard me out, agreed to a slight increase, but didn't give me everything I wanted. That's politics. You win some, and you lose some.

The President is extremely open-minded. He encourages frank discussion. He's flexible on most subjects. The thing is, if I were to disagree with him in principle, then I'd want to step down. If I couldn't live with a decision, then I'd resign. I would not compromise in principle. If I did, I'd be no good to myself or to him.

JE: As the top Black in the Reagan Administration, do you feel any special obligation to voice the hopes and aspirations of black Americans to the upper echelons of the administration.

SP: Yes, very much so. I've met with many black Republican leaders. I've tried to communicate many of my concerns to the President and members of the cabinet. And we've made some real progress. For example, we've developed the Minority Youth Training Initiative (MYTI). Our goal is to train young people—with funding help from the Department of Labor—in skills needed in building and maintaining public and private housing.

Yes, I feel a special responsibility to tell the administration what's on the minds of black Americans. Right now, my efforts are directed toward the problem of unemployment, particularly black unemployment. Black unemployment is staggering. Unemployment is terrible for anyone, but it's always worse in the black community. It's generally twice the rate for whites in the adult world. And 50 percent of black teenagers are unemployed. That's why we developed the Minority Youth Training Initiative. We've got to do better. There are too many Blacks out of work.

JE: Unlike most Blacks, you've been, since you were old enough to vote, a registered Republican. What explains your attraction to the Republican Party?

SP: There are a number of reasons. I grew up in a Republican area—Nassau County, New York. In fact, it was even more Republican back then. My father was a Republican. And, at that time, most of my friends were Republicans. It was only natural for me to become a Republican.

When I went to college, I was still undecided. I left open the possibility that I might become a Democrat or a Republican or an Independent. I hadn't yet made up my mind. Then I went into the service. After I got out, I went to law school and made several close friends, including George Ives. He was the son of Senator Irving Ives (R-N.Y.). We became good friends. And he introduced me to his father. I got to know him very well. He was a splendid man. He fought hard for his beliefs. I had the pleasure of working on his senate campaign. I also got to know a number of other leaders in the Republican Party, including Senator Kenneth Keating and Governor Nelson Rockefeller, both of whom I admired. All of those experiences—my background, my father, my peers, and my political contacts—made me want to join the Republican Party.

Moreover, I believe that Blacks should be active in both political parties. I think they make a tremendous mistake by being involved only in the Democratic Party. If Blacks limit their involvement to the Democratic Party, then that party is going to take them for granted. I've seen this happen. It happened in New York City. Blacks have not received their fair share of high-level appointments because the Democrats have them in their hip pocket. This also affects the way in which Blacks are viewed by the Republican Party. Instead of courting black votes, they say,"What the heck, they're going to vote Democratic anyway. Why should we do anything for them?" So Blacks lose on both counts. As a result, Blacks would be wise to become active in both parties. They must become more sophisticated in their voting. Nobody should be able to to take them for granted. If one side ignores them, they should go to the other side. That would force both parties to be more responsive to their needs.

JE: Won't the Republican Party have to make several major concessions in order to attract black voters? Why should Blacks register as Republicans so long as the party takes many of the stands it does?

SP: You're right. The Republican Party will have to reassess some of its positions, particularly in the area of civil rights. Moreover, Republicans will have to do a better job of presenting their story. That story hasn't been told very well. We've made some progress, particularly in terms of black businessmen. We've also made some inroads with black educators. But too many Blacks hold false views about the Republican Party and what it stands for. We've got to change that.

JE: How do you feel when black leaders, many of whom you have known for many years, attack your motives and suggest that you're working against the best interests of black America?

SP: It hurts. Actually, the great black leaders, men like Benjamin Hooks, have never said anything negative about me personally. I just received a letter from Ben, who has been extremely kind. Others, like Vernon Jordan and Jesse Jackson, have responded similarly. I don't get flak from guys like that. The great black leaders don't make negative comments. Instead, the criticism comes from the lesser-known ones. And even here, their criticisms are minimal. No, most black leaders know my record. They know I'm committed to civil rights. They know where I stand. I've been active in the movement for many years. I was the attorney who argued the case of *New York Times* v. *Sullivan* (1964) before the Supreme Court on behalf of Dr. Martin Luther King, Jr. I was on the board of trustees of the NAACP Special Contribution Fund. I've been chairman of several New York Urban League dinners. I've spoken all over the country on behalf of various civil rights causes. I've also given a substantial amount of money to the movement. My record in this area speaks for itself.

JE: What are your major goals as secretary of Housing and Urban Development?

SP: I have four main goals. These are: (1) to provide cost effective housing for the most needy in our society, (2) to ensure fair housing and equal opportunity, (3) to encourage home ownership, and (4) to assist in the development of stronger communities while delegating to state and local governments greater responsibility for planning and operating their own community and economic development activities.

JE: Although you've advocated increased housing for the poor, isn't it true that the Reagan Administration has drastically reduced the funds earmarked for public housing?

SP: Prior to 1981, the federal government sought to solve the problems of providing housing for the poor mainly by constructing new buildings under the assumption that the problem was a shortage of housing. Bipartisan recognition of the failures of the Section 8 New Construction Program has triggered a search for better ways to house the poor.

Based on extensive research and program operation, we believe that, in most communities, the major housing problem of the poor is housing affordability, not housing availability. Good quality housing or housing on which only minor repairs are necessary is widely available, but it costs too much to be affordable to the poor.

Rather than addressing the housing needs of the poor through a large and costly housing production program, we have proposed a program which focuses on housing affordability for the poor. Our proposal for Housing Payment Certificates (vouchers) helps poor people afford good housing in the broader community, as opposed to being isolated in the projects. We consider this proposal the most humane, most socially positive and cost-effective means of meeting the shelter needs of our nation's poor.

JE: To what extent is the Reagan Administration committed to fair housing and equal opportunity? What hard evidence can you cite to support your claims?

SP: Fair housing and equal opportunity are issues to which I am personally committed, and HUD intends to continue its systemic efforts to ensure equal opportunity and fair housing.

This department is actively working to eliminate discrimination in the housing market. Since this administration took office, more than $5 million have been provided to state and local governments for the enforcement of federal fair housing objectives. There has been a marked increase in state and local processing of fair housing complaints, and the number of states and local agencies recognized by HUD—as having fair housing codes essentially equivalent to Title VIII—has increased from 38 to 69, with several more expected to enter the program in the near future.

The administration recognizes that a balanced voluntary and statutory program for developing and enforcing the nation's fair housing standards will ultimately meet with the greatest success. Therefore, HUD has moved to increase local voluntary actions through the expansion of the number of Community Housing Resource Boards by 44 percent over the last two years. These boards assist the department in monitoring and evaluating affirmative marketing agreements which members of the housing industry have signed. We have succeeded in increasing the number of participating local realtor associations by nearly one-third in the last two years. Further, we are continuing to improve the processing of individual and systemic complaints of housing discrimination.

JE: What have you done, as secretary, to bring more qualified Blacks into top decision-making positions?

SP: We have tried to increase the opportunities available to Blacks within the agency. In the 1950s, there were relatively few Blacks in government above the menial and clerical levels. In fact, between 1948 and 1961, only four sub-cabinet positions and one presidential executive staff position were held by black Americans within the federal government. Now, 30 years later, the picture has changed dramatically.

For example, since I was sworn in as secretary of HUD in January 1981, I have made 48 career and non-career Senior Executive Service (SES) appointments, and one supergrade appointment, at HUD. Of those 49 appointments, 8 have gone to Blacks. This means that Blacks comprise 16 percent of the appointments I have made to date.

We have come a long way in the past three decades. But I also want to emphasize that we still have a long way to go in the fight against bigotry. I know how subtle and stubborn bigotry can be. I also know what the struggle to overcome it entails—in the courts, in the schools, in the media, and in the marketplace.

Each of us must contribute to this process in his—or her—own way. As a lawyer with experience in government and politics, I have unwaveringly worked for equal rights in those areas. Moreover, as a cabinet officer in the Reagan Administration, I have exerted influence wherever and whenever possible in the interest of equality for black people.

JE: Finally, what are the major frustrations you face as secretary? What are the most difficult aspects of your job?

SP: Oh, there are many. First, how do you get people to understand what you're doing, when the press won't report it? Second, how do you convince people that more is not necessarily better? Third, how do you prove to people that we can't spend what we don't have? Fourth, how do you explain to people that government can't solve all problems? Each of these poses different frustrations. It's easy to spend. And it's easy to promise the moon. Obviously, people would like more than they have. And they respond to those who make inflated promises. But what happens when these promises don't pan out? How will the public respond? No, there comes a time when you've got to level with the public. There comes a time when you've got to tell them the truth, even if it's not always popular. I've tried to do that as secretary of HUD. I can only hope that the public will understand. It isn't always easy to be truthful with people. Sometimes they don't want to hear the truth.

Donald F. McHenry, Jr.

Getting Beyond Race

Donald F. McHenry, Jr., was born on October 13, 1936, in St. Louis, Missouri and grew up in East St. Louis, Illinois. He received a Bachelor of Science degree from Illinois State University in 1957 and a Master of Science degree from Southern Illinois University in 1959. In addition, McHenry has completed post-graduate studies at Georgetown University.

A career diplomat, McHenry has studied, taught, and worked primarily in the fields of foreign policy and international law and organizations. He joined the United States Department of State in 1963 and served eight years in various positions related to American foreign policy. In 1966, he received the department's Superior Honor Award. In 1971, while on leave from the department, he was a guest scholar at the Brookings Institution in Washington, D.C., and an international affairs fellow of the Council on Foreign Relations in New York. In 1973, after leaving the State Department, he joined the Carnegie Endowment for International Peace in Washington, D.C., as director of humanitarian policy studies. In 1976, he served as a member of President Jimmy Carter's transition staff at the State Department before joining the United States Mission to the United Nations.

In September 1979, President Carter nominated McHenry as United States permanent representative to the United Nations. He served in that position until January 1981. As chief United States representative to the United Nations, he also served as a member of President Carter's Cabinet. At the time of his appointment, McHenry was the United States deputy representative to the United Nations Security Council, a position to which he was appointed in March 1977.

During his diplomatic career, McHenry represented the United States in a number of international forums and as the United States representative on the United Nations Western Five Contact Group.

He was the chief United States negotiator on the issue of Namibia.

McHenry has taught at Howard and American Universities and the Georgetown University School of Foreign Service, all in Washington, D.C. He is the author of *Micronesia: Trust Betrayed* (Carnegie Endowment, 1975) and numerous articles and reviews in a variety of professional journals and magazines.

McHenry is currently university research professor of diplomacy and international affairs at Georgetown University and president of International Relations Consultants, Inc. In addition to serving on several corporate and university boards, he is a member of the Council on Foreign Relations and the editorial board of *Foreign Policy* magazine.

JE: Can you recall the time and circumstances when you first learned of your appointment as United States ambassador to the United Nations? In retrospect, why do you think you were selected for the position?

DM: Yes. I was asked to come down and meet with President Carter. I was in New York at the time. It was fairly obvious what the subject of the conversation was going to be since Andrew Young had resigned as ambassador. I figured that the conversation could have been about one of three things: (1) my own ideas about the kind of person who should be appointed; (2) an attempt by the administration to judge my reaction if someone else were appointed; or (3) the possibility of my accepting the post. In the end, the conversation wound up involving all three elements. However, we never actually discussed the possibility of my being named to the position. The President had obviously thought the matter over very carefully and had discussed it with several top aides. The conversation ended with the President indicating that he would talk to Secretary of State Cyrus Vance and others and get back to me once he had made a decision. As I was walking out of his office, he said, no, he had already made up his mind, and he wanted me to take the job.

JE: Did you decide to accept the offer at that moment, or did you think the matter over before making a decision?

DM: I think it was on the spot, but that's sort of misleading, obviously. I had had a number of days during which to think about it, because I, like everybody else, was speculating on who was going to be named, and, of course, the press had been bugging me about the matter. There had been a lot of speculation about it. So I had given it considerable thought prior to being asked. The only concern I had as far as accepting the post was to ensure that the conditions of the job and the circumstances of the work were, in my judgment, sufficient for me to perform the job as well as I would want to.

JE: What was your immediate reaction to the offer? Did you have any apprehensions or doubts about accepting the position?

DM: No, I didn't have any doubts that I should take it. I mean, there was nothing compelling about taking it. I did have to be convinced that the conditions and the working relationship were such that I could succeed at it, and that depended very much on the President and his perception of the job. I think it's fair to say that he made it sufficiently clear, in the course of our conversation, that his perception of the job was close enough to my own that one could succeed. Obviously, that is a very difficult job. I had discussed it at length with a number of people at the time. So there was ample time to give the matter sufficient thought. You have to remember that this is a position which I have known as an academician since my undergraduate days in college and had known professionally since I went into the State Department in 1963. I had worked closely with Ambassador Adlai Stevenson and his successor and had known many people involved in international organization affairs for quite some time.

JE: Can you discuss some of the conditions or concerns you had about the post?

DM: I'm not using the term "conditions" in the sense of demands, but in the sense of the atmosphere, the working relationship, the philosophy of the job, and certain aspects of policy. I wanted to be assured of access to the President, of the ability to get a hearing—not necessarily to accept my policy views, but to ensure that there would be a fair and timely hearing on those views. I wanted to be assured of the president's commitment to the philosophy of international organizations and the process of problem solving which such a commitment requires. And particularly in government, I wanted to be assured of access to information. Without information an ambassador is almost useless. Being informed is a very important aspect of the job.

JE: Much has been said and written about President Carter's foreign policy. How would you assess his record in this area? What were his major triumphs and failures?

DM: It's too early to rate President Carter's foreign policy. In fact it's too early to rate his administration in any sense. One of the disadvantages of modern times—namely, the ability to produce books and films at blitzkrieg speed—is that we tend to rate without assessment, and without the perspective, I believe, which is required for assessment. I would simply say that I think just as with President Truman, aspects of

Mr. Carter's policy will stand out more than others. And some things that today's pundits have singled out for criticism will fall by the wayside with the passage of time. That's true of his policies concerning the Panama Canal, human rights, the Middle East, and nuclear nonproliferation. I think that his efforts to restore American communications with the newly developing nations—the Third World—these things will all stand him in very good stead historically. I think that this kind of changing attitude is true of most presidents, even some who have an enormous stigma attached to them. Richard Nixon stands out more today, in terms of his foreign policy, than many thought he might after the Watergate scandal. President Johnson will stand out for his domestic program, despite efforts to dismantle it, and despite Vietnam. There are some presidents who don't make it—there are some Hardings and Grants of this world who don't have any redeeming policy virtues, I guess. But I think the attitude towards President Carter will be reasonably positive.

JE: A few moments ago, you mentioned Ambassador Stevenson. Did he serve as a role model? Did you try to imitate his style or approach?

DM: I started following his career long before he came to the United Nations. I grew up in Illinois. I was a high school student when he was elected governor. I saw the positive things he accomplished. He succeeded a very corrupt political machine, and brought integrity to government. I followed him in the presidential campaigns of 1952 and 1956. I was a collector of books both about and by Stevenson. So it was an old association. And when I went into the State Department in 1963, he had been at the United Nations almost three years. I went into the Bureau of International Organization Affairs, where his office was down the hall, and on occasion when there was a subject which I was working on that he was interested in, I would meet with him to discuss the matter. I spent some time at the United Nations, as a very young officer, giving orientation tours. And then later I served on the delegation while he was still there. So from 1963 until his death in 1966, he was someone I was reasonably close to. He was a man of enormous intellectual capability, extraordinarily articulate, a great writer, a superb listener—a man who was inspirational to the people around him, but a man who came at the wrong time as far as the presidency was concerned. He ran against "God" (Dwight D. Eisenhower) in 1952, and against "God" again in 1956 (Eisenhower). Almost everything he advocated was later adopted by the government, including a test ban treaty. Many of his warnings, unfortunately, came true—the warnings right before the election in 1956—concerning Eastern Europe and the Middle East. But his warnings came at the wrong time, and by the time he was gone, it was time for a younger, more dashing generation.

JE: Can you recall your maiden speech as United Nations ambassador? How was it received? Were you nervous or apprehensive?

DM: I can't recall the speech. You have to remember, now, that there are five American ambassadors at the United Nations. So delivering speeches was sort of old hat, and I wouldn't see that much difference between delivering it as the deputy permanent representative or delivering it as the permanent representative.

JE: Much has been said and written about your style or approach in comparison to previous ambassadors. In what ways was it most similar and most different from that of the present ambassador, Jeane Kirkpatrick?

DM: I have made it a policy not to make that kind of comparison with my successor. What I can do is to talk about my own style, my own approach, and you can make the comparisons. In the first place, I think an ambassador, in order to succeed, needs to be a good listener. That was one of the hallmarks of a Stevenson or a William Scranton, both of whom were enormously successful. Scranton wasn't there long enough and didn't receive the publicity, but nevertheless he was tremendously successful, succeeding Daniel Moynihan. I think an ambassador has to be reasonably open in terms of considering the views of others, not just listening to them, but recognizing the fact that we don't have all the right on our side. Moreover, an ambassador must understand the necessity of living with diversity—diverse economic systems, diverse political systems, diverse cultures, even diverse intellectual abilities and interests. Unless an ambassador is extremely adaptable, it's very difficult to operate in a multilateral context.

As an ambassador, you must have an appreciation of diversity. The moment you start lecturing to people or talking down to them, as if you are the source of all wisdom, as if your way of life is the only one that exists, as if everyone else is somehow bad, then I think you're headed for failure.

My own approach was, I suppose, consistent with certain aspects of my personality. It was a quieter voice, a much less public profile. Publicity is bad for diplomacy in my judgment. It makes it very difficult to accomplish your task. Just as it is important to work well with other nations and their representatives, it is also important to work well with your staff. When the time comes that I know as much about a subject as my staffer who is working on that subject full time, then either the staffer isn't doing his job, or I'm not doing mine. He's either not spending enough time studying his task, or I'm spending too much time on the details and not enough on the overall direction. It's very important to have a good staff and to give them the room they need to perform—and under the right circumstances they will.

JE: How well did your childhood and formal education prepare you for a career in international affairs? Did they equip you well to become a diplomat?

DM: My childhood was probably as far away from international diplomacy, I guess, as anybody can get. I grew up under very poor conditions, not as poor as some, but poor. My exposure to international affairs was minimal. I never traveled. I studied languages the old-fashioned way, which made it more a drudgery than anything useful. I never knew anybody who traveled abroad, except the soldiers who came back from World War II and Korea. On the other hand, I developed a strong interest in government, public affairs. I immersed myself in it as a debater in college. I suspect if there was anything which contributed to my own philosophy, in terms of foreign affairs, it was the discipline of debate, the necessity of shifting back and forth from one side of a question to another—arguing one side one day, the other the next. Debating forces you to examine both sides—or many sides—of an issue. You can't build a case unless you thoroughly understand the arguments of the other side. It also brings an appreciation of logic, as opposed to emotion, and the various other things one can use in structuring an argument. I don't know. But I suspect that that was a great, great influence.

JE: With your many interests and talents, why did you focus on the international arena, as opposed to civil rights?

DM: I had a very long debate with myself about that question, particularly in the 1960s. As a student, I had been somewhat involved with the National Association for the Advancement of Colored People and various local activities related to civil rights. As a young teacher, on occasion, I might go off with some of my students or give them a ride to some function. But my own interests centered on foreign affairs, and at some point in the 1960s I did ask myself why I should be involved in foreign affairs—trying to do things so far away—when there were so many things to be done in the United States in terms of discrimination, or poverty, or social reform. The answer to that question is an answer which can historically be found in two individuals—you can find it in terms of the great debate which Booker T. Washington engaged in many years ago, when he argued that we can be as separate as the fingers on a hand, but still a part—in other words, each having a function or something to do. Or you can find it in that Sunday television program which

Roy Wilkins participated in some time back, in which he was ridiculed by Stokely Carmichael and others as being too conservative, or old hat, and that the future lay in the efforts of groups such as the Student Nonviolent Coordinating Committee. Wilkins was asked whether Carmichael's comments had upset him, causing him to question his own methods. His response was that, no, it didn't bother him. Stokely Carmichael and his group could demonstrate in the streets or hold their sit-ins, so long as Mr. Wilkins had his lawyers to get them out of jail. We all have our own calling. We all have things at which we have particular expertise or particular interest, and there is no reason why any individual or group must devote itself exclusively to one area. On the contrary, there's a certain amount of trailblazing which needs to be done in international affairs. The debate was easy to resolve. Foreign affairs was my interest. It was where I could make my contribution. And in a real sense, it was also a contribution to these other things that were being done. Presumably you open up education so that people can better prepare themselves for a wide variety of fields. And this was one of them.

JE: Did race prove to be an asset as well as a liability as United Nations ambassador? Did it bring with it advantages as well as disadvantages?

DM: I was never conscious of it being a liability, except perhaps, among a segment of the public which thought that I might be partial in some areas. Yes, being Black had certain advantages. There's a feeling on the part of some that you have a particular sympathy or empathy for their cause. This was true of some, particularly Third World, delegates or, more particularly, of certain Africans and Arabs. Some miscalculated the importance of race, on which occasions it posed certain problems. But in terms of my own work, there was only one area where I felt it affected my work, and that was on the Middle East. On the part of some Arabs, but not all, there was the feeling that certain positions were more acceptable than others. This was even more true in the case of the Jewish community. There was the view that anything that involved Israel ought to be left to the Jewish community. For example, Mayor Edward Koch of New York stated that if you are Black, you are anti-Jewish and anti-Semitic. That was a stupid statement on his part, revealing a great deal of prejudice. I didn't have anywhere near the problem with the South Africans, where you might think I would have more difficulty. If I had to put my finger on any one issue, then, it would have to be the Middle East, where race proved to be a factor.

JE: As United Nations ambassador, you were very sensitive to the suggestion that you were a "black ambassador" of the United States. Why did you attempt to downplay race?

DM: I've never seen anyone described as the "white ambassador." As ambassador, you represent the interests of the United States. No one can do anything about the fact that they may be black, or white, or Jewish, or Catholic, or Polish-American, or any number of things. In my own view, it wasn't particularly relevant to the performance of my job. And there were circumstances where people looked beyond it. They might marvel at it, but after a while they forgot it. I don't think it's useful to think of individuals in terms of these designations. I have long been against ethnic politics, and I think we'd all be much better off if our political leaders would rise above it, although that's rarely the case.

JE: In what sense are you against ethnic politics?

DM: There are times when we become so involved in doing something because *an* ethnic group would be pleased, that we lose sight of what we're trying to accomplish. Political leaders must act for the United States, not for the narrow interests of a particular group. In the international arena, such action skews foreign policy and makes us forget what our interests are. We've done this on a number of occasions. We did it in terms of the Greek-Turkish dispute over Cyprus. We do it all the time with regard to the Middle East. We've done it in the past, historically, with regard to the Italians or Irish or any number of other groups. In fact, I did an article on this subject for *Foreign Policy* magazine, in which I said that foreign policy should be captive of no group. It ended up making virtually every interest group mad. Jewish-Americans were mad. Black Americans were mad. They all were mad. Blacks think they ought to determine American policy towards Africa. Hispanics think they ought to determine policy in Latin America. Jews think they ought to determine policy in the Middle East. The Irish believe that the Irish ambassadorship, the ambassador to Ireland, belongs to them. The Italians believe the same damn thing. And it's not good. It doesn't make sense. More important, it makes for bad policy.

JE: To what extent does race influence how you view the world, the political system, and social change? Is it *the* controlling factor, or *a* factor?

DM: It's *a* factor. And at times and on some issues, it is more important than others. But it is *a* factor. I get very impatient with people who, whatever the situation in the past, are so consumed by the factor of race, that they can't move on. They can't see changes and take those changes for what they are. They're still suspicious. They're still held back, believing that, in the final analysis, race will be *the* key to their success. Let me cite an example. In the little community in which I grew up, I've been working with several local groups to bring about community redevelopment. One of the men who has been working with me on this project is so bad in terms of his suspicion of whites, that it's very difficult for me to work with him. It's very difficult for two reasons: First, if you're going to get anything done, you're going to need the cooperation of everybody; and second, I don't want to generalize any more about all whites than I want them to generalize about all Blacks. I don't want to be guilty of the same thing I think many of them have been guilty of. How do I overcome this problem? I don't know. I may not, in this instance. If I can't, there's no way I can work with this individual. Others might be able to, but I can't.

JE: In your role as ambassador, what were the best moments, the moments that most stand out, the moments of which you are most proud?

DM: I'm afraid I can't answer that question. I don't spend much time looking back. At some point, I guess I will, but I haven't done so. I had a series of goals, a series of things I wanted to accomplish. I wanted to build a staff, the very best staff there was. And I did it. It wasn't as good a staff as it should have been when I took over. I wanted to do that, while at the same time making a contribution to affirmative action. I wanted to hire more women, and not simply because they were women, but because they were extraordinarily qualified. I wanted to do that with Blacks. I wanted to do it with Hispanics. I wanted to demonstrate that you could do that and not only maintain the caliber of the staff, but improve it one heck of a lot. I wanted to ensure that I was running the mission across the board, giving it direction, and not, in a sense, being pigeonholed into handling a particular item or items. That was very difficult for some people to understand. Every agency in Washington felt—and that's not ususual—that here was an opportunity for them to take over some aspect of the job, whether it was the disarmament people, or the economics people, or the telecommunications people—any of the tremendous range of issues that one has to handle. It meant boning up on certain subjects that I knew very little about, while ensuring that the work was done and done extraordinarily well. I also wanted to develop a better understanding of the United Nations in this country. Unfortunately, I didn't succeed too well on that count. We were sidetracked by Iran and the Middle East, what with the 1980 presidential campaign. I think it's important to recognize, however, that in the field of international relations, you have to accept the fact that your contribution may be only a fraction of what's required. Solving a problem may take many years. Most problems are the product of years of trying—and failing. It's unrealistic to expect that any one person can, in the span of a year or two, resolve a problem that has evolved over a long period of time.

JE: As ambassador, was it difficult for you to espouse views or represent policies with which you may have personally disagreed?

DM: I never found myself in a position where I disagreed on the point of principle. There was one time when it came close to that, but the policy went my way. And those are the only times, I think, when you have an obligation to ask yourself whether you ought to continue. There will be many times when you have a different view of what ought to be done, or the way it ought to be done. That's the nature of government. That's really the nature of man. We all view things from a different perspective. As long as we're working within an acceptable policy range, those differences are to be expected. You win some, and you lose some. But when you conclude that you're outside that policy range, and you can't live with it, then, I think, you're obligated to leave.

JE: In 1973, you *did* leave the State Department following the American invasion of Cambodia and the appointment of Henry Kissinger as secretary of state. Was this decision difficult to make, both personally and professionally?

DM: Yes, very much so. I left initially in 1971 and went on leave. I had already stayed longer than I had planned. In 1969, after having been there six years, I had planned to leave. I had even telephoned the movers and made plans to teach in the Midwest. However, I was persuaded to stay by incoming Secretary of State William Rogers. I had worked with him earlier. And so I did stay for that two-year period. It was a period that was extraordinarily useful to me in terms of learning and exposure. But it was a very difficult period in terms of policy. I didn't agree with Vietnam. I didn't agree with Cambodia. I didn't agree with the appointments of Clement Haynsworth and Harold Carswell to the Supreme Court. And there were a number of other issues. So, in 1971, I went on leave. I chose the leave route, I guess, because I didn't, at the time, have my finger on another job. I hadn't looked. The events driving me to take leave came very quickly. I went to the consul, and I went to Brookings, and I thought that maybe I would wait out the administration. I didn't. They got back in. And I left. But leaving, as I said, was only a question of timing. I would have left in 1969, because my intention always had been to go into and out of government, to alternate between academia and government service. My decision to leave was only a question of when.

JE: Today, many Americans have a very negative opinion of the United Nations. There are those who argue that it's ostensibly a debating society; others believe that it is inimical to the interests of the United States; and still others believe that it is irrelevant and has outlived its usefulness. How do you view the United Nations?

DM: I view it in much the same way that people viewed it in

1945—namely, as an institution which contains within it the best hopes of mankind. But that means that it's an institution towards whose ideals one is constantly striving. It doesn't mean one has to attain them. There's no such thing as an instant utopia. There's no such thing as instant cooperation among nations. And when you fall short of those ideals—and there will be inevitable low points—you don't immediately toss such an institution out the window. It takes a long time to build institutions. It's taken this country, under its present Constitution, almost 200 years—and more than 200 years under the Declaration of Independence. You could go through those documents and discover any number of areas where we've fallen short. The same thing is true of the United Nations, except that it's working under much more difficult circumstances. It has no army, raises no money, and has no police. And yet it's done pretty well.

JE: If President Reagan were to call you this afternoon and ask for your views on the direction of American foreign policy, what would you tell him? What basic tenets or principles should our foreign policy reflect?

DM: Mr. Reagan is not likely to call me, I can tell you that. Our foreign policy is in a mess. It will require a drastic overhaul. We are currently out of step with our adversaries, with the so-called "neutrals" or Third World nations. We're also out of step with our allies which is clearly evident in a number of problem areas. You could make a list of things where the United States is odd-man-out. *Time* magazine recently ran a story pointing out the differences between the United States and several of its closest allies. One of the problems we face is our obsession with Communism, our unwillingness to live with diversity, the fortunate but unfortunate fact that we have not gone through the adversity of war—and I don't mean our soldiers going off to war, I mean within our own territory. I'm not saying we ought to do it, but there is an experience and a perspective which comes about from that, which we don't have. We are only now undergoing some of the adversity which much of the world has experienced for some time. We now have considerable economic difficulties. There's competition with regard to world trade. We now require certain natural resources. Some of our solutions to world problems haven't worked. I mean, we haven't stopped Communism by throwing money at the problem. We haven't achieved modernization by sending economic and technical assistance. The problem is still there. We're wracked with frustration because we don't know how to handle things. We have simplistic solutions to complex problems, like—stop the Soviets and Cubans. Or pull yourself up by your own bootstraps. Or keep the Japanese out. None of these work. And, of course, the great frustration is that, despite our enormous economic strength and our tremendous military power, people step on us or criticize us. And we take that, either as weakness or a reluctance to fight back. Take our hostages, and we'll blow you off the map. Many people believe that. And if we don't, some people look upon that as weakness. If the representative of some tiny little country gets up and criticizes us and we don't spew back with as much invective and hot air as we have got, or if we don't cut off their aid, we're seen as sitting there and allowing people to take advantage of us. Neither of those is true. The taking of hostages does not demonstrate weakness on our part. We could blow Khomeini off the face of the earth if we wanted to. On the contrary, studied patience and quiet diplomacy demonstrate strength, in my judgment. It's hard to get people to accept that, but it's true.

JE: How would your foreign policy differ from President Reagan's, for example, as it relates to Third World countries? Would it produce considerably different results?

DM: Yes. These countries have to evolve. And, in terms of their evolution, in the course of trying to develop their own systems of government, they're going to experiment with some things that we may not like, which will prove quite frustrating for us. But they must have that opportunity. They've got to go through it. We went through it. Europeans went through it for 500 years. They are no more perfect than we are. And, their evolution is going to cause us some genuine concern. It's not wrong to be concerned. But we can't control events in those areas. We can't look upon every development, every coup, every arms shipment as a threat to either the strength of the United States or to our manhood. We will have to learn to live with change. We will have to learn to live with diversity.

JE: What was the most difficult problem you faced at the United Nations? What made it so?

DM: The Iranian situation was certainly the longest in terms of duration and intensity, but it wasn't the most difficult. The most difficult was trying to forge peace in the Middle East. This was true for many reasons. In the case of the Arabs and Israelis, you're not dealing with substance. You're dealing with emotions, the result of many years of conflict and mistrust. Both sides spend more time dwelling on the past than they do on the present or the future. If you sit down with either side, instead of trying to deal with the facts at hand so that we can influence the future, they will talk about what happened years before. Neither is very honest in terms of what their objectives are. They camouflage their positions in all kinds of things. If it's Israel, they camouflage it in security, when they really mean religion and a few other things. If it's the Arabs, they camouflage it in self-determination and all kinds of high-sounding things, when they really mean to devour Israel. The thing which makes it more difficult is that the United States has no policy. Our people privately know what needs to be done but, publicly, they won't do it. It raises such political issues as who's going to vote for whom, and who's going to contribute to what in terms of the next election. The result is that there's no foreign policy.

JE: Have you ever harbored thoughts of becoming secretary of state? Is that a long-term personal goal?

DM: No, not really. It's not something I would shy away from, but it's not a particular goal of mine. A reporter once wrote that that was my ultimate objective. I wrote him a letter, in which I asked him if he had seen a psychiatrist lately, because something was obviously wrong in his head. No, I wouldn't shy away from it. It's a challenging position. It's the pinnacle of the diplomatic world. There's a lot to be done. But it's a position that only about 50 people have held in the history of this country. It's not likely to be readily available. Those positions, like mine at the United Nations, require the right kind of preparation; they also require an extraordinary amount of luck—that is, the right preparation, as well as being in the right place at the right time. After all, there are hundreds of people who are just as qualified and could hold almost any post in government. Who gets what depends on a host of factors, many of which have little to do with professional competence.

JE: Finally, as ambassador, how did you deal with the inevitable tension and frustration which are part and parcel of the job? Was it difficult to leave the problems behind when you went home at night?

DM: I've always tried to be calm about things. I've always tried not to let anything upset me. In fact, when I'm upset, my tendency is to get extraordinarily quiet. I even do that with my children. A lot of parents will blow off steam, punish the children, that sort of thing. My tendency is to get very quiet. It drives them up the wall, because they know what it means. I think they would rather I said something to them or told them how I felt, but I tend to hold back. As ambassador, I operated in a very similar manner. I always try to do the best I can—to do as much as I can. When I reach the point where I can do no more, that's it. I don't think about it. I've done everything that I reasonably can do. I've stretched myself to the limit, and when I reach that point, I've just reached it. I'm satisfied. There's nothing more I can do. So why be concerned about it? Why say, I could have, I should have, if I have. At that point I know I've done the best I can, and I don't worry. Whatever happens will happen. There's nothing more I can do about it.

Clarence Thomas

American Ideals, Policy Dilemmas

Clarence Thomas was born June 23, 1948, in Savannah, Georgia. He received a Bachelor of Arts degree in 1971 from Holy Cross College, in Worcester, Massachusetts, and currently serves on the board of trustees of that institution. Upon graduation, he attended the Yale Law School, in New Haven, Connecticut, from which he received a Juris Doctor degree in 1974.

From 1974 to 1977—during his first two and one-half years after law school—Thomas served as an assistant attorney general for the State of Missouri. He was responsible for the State Tax Commission and Missouri's Department of Revenue. He argued numerous cases for the state before the appellate courts and the Supreme Court of Missouri.

Thomas's legal career extends beyond the legislative and executive branches of the federal government to both the private sector and state law enforcement. Indeed, from 1977 to 1979, he served as an attorney for the Monsanto Company, an international petrochemical company in St. Louis, Missouri.

Thomas arrived in Washington in 1979 as a legislative assistant to Senator John C. Danforth (R-Mo.). In this capacity, he was responsible for issues in the areas of energy, the environment, and public works projects.

In 1982, Thomas was appointed commissioner and chairman of the U.S. Equal Employment Opportunity Commission (EEOC) by President Ronald Reagan, following Senate confirmation. His term expires July 1, 1986. He is the eighth chairman of the commission since its establishment in July 1965.

The EEOC was created by Title VII of the Civil Rights Act of 1964, as amended, to eliminate employment discrimination based on race, color, religion, sex, or national origin. In 1979, the commission received additional jurisdictional responsibilities as part of the Reorganization Plan No. 1 of 1978. These included enforcement of the Age Discrimination in Employment Act of 1967 (ADEA), as amended; the Equal Pay Act of 1963 (EPA), as amended; and Section 501 of the Rehabilitation Act of 1973, as amended.

On August 17, 1982, under Thomas's leadership, the EEOC unanimously endorsed and announced a headquarters reorganization plan designed to enhance the policymaking role of the commissioners and to place major operational responsibilities on a small team of office heads reporting directly to the chairman. The changes—aimed at strengthening the commission's capacity to vigorously enforce federal legislation that prohibits employment discrimination— consolidated functions under single offices to provide clearer lines of functional responsibility. The EEOC also approved a new mission statement which read, in part: "To ensure equality of opportunity by vigorously enforcing federal legislation prohibiting discrimination in employment through investigation, conciliation, litigation, coordination, regulation in the federal sector, and through education, policy research, and provision of technical assistance."

JE: In what ways, if any, did your early childhood shape who you are and what you believe about civil rights?

CT: I was raised by my grandparents, who played the single most important role in my life. My grandfather was raised by his grandmother, who, according to him, was freed from slavery at the age of nine. He had a third-grade education and was barely literate. He believed in this country and its values. He believed that this is the land of opportunity—and fought hard for equal opportunity. He knew that discrimination existed and that its existence undermined the values in which he believed and the principles upon which this country was built. It did not matter that he worked harder than anyone I have ever known. It did not matter that he obeyed the laws. It did not matter that he was religious or that he was a good provider. It did not matter that he exemplified and embodied all that is good about this country. His efforts were all but neutralized by racial discrimination and prejudice. So he turned to fight discrimination. As he fought, I fight today. And like my grandfather, I am firmly committed to preserving and advancing the fundamental values of this country—values rooted in the rights of the individual, but values so often paid only lip service.

JE: How do you view the problems of race and racism?

CT: I adhere to the principle that individuals should be judged on the basis of individual merit and individual contact. No one should be rewarded or punished because of group characteristics. Unfortunately, this principle has not been made a reality. So today we are faced with the challenge of making this country color-blind after it has seen color for so long. And the critical question facing us is how to approach this challenge. Should we push for immediate *parity* or the fairness that has never really existed? Parity tends to show quicker change at least on paper. But is unfairness under the guise of parity any better than just plain unfairness? Should you concede your promotion in the name of parity for those who traditionally have been discriminated against?

On the other hand, it is difficult to tell those who have lost out in the past because of discrimination that we now, as a matter of policy, believe in fair play. This difficulty is exacerbated when we look at the socioeconomic plight of the affected groups and the inextricable relationship of that plight to unlawful discrimination. It is further complicated by the inconsistent but common practice of doling out preferences in this society to various groups for any number of reasons.

I opt for fairness—that is, treating individuals as individuals, neither preferring them nor deterring them on the basis of group characteristics. But I choose this option knowing full well that fairness, though an underpinning of this country, has never been a reality. I choose this option with the painful awareness of the social and economic ravages which have befallen my race and all who suffer discrimination. I choose this option with the enduring hope that this country will live up to the principles enunciated in the Bill of Rights and the Constitution of the United States: that all men are created equal and that they will be treated equally. But more than hope is necessary. These rights must be protected, and the laws protecting them must be vigorously enforced.

It is a sad fact that anti-discrimination laws have *never* been enforced in this country. The current tendency to parcel out rights and preferences on the basis of group characteristics is a poor substitute for protecting an individual's rights. I am certain, for example, that you would not be satisfied with a law enforcement official's offer to take your neighbor's television to replace the one stolen from your home, instead of preventing the theft or arresting the thief. Such an ersatz enforcement policy, though tempting and politically saleable, merely paints a veneer over the historical lack of enforcement of civil rights laws.

JE: Many Americans believe, rightly or wrongly, that the Reagan Administration has abandoned equal employment opportunity and has, in the process, encouraged widespread non-compliance. Do you agree?

CT: No. Those who read any signals coming from anyplace in this government to justify non-compliance with any of the equal employment opportunity laws of this country are doing so at their own peril.

When it comes to equal employment opportunity, the EEOC is the federal government's lead law enforcement agency. As chairman of the commission, I am determined to enforce the laws against discrimination—effectively, efficiently, and equitably.

Our effectiveness, however, is somewhat diminished by the limitations on our power. For example, like anti-trust statutes, civil rights laws have codified important national policy, and both areas of the law have established meaningful remedies. But unlike the treble damages for violators of anti-trust laws, the monetary damages and injunctive relief provided by civil rights laws have not encouraged meaningful compliance. Achieving that goal is the true measure of our effectiveness. Certainly, individual rights should be at least as important as commercial rights and obligations.

If I had my way, the equal employment opportunity laws would have at least as many teeth as the anti-trust laws. Violators would be put on notice that the EEO laws employ the same sanctions as other important federal statutes. No one would be allowed to escape the sword of justice by raising objections and considerations which have their place in the halls of Congress, not in the courts of law. Competing social concerns, cost considerations, and the negotiation of delays in the imposition of remedies would not be standard fare. With more meaningful sanctions in place, we could safely move away from the present tendency to parcel out advantages and preferences, *without* endangering the status of the equal employment opportunity laws.

Unless accompanied by these or other meaningful sanctions where discrimination is found, the call for a color-blind Constitution and a color-blind society rings empty. It makes no sense to talk about rights unless we intend to protect them and we have the clout to protect them. Unless we have the means and the will to aggressively protect individual rights, it is meaningless (if not fraudulent) to demand a color-blind society after this country has seen color for so long.

JE: For many years, the EEOC has been the subject of fierce criticism. What explains this fact?

CT: From the very beginning, the EEOC has been an easy target for public criticism and public flogging. Created during the euphoria and optimism of the mid-1960s, the EEOC was given the mandate to seek out and to root out the employment discrimination which poisoned our free enterprise economy and which relegated millions of Americans to second-class citizenship. The magnitude of these marching orders and the magnitude of resistance to them, however, were greatly underestimated. Despite the law and the great expectations, employment discrimination still persists.

Being forgiving and understanding when great enterprises fail and great expectations are shattered is difficult. When this occurs, someone or some group always points the finger of blame. This is one of the reasons that the public has viewed the EEOC and other programs established during this period with extreme skepticism.

The EEOC has fallen prey to the general disillusionment surrounding many of the Great Society programs. It has received unfair criticism for emphasizing its role as an investigator and conciliator of charges at the expense of its role as a litigator. Yet, Congress and the Supreme Court have repeatedly emphasized that the EEOC *must* attempt to resolve discrimination by settlement and that the discretion to bring suit may only be exercised after we have exhausted our obligation to conciliate. At the same time, the commission has been charged with administrative inefficiency when that so-called inefficiency was caused by the fact that EEOC invested its limited money and human resources in programs rather than administration.

In light of the lofty goals Congress has set and uninformed critics' judgments, questioning the worth and value of the commission as an institution is easy. I understand this point of view, but I do not subscribe to it. I am not surprised by the so-called shortcomings of the agency I lead. I am only surprised that an agency which has such limited powers and which must function in such a skeptical environment has accomplished so much.

JE: To what extent has the press contributed to the misunderstanding which surrounds the EEOC?

CT: As we become more and more physically removed from the events of the day, we rely more and more on the media to provide us with the facts surrounding those events—to assist us in fully participating in our democratic system. With its constitutional guarantees of freedom, the press has the attendant responsibility of at least being accurate, objective, and fair in reporting the news. The press must live up to this responsibility—reporting the tough issues in the proper context and eschewing the use of shorthand references and loaded signals such as "forced busing" and "reverse discrimination" which inflame rather than inform.

Long ago, I decided not to become defensive about my own press coverage. Suffice it to say, I have been zapped. I sometimes wonder why this bigot is using my name when he talks to the press and why people are surprised to learn upon meeting me that I am not *the* Clarence Thomas they read about.

More important, however, the press must realize th₁ ₍ there is not total agreement, even within the black community, on the merits of all civil rights strategies or social programs. We are not a monolith and we certainly are not clones. There are as many shades of black sociopolitical thought as there are in any ethnic group. Just as we don't look alike, we don't think alike. It is critical to balance these varying opinions in our national debate. Moreover, to effectively service our democratic process, we must strive to achieve and maintain a truly democratic press—one with balanced composition as well as views.

JE: Many critics of the EEOC contend that the agency has fueled these flames by failing to prosecute large businesses for employment violations. Are they correct?

CT: No. Unfortunately, in too many instances, businesses have been unnecessarily subjected to practices and conduct which do not serve to enforce the civil rights laws effectively. Rather, such conduct has often proven punitive and counterproductive. If civil rights laws are to be institutionalized and cease to be a case of "good guys" versus "bad guys," then such conduct must be kept to a minimum and ultimately eliminated.

In essence, this approach to civil rights enforcement becomes "undue process" as opposed to "due process." That is, the mere process of determining the culpability of businesses becomes the punishment. Expensive, confusing, and sometimes contradictory enforcement practices have punished the good *along with* the bad. The net result is that those who have obeyed the laws are subjected to the same undue process as those who do discriminate. From an economic standpoint, the *cost* for those who *do* discriminate is the same as the cost for those who *do not* discriminate. This approach to civil rights enforcement eliminates the incentive for complying with the laws and fails to allocate properly the disincentives for violating them. If civil rights laws are to be effectively enforced, this lack of differentiation cannot continue.

Even if a business does discriminate, it is entitled to a fair, professional determination of its liability. Being in violation of the law does not give the enforcement agency license to do as it pleases. I believe that the EEOC can and must be fair—but tough as nails. In order to clear the air, let me say, in no uncertain terms, that the civil rights laws in employment *will* be enforced in a fair and professional way. There are some who claim that this administration has turned its back on civil rights enforcement, that it has no civil rights policy, and that it is determined to turn the clock back in the civil rights field. As chairman of the EEOC, I state for the record that this is utter nonsense. I will have no part in turning back the clock or in seeing past progress undermined by current laxness. President Reagan supports a vigorous enforcement program, and that is exactly what I have attempted to do at the EEOC.

JE: Why have most, if not all, national civil rights organizations criticized the EEOC and its policies?

CT: Although many civil rights leaders tenaciously cling to past policies designed to solve these problems, the net results are often in diametric opposition to the original purpose of the policies. A recent series of articles on affirmative action in the *Washington Post* summarized the problem this way: "While affirmative action has accelerated the progress of certain groups, it has *not* affected broad traditional patterns of inequality." In other words, the best prepared amongst us are the beneficiaries of programs and policies which are, or should be, designed to help the least prepared.

This brings me to the corollary of enforcement. To say that we will pursue vigorous enforcement of civil rights laws does not mean that we will accept—uncritically and unthinkingly—present approaches and assumptions about civil rights programs. There are numerous examples of programs set up to assist minorities for which there is no proof of concrete results.

Do not misunderstand. I am not saying that policies flowing out of the civil rights movement have failed to achieve any positive results. However, it is imperative that we pinpoint the sources of the statistical disparities if we hope to develop workable and successful policies. Statistical disparities in employment, for instance, may indicate discrimination in the workplace, or they may indicate inadequate job preparation.

We must not continue, year after year, to base decisions on the same assumptions about the nature of the problem or the requirements for a solution. I intend to use my EEOC office to question old assumptions; to develop new approaches to old problems; to gather information, to analyze it, and use it to check the validity of current policies. I intend to use the enormous volume of data which the EEOC has collected over the past fifteen years to aid in future policy development. There is too much left to be done in the area of equal employment—we cannot afford to devote significant time and energy to policies or programs which effect no measurable progress.

JE: Is the traditional approach—advanced by the major civil rights organizations—likely to prove effective in these areas?

CT: No. I would suggest that in certain areas we have been less than responsible in our refusal to attack sacred cows. One such issue is affirmative action. Few issues have generated more controversy than this one. Due to its extreme complexity, affirmative action is an issue that does not lend itself to an absolute "for" or "against" stance. It is easy for people of good faith to agree with the premise of affirmative action while disagreeing with some of the *components* of the policy. Even when we consider results, we see no conclusive findings. There are, of course, conflicting reports on successes and failures. But we cannot ignore the facts. Among these is the fact that black men are still dropping out of the labor market at a frightening rate. One recent study showed that black male participation in the civilian labor force dropped from 74.1 percent in 1960 to 55.3 percent in 1982. That is an alarming drop of 18.8 percent. Moreover, even though the income of the most fortunate minorities has reached parity with whites, the income of the least fortunate continues its relentless downward trend. Clearly, something is wrong, and even with the strong laws presently on the books, we have failed to make things right.

Don't misunderstand. I would be the last person to disagree with the assertion that we must do more than simply stop discriminating if we hope to eliminate the effects of a history of discrimination. In fact, the EEOC continues to employ affirmative action remedies with court approval.

I firmly believe that the true measure of a society lies in the way it treats its less fortunate citizens. But I do not see many positive results of past policies affecting a majority of the oppressed.

My point is that the ultimate objective is progress. We simply cannot continue progressive movement if we do not stop to make sure we are still on course. If a policy is working, then there is no reason to abandon it. If it is not working, then we must develop an alternative approach. We will not develop such viable alternatives if we do not take the first step in raising questions about the particular tactics in our overall strategy. We certainly will not be able to develop effective policies if we continue to allow ourselves to be polarized in senseless, symbolic debate.

JE: In general terms, your philosophy seems to mirror that of most civil rights organizations. Yet, you strongly disagree with many of the programs and policies advocated by these organizations. How do you explain this fact?

CT: I try to approach my responsibilities with a certain open-mindedness. You must have the courage to question established beliefs and practices, and you must have the wisdom to choose the best among options—even when those options appear at first to be politically unpopular.

For example, there has been an established agenda of important civil rights concerns. And, of course, there are the—quote—right positions to take on these matters. The "right" position to take on the issue of eradicating employment discrimination often is support for affirmative action programs. The right position to take on educational equality is support for busing. The right position to take in handling the problems of the poor is support of an unlimited public welfare system.

These positions are seldom reevaluated. Rarely do we analyze whether, in fact, the policies which benefit from such unquestioned support really are accomplishing their intended purposes. As a matter of fact, the mere *suggestion* of alternatives often is attacked as a sign of anti-civil rights and anti-minority sentiment. I will not travel down that road.

It only makes sense that to continue moving forward, we must be forward thinking individuals. We must continually reevaluate the methods we are using to reach important objectives. This is as true in government as it is in industry. The great civil rights victories we have witnessed were not won as a result of blind allegiance to the status quo. They were won when a nation opened its eyes with the courage to ask questions, the commitment to seek answers; and the dedication to work for progress.

Similarly in business, we are not preparing now to enter a new age simply by screwing rusty bolts onto brave new wonders of technology. We are retooling—raising our assembly-line consciousness to new levels of computer literacy.

You simply cannot accept old answers to new, difficult questions. You cannot exert leadership—as you must—by continuing to participate in a counterproductive exercise of follow-the-leader.

JE: To what extent is your strained relationship with the civil rights establishment attributable to the fact that you are both a black Republican and an ardent defender of President Reagan?

CT: My image as a black Republican, working in the Reagan Administration, is not the important factor. I would hope they could see beyond this fact. Rather, the challenge itself is what is crucial. As President Kennedy said: "I do not shrink from this responsibility, I welcome it." I do not believe that black Americans will accept or reject my ideas on the basis of my party affiliation. They are far too intelligent for that. They know that the great problems facing our country cannot be solved through narrow-minded partisan proposals from either party.

I am a black Republican and proud of it. And I am aware of the image problem I suffer because of my political affiliation and my association with the Reagan Administration. Because of this association, many of us are perceived by our fellow Blacks as being "conservative, opportunistic Uncle Toms." It is presumed that we are not concerned with or sensitive to the problems of Blacks in this country. Consequently, many

Blacks have chosen not to work with me and other black Republicans in this administration. That stance has had a paralyzing effect on the progress of Blacks.

While I am aware that we are presented to the American people as uncaring, unfair, and even *unjust*, I refuse to live with such an untrue image—either personally or politically. However, I gladly accept this iconoclasm and abuse to do what I believe is right and necessary. It is a small price to pay.

JE: Prior to your becoming chairman, critics charged the EEOC with widespread administrative mismanagement. Were these charges well founded?

CT: To a large extent, yes. When I took over as chairman, I faced a serious challenge. In prior years, the agency experienced a growing backlog of cases. Unfortunately, much of the backlog resulted from the misplaced fervor of agency staffers rather than from the merits of the claims being handled. The cynicism of the early 1970s, coupled with the EEOC's litigation power, gave rise to an adversarial approach to meeting our law enforcement responsibility. Employers were all too often viewed with suspicion and mistrust. It was an approach which frequently limited the agency's effectiveness in doing the critically important job it was created to do.

The result of that attitude was that many employers, who earlier might have been willing to voluntarily change their hiring and promotion practices, adopted a dramatically different posture. "See you in court" became the characteristic employer response.

Moreover, there was a widespread view of the EEOC as an ineffective and inefficient bureaucracy. From the very beginning, the EEOC was staffed and run by idealists who were long on dedication to enforcing civil rights laws and short on administrative experience.

This problem was a matter of record. And I was well aware of the criticism of the EEOC prior to becoming chairman. I had read the Government Accounting Office reports which focused on the commission's administrative and management problems. I had also read numerous letters—complaints from people who had filed charges with the EEOC—only to become disappointed with the agency's handling of those charges. On the other side were the complaints of private employers who talked about burdensome, unreasonable requirements and procedures.

Well, you can imagine my dismay in finding—after only a few weeks at the EEOC—just how much of the criticism had been based on fact. The administrative and management practices of the organization, I found, were sometimes merely inefficient while other times they were totally ineffective. The sad result was a frequent delay in processing cases and a sense of confusion and resistance among employers.

JE: As chairman of the EEOC, what have you done to correct these problems?

CT: After studying the problems, the commission developed and instituted a plan of action—a comprehensive agency reorganization designed to bring about several important structural changes in management style and scope. These changes reflect the spirit of cooperation which I believe gave rise to the EEOC in the first place.

On the management side, our goal has been to foster an organization where team building, collective accountability, and shared goal achievement are encouraged and rewarded. Individual initiative and innovation are now strongly encouraged within the context of the congressionally mandated mission of the agency. I am confident that this new arrangement and new set of priorities will prove beneficial to all concerned.

As a result of this reorganization, the commissioners are assuming stronger leadership roles in the development of program policy. They are assisted in meeting this task by our newly formed Office of Program Research (OPR). Before the OPR was established, we had no way to measure the sociological, economic, and industrial impact of our policies. This office will also provide the critically important data we need to distinguish employment barriers set up as a result of employer discrimination and those caused by other social and economic problems. This is vital information for the work ahead. It will be critical to the agency in reaching enlightened policy decisions.

We also have established an Office of Legal Counsel to provide the commission members with objective legal advice—the crucial facts and analysis they need in staying abreast of the current state of the law. This development has freed our already overburdened General Counsel's Office to pursue its primary role as prosecutor and ensure that it can handle the agency's caseload according to the highest standards of the legal profession.

Furthermore, we have replaced the Office of Executive Director with the Office of Program Operation and the Office of Management. This development will enable the EEOC to effectively serve those people who rely on it for protection without becoming bogged down in the muck and mire of administrative problems.

However, administrative reorganization alone is not a panacea for the ills of the agency. Follow-through is equally important. In view of this need, the EEOC is undertaking a thorough, methodological examination of policies and practices which have been initiated in the past.

We must know what works and what does not work in order to effectively carry out the agency's congressional mandate. This examination, however, will be conducted in a responsible manner. We owe this to the individuals who rely on the commission for protection. We also owe this to those dedicated persons who have worked so hard to make the EEOC effective. But, with an eye to the future, we must be willing to critically appraise past efforts. We must have the courage to rethink our positions in critical areas. In so doing, I hope to take the EEOC into a new era—one characterized by responsibility, objectivity, and cooperation.

JE: In your view, what can and should be done to achieve equal employment opportunity?

CT: Clearly, strengthening the sanctions available for Title VII violations would do much to offer incentives to employers to erase every vestige of employment discrimination. Federal leadership requires that we look for such weaknesses and that we work diligently to correct them.

The federal government has a profound obligation to exert progressive leadership to foster a national consensus around the issue of equal employment opportunity. In recent years, we have witnessed the steady erosion of the national consensus on civil rights. This is a dangerous trend. It was, after all, this very consensus which led to successful challenges of the most obvious barriers to equality in this country—segregated public carriers, cafeterias, and washroom facilities; separate local unions for Blacks and whites, males and females; mandatory retirement ages, which were, of course, lower for Blacks than for whites; race and sex-biased recruitment; word-of-mouth recruitment; and subjective promotion decisions.

Many of these practices were discontinued, in large part, because most people *agreed* they were wrong. That same agreement does not always exist as we move beyond the more blatant traditional barriers to the less obvious, but no less devastating, *systems* of discrimination.

Questions of fairness become much more difficult to address as we move from the front lines of civil rights demonstrations to the inner sanctums of corporate boardrooms. While it was easy to agree on methods for attacking blatant acts of discrimination a generation ago, it is rarely easy these days to agree on the most equitable methods for allocating scarce resources. Widespread confusion, even hostility, can only be exacerbated by a lack of clear, consistent positions taken by the federal government.

Consequently, every agency in the federal government must demonstrate full, unequivocal support for equal opportunity—an unwavering commitment to fundamental principles of justice and fair play. Clearly, the federal government must set the example for others to follow.

JE: From your perspective, is discrimination the major barrier to equal employment opportunity?

CT: It is *a* barrier—an important barrier—but it is not the only barrier. We must have the courage to admit that, while discrimination continues to have a pervasive, destructive impact on minority and female expectations in this society, there are other socioeconomic factors which historically have contributed to limit the opportunities of a great many people.

We must begin to recognize the important need for private individual responsibility to augment the efforts of government enforcement. Today, we are facing some difficult socioeconomic challenges—challenges every bit as tough as the legal ones we faced a generation ago when we boldly marched forward into a new era of legal justice. The objective today is the same. The tactics, however, must be different.

Clearly, this new approach is made necessary by our ever changing environment. We live in a dramatically different political, social, and economic world today from the one that existed yesterday when we sat in, walked out, and spoke up for our rights. In many respects, the problem of discrimination has also changed. Yesterday, we confronted clear-cut acts of blatant discrimination. Today, we face less obvious, but no less pervasive, effects caused by discrimination. Moreover, the problem of discrimination is compounded by a lack of preparation.

Even though all signs point to continued recovery from our latest recession, many jobs which were lost during the recent hard times are not being replaced. Many companies have retooled in order to profit in the new information age. The people who are destined to "make it" in this new era are the people who are also retooling—developing the high-tech knowledge they will need to keep pace. The people who are falling behind are the ones who are fine-tuning an assembly-line mentality in a nation hungry for computer literacy.

JE: What are the main factors which contribute to black unemployment?

CT: Recent government reports reveal that a fragmented family structure, poor education, and a variety of other social ills have served to keep too many minorities on the socioeconomic treadmill. For example, one out of every six black children between the ages of fourteen and seventeen is out of school. Forty-five percent of Hispanics who enter high school fail to graduate. It is no wonder, then, that a frighteningly high number of black and Hispanic adults are functionally incompetent in reading, writing, and arithmetic skills. Unable to read the want ads;

to fill out a job application; to correctly count their change when they shop. In a technological revolution, these people are the casualties. And the law can do little, if anything, about it.

This is not to say that minorities and women are to blame for the problems they face in the employment arena. Not at all. Discrimination *is* a continuing problem. And even the broader problems I have discussed can be linked to a history of rigid, institutionalized discrimination based on race, sex, and national origin. But even as we recognize the link between these problems and discrimination, even as we recognize that single-parent households are both the cause and effect of poverty, it still is difficult to fashion legal solutions.

JE: Do the American people, from your perspective, firmly support the principle of equal employment opportunity?

CT: Yes. The EEOC was created because we, as a nation, are committed to this principle. Any retreat from this principle would be an unforgivable violation of the public trust. But upholding the principle imposes a heavy responsibility—a difficult responsibility—as we struggle to adapt to a changing economic order.

JE: What role can and should the EEOC play in eradicating employment discrimination?

CT: As I stated earlier, I am committed to making sure the law is enforced as effectively as possible. I also am committed to making sure the law itself is strong enough to accomplish its important purpose. My one regret is that the laws I am sworn to uphold are *not* as strong as I believe they should be. When it comes to civil rights, I am a tough law and order man. I don't believe in leniency for violators.

As I have noted on numerous occasions, the remedies available under Title VII are not as compelling as the civil and criminal penalties available under other federal statutes. The back pay and reinstatement relief that Title VII offers to discrimination victims are not designed to *penalize* the people responsible for the victimization—the people who discriminate. I am appalled at the fact that there are greater penalties for breaking into a mailbox than there are for violating someone's basic civil rights. In light of this inequity, I have repeatedly called for tougher sanctions for EEO laws. It is my hope that this will encourage employers to eliminate every trace of employment discrimination.

As I see it, my duty is not only to effectively enforce the laws, but to do all within my power to make sure there are effective laws to enforce. In the meantime, I will not sit back and become preoccupied with the apparent weaknesses of our enforcement apparatus.

Laws have authorized the commission to utilize several tools, which, for whatever reasons, have long been underutilized. As I have mentioned, doing an effective job means that the commission must use its statutory power to increase public awareness, to increase public access, and to help employers voluntarily comply with the law. It also means that we cannot allow a failure of voluntary compliance or lack of public awareness to leave rights unprotected.

I am prepared to aggressively use the power of my commissioner's charge to eliminate deep seated systemic problems which otherwise may take years to correct. And I know I will not have to look too far to find violations, either. Right in my own backyard, professional organizations—law firms, accounting firms, associations—are trying to sweep invidious patterns and practices under a carpet of facially neutral policies.

I will accept no equivocation on basic questions of right. I will accept no excuses for failure to correct injustices. I am particularly annoyed by the complaint I hear too often that compliance with civil rights laws is too burdensome—too costly. I find this excuse totally unpersuasive. I happen to believe that it is extremely difficult to valuate basic civil rights. These rights cannot be bought, sold, or disposed of solely for economic expediency. They cannot be traded away simply because it is cheaper to discriminate than to be fair. When Congress enacted Title VII of the Civil Rights Act of 1964, it demonstrated its belief that, as a nation, we cannot attach a price tag to the guarantee of basic rights. The EEOC will continue to follow that congressional mandate.

JE: Many critics contend that the EEOC has failed to aggressively prosecute cases of employment discrimination. Is there any truth to this charge?

CT: No. The commission has tenaciously championed the rights of the individual, as well as effective, meaningful remedies for individuals who have been victimized by discrimination in precedent-setting cases.

For example, in the area of sex discrimination, the EEOC has fought industry pressure by repeatedly insisting that women retirees be paid the same benefits as similarly situated men. Our recent victory in the Second Circuit in *Spirt* v. *TIAA* (1982) on that issue is a testament to our commitment to individual rights. Similarly, EEOC firmly supported the right of an individual woman to be treated on the basis of merit in being considered for promotion to partnership in a law firm. The commission was recently vindicated by the Supreme Court in its unanimous decision in *Hisbon* v. *King and Spalding* (1981).

In the area of age discrimination, the commission has achieved record breaking settlements in the cases of *EEOC* v. *Liggett and Myers, Inc.* (1982) and *Smallwood* v. *United Airlines, Inc.* (1981). In the United

Airlines case, the commission helped obtain an $18 million jury verdict for individuals who had been denied the opportunity to transfer to flight attendant jobs because of their age. Approximately $7 million in relief was obtained in the Liggett and Myers case on behalf of individuals who had been forcibly retired.

JE: What lessons should be learned from these and other similar cases?

CT: The lesson to be learned from such cases is that in situations where the rights of the individual are threatened, the courts will act swiftly and without hesitation. Where, however, individuals are classified and treated as simply components of larger groups defined according to race, sex, or national origin, the courts will be exceedingly skeptical. The recent decision in *Firefighters* v. *Stotts* (1984) can be viewed as a somewhat ambiguous and simplistic application of this principle.

JE: Given these decisions, how would you describe the mission of your agency?

CT: The EEOC will continue its historic mission of protecting and maintaining the rights of the individual in an increasingly complex matrix of jobs and employment opportunities. The commission has demonstrated its commitment to individuals through the relief it has sought in the courts and through its administrative processing of charges.

The EEOC has demonstrated its willingness to use innovative and creative techniques in the war against employment discrimination. As part of our $42 million predetermination settlement with General Motors (1984), the commission persuaded General Motors to establish an unprecedented $15 million endowment and scholarship fund to be used to prepare minorities and women for managerial and high-technology jobs.

The creativity and flexibility demonstrated by the General Motors settlement is evidence of our commitment to developing innovative means of fighting employment discrimination. In order to lay the foundation for better litigation and better settlements, we have emphasized the investigation, rather than the settlement of charges. Similarly, through our expanded presence program, we have attempted to make our services more accessible to those persons not located near the EEOC offices and to persons whose primary language is not English. We also have implemented a voluntary asistance program designed to enhance employer and union understanding of the responsibilities imposed by laws prohibiting discrimination in employment.

Finally, in order to prevent the EEOC's programs from being overshadowed by charges of administrative inefficiency, we have weeded out those practices which diverted attention from the agency's programs. Simultaneously, we have strengthened management practices throughout the agency.

JE: How would you assess the overall progress that has been made in eliminating racial discrimination?

CT: Today, black people can—and are—voting in every county in the country. There no longer exist "White Only" signs or buses to desegregate or lunch counters to sit in. Those battles have been won. And the hard ground of injustice and intolerance, broken first by Blacks, is now being tilled by others long denied.

However, the task of making America "one nation under God" has yet to be realized. The great architectural wonder built of truth, right, and law—that majestic bridge that was to link the minorities of America to the mainland of American life—dangles half complete, a great heaving, swaying witness on the landscape of the conscience of our nation. Though the pillars have been sunk and the steel forged, the ties have not yet been placed and soldered. The job has yet to be completed.

Segregation and discrimination are still, despite thirty years of progress, a stultifying way of life for most minority Americans. The grim unemployment statistics for minorities bear this out. Housing patterns and high school dropout rates are stark witnesses. The absent minority voices in the classrooms, where the law, medicine, engineering, and computer science are taught, sigh like ghosts of a future still denied. The task remains to be finished.

JE: Many Americans believe, in spite of these facts, that the battle for racial justice has been won. They are tired, they say, of minority pleas for special consideration and compensation. How would you respond?

CT: I have heard it said over and over again that we, as a nation, have done enough; that the doors of opportunity for women, Blacks, Hispanics, and others have been opened; that the present laws against discrimination are sufficient; and that people are tired of the plight of minorities.

Well, let me assure you, no one is more tired of their plight than this nation's minorities. No one is more worn out by the fight to stay alive, to find a job, to be treated with dignity and respect than the minorities. To stand in the midst of the squalor of East Harlem and look out toward the towering spires of power in mid-Manhattan, less than thirty, forty blocks away and say—"There the doors of opportunity are open"—is to say nothing. The question is, "How do I get there?" Those forty blocks, those short forty blocks are, for many, a lifetime journey. For some, they are as far away as ancient Mesopotamia. They are a space of another time, another place, another race.

I know! I was not born to affluence or privilege. No tender hand rocked my cradle and said, "My son will follow in his father's footsteps to Holy Cross College and Yale Law School." The footsteps for me led to the hard ground of my grandfather's farm. The footsteps for me were unceasing ones, not nine to five, or even nine to nine, but dawn to midnight and beyond. But I was one of the lucky ones. My grandparents had a vision and a faith unblurred by time and toil. They saw beyond that farm outside Savannah. They saw beyond the segregation and degradation that had been their lot. They saw in their minds' eyes the long-locked doors of opportunity squeaking open. My grandfather and grandmother had faith that I could make it through and the wisdom to know I had no choice.

JE: As chairman of the commission, how do you view your responsibility to open those doors?

CT: It was Luke who said, "For unto whomever much is given, of him shall much be required—and to whom men have committed much, of him they shall ask more." I am one of those to whom much has been given. From me—and people like me—society demands much.

It demands redress of generations of wrongs, not only in the legal sense but in the hearts of men and women. It demands not only justice, but compassion. It demands that the crusade for civil rights continue unabated until every man, woman, and child in this country has an equal opportunity for education, employment, and life, liberty, and the pursuit of happiness.

Much is said these days about the need for the law to be color-blind. I agree with that. I believe that our achievements and our failures should be measurements of our individual abilities and efforts. I believe that a person should be accepted in a school because of his or her ability; hired for a job because of his or her experience; promoted *in* a job because of his or her achievements. I believe firmly in the rights of the individual. That success should be the reward of individual effort.

This is the *ideal*. It is one to which all Americans, in some sense or another, aspire. And yet, this is obviously not the reality. Instead, for many easily identifiable groups, the idea of individual achievement has been effectively stymied by the reality of discrimination. The individual members of these groups have not, historically, been judged on the basis of individual merit but, rather, on the basis of characteristics ascribed to the group to which they belong.

This is the fundamental problem. How do we, as a nation, reconcile the ideal of individual achievement with the reality of group discrimination? How do we redress the problem of discrimination against particular groups without seriously undermining the importance of individual achievement?

The dilemma created by this situation strikes at the heart of what we stand for as a nation. This is the reason why honest, intelligent men and women of good conscience can and do differ as to the best ways in which to combat the effects of historical discrimination.

JE: Finally, is the Constitution, as is often said, color-blind? If so, how did America move so far from its stated ideals?

CT: Justice John M. Harlan, in *Plessy* v. *Ferguson* (1896), wrote a courageous dissent in which he argued that the Constitution was color-blind and that the laws of our nation were intended to be implemented in a color-blind fashion. His argument was simply that the laws of this land should be implemented in the spirit of the Constitution; the spirit which recognized the equality of all our citizens.

But while Justice Harlan's dissent was admirable in its forthright assessment of the ideals outlined by the Constitution, it was not accurate in its examination of the factual components of that document. For though the Constitution is stirring in the ideals which it espouses, it did not fully embrace those ideals. In that very document, Blacks counted as only two-thirds of a human being.

Clearly, though the framers of the Constitution may have intended it to be a color-blind document, it was not color-blind at its inception, nor has it been made color-blind through interpretation. This has, in essence, been a color-conscious nation for over 200 years. It is, therefore, nearly impossible to move in one—or even three generations—from being a color-conscious nation to being one in which color is not taken into account. Two centuries of segregation, discrimination, prejudice, and denial of basic human rights have done their work too well for that.

Yet our laws—even Title VII, from which the EEOC draws its authority—clearly state that individuals are to receive treatment which *does not* take into account their color, race, sex, or national origin. The laws are designed to protect those persons of equal qualifications who are entering or have already entered the job market. They are not, however, designed to train people for employment or to overcome years of inferior schooling or to eradicate the hopelessness that generational poverty breeds. They are not designed to create equality but, rather, to make a place for those who are already equal. They are designed to help the seekers, those already on their way.

Because of the historical color consciousness which has affected the lives of so many Americans, we find ourselves in a situation in which a color-blind application of the law appears to insulate and reinforce socioeconomic disadvantages. Unfortunately, civil rights laws in general and equal employment opportunity laws in particular simply lack the ability to eliminate these disadvantages. But they must be eliminated.

We, as a nation, have come too far toward justice, toward full equality, to allow contravening winds to forge a halt in the march to making the vision of America a reality. But still, the task is not yet done. We cannot cry out against injustice in El Salvador and be immune to it at home. This is hypocrisy. We cannot defend the human rights of the people of Central America, Asia, and Africa and deny those same rights to American children here at home. We must make real the ideals of America for all our citizens. The fruits of our labors will be freedom. Our gift will be the true greatness of America.

PART THREE

The Judicial Branch

Theodore R. Newman, Jr.

Of Dreams Deferred

Theodore R. Newman, Jr. was born July 5, 1934, in Birmingham, Alabama. He graduated from Brown University in 1955 with a Bachelor of Arts degree in philosophy. He then attended Harvard Law School, from which he received a Bachelor of Laws degree in 1958, concentrating in constitutional law and jurisprudence.

After a three-year tour of duty with the United States Air Force as a judge advocate stationed at Laon Air Base, France, Newman served as an attorney in the Civil Rights Division of the Department of Justice from 1961 to 1962. He then entered private law practice as an associate with the firm of Houston, Bryan, and Gardner in the District of Columbia and in 1968 left that firm to become a partner in the firm of Pratt, Bowers, and Newman, also in the District of Columbia.

In November 1970, Newman became an associate judge of the Superior Court of the District of Columbia. He served on that court—the court of general trial jurisdiction for the District of Columbia—until October 1976.

In October 1976, Newman was appointed to the District of Columbia Court of Appeals as chief judge. The District of Columbia Court of Appeals is the court of last resort in the District of Columbia court system.

A fellow of the American Bar Foundation of the American Bar Association, Newman is a trustee of Brown University. Formerly president of the National Center for State Courts and chairman of the Judicial Council of the National Bar Association, he was awarded an honorary Doctor of Laws degree by his alma mater, Brown University, in June 1980.

JE: Let's begin with some background information. Can you talk about the time, place, and circumstances in which you grew up?

TN: I was born in Birmingham, Alabama, where my father was a pastor of an African Methodist Episcopal church (AME). We lived in Birmingham for a year and a half. Then we moved to Pratville, Alabama, a small rural town, where he pastored another church for a year. And from the time I was two and a half, we lived in Tuskegee, Alabama, where my father again pastored a church and later became a presiding elder in the AME church. My mother is a school teacher, now retired. My father retired from the church in 1983.

Tuskegee is a unique southern city because of the presence of both the Tuskegee Institute and a large veterans hospital, which was predominantly, if not 100 percent, black staffed at the time I was growing up. Tuskegee was something of a cultural oasis in the south. The money in the town was primarily black although Blacks didn't leverage their money in those days. The culture in the town centered on the college campus. The intelligentsia was primarily black. It was largely a self-contained community, where one had little contact with the white establishment, save for when you had to shop for clothes, go to the department store, and take part in other activities in town. I lived close to the college. The racism of the South was clearly apparent when I went downtown. This caused me to better appreciate Tuskegee, which was an atypical community. Had I not ventured out of Tuskegee, I would have had a very limited view of the South, not understanding the lingering legacy of racism which clearly existed.

The best schools in the area were black, both elementary and secondary. In that sense, too, it was an atypical environment. My peers placed a high premium on education and everyone expected to attend college—and not just *any* college, but a first-rate one. No one in that small environment thought I was crazy when I announced, at a very young age, that I intended to one day attend an Ivy League university and Harvard Law School.

JE: When did you first develop an interest in law and begin to think in terms of being a lawyer?

TN: I am told by my parents that I first decided to be a lawyer by the time I was seven or eight years old. My impression is that that desire was a sublimation of my father's desire to have been a lawyer. I don't ever remember having wanted to be anything else *but* a lawyer.

JE: Was politics a much-talked-about subject in your family? If so, what did your parents teach you about politics and the political process?

TN: My interest in law closely paralleled my interest in politics. The first presidential election I recall was that of 1944, which pitted Dewey against Roosevelt. I was ten years old at the time. My father was a very active Republican and continued to be well into his seventies, at which point he was forced to curtail his activities due to poor health. I was not surprised by Dewey's defeat, but I was disappointed.

At that time, it was unusual for Blacks to be involved in politics at all and virtually unheard of for Blacks in the South to be actively supporting Republican candidates. As I said, my father was a lifelong Republican. The party symbol of the Alabama Democratic Party back then was a white rooster with the logo: "White Supremacy For The Right!" Daddy had a window shade which prominently displayed this slogan, and whenever he was talking politics to someone, he would pull down the shade and say, "If that's what you believe, vote for the Democrats." This was not an uncommon view among Blacks in the early 1940s. Come the 1950s, when the country was voting for Dwight Eisenhower, Blacks were still voting for Franklin Roosevelt. My father is still voting for Abraham Lincoln.

JE: At what point did you develop a serious interest in the law? What triggered that interest?

TN: I've always been something of a rebel. I've always had a profound sense of justice and, concomitantly, of injustice. I witnessed repeated instances of legal deprivation. Blacks could not obtain counsel, since all of the lawyers were white. I observed numerous instances in which Blacks dealt with white lawyers to their economic detriment. These frequently involved battles over the legal ownership of property in which the white lawyer would end up owning the property. I developed a deep sense of outrage that black people were being ripped off because there were so few lawyers who would honestly and sincerely represent their interests. I concluded that the solution lay in black lawyers. And I vowed that I would be one of them. I wanted to make a contribution to freedom and justice in Alabama. Moreover, I realized that ultimately the struggle for human rights would center on the law and that the great issues of the day would be played out in the courts of this land. I wanted to be part of that effort.

JE: Did you believe, from the very beginning, that you would succeed as a lawyer? If so, what factors contributed to your feeling of confidence?

TN: I always knew I would succeed. It goes back to my parents. They reinforced my belief in myself. They repeatedly told me that I had the requisite ability—as much ability as anyone else. I recall them saying, "If you work at it, and you will—because we will make sure you work at it—you will succeed." No, I never had any doubts. As I said, when I was seven or eight, I was already telling people that I was going to attend an Ivy League university and Harvard Law School. Some of them, outside the small environment in which I grew up, thought I was touched in the head. Who the hell did I think I was, that I was going to reach such heights? But I never had any doubts about it. My critics now will tell you that I am, at the very least, uppity, with a touch of arrogance.

JE: Youngsters often role model movie stars, or baseball players, or rock stars. Did you model judges? If so, which judges did you most admire?

TN: Yes, to a certain extent. It occurred during my college years, when civil rights litigation was on the upsurge. A number of judges, especially United States district judges and Court of Appeals judges, stood out. These included the likes of Waties Waring in South Carolina, Skelly Wright in Louisiana, Frank Johnson in Alabama, and Elbert Tuttle, Richard Rives, and John Brown on the Fifth Circuit Court of Appeals. These and other judges later became the subject of Jack W. Peltason's much-talked-about book, *The Fifty-Eight Lonely Men*. These district court judges, particularly in the South, became my role models, my idols, to the extent that I had any. I had profound admiration for Thurgood Marshall from an early age. He had litigated the famous Alabama case of *Gomillion* v. *Lightfoot* (1960), which involved my hometown of Tuskegee. I knew Gomillion all my life. The Tuskegee Civic Association was very, very active in voter registration. I heard as many sermons from the pulpit by my father on voter registration as I did on Christianity. His Christianity was as much unitarian in terms of the teachings of religion, especially in its application to the problems of today, as it was rooted in a study of biblical times and practices. As a result, the civil rights movement—and the litigation strategies associated with it—brought me in touch with my heroes.

JE: Did your heroes multiply and/or change once you turned to the study of law?

TN: Yes. I probably should add a footnote. At that juncture, I had no thought or expectation of becoming a judge. My goal, as I stated earlier, was to return to Tuskegee and practice law there once I completed my studies.

As for your question, yes, my list of heroes increased. When I enrolled in law school—and to some degree, while I was in college—my primary interest was jurisprudence. I was a philosophy major in college. One of my favorite courses was jurisprudence. I took as much jurisprudence as I could in law school. I was particularly impressed by the work of Roscoe Pound, the great American jurist, who wrote masterfully on the subject of law as an instrument of social control and social change. I also fell under the spell of Charles Hamilton Houston, a brilliant legal mind and one of the giants in the field. Both men had a profound influence on me and my view of the law.

JE: How would you characterize your judicial philosophy? How do you view the role of a judge?

TN: I'm at a loss to answer that question, because I'm not sure what terms mean anymore. The liberal-conservative dichotomy is a floating dichotomy based upon who is defining the term. For example, if Edmund Burke is a symbol of conservatism, I would argue that I am a true conservative. Burke's philosophy, simply put, is that government ought to stay out of the individual's private life. In this day and age, conservatives want to keep government out of people's economic affairs, but are quite willing to permit governmental intrusion into the bed-room. My conservatism, however, extends to the latter as well. I want to keep the police outside my home unless they have a clear constitutional justification for entering it. That view is now called liberal. But in Burke's terms, it is classical conservatism. As a result, I don't really know how to describe my philosophy, as measured by such labels.

I can, however, tell you what I believe. I believe that it is important to protect individual rights from governmental intrusion. As I've frequently said, the constitutional protections were not designed to make the constable's task easier. They were designed to make it more difficult; they were designed to put some weight into his saddlebags. And I think that weight should remain in the constable's saddlebags, as a way of protecting the rights of the individual against the powers of the state. I've always had a keen interest in the rights of the individual. In terms of the relationship of the individual to the state—in terms of the law— I am an Edmund Burke conservative.

JE: Where would you place yourself in terms of the judicial activist-judicial restraint dichotomy?

TN: That would take forever to explain. I don't think that dichotomy exists as it relates to most subjects that come before a judge. Clearly, someone has to decide these matters. And a decision not to decide is, I would argue, a decision to decide. Let me give you an example. Suppose your car is out of control, traveling down a mountain road. You have three choices: to jump out, stay in, or not make a decision. But the latter is a decision to stay in. This is equally true with respect to judicial decisions.

Take the famous reapportionment decision, *Baker* v. *Carr* (1962). The Supreme Court had three choices: to get in, stay out, or do nothing. By doing nothing, they are staying out and endorsing the status quo. But they *are* making a policy decision by staying out. And, in my view, that is as activist as getting in.

I recognize the argument that the question is not whether the issue must be decided, but what branch of government or what entity should decide it. But that argument really misses the point. Clearly, I would describe myself as an activist. Given my background, training, and experience—and the role of the courts in protecting the rights of black Americans over the last thirty or forty years—it should not be surprising that I would describe myself this way. I do recognize areas where the courts probably should not get involved, but I think the courts must assume the role of protecting the rights of the individual against the powers of the state. And if that makes me an activist, then I plead guilty.

Judicial activism, I would add, is one of the things that has made our system of government work as masterfully as it has with minimal change in the Constitution. In my view, one of the frustrations that Marx and Lenin must feel—wherever they are now—is that they did not think our system of government would be able to adapt to social change. They could not foresee a Theodore Roosevelt or a Franklin Roosevelt. Our system has, through a mechanism of internal corrections, proved capable of responding to social change. Central to this process is the pivotal role of the Supreme Court and the federal judiciary. Had we not learned how to adapt, we would have long ago experienced revolution. By legitimizing change—and making it possible—we have avoided revolution and its attendant consequences.

JE: To what extent did race influence your decision to become a judge? Has it affected your view of the law?

TN: It has had a significant impact, no question about it. My decision to become a lawyer and, later, a judge, was bound up in the injustice which I saw and experienced as a youngster growing up in the South. I was angered by the injustice that the legal system heaped on Blacks.

JE: Has that interest intensified over the years?

TN: Yes, very much so. I have come to recognize, as a result of increased exposure to the broader world, the systemic injustice between the haves and the have nots. Blacks represent a disproportionate percentage of the have nots.

JE: Has race proved an asset or a liability in achieving your goals?

TN: Race has been a persistent factor. Our society is racist. And that's not just true in the United States. I've had the opportunity to travel extensively throughout the western world and have witnessed the attitudes of the northern Italians toward the Sicilians. I've seen the attitudes of the French toward the Algerians. I've observed the attitudes of the Rhineland Germans toward the Bavarian Germans. Every society has some group that comprises its "niggers"; every society has its own version of the caste system. Every society has its haves and have nots. And often this caste is based upon an identifiable group characteristic.

As a result of these experiences, my exposure has both broadened my perspective and reinforced my childhood perceptions, to wit, that there are always people on the periphery of society—and that these people need protection.

JE: As a judge, is it difficult for you to separate your own values, your own beliefs, from what the law says and act in ways that may contradict what you personally believe or feel?

TN: That's a question that concerns not only judges but anyone who is in the position of having to make decisions. We are the sum total of our human experiences, and there is absolutely no way that I can ignore my background, training, race, values—all of those things that go into the making of who and what I am. If I had grown up white in my hometown of Tuskegee, it is less likely that I would have the mindset I do. So, I'm not sure—however hard you may try—that it's possible to divorce yourself from all those things that make you who you are.

Young people are frequently schooled to believe that we are a government of laws and not of men; that somehow judges are able to separate themselves from the very things that form their personalities; and that judges simply read the law as written and interpret it on the basis of the words themselves.

Anyone who believes that does not understand the law. One of the most tragic appointments to the Supreme Court that I have seen in my lifetime was that of Justice Charles Whittaker, who at his confirmation hearings, in response to a question about how he viewed his role as a justice, stated, in essence, "I take the Constitution in one hand, and the statute in the other, and I balance them and see if they jibe." At that time, I was still in school. But I said to myself, if that's what he thinks constitutional adjudication is all about, then he's badly mistaken.

JE: What prompted your decision to give up private practice to serve on the bench?

TN: By the time I was well into private practice, I had two career interests, basically. One was judicial; the other was political. There came a time when it was politically feasible for a Black to be elected county attorney in my home county in Alabama. At that time, I was in private practice and very, very active in Republican party politics. Incidentally, in November 1983, I changed my registration to Democrat. I enjoyed politics. And, of course, being a judge here in Washington, that's the name of the game.

Several people in my hometown invited me to discuss with them the possibility of returning to Tuskegee and running for county attorney. At that point, I was forced to evaluate what I wanted to do with the rest of my life. Those two interests—judicial and political—were very prominent at the time. This is best illustrated by the fact that my former wife gave me two photographs: one of the Capitol of the United States, the other of the United States Supreme Court. She gave me both because I hadn't yet decided which way I wanted to go.

I went back to Alabama and talked to several knowledgeable people and did my own analysis of the situation. I concluded that a Black could be elected as county attorney, and that I could be that person. I also concluded that it would be possible, in my lifetime, to elect a Black to Congress from that district. It has not happened yet, and I was perhaps overly optimistic in my assessment.

I had to make a decision. I have always been fiercely independent and have not taken kindly to people telling me what I could or could not do. Still, I had enough practical experience in politics to know that, as an elected official, in an arena where the beginning is the word and the word is money (campaign money), there would come a time when a major contributor would say, "Ted, you owe me this one." And I would face a difficult dilemma. I concluded that I was not independently affluent enough to survive in the political arena because the day would surely arrive when I would have to say, "Go to hell, I quit." So, I decided that a political career was not for me. If I had had Rockefeller's bankroll, it might have been a different matter. Or if I had had independent means, less than Rockefeller's, so that if I said, "Hey, I can't go for this, I'm going back to do something else," something else would have been readily available. As a result, I dismissed the idea of a political career and began to think in terms of either remaining in private practice or pursuing a judicial career.

As hokey as it may sound, I concluded that I could have a greater impact on society as a judge than I could as a private practitioner. Moreover, if people who were "the good people" in the practice of law continued to say no to judicial appointments, they forfeited their right to criticize those who were less good and ended up on the bench. So, in that sense, probably, the motivating factors were of an altruistic nature.

JE: As a judge, you have considerable power, both within and outside the courtroom. How difficult is it to avoid becoming overwhelmed by your power and using it in an arbitrary and capricious manner?

TN: You still have to have your car repaired; you still have to pay the cleaning bill; you still have to deal with your golf partner; and you still have to carry out the trash at home. You're right, though, it is a problem. However, there are enough forces at play—unless you're a total egomaniac—to keep you on a fairly even keel. In the end, it really depends upon the makeup of the individual. One of the qualities to look for in selecting judges is appreciation of the limits of power. And power does have its own limits. It has always been interesting to me—both in terms of the judicial branch and government in general—to discover that the higher you climb toward the top, the narrower your degree of freedom of choice becomes. I suspect I had at least a *feeling* of more freedom of choice as a trial judge, when I had less right to make law, than I have now. And there are some institutional reasons for this. This court is collegial. I can't do anything with one vote. If we're sitting in a division of three, I've got to persuade one other person, at least, to agree with me before I can do anything. If we sit *en banc*—as a full court of nine—then I've got to sway at least four additional votes. That affords me less free choice than I had as a trial judge. Often as a trial judge—and this was the most awesome responsibility I had—by a slightly different formation of the tongue, I could give 20 months or 20 years as a criminal sentence. I know of no place in our society where one human being has a greater capacity to play God than a trial judge at the moment of sentencing in a criminal case, particularly in a jurisdiction like this one where the range of sentence options is vast.

Moreover, the longer you live, the more you see instances of today's hero and power figure, who become powerless or forgotten tomorrow. And you begin to realize how transient your power actually is. I will never forget my parents' advice: "Be nice to people on the way up the ladder because those are the same people you will see on the way down. And if you're not nice to them on the way up, they will stomp on your toes and fingers when you're on the way down." Such advice has kept me from floating too far up in the clouds, from becoming overwhelmed by my own power.

JE: To what extent does being a judge affect your personal life? Can you leave your work behind when you go home at night?

TN: You're a judge 24 hours a day. I'll modify that a bit. As a public figure, you must recognize that you're constantly under public scrutiny and that your life is no longer totally your own. I have often said, I am three people. I am Chief Judge Theodore R. Newman, Jr.—that's one. I'm Ted Newman—that's two. And the third is what I *really* am—a combination of the two. I try never to allow Ted Newman to prejudice the reputation of Chief Judge Newman.

However, at one time in my life I concluded that all of Ted Newman could not be sacrificed to Judge Newman. You are the combination of both. And your life can't be a totally judicial life, otherwise, you can't do your job properly. You've got to know the woof and warp of society. On the other hand, you've got to recognize the limitations that being in the public eye places on you.

JE: What qualities, do you think, make you a good judge?

TN: I will answer that question by telling you what qualities I think are necessary to being a good judge—and I will differentiate between being a trial judge and a judge at the appellate level.

For a trial judge, I think you need a good deal of common sense, some intellect, a willingness to work hard, and a sense of fairness and compassion. I think you need all of those qualities as an appellate judge, but I think you probably need a heavier dose of the intellect and a broader philosophical and jurisprudential perspective. Whether society likes it or not, judges *do* make law. The appellate function has two major components: One is the error review function. Did the person receive a fair trial? Was the law followed? Those kinds of things. The other and more significant component relates to its lawmaking or jurisprudential function. At that level, I think you need a broad-based person, one who has a keen understanding of the relationship of the various segments of society, the key elements of government, and an awareness of what society should be and the role of the judiciary in realizing that ideal. This is not to denigrate the need for intellect on the part of the trial judge. I have many friends on trial courts, and I was once a trial judge myself.

JE: Is the judicial system, as many believe, stacked against black Americans?

TN: The American legal system, like our society in general, is infected with racism. That is a fact. In addition to it being a fact, it is clearly perceived as being a fact. And I am firmly convinced that perceptions are, in fact, the reality because we tend to pattern what we do on our perceptions of reality, as distinguished from abstract reality. Clearly, there is a perception in our society, which I think is valid, that our legal system is imbued with racism.

When a black person walks into a courtroom and all the rest of the players that he sees are different from him, he is understandably concerned as to whether or not, on a fundamental level, they understand the dynamics and realities of his life. And he wonders, given the dynamics of racism, whether or not he'll get a fair shake.

I think it's crucial that in any structure—governmental or otherwise—where people are going to make decisions affecting other people, that the system be representative. There must exist not only the commonality of human experience but the perception of that commonality. In that regard, we have a long way to go.

JE: Are you satisfied with the progress that Blacks have made in terms of judicial appointments?

TN: Yes and no. It depends on when and where. The record of the Reagan Administration is abysmal as it relates to the appointment of women, Blacks, Hispanics, and Asian Americans. The record of the federal courts is equally abysmal. And the record of the state courts is only slightly better. For example, we've never had a Black on the Illinois Supreme Court, despite the large number of blacks who live in Chicago. We've got only eleven Blacks now on state supreme courts, including four on this court in the District of Columbia. There are only seven elsewhere—one in Pennsylvania, one in Maryland, one in North Carolina, one in Virginia, one in Florida, one in Alabama, and one in California.

JE: Are black judges different, in terms of their attitudes and values, than their white counterparts? Do they bring a different perspective to the court?

TN: Yes. Because his or her background and experiences are different, I would expect a black judge from Harlem to view the world differently than a white judge who was raised in Scarsdale. That's inevitable. It's to be expected. It goes back to perception. If a Black enters an environment in which all the levers of power that affect his life are controlled by whites, what does that say to him about the powerlessness of being black? Doesn't it reinforce that sense of frustration, futility, inferiority—all the rest of the things that are the concomitants of racism?

JE: It's often said that the Supreme Court follows the election returns. Does this view accurately reflect the record of the court, particularly under Chief Justice Warren Burger?

TN: I suspect the Supreme Court has handed down decisions which, in the opinion of some, may reflect current political realities. I won't deny that a legitimate argument could be made on that score. For example, Franklin Roosevelt's "court packing" scheme *did* reflect a desire to change the philosophical makeup of the court. But that occurs less frequently than some judicial critics would have us believe. Yes, the courts do reflect changes in society, but not as rapidly as from one election to another. Society had changed markedly from *Plessy* v. *Ferguson* in 1896 to *Brown* v. *Board of Education* in 1954, but the changes took nearly 60 years. To as great an extent, if not greater than the election returns, the court's decisions reflect the values of the men and women who serve on it. That's quite natural. For instance, I wouldn't expect Ronald Reagan to appoint the same kinds of individuals to the bench as Edward Kennedy might. They have entirely different world views. And that's legitimate.

JE: What would you say to young Blacks and others who contend that the Supreme Court has abandoned the quest for racial justice—that the present court has attempted to thwart much of the progress made by the Warren Court?

TN: I would disagree. This relates to my theory of history which I see as one of thesis, antithesis, and synthesis. I think it's important that we, as Blacks, use every resource at our command to make sure that the antithesis is contained. We must make sure that the retrenchment goes no further backward than necessary. I agree with Marcus Garvey's contention that nobody is going to turn over to you any lever of power—that you are going to have to develop those levers for yourself. Yes, we will have allies in that struggle, but in the end, we will have to do it for ourselves. We must make the system respond to our needs because it is in our interest to do so.

One reason, for instance, that I don't become bitter when I start becoming frustrated is that I don't know what alternative exists. Revolution is not a viable option. The last time I looked, Blacks did not have control of Fort Knox and the gold reserves there. They did not have control of the First Airborne Division, or the air force, or the navy. Revolution is a dead end. Instead, we must make the system respond by developing those levers of power that bring about social change.

JE: Does it concern you that young people seem less interested and involved in the civil rights struggle today than they were in the 1960s?

TN: Yes. But as I've said, history is cyclical. When I was in college in the 1950s, we were known for panty raids and swallowing goldfish. We were an uninvolved generation. Fifteen years later the lunch counter sit-ins were led by college students, as was the Vietnam protest movement. We are now in a period similar to the 1950s, marked by less activism and participation. But that too will change: Life, history, and society operate on that cycle.

JE: How would you describe the legacy of the Warren Court and the role it played in advancing the cause of racial justice?

TN: It played a significant role in that effort. It reflected the view that government had a responsibility to translate the American dream into a reality. It made an important contribution in that direction, but it did not *solve* the problem. This reminds me of the title of a speech that I have delivered several times—"The Battle Is Not Won; Nirvana Is Never." That state of blessedness, that state of human perfection will *never* be realized. Instead, it's an unending process of trying to make society better in terms of its goals and aspirations than it is presently. But to give up because we have not achieved Nirvana is a cop-out. There is no rational alternative but to continue the process of trying to make society better. Martin Luther King, Jr.'s dream will *never* be accomplished in this society or any other. But that doesn't mean the battle is not worth fighting. Just because you won't attain perfection doesn't mean you shouldn't battle toward improvement. There's no alternative but to continue the struggle.

JE: How would you compare the record of the Warren Court with that of the Burger Court in terms of civil rights?

TN: Thus far, at least, in strictly civil rights terms—that is, on race-related questions—there has not been a significant retrenchment under Chief Justice Burger. The retrenchment has occurred more in the area of civil liberties—for example, in areas concerning the rights of criminal defendants. Obviously, the record of the Burger Court in civil rights is not as striking as that of the Warren Court, but it has not, in my view, departed significantly from the progress made by the Warren Court in the field of civil rights.

JE: Much has been said and written about Justice Thurgood Marshall, the only black member of the Supreme Court. You've known him for a number of years. How would you assess his contribution?

TN: Thurgood Marshall is a giant. He is the culmination, I would argue, of Charles Houston's dream—of the litigation approach to racial justice. I regret that Charles did not live long enough to see its culmination in Thurgood Marshall.

Thurgood has a keen intellect. He has a profound sense of justice. He is a superb tactician. He has a marvelous sense of humor. He has a keen awareness of who he is. He comes out of a common human experience that reinforces such qualities. Thurgood's a giant.

JE: I assume you've read Bob Woodward and Carl Bernstein's book, *The Brethren*. In their book, the authors picture the justices as arrogant, petty, racist, quarrelsome, and second-rate in terms of intellect. Is that an accurate characterization?

TN: I don't think so. Those who expect a collegial court not to be involved in internal controversy are living in a fantasy world. They seem to expect human beings to behave as something other than human. People who are surprised that there is internal friction on the court need only examine their own marriages. If they were to tell me that they have marriages that are free of internal strife, disagreement, give and take, push and shove, I wouldn't believe them. Any time you have two people who have to work together, you're going to have that. If you don't, then one of them is useless in the relationship because he or she is simply a mirror of the other. And you don't need that mirror to create a collegial body.

Moreover, you must remember that the easy cases do not reach the Supreme Court; they are decided by the lower courts. The Supreme Court hears only the tough ones about which people are going to disagree, at times intensely. There's going to be friction; it's inevitable. Instead, you work to control it. You work to keep it from becoming public.

As I see it, that was the great tragedy of *The Brethren*—people violating their oath of confidentiality and yacking to the press about matters that were supposed to be secret. But was I surprised? No. I would have been stunned to read that such things didn't go on.

JE: Would it be better, in your view, if the Supreme Court were to shed its cloak of secrecy and speak more directly to the American public? Don't you think it would dispel many of the myths about the court?

TN: I tend to think it would do more harm than good. It's a hard balance to strike. Keep in mind, the only resource the judicial branch has, in terms of its power, is public acceptance. The courts have no other resource to enforce their orders. I recall the comment made by one president, who observed: "The Supreme Court has made its decision, now let's see them enforce it." He was telling the truth. If the executive branch refuses to enforce a court decision, the court can do nothing about it. For example, we don't have a single person on the staff of the District of Columbia Court of Appeals empowered to enforce an order of our court. The enforcement lies in the executive branch. In this regard, the judicial branch is the least powerful branch of government. Its power springs from public acceptance.

If you bring everything out in the open, what will that do to the public's perception of the court? I think it would damage it. It may be necessary to preserve illusion or at least a degree of illusion. It's important that the public believe that this is a country of laws, not of men. That's probably a myth but a very necessary one.

JE: How does social class affect the dispensation of justice? Isn't the system riddled with class distinctions?

TN: Oh, it's a tremendous failing, but I would hate to have to prove it. Don't forget, race has an impact on economics. There is a direct relationship between race and class. Yes, money plays a very important role in our society. An indigent criminal defendant in the District of Columbia is represented by a lawyer who presently makes $20 an hour out of court and $30 an hour in court. Legislation has been proposed to raise that to $35 both in and out of court. If I were a millionaire charged with a crime in the District of Columbia, I would not be talking about hiring a lawyer to whom I would pay $35 an hour—rather, I would much prefer one who would charge $350 an hour. And I would get a much more qualified lawyer. That's inevitable. To expect it not to exist is to live in a fantasy land. Instead, you try to ensure that no one, because of his or her economic position, is deprived of quality representation. No system will ever exist in which the manual laborer will be able to afford—or have the state provide to him—the quality of representation available to the president of General Motors. That will never happen. Rank has its privileges. Economic clout will always be unequal. Instead, we must do everything possible to provide quality representation to the less privileged among us.

JE: Finally, now that you've reached the zenith of your legal career, do you intend to remain on the bench until your retirement? Are there other goals that you would like to achieve, or have they all been realized?

TN: No, they haven't. My answer has more to do with Ted Newman, the individual, than it does with Judge Newman. I still have two careers that I would like to pursue—that is, if circumstances permit. First, I would like to return to private law practice for about ten years. I've been on the bench now for fourteen years—six years on a trial court, and eight years here. And you reach a time when you become tired. Psychologists call it "burnout." The studies with respect to judicial burnout tend to indicate that this malady sets in after from six to eight years on a particular court. The more Type-A personality you are, the more likely it is that you will suffer from burnout. I think that everybody who knows me would agree that I'm a classic Type-A personality.

After about ten years of private practice, I would like to start another career—namely, law school teaching. I received such an overture when it became known publicly that I was looking at various career options. It came from a very prestigious university—one of the finest, if not *the* finest, in the nation. And my response was, "Not yet." But I do hope to pursue such a career in the not too distant future.

Let me add this final point. The place I want to teach is not my alma mater but Howard University. I want to put something back. I've been very, very fortunate. I've been blessed. I'd like to extend a helping hand to others. And the way I'd like to do that is by teaching at Howard. Teaching there would give me tremendous satisfaction.

Richard C. Erwin

The Courts as Policy Makers

Richard C. Erwin was born August 23, 1923, in Marion, North Carolina. He attended Johnson C. Smith University, from which he earned a Bachelor of Arts degree in 1947 (after serving three years in the United States Army). He later enrolled in Howard University School of Law, receiving a Bachelor of Laws degree in 1951. He also holds honorary Doctor of Laws degrees from Pfeiffer College and Johnson C. Smith University, his alma mater.

Prior to Erwin's appointment as United States District Court judge for the Middle District of North Carolina in 1980, he served as a judge on the North Carolina Court of Appeals (1978-1980), becoming the first Black in the history of North Carolina to win a statewide race for any elective office. When he stood for election in November 1978, he received more than 60 percent of the vote. He elective positions. He was a member of the Winston-Salem/Forsyth Associations and as president of the Forsyth County Bar Association. He was involved in the private practice of law in Winston-Salem, from 1951 to 1977.

In addition to his judicial experience, Erwin has held a variety of elective positions. He was a member of the Winston-Salem/Forsyth County School Board and a member of the North Carolina General Assembly. He has served as a member of the North Carolina Penal Study Commission, the General Statutes Commission, and the Steering Committee to initiate the Constitution Study Commission.

Erwin's commitment to education is reflected in several other positions he has held, including service as a member of: the Board of Visitors of Johnson C. Smith University, the Board of Visitors of North Carolina Central University School of Law, the Board of Visitors of the Divinity School of Duke University, and the Board of Trustees of Bennett College (on which he served as chairman).

JE: Can you briefly trace the career steps which led to your appointment as a United States District Court judge for the Middle District of North Carolina?

RE: Yes. I finished high school in Marion, North Carolina in 1940. Thereafter, I attended Johnson C. Smith University in Charlotte, from September 1940 until April 1943, at which time I was inducted into the United States Army. I served a three-year hitch in the army and returned to Smith in the summer of 1946, completing my studies in June 1947.

After finishing college, I stayed out one year. Then I entered Howard University School of Law in Washington, D.C., in the fall of 1948. I completed my studies in 1951 and took the North Carolina bar that same year. Shortly thereafter, I established a private law practice in Winston-Salem and remained in private practice until December 1977, at which time I was appointed to the North Carolina Court of Appeals.

During the period 1951 to 1977, I was involved in a variety of activities, in addition to the practice of law. I held many positions within the United Methodist Church. I served on the Winston-Salem Board of Education, which was later consolidated with the Forsyth County Board of Education. In 1968, the board was changed from an appointed to an elected board, at which point I decided not to run. I later became involved in the Citizens Coalition of Forsyth County, which was the successor to the Urban Coalition of Winston-Salem. I served as a member of the Winston-Salem Foundation, a public charity in Winston-Salem. I also served as president of the Forsyth County Bar Association, and, in 1974, I was elected to a seat in the North Carolina General Assembly. I served in the 1975 session, the 1976 short session, and was re-elected in 1976 for the 1977 session. I resigned from the General Assembly, effective January 3, 1978, to become a member of the North Carolina Court of Appeals.

In 1977, the General Assembly voted to add a panel to the North Carolina Court of Appeals. The Court of Appeals closely resembles the federal judiciary. It serves as the first echelon of appeals, satisfying the constitutional requirement that, in the event a party is convicted, or a party has a case in court and that party is not satisfied with the trial judge's opinion, that party is entitled to one appeal in a state court—that being the North Carolina Court of Appeals.

I was appointed to the Court of Appeals in January 1978 and was required to stand for election later that year. North Carolina law provides that if a person is appointed to the bench, that person must stand for election in the next general election. In my case, I faced opposition in both the primary and general elections. After winning the general election, I began to hear rumors that I was being considered for a seat on the Fourth Circuit. That proved not to be the case. Shortly thereafter, I was advised that my name had been submitted for a seat on the United States District Court for the Middle District of North Carolina. And, as you know, I was nominated for that position by President Jimmy Carter and confirmed by the United States Senate.

JE: How well did your legal training prepare you to be a judge? Did it prove to be a valuable training ground?

RE: A law school education provides you with the fundamentals and foundations to be successful, whether it is to practice law or go into a law-related position. It introduces you to subjects that demand thought, organization, concentration, and, to an extent, a commitment to community service. As law students, we were taught that, should we do well, we ought to be willing to donate some of our time to public service as opposed to concentrating exclusively on money-making pursuits.

I always shared that view. I come from a religious family. My brother is a Methodist minister. I suppose that may have been one of the reasons why I've always been close to the church. I've always had the feeling that I should be involved in some activity other than simply the practice of law.

JE: Your appointment to the Middle District Court was opposed by North Carolina Senator Jesse Helms, who argued that, as a state legislator, you argued for the repeal of the state's right to work law and that you were too pro-labor. This, in his view, could cloud your objectivity as a judge. How important was Helms's opposition? Did it prove to be a major hurdle?

RE: No, his opposition was not difficult to overcome. His objection to my nomination was, to a large extent, totally irrelevant. I was a member of the General Assembly for approximately three years. During that time, I voted on more than 3,500 bills. In my role as a legislator, I had the responsibility of presenting matters for consideration by the General Assembly. Those bills or ideas came either from me or from my constituents. My role as a legislator was to send them forward with the hope that there would be sufficient support for their adoption. Obviously, I took many stands on the issues which came before the General Assembly. That is a job of a legislator.

The role of a judge is different. A judge is required to follow the law. He does not have the right to proceed in any given direction other than that required by the law. I think you would find in studying my judicial background, that I have followed the spirit and the letter of the law, as opposed to following my own beliefs or preferences.

I am often asked whether I think Senator Helms's opposition was racially motivated. I've never been able to establish that fact. I always tell such persons that they should ask the other side or even Senator Helms. In my opinion, he was sincere in his support of the state's right to work law. But his concern was totally irrelevant to my nomination. I think he went too far. During the hearing, I had an opportunity to talk to him and explain my position. As a result, he finally backed off.

JE: How would you describe your judicial philosophy? Do you view yourself as an advocate of judicial activism or judicial restraint?

RE: That's a difficult question to answer. Although this dichotomy is often raised, it is extremely difficult to define. The rules are very clear: if a case comes before you, and you have jurisdiction, you must hear and decide the case. Now, if you are asking me, do I tend to favor judicial remedies more often than new innovative remedies, then I would probably come closer to the position of judicial restraint. However, I would not describe my own philosophy that way. It doesn't tell you very much about how I view the law or how I weigh the facts in deciding a case.

JE: To be more specific, do you tend to defer more to the state legislature or to the national legislature?

RE: It would depend upon the issue. For example, consider the issue of age discrimination in employment. This involves an act of Congress, and, as such, I would be required to implement the law. So, there's no real problem in this regard. The term "activist" is more applicable where there is no legislation, or where there is discretion as to whether a particular problem falls under a given statute. That's not a problem when the statute is clear. In such cases, you have a remedy. Most of the time, the courts have precedents to govern their decisions.

JE: What qualities should a judge possess? Are these difficult to develop?

RE: Actually, they're very simple. A judge should treat every party in his court as he would like to be treated, were he a party to the case. Basically, it boils down to following "The Golden Rule." Now, to do that, you must be secure in yourself, whether you're right or wrong. Moreover, you must not care what other people may say. If your goal is popularity, then you shouldn't be a judge.

JE: How do you view the importance of such traits as intellectual acumen, technical competence, and research capability? How critical are these attributes?

RE: Obviously, a judge must be able to recognize the problem, identify the relevant issue, and understand the law in order to hand down the correct judgment. I view myself as a technician as opposed to a scholar. It may be good to have a scholar on the Court of Appeals, but such a person may not be well suited for a trial court. As a trial judge, you must follow certain prescribed rules: existing statutes; prior decisions; and rulings of the Supreme Court, Court of Appeals, and District Court. That doesn't leave much room to be a scholar. A scholar is better suited for a court with more discretion.

As a District Court judge, I have discretion—but it's in limited areas, such as evidence or sentencing. You don't have the option of dismissing a case unless you are doing so on the basis of some competent authority.

JE: How would you explain the fact that two courts, hearing the same case, will often reach two entirely different conclusions?

RE: I think it's attributable to the membership of the court, as well as the prevailing public view at the time the opinion is rendered. For example, consider the cases of *Plessy* v. *Ferguson* (1896) and *Brown* v. *Board of Education* (1954). In the former, the Supreme Court held the doctrine of "separate but equal" to be both equal and constitutional. In the latter, it held "separate but equal" to be both unequal and unconstitutional.

In the *Plessy* case, the court held that, as long as a state maintained a separate but equal facility, the separation of the races was constitutional. The court completely reversed itself in the *Brown* case. But bear in mind that when the *Plessy* opinion was rendered, Blacks had been free for less than fifty years. It was very difficult for whites to accept the fact that those people who had built the farms, had worked the land, and who were slaves were actually citizens of the United States. It was equally hard for the Supreme Court to accept this fact. The court simply mirrored the popular sentiment of the country.

JE: As a judge, do you attempt to weigh the impact of your decisions on society, before handing down a ruling?

RE: No. That's not necessary. My job is to decide the issue before me. And if I decide the issue, it is immaterial how society will view that decision. If such considerations enter into your decision, there is a good chance that you may not make it. I'd rather just decide the case and let the chips fall where they may. As a judge, your job is to make the right decision. And after you make it, you're finished with it. Then it's up to the executive branch to enforce it.

JE: As a judge, is it possible to be truly objective—to put aside your own values and beliefs?

RE: It's possible to be objective, but it's not possible to divorce yourself from your past: who you are, what you believe, where you come from. A judge should not be expected to be value free. For example, everyone knows that a black man, born and reared in North Carolina as I was, is likely to have experienced some form of discrimination, particularly if he is my age. Even so, I don't have a problem hearing a case wherein there's a charge of alleged discrimination of a black person by a white employer. And I don't side with one party or another because of race. I try to decide the case on the evidence. You cannot decide a case outside the record.

JE: Do you feel any pressure—from your colleagues or others—when you're ruling on a case?

RE: No. I make my own decisions. If another District Court judge doesn't like it, he can do very little. If the Court of Appeals believes I acted wrongly, they can always reverse my decision. I never solicit advice from colleagues before rendering a decision. Oh, I may ask them about a particular piece of evidence, and whether or not they would admit it, but I never ask them how they would rule in the case. That's my job!

JE: What factors led to your present appointment? Did you expect to be nominated to the Middle District Court?

RE: To become a federal judge, several conditions must exist. First, there must be a vacancy on the court. Second, your politics must reflect that of the President, who makes the appointment. Third, the senator from your state must know you well enough to speak highly of you if your name is proposed. If all three things don't fall into place, you won't be nominated.

Other factors are also important. Certainly, I was helped by the fact that I happened to be a member of a minority. When I first stood for election in 1978, I carried approximately 60 percent of the vote. That proved helpful, as the senator could argue that I had already won the approval of the voters. And, of course, the fact that I was already on the Court of Appeals was also helpful as I possessed actual judicial experience.

JE: Chief Justice Warren Burger has expressed dissatisfaction with the performance of the bar, particularly as it relates to the Supreme Court. How would you rate the skills of the attorneys who come before your court?

RE: Like any other field, there are good attorneys and bad ones. In most civil cases, the lawyers who appear in my court are quite adequate. This is less true in criminal cases, where you may find a larger number of less qualified attorneys. The latter stems from the fact that in criminal court many of the rules and procedures differ from those of the state. And it requires more of a lawyer. For example, if you don't do certain things, your right to do so is considered waived. That can make a big difference.

JE: In your view, would increased minority representation on the federal bench significantly affect the workings and decisions of the court?

RE: I'm not sure it would result in any profound changes. I do believe, however, that the public would—after a given period of time—develop greater confidence in the courts. There are instances, I believe, where a white person would rather be tried by a black judge than a white judge. I think that's understandable, very understandable. This is especially true in cases involving the massive power of the state versus the power of a single individual.

JE: When you consider black judges as a group, do they differ in any significant way from white judges? If so, how?

RE: I think there are differences, but it's a question of degree. I'm not sure how deep those differences actually are. After all, we all must follow the same precedents. We all must read the same rules. We're all governed by the same constitution and statutes. Black judges may, however, be a bit more liberal than white judges in their interpretation of those statutes. But, really, you can't generalize.

JE: Do you believe that the courts should mirror the racial composition of society?

RE: Certainly, I think that should be the goal. But I would not like to see an iron-clad quota system. At times, for example, a president may have made a commitment to a particular individual and should be permitted to honor that commitment. There should be some flexibility in the appointment process. But, excluding such exceptions, I think the courts should reflect the makeup of society. I think it would be good for the courts and good for society.

JE: Many poor people and minorities argue that, because of their lack of representation on the bench, it is less likely that they will receive a fair trial. Do you agree?

RE: I think it's quite natural that they would feel that way. Poor people and minorities are not generally represented in the judiciary. The one thing they have going is that there's a court upstairs—a court to which they can appeal. This ensures that if they receive unfair treatment they can challenge the decision of the lower court.

JE: Is the federal judiciary less committed today than previously to the cause of civil rights?

RE: No. I don't think that's true in the case of the courts. It may be true, however, of the executive branch. The courts have not backtracked in this area, although their focus may be different today.

JE: Are you concerned that the ideological balance of the Supreme Court has shifted dramatically in recent years, to the point that conservatives now dominate the court?

RE: Yes, I'm concerned about it, but it's a fact of life. There's not too much one can do about it.

JE: From your perspective, is the era of affirmative action over, given the decision of the Supreme Court in *Regents of the University of California* v. *Bakke* (1978)?

RE: I don't agree with the court's ruling in the *Bakke* case. If you've been the victim of discrimination and you're behind, then you've got to have a way to catch up. The *Bakke* decision didn't do that. It ignored the historical reality of segregation and the present likelihood of catching up without some form of special consideration. I think the ruling was a mistake.

JE: How do you view the issue of reverse discrimination? Is there such a thing and, if so, is it ever justified?

RE: I'm not sure that reverse discrimination is a valid contention, at least at this time. Bear in mind that what the courts were attempting to do was correct a wrong. Today, the same person who discriminated against minorities is not willing to accept the same treatment. He is not willing to assume responsibility for what his foreparents did. Perhaps the white majority should be required to make some contribution to correcting past inequities. It's alleged that preferential treatment amounts to reverse discrimination. I don't think that's the case. In my opinion, what the courts have attempted to do is to put the disadvantaged on the same footing with those persons who have always enjoyed the advantage. That's not reverse discrimination—that's justice.

JE: Do you believe there should be a permanent "black seat" on the Supreme Court?

RE: No. I would not want to see a permanent "black seat." I do think, however, that there should always be at least one Black on the Supreme Court. But I don't think they should each have to follow the same seat. For example, suppose we were in the midst of a presidential campaign, and the president, knowing that Justice Thurgood Marshall is both old and in declining health, should go ahead and appoint a black person, without regard to the fact that Marshall is still on the court. Then, if Marshall should resign or retire, his seat could be filled by either a black *or* a white person. I just don't believe there ought to be *a* "black seat" or *a* "white seat." However, if that's the only way this goal can be accomplished, then so be it.

JE: In recent years, a spate of books have been published about the Supreme Court, including the best-seller *The Brethren*. Do you think the book presents an accurate picture of the court?

RE: At the appellate level, one can find all types of personalities on the bench. I served on the Court of Appeals with twelve people, and they all had different personalities. They fit various and sundry categories. Still, we found a way to work together. We decided our cases in panels of three. Now, to do it in terms of twelve individuals, I doubt that would be possible, as each judge is entitled to his input. It's highly unlikely that twelve judges would agree on a single opinion.

After all, judges are human beings. They exhibit the same qualities—good and bad—that are common to the rest of the population. Despite this fact, judges must strive to merit the respect of the community. In the end, their greatest power is public acceptance. Judges must act with dignity and decorum. If not, they could seriously undermine the esteem in which they are held.

JE: In that same book, the Supreme Court is described as an elitist institution—that the justices expect and demand deferential treatment and acquiescence. Is this a healthy state of affairs?

RE: It's par for the course. That's how they've been treated over the years. Moreover, presidents have been treated that way. And Congress has been treated that way. I won't criticize them for that. After all, there are only eight justices and one chief justice. There aren't 400 people on the Supreme Court. Why shouldn't they receive the same treatment accorded the President and the Congress? So, no, that doesn't alarm me.

JE: To what extent are Blacks well served by the reapportionment schemes currently in practice in most states?

RE: In the case of North Carolina, I think the impact of the "one person, one vote" principle has begun to be felt. I think we've made considerable progress in this area. In the end, I would like to see us move toward single-member districts. And this should apply to both the House and Senate, if we're serious about equal representation.

JE: Do you believe that multi-member districts and at-large elections weaken minority voting strength?

RE: Yes, there's no doubt about it. The question arises, however, whether there are enough minorities to create a single district or to put that minority in a district where they have a chance of winning. Still, the single-member district promises the greatest results. It's always better for a minority to be a big fish in a small pond than a small fish in a big pond where the likelihood of winning is negligible.

JE: Do you believe that the bar examination discriminates against minority applicants?

RE: Let me answer the question this way. If a black student and a white student have received the same training from the first grade through high school and through college and law school, there ought to be no problem. The problem arises when some of the black students who have attended college and law school have not received an equal education.

There are more poor Blacks attending law school today than there are poor whites. Many of these students fare badly on the bar examination. Part of the problem may be due to poor writing skills or poor communication skills. Many of these students may possess the requisite knowledge—comparable to their white counterparts—but may not be able to explain the answers clearly. Both groups may know the identical amount of law, but the ones with the best writing and communication skills are naturally going to do better on the test. That's the reality. I'm not sure how you offset that advantage.

In addition, other factors also influence bar passage, including such informal factors as who you know, who your parents are, and where you went to school. These factors are especially unfair, as they are often used to reward some students and not others. In the past, these factors have victimized Blacks. Many lack the social and political contacts required to succeed in the legal profession.

JE: Do you favor the passage of the Equal Rights Amendment? If so, why?

RE: Yes. I support the Equal Rights Amendment. Its failure can be attributed, in large part, to the attitudes of white males. They simply don't want women to be as "equal" as they are. They relish the special position which they enjoy. As far as Blacks are concerned, I think that most Blacks understand the importance of equal rights—for women as well as for men—and would, if given an opportunity, vote for the Equal Rights Amendment.

JE: In your view, have the courts eroded the right of privacy in recent years? If so, how?

RE: Yes. A good example of this is *United States* v. *Palmer* (1981), a case which I decided. I think my ruling was correct. The State spent considerable money in investigating the case. Despite the fact that the government agent made a serious error in the case, the State wanted to win a conviction. They found a way around the error by arguing that, at the time Palmer signed the property receipt, he incorrectly identified the building in which the property was seized. The government was oblivious to the question of whether or not the warrant was properly issued.

I think there are some areas, even today, where individuals should enjoy the right to privacy. The courts have continued to chip away at this right, inch by inch, to the point where the individual's right is clearly in jeopardy.

JE: In what area(s) should a citizen's right to privacy be protected?

RE: In his home, in his office, and in his automobile—if he's not violating any motor vehicle laws. As for the latter, if you have something on the front seat, and a policeman looks in and sees it, that comes under one set of rules. But if you have that same item in the trunk, glove compartment, or under the seat, where it cannot be seen, I think your right to privacy ought to be safeguarded.

JE: Do you take a similar view when it comes to the issue of abortion or gay rights?

RE: Yes. I think both should enjoy the full protection of the Constitution. In the end, it boils down to a question of privacy. I'm very reluctant to permit governmental intrusions into these and various other areas. I don't think the government has any business telling men or women what they can or cannot do with their own bodies. That should be a matter of individual choice.

JE: How would you respond to the old adage that "We are a government of laws and not men"?

RE: To me, it means that all activity, generally, is controlled by the Constitution, a statute, or some principle of law and that those who have the responsibility of enforcing the law do so on the basis of these written documents.

Now, with a government of men, a judge could, in a given case, disregard the law and decide the case on the basis of the way he personally felt about the matter. That violates what America is all about. The laws govern the courts. And those persons charged with the responsibility of executing the laws should follow the law and not substitute their own beliefs for what the law says.

JE: Another adage suggests that the courts often follow the election returns—that they tend to mirror the dominant political wisdom of the times. Is this an accurate view?

RE: No. I don't subscribe to that viewpoint, particularly as it relates to the federal judiciary. I know that some courts, particularly state courts, often follow this practice. But that's not the case in the federal courts. After all, why should a court follow the election results? The public is not voting on the law or what it ought to be; they are voting for their elected representatives.

JE: Does it concern you that most Americans know very little about the court system and the legal process? If so, what explains this fact?

RE: I think it stems from two reasons. First, the average citizen is required to vote for too many offices. As a result, he has difficulty understanding the offices for which he's being asked to vote. At the judicial level, there are so many judges running that the public finds it impossible to distinguish between the candidates, let alone the courts. Most voters don't even know the difference between the Court of Appeals and the State Supreme Court.

Second, very little political activity takes place in the judicial arena. When I first ran for judge, a pollster called twelve people before one could properly identify the Court of Appeals. Most judges wage low-key campaigns. As a result, the voters know little or nothing about the various candidates. Moreover, most voters do not know what to look for in picking judges. They don't know how to evaluate the candidates. This exacerbates the problem and contributes to widespread apathy and indifference.

JE: In your view, should all judges be required to stand for election?

RE: I'm not sure. The real issue is not whether judges are elected or appointed; rather, it is what individual or group is going to do the appointing. Once you resolve that issue, you won't have any problem with appointing judges. That was the problem we faced in 1977 in the North Carolina General Assembly. The defense bar said, "We're not going to let the plaintiff bar appoint our judges"; and the plaintiff bar said, "We're not going to let the defense lawyers appoint our judges."

So, once you settle this matter—and write it into the Constitution—I believe the problem will resolve itself. After the initial appointment, I think that perhaps judges should be required to stand for election, provided the legislature can decide the percentage required to win. I'm not sure whether it should be 60 percent, or 65 percent, or whatever.

JE: As a judge who happens to be black, are you generally assigned those cases involving black litigants?

RE: No, not at all. We're assigned cases on the basis of a set formula. No consideration is given to the race of the litigants in terms of who hears the case. It doesn't work that way.

JE: Looking at the federal judiciary today, do you think that Blacks still have good reason to look to the courts with confidence and optimism?

RE: Yes. Had it not been for the federal courts, I suspect we would have faced a serious revolution in this country. The courts have served to diffuse that possibility and demonstrate to all Americans—black and white—that justice is color-blind.

JE: How do you view the problem of school desegregation today? Have the issues changed with the passage of years?

RE: Yes. The problem of school desegregation has changed dramatically since the Supreme Court handed down the *Brown* decision in 1954. There are many new issues today that did not occur to the court back then. Clearly, we still do not have a completely desegregated school system throughout this country. There are large pockets of segregated schools, despite the decisions of the courts.

In this regard, I believe that firm steps ought to be taken—in terms of summary judgment—if such cases come before the court—in order to speed up the process. Then, too, it depends on the nature of the community or the neighborhood. The South has done much better than the North where the problem is much different. This is best seen in the related concepts of *de jure* and *de facto* segregation. The South imposed legal segregation; the North sanctioned unofficial segregation.

JE: As a lifelong resident of North Carolina, do you discern a different attitude toward race today than you did as a boy growing up in the state?

RE: Yes, very much so. Let me give you a good example. In 1946, black people in the community in which I grew up (Marion, North Carolina) were not permitted to vote. In 1948, everything changed and black people could vote for the first time. Everybody knew that the reason was race. When Blacks were finally permitted to vote, all Blacks but one registered—and that person lived in a different precinct. The Democratic Party chairman asked, "Where does he live?" And we told him. He said, "Oh, hell, take him back next week. I forgot to tell the registrar to permit him to register."

Now, compare that with 1978, which was when I stood for election as a judge. The same people in the community said, "When you get ready to open your campaign this fall, we want you to come up here and open it in Marion." And we did. The situation was completely different. The clerk of the court and the registrar of deeds, both of whom were white, poured the tea and the punch at the reception. That wouldn't have happened thirty years before, but it happened then. And, of course, the sheriff and I became good friends. He supported me, and I supported him. The Democratic political establishment in Marion realized that all of the Democratic candidates would benefit from black registration. And so they pushed it. That was a significant change, as far as I am concerned.

JE: In your view, does the death penalty discriminate against the poor and minorities?

RE: Yes. Nearly half of those on death row in North Carolina today are black. And, typically, if you look at most states throughout this country, you will see an overwhelming number of minorities, disproportionate to their numbers in the population.

I doubt that Blacks commit more crimes of this kind. Bear in mind, most police officers and most deputy sheriffs are white persons. I don't know whether they work harder to catch black people than they do white people, or whether the fault lies in the judicial system.

JE: What is your philosophy when it comes to sentencing? Do you tend to hand down long sentences?

RE: My philosophy is very simple: Individuals charged with the same offense, who are similarly situated, should receive roughly the same sentence. That means that you must have a pretty good recollection of the sentences you have handed down in the past. It also means that you must look at the spectrum of possible sentences—that is, the minimum and maximum sentences the law prescribes, and where, in terms of that spectrum, the defendant's conduct falls. Should he receive a heavy sentence, a moderate sentence, or a light sentence?

In the area of drug cases, for example, I tend to favor longer sentences than I did originally—simply because this area of activity is on the increase. Drug dealers are victimizing many poor people, as well as encouraging them to commit serious crimes in order to satisfy their habits. I would not call myself a "hard" judge, but I think I'm hard enough. I impose some fines, particularly in cases where the defendant has the ability to pay. There's no point in imposing a fine if a person can't pay it.

JE: What are the most difficult adjustments you've had to make as a District Court judge?

RE: There are certain habits that you must break if you're going to be a judge. One of the greatest problems I had was my tendency to smile. You cannot, particularly in criminal court, have a smile on your face. That's one of the big things I've had a problem with.

I suppose the other was my tendency to introduce humor into the proceedings. That's all right in a civil case but not in a criminal proceeding. I often made humorous remarks because I felt the situation warranted it. But I probably should not have done so. I've had to learn to be more stern.

JE: Not long ago, civil rights attorney Julius Chambers bemoaned the fact that fewer and fewer black lawyers are choosing to specialize in civil rights litigation. Does this trend disturb you?

RE: Yes, it does. I feel that the change in the economy and the expenses required to maintain a law office are so significant that many young lawyers are more likely than not to look for cases which will generate revenue quicker than a long, drawn-out civil rights case. Civil rights cases are harder and less lucrative, which serves as a damper.

Today, we have a new generation of civil rights lawyers, many of whom will take cases where there's only a borderline prospect of recovery. I don't object to their taking such cases, but I believe the plaintiff at least ought to be willing to pay their expenses. And, in the event of recovery, I try to allow a fee sufficiently large to reward them for their efforts. In truth, there's very little money in civil rights litigation, which encourages many lawyers to take peripheral cases in order to survive. It's a trend I don't like.

JE: When you fantasize about your own career, do you ever fantasize about the possibility of an appointment to the Supreme Court?

RE: No. It's highly unlikely that a District Court judge would ever be appointed to the Supreme Court. That has never occurred. You don't pass over all the other circuit judges in the country. You might think about being appointed to the Fourth Circuit if a vacancy should occur, but you've got to get to the Court of Appeals before you can realistically think about a Supreme Court appointment.

JE: Have you given much thought, then, to being appointed to the Court of Appeals?

RE: As I've stated, that's the position for which I was initially considered. No, I don't give it much thought; really I don't. If I were offered the appointment, I'd have to make a decision. But I'm not sure I'd take it.

JE: What is the appeal of being a judge, as opposed to being a legislator?

RE: That's easy. How long would I last as a legislator? I'd have to run every two years. No, I prefer being a judge. I would trade my judgeship for a seat in the United States Senate but not for a seat in the State Senate or General Assembly. There are several advantages to being a judge, one of which is that you don't have to deal with the political vagaries of elective office.

JE: Finally, what do you most like about being a judge? How would you like to be remembered?

RE: Generally, I very much enjoy my work. Of course, there are frustrations, like any other job. But the satisfactions far outweigh the drawbacks. Most of all, being a judge gives me the opportunity to serve. And that's a good feeling. It's satisfying to know that you played a small part in making the system work. My goal is to ensure that every citizen, regardless of race, color, or creed, receives a fair shake. And, after all, isn't that what the law is all about?

Julius LeVonne Chambers
Correcting Political Inequities

Julius LeVonne Chambers was born on October 6, 1936, in Mt. Gilead, North Carolina. He attended North Carolina College at Durham (now North Carolina Central University) and received a Bachelor of Arts degree in history in 1958. He then went to the University of Michigan, earning a Master of Arts degree in history in 1959. Upon graduation, he attended the University of North Carolina School of Law, receiving a Bachelor of Laws degree in 1962. After completing his degree, he was appointed as a teaching associate and taught first year classes at Columbia University School of Law from which he also received a Master of Laws degree in 1963.

Chambers was appointed the first legal intern with the NAACP Legal Defense and Educational Fund in 1963 to 1964 and worked principally in civil rights cases in Virginia, North Carolina, Georgia, and Alabama. His tenure with the Legal Defense Fund was followed by several law-related positions including: guest instructor at Harvard University; lecturer at the University of Virginia, Columbia University, and the University of Pennsylvania; member of the Inter-Government Task Force for the City of Charlotte; chairman of the board of the Charlotte Bureau on Employment Training and Placement; and United States commissioner for the Western District of North Carolina.

In 1963, Chambers set up private practice in Charlotte, North Carolina. He has worked primarily in the civil rights area and is presently senior partner in the law firm of Chambers, Ferguson, Watt, Wallas, and Adkins. He is a member of the American Bar Association, the National Bar Association, the North Carolina State Bar Association, and the North Carolina Association of Black Lawyers.

Chambers serves on numerous committees and commissions. Among them are the Constitutional Review Committee of the North Carolina Bar Association, the Board of Trustees of the Center for Law and Social Policy, and the Board of Directors of the National Health Law Program. He is president of the NAACP Legal Defense and Educational Fund.

Chambers has argued several major civil rights cases, including the landmark case of *Swann* v. *Charlotte-Mecklenburg Board of Education* (1971), in which the Supreme Court affirmed a comprehensive district court desegregation order for Charlotte, North Carolina. In doing so, the court called for the desegregation of the public schools, necessitating a comprehensive plan of cross-town busing.

JE: Can you discuss those early events and forces which most shaped your view of yourself and the world around you?

JC: Yes. I was born in 1936 in Montgomery County, a small rural area of North Carolina, and attended elementary and secondary school there, graduating from high school in 1954. During that period, society—particularly in the South—was racially segregated, and the community in which I was raised was very poor. My father was an automobile mechanic and, ever since I can remember, was engaged in a business of his own, first running a garage and, later, a garage service station. Like most kids of that period, I did the kinds of things that young people do in a very limited environment with limited opportunities.

JE: Did your family take an active interest in politics? If so, what did they teach you about the political system?

JC: With my father, politics was discussed at times—particularly in terms of would-be candidates for president. My father was not too interested in state and local government, perhaps because Blacks were actively discouraged from participating in the political process. Blacks saw more opportunity and felt a greater obligation to vote in presidential elections. As you recall, during that period, America was just coming out of the Depression. There was some interest among Blacks in trying to influence national events. On the other hand, there was a feeling that not very much could be done, statewide, to change things. As a result, we had little interest in state and local politics.

JE: At what point did you first develop an interest in politics? What provoked your interest?

JC: It first blossomed, I think, in high school, when I began to develop an interest in student politics. I served as president of the student government association during my junior and senior years. My interest flowered further in college, when I became deeply involved in student politics and, subsequently, in politics off campus. I served as a class officer in college, and as president of the student body for two years (during my junior and senior years). I was also active in the student state legislature and the national student association. I did not, however, become involved in any state or national political campaign during that period, although I was increasingly interested in such matters. My interest really took hold in law school when I became fascinated with state and local politics. That was during the period of the sit-ins, when there was a growing interest among young people, particularly Blacks, in the possibilities of elective office and influencing state and national elections.

JE: When did you first give serious thought to becoming a lawyer?

JC: I first entertained the thought several years prior to law school. I had had several personal experiences that led me to want to serve the needs of minorities and disadvantaged people who weren't able to afford counsel, and who were, in fact, badly represented.

Let me give you an example. While I was in high school, my father needed a lawyer to assist him in collecting a debt. He was unable to retain counsel. That experience caused me to appreciate the need of Blacks to have adequate counsel.

Other examples also come to mind. When I was in college, I had occasion to ride a bus from Durham to my home and was ordered to move from the front of the bus to the back. I contacted the NAACP, requesting assistance in challenging that practice (that was several years before the Montgomery Bus Boycott). I was advised that there wasn't anything the NAACP could do, although it was sympathetic to the problem. Again, I felt that the civil rights organizations should have been able to do more in attacking discriminatory practices. These and other experiences stimulated my interest in the law and strengthened my desire to become a lawyer.

JE: Did you know any black lawyers in Montgomery County? If so, did they influence your decision to become a lawyer?

JC: There were *no* black lawyers in Montgomery County. The black lawyers I knew lived in other parts of the state. For example, I knew Conrad Pearson in Durham, who was associated with the NAACP Legal Defense and Educational Fund. I also knew Floyd McKissick who graduated from law school later. And when I was at North Carolina College at Durham, I knew several people who had graduated from law school and were practicing law.

JE: Did you believe, from the very beginning, that you would succeed as a lawyer—that you had what it took to overcome the obstacles that stood in your way?

JC: Like most law school students, I had certain fears and anxieties, particularly the first year. Most people are apprehensive about pursuing an unknown field of study. None of my family had been lawyers, and, as I've said, I had little contact with lawyers, black or white.

Moreover, I had no real understanding of the law or, for that matter, what law school entailed. So the first year of law school was quite a challenge. After that, I felt that I knew how to study, what the professors expected, and how to compete in a law school environment. Throughout the three years I was there, I spent a substantial portion of my time studying and trying to be as well prepared as possible. But I was not as apprehensive the last two years. I had a much better handle on the subject itself as well as on the demands of law school.

JE: As a college student, were you actively involved in the civil rights movement?

JC: No, not as an undergraduate. I worked closely with a friend who was president of the student government association at the University of North Carolina–Chapel Hill. We worked with the student state legislature. But I was never actively involved in the sit-ins or demonstrations. Moreover, as a law student, I was discouraged from participating in such activities, for fear that it would hurt my chances of becoming a lawyer. At that time, passing the bar was a bit more subjective, and open to abuse, than it is presently.

JE: Why did you choose to attend the University of North Carolina School of Law? How well did it prepare you to practice law?

JC: Chapel Hill was my second or third choice. I much preferred the University of Michigan, where I had been a graduate student. However, Michigan had its quota of minority students for law school. I was encouraged by the then dean of admissions at Michigan to attend Howard or North Carolina Central or Texas Southern or Southern University. At that point, I looked at Chapel Hill and thought seriously about what one should consider in selecting a law school.

I intended to practice law in North Carolina. I appreciated that most of the judges and, in fact, most of the lawyers were graduates of Chapel Hill. I also knew that Chapel Hill devoted considerably more attention to North Carolina law than did the other schools. I felt that Chapel Hill would afford me a better legal education, a greater opportunity to make contacts, and a more solid foundation to practice law in the state. As a result, I selected Chapel Hill.

JE: How would you assess the quality of instruction you received?

JC: I think it served me well. I know that other schools, such as Harvard, Yale, or Columbia, would have offered more competition—that they would have prepared me better, perhaps, for a federal or national practice. But given my objectives, Chapel Hill proved to be a wiser choice. Moreover, my horizons were not as broad as they are now.

At that time, I anticipated practicing in North Carolina and specializing in civil rights litigation, but I expected that I would have to practice mostly state law in order to survive. Civil rights was not a lucrative area in which to specialize. One also had to do the bread-and-butter type of litigation.

JE: Did any particular lawyer or judge influence your view of the law and your role as a lawyer?

JC: I was very impressed with Dean Henry Brandeis at Chapel Hill and with Dan Pollit at that same institution. I was similarly impressed with Albert Turner, who was dean of North Carolina Central.

I was discouraged by several of my professors at Chapel Hill from specializing in civil rights litigation because of the stigma attached to that type of law. But I had watched Dean Brandeis in his role at the law school and in his private life and was very much impressed. Dan Pollit had been actively involved in the area of civil rights and civil liberties, which also impressed me. Their activities, I think, persuaded me that it was possible to make law responsive to the needs of minorities and the disadvantaged.

JE: Did these two men serve as role models for the kind of lawyer you hoped to become?

JC: Yes. And others—not associated with the school—also had a profound influence on my view of the law. They saw the law as a means for improving opportunities for the powerless and dispossessed. They would look at a state constitution or a federal statute and talk about how that document might be interpreted in order to effect social change—change that was not generally accepted at the time. Another major influence was Thurgood Marshall, who emphasized the importance of using the law as a means of promoting rights and opportunities. As a law student, I often met with other students to discuss how we could contribute to that effort.

JE: Did you personally know Thurgood Marshall? If so, how did he impress you?

JC: I first became acquainted with Marshall in 1961. After I was elected editor of the Law Review, I attended a meeting of the Legal Defense Fund where I had an opportunity to meet Marshall and talk to him about the possibility of joining the organization.

As for Marshall himself, I was very impressed with his leadership ability, his commitment to recruiting lawyers and non-lawyers into the movement, his understanding of the direction the movement should take, and the boundless time and effort which he invested in the cause.

I was similarly impressed with his legal ability, his personality, and his talent for swaying people. He was the inspiration behind the Legal

Defense Fund. His objective was to recruit young lawyers into the organization, involve them in civil rights litigation, and encourage them to specialize outside the organization in civil rights matters.

My admiration for him has grown with the years. He has continued to pursue these goals and has made a significant contribution to this area of the law and law generally. He has served as a role model for large numbers of lawyers, particularly minority lawyers. Minority lawyers can look to him, to William H. Hastie, and to Charles Hamilton Houston, for example, and say that it's possible to accomplish something positive, to make a contribution. And Marshall has done well in that regard. As the only black Supreme Court justice, he has meant much to minority lawyers and to minorities generally. He has proved that it's possible for anyone to achieve regardless of color.

JE: Do you think there should be a permanent "black seat" on the Supreme Court?

JC: It very much depends on who's president at the time, just as the president in power at the time Justice Abe Fortas resigned from the bench, for example, decided that there shouldn't be a permanent "Jewish seat." President Reagan could easily decide that there should not be a permanent "black seat." So I think it depends, to a very large extent, on who is president at the time. Too frequently, whites satisfy their guilt by moving a Black into a position and saying, "See, I'm not prejudiced," and then fail to appoint another Black once that person leaves the scene. It's quite possible that once Marshall steps down, whoever is president will decide not to appoint a Black to replace him.

JE: Upon graduation from law school, you served as a legal intern for the Legal Defense Fund. What did that experience teach you about the law?

JC: It was a real eye-opener. I served as an intern during the sit-ins and demonstrations—at the time when Martin Luther King, Jr. was leading the civil rights movement. At the time, the Legal Defense Fund was inundated with all kinds of litigation. That experience exposed me to the real practice of law. I hadn't had anything like that in law school—that is, how one might develop legal theories to deal with unexpected and unusual situations. For example, at the time I was in law school, trespass was considered a routine criminal prosecution. I could either forbid someone to come on my property, or I could tell someone to get off after he or she had come on my property. With the advent of the sit-ins, we were forced to develop new theories of how the Constitution or federal statutes limited state application of the trespass law, and we ended up with public purpose being served by private businesses that warranted a different application of the trespass law. Several cases grew out of the sit-ins, resulting in modifications of the trespass law, even in North Carolina, that have changed what people view as the appropriate and legal means for directing someone off one's property.

I also saw how the Constitution evolved, with the "separate but equal" theory to *Brown* v. *Board of Education* (1954), and then how *Brown* was to be interpreted over the years to include not just schools but all places of public accommodation.

Not all of this happened during my year with the Legal Defense Fund, but the approach, the planning, the outreach, and the process were things that I experienced firsthand that year. It was all quite helpful.

JE: How do you view the often-quoted adage that ours is "a system of laws and not of men"?

JC: Somewhat skeptically. I know, at least in the public law area, that the courts are frequently influenced by public opinion. The Supreme Court, for example, moves back and forth, depending on public acceptance or reaction to decisions of the court. Lower federal courts and state courts are also influenced by public opinion and, in some cases, much more than I think is appropriate. When I see that, I begin to ask whether we are a government of men and not law.

There are, however, some judges who, despite public opinion, are brave enough to render decisions that reflect judicial courage. On the other hand, there are others who, for a variety of reasons, are reluctant to do so, at least at a pace that some people would like to see.

I observed instances of the latter during the school desegregation period, which, in some areas, is ongoing. I observed the reluctance of the courts to apply *Brown* to require desegregation of schools—so reluctant that it took 15 or more years before they ordered the schools to desegregate. Then, to see the Supreme Court back off of that commitment due to vocal citizen opposition to busing was quite disturbing. So as a general proposition, we might say that ours is a nation of laws and not of men. But in reality, one must appreciate the fact that law does not interpret itself—men must interpret it. In that sense, the law is man-made and interpreted by man. It means what man says it means.

JE: As you view it, should the law be used to effect social change?

JC: Our system of government is composed of three branches, with the legislature constitutionally empowered to make law and regulate the activities of people. We can all appreciate that the legislature, elected by popular vote, is sometimes unable to do what is right or what is fair. In such cases, I believe the courts have the responsibility of declaring what the law should be in terms of the governance of men. The courts must play this role, especially in the public and private law areas, because there are times when the legislature is unable even to decide what a contract should be—for example, a contract governing the private activities of people. In that sense, I think, the courts have to step in and decide whether the legislature has been fair to minorities and the disadvantaged, and if they conclude that it has not been, to require that the legislature act to ensure opportunities for the underprivileged. Unfortunately, when the courts assume such a posture, they are frequently charged with exceeding their constitutional authority. There are times, however, when the courts must take an activist position. When the courts see evidence that the legislature is beginning to respond, they must step back and allow that body to act and decide.

This is best illustrated by what is happening in the area of voting rights, where we have the courts becoming more active in ensuring that all citizens are allowed to participate on an equal basis in electing their representatives. If we really want a less active court, we should ensure that the legislature is fairly representative of all people within a particular state or nation.

So I see the courts having to implement the evolution of law when the legislature is unable to act and/or when the executive will not act to ensure that all people are guaranteed equal protection under the law. To do less would be a violation of the constitutional mandate of the courts.

JE: Do you believe that justice is blind—oblivious to color, status, influence, and wealth? Is such objectivity even possible?

JC: I think that status and position do, at times, influence judicial decisions. I think it's unfortunate, but I think it's important to recognize that fact. After all, judges are human. They like to be liked. They like to socialize. They like to intermingle.

Additionally, judges have grown up like I have. They've been exposed to various experiences. If their experiences with certain people and groups have been positive, they tend to believe in such people and groups. If, for example, they've been taught not to associate with members of a minority, and that's how they've been raised, then that's how they will behave as judges. They cannot divorce themselves from their backgrounds. They're products of their environment and upbringing. It's difficult, if not impossible, for judges to separate themselves from the forces which shaped them. And I think that their experiences will affect how they decide various cases.

As a lawyer, some of the things I've been taught about dealing with judges are the need to appreciate the history or background of each judge and the need to develop a case that will help him to appreciate the need for some change or relief in a particular area. A lawyer must understand the background of the judge—what he thinks, how he reacts, what he values. These factors play a salient role in the decisions he renders. Not to understand these forces is both naive and, at times, dangerous.

JE: At what point in your legal education did you decide you wanted to specialize in civil rights litigation?

JC: It occurred during law school. I was among the first group of Blacks, although I wasn't *the* first, to go to law school at Chapel Hill. Floyd McKissick and others preceded me, I suppose, by five or six years. But, at the time, Blacks at the law school were experiencing a number of problems. This was at the outset of the civil rights movement of the 1960s, and there was an urgent need for lawyers to represent the civil rights activists. At that point, I felt an obligation to use whatever ability I had to play a role in trying to effect some change, however small, in society. I appreciated that, despite my training, I was still just a minority lawyer. That was brought home quite forcefully during my last year of law school when I applied for employment with a number of law firms across the state. Despite what I considered to be my qualifications, I failed to secure employment. No white firm was interested in hiring a black lawyer at that time. And so I saw that, unless there was a substantial change in society, I would be victimized, as would other Blacks who came along later. It seemed to me that it was better to devote my life to trying to effect that change than to trying to ignore what I knew existed.

JE: What qualities, in your view, make you a good lawyer?

JC: I don't really like to talk about myself. There are, however, some qualities that might have contributed to my success—namely, that I studied hard, I took my work seriously, and I participated actively.

Since that time, I have worked hard to perfect my skills. I continue to study the law and its development. I try to study those theorists and practitioners who are involved in the definition of the law. And I think that helps me to understand the law and use it in ways that are socially responsible. Moreover, as a courtroom lawyer, it is vital to be prepared—to organize a case effectively. I try to use those skills developed in law school to prepare the strongest case possible. That requires time, effort, and organization.

JE: How would you respond to the charge that the legal system is stacked against black Americans?

JC: I would not accept such a broad statement. I think it's difficult for the poor and the disadvantaged, regardless of color, to obtain equal justice—at least, as a general proposition. But I don't think the failings of the system are limited only to racial and religious minorities. I think they pervade the whole society.

When I first started out as a lawyer, I would have accepted that premise without question. But things have changed and continue to change. Today, we have many black judges on the bench. We have Blacks in the prosecutor's office. And we have Blacks in the clerk's office. That wasn't the case twenty years ago.

Moreover, many white judges are much more sympathetic today to the plight of the minorities and the disadvantaged. For example, in Charlotte, the state district court, the present court is much better than it was five or ten years ago.

So while certainly there are some judges who still harbor various prejudices, the overall picture is much improved. Although the courts are much more committed to fairness and equity, I do not mean to suggest that judges are completely free of prejudice. But the situation is considerably better.

In addition, public attitudes have changed in profound ways. Citizens are much more sensitive to the injustices of the legal system. They are not afraid to speak out when such injustices occur. The attitudes of the media have also contributed to public enlightenment. The media are much more vigilant today. They frequently report injustices and call attention to judicial wrongdoing.

There are, however, several problems that make it difficult for the poor and the disadvantaged to receive fair and equal justice. For one thing, going to court is expensive. And that disturbs me. In fact, it's so expensive that I doubt most people can afford to pay for competent legal representation. In criminal cases, the costs of conducting an investigation, calling witnesses, and paying lawyers' fees make it increasingly difficult for a person to afford counsel. This problem is offset, to some extent, by the public defender system. It is further mitigated by the Legal Services Corporation—which President Reagan wants to eliminate. Still, there are several means available to offset the problem of escalating legal costs. It's important that we do everything possible to ensure the equal administration of justice. The system is not perfect. We have still not achieved the goal of equal justice. There is the danger, despite the protections I've mentioned, that the poor and the disadvantaged may not receive equal justice. We must be on guard against that. In short, the system is not perfect, nor is it bankrupt. The truth lies somewhere in between.

JE: In recent years, you've spoken out vigorously against local at-large elections. Why?

JC: I think that local at-large elections of public officials foster the same type of apathy and indifference that we have witnessed at the state level. In this regard, we have filed several lawsuits to ban at-large elections. We support district representation in local elections as well as state contests because it serves to heighten citizen interest and involvement. District representation makes people feel that they're part of the government. People know their representative. And that promotes good government.

JE: You've also advocated the elimination of state legislative districts with more than one senator or representative. To what extent do these districts dilute black voting strength?

JC: Obviously, we must talk in generalities, because some districts contain few if any Blacks. But, generally, where we have at-large elections, or multi-member districts, Blacks are unable, for a variety of reasons, to participate meaningfully in the electoral system.

I mentioned earlier, if you recall, that my father was less involved in state politics than in presidential politics, because he didn't think that his vote would have any impact on what happened. Politicians were elected regardless of what he said or did. I think the same thing affects people, particularly minorities, in multi-member districts where they are significantly outnumbered. They can't elect candidates or even influence the outcome of the election. Once we add to that such devices as bloc voting or numbered seats or majority vote requirements, it is clear that minorities are in a disadvantaged position. So, multi-member districts, I think, limit opportunities for minorities to participate in the electoral system.

JE: What can and should be done to promote political access for black Americans?

JC: One is district representation, about which I've already spoken. Single-member districts would be a great improvement. Another is getting Blacks more involved in the political system itself—encouraging Blacks to run for office and better appreciate the importance of elected officials. The election of Harvey Gantt as mayor of Charlotte is a good example of what can be done in this regard.

JE: Are you satisfied with the progress that Blacks have made in terms of elective office?

JC: Despite considerable progress in this area, we have a long way to go. We must remember, however, that Blacks are still a minority—that Blacks are not registered to the same extent as whites. Moreover, Blacks do not vote in large numbers as do whites. This has produced a situation in which Blacks have failed to elect public officials proportionate to their numbers in the population.

But that too is an evolving process. It will take time, but it will come. I've been pleased with the growing awareness and interest of Blacks in the electoral process. For example, take the presidential candidacy of Jesse Jackson. Many Blacks were enthusiastic about his candidacy; others were less so. However, as a result of his candidacy, more and more Blacks are now taking an active interest in electoral politics. And that is a good thing. Prior to his candidacy, too many Blacks were sitting on the sidelines. They have now begun to feel more a part of the system.

JE:　How do you respond to the charge that Blacks have erred by aligning themselves, for the most part, with the Democratic Party—that it would be politically wiser for Blacks to penetrate both political parties so that no one party could take the black vote for granted?

JC:　I would like to begin with a caveat. Blacks have not been particularly well served by the Democratic Party. There are far too few Blacks in positions of power and responsibility. This is true, despite the fact that 90-plus percent of Blacks vote democratic.

I think it's a developing process—that while Blacks have made some inroads within the Democratic Party, Blacks still must push for greater representation. The question remains whether Blacks should dissipate their strength by withdrawing their support and joining the Republican Party.

Moreover, if the Republicans really want to promote black participation, they will select candidates who are sympathetic to the interests of minorities and not run candidates who espouse racist views or who adamantly are opposed to virtually every civil rights measure that is proposed.

To tell me that, in order to promote greater influence within the Republican Party, I need to vote for that party, or become active on behalf of candidates who champion such views, strikes me as ludicrous. That course of action doesn't make sense, at least to me.

The problem is that we still need to maximize our influence within the Democratic Party, and to split that vote now could prove detrimental to our long-term progress. In addition, if we were to take that proposition seriously, we ought to be looking at candidates and programs that express sympathy for the plight of black Americans. And I don't see that, at least now, in the Republican Party.

JE:　Would you recommend that Blacks form an independent third party, as they have done, on occasion, in states such as Alabama and Mississippi?

JC:　No. I think that would prove devastating. I don't think there's any possibility of such a movement, nor would I support such an effort. From what I've seen in Alabama, it has not proven effective. I have listened to the third party argument and give it as much credence as I did Marcus Garvey's "Back to Africa" scheme. I just don't think it's feasible.

JE: How would you respond to those who argue that the struggle for equal justice has already been won—that the civil rights movement of the 1960s settled most of the pressing issues involving race?

JC: I think that's a rather limited view of what occurred. As I see it, the courts and most Americans no longer believe in racial segregation. But most people and most courts do not yet appreciate the need for further assimilation and the sharing of power. For example, if we talk about school integration—that is, bringing together Blacks, Hispanics, and whites—we still are sharply divided in terms of what policies would best allow these groups to study together, to live together, to work together. For example, the court decisions I've seen which deal with this problem have been very unsympathetic to the need for special programs to allow Spanish-speaking Americans to learn English, to study mathematics in English or Spanish, or to do whatever is necessary to make educational progress. Likewise, the courts have shown little sympathy for the plight of Blacks in terms of bringing them to a position that will enable them to compete on an equal basis. We impose tests, for example, for the purpose of classification in the schools, not appreciating the difficulty that some Blacks have in taking certain kinds of examinations and not appreciating the possibility of using other measurements for determining students' ability to work in particular contexts.

So, while we have outlawed legal segregation, we have done very little to resolve those problems that remain. For example, North Carolina Central University (a predominantly black institution) and the University of North Carolina–Chapel Hill (a predominantly white institution)—both within a ten mile radius of each other—demonstrate how difficult it is to bring about an integrated student body and an integrated faculty.

Obviously, neither school can say that it will not hire a black or a white faculty member. But what happens once that faculty member is hired? How is he or she treated? How do the students relate to that faculty member? Does the school make a conscious effort to involve that faculty member in the life of the institution? Those are problems that we're still wrestling with today, problems which will remain, I think, for some time to come. However, I don't think the courts have closed their doors to finding solutions to these problems. One can look at places like Detroit, where serious thought was given to a proposed remedy and where the courts talked about possible relief measures. That represents a positive step in the right direction.

JE: Looking back over your career, what do you see as your most important civil rights cases?

JC: I would cite several cases. First, *Coppedge* v. *Franklin County Board of Education* (1965). Filed in 1965, an order was entered in the case in August 1967 holding that, because of the extensive intimidation and harassment of parents and pupils, the school board should be required to institute a plan other than freedom of choice.

This was the first instance of any court in the South requiring that a school board adopt a plan other than freedom of choice for desegregation of schools. The district court directed that the school board institute a geographic attendance plan effective with the 1968–1969 school year. Through the summer, the school board continued to procrastinate, and on August 5, 1968, the court drew its own plan for desegregation of the schools in Franklin County. The school board appealed, and the Fourth Circuit again denied its application for a stay and affirmed the decision of the district court. Faced with this order, the school board assigned students across racial lines to all schools but then segregated the students within the schools. The plaintiffs and the government moved the court for further relief and for contempt and counsel fees. Relief was granted to plaintiffs.

Another important case was *North Carolina Teachers Association* v. *Asheboro City Board of Education* (1965). This case involved the dismissal of twelve black teachers at the close of the 1964–1965 school year. The district court found no discrimination in the dismissal of the teachers. The court of appeals, however, reversed and directed that three of the teachers be reinstated, that five be offered employment for 1968–1969, and that three of the teachers be awarded damages.

Still another case was *Smith* v. *Hill* (1966). This was a vagrancy case, which involved a directive from the recorders court judge to arrest as vagrants all black "loafers" and put them to work in the cotton fields. The district court found that the vagrancy statute under which the plaintiffs were arrested was unconstitutionally vague; enjoined further enforcement of this ordinance; and ordered that the judge, police chief, and arresting officer pay plaintiffs' costs and counsel fees.

Finally, there are two related cases. *Newberne* v. *Duplin County Board of Education* (1966) and *Godwin* v. *Johnston County Board of Education* (1967). These are two instances in which the plaintiffs attempted to impose an obligation upon the state board of education to withhold state funds until the school systems completely desegregated. These proceedings also sought injunctive relief to require affirmative action on the part of the state board of education to require desegregation of the local schools.

JE: Finally, what do you see as the future of civil rights litigation? What types of cases would you like to see adjudicated?

JC: One immediate problem, I think, is preserving what gains we have made in the last decade or so. In terms of the future, we are likely to encounter cases dealing with equal employment, equal educational opportunity, and other related issues.

More important, it is vital that we develop a system whereby the two societies—black and white—can live and work together, appreciating differences that exist among people and using those differences to create a stronger society. This is a difficult problem. It is, I suspect, one that will be the subject of future litigation.

I would like to see more attention directed to training opportunities for minorities and to ensuring that they are able to enroll in college and graduate. Minorities must be able to obtain employment without the hardships they presently face. Advanced education is an important step in that direction.

Another area that concerns me relates to program access. Minorities must be able to take advantage of the opportunities that presently exist. This is not always the case. For example, I know several people who require medical assistance. It's true that we have programs such as Medicare and Medicaid. However, these programs are structured in a manner that makes it difficult for many minorities and disadvantaged people to avail themselves of them. Either they don't qualify, or they can't meet the minimum requirements. That's wrong, terribly wrong. All Americans, regardless of race or income, should be entitled to decent medical care.

Another area is public housing. Yes, we have public housing. But in order to qualify, renters have to earn a certain amount of money. If the program is intended to help the poor, then such requirements don't make sense. These people frequently end up on the streets or in substandard housing. As a society, we must do better. We're willing to spend huge sums of money to kill people, but we're unwilling to spend a similar amount to feed, clothe, and house people. That says something about our priorities. And I don't like what it says.

PART FOUR

Interest Groups

John E. Jacob

Public Policy and
Black Employment

John E. Jacob was born December 16, 1934, in Houston, Texas, and received his Bachelor of Arts and Master of Social Work degrees from Howard University. He is president and chief executive officer of the National Urban League, one of the nation's most respected community-based social service and advocacy agencies. As president, Jacob directs an organization that serves millions of Americans. Structurally, the National Urban League includes a national headquarters in New York City, a Washington Operations Department, a research arm, four regional offices, and affiliates in 113 cities.

Jacob has served as president of the National Urban League since January 1, 1982. Prior to that, he was executive vice-president of the National Urban League, appointed to the post on February 1, 1979, to oversee the daily operations of the organization. From 1975 to 1979, he was president of the Washington, D.C. Urban League and introduced a number of innovative programs, including the first comprehensive study of black community needs. From 1970 to 1975, he served as executive director of the San Diego Urban League, where he vastly expanded the programs and services of that affiliate. Jacob began his Urban League career in 1965 as director of Education and Youth Incentives at the Washington, D.C. Urban League and served in a number of important administrative positions, among them acting executive director and director of Community Organization Training in the Eastern Regional Office of the National Urban League.

In addition to his present duties, Jacob serves as vice-chairman of the Howard University Board of Trustees and as a member of the Board of New York Telephone, National Conference of Christians and Jews, Local Initiatives Support Corporation, New York Foundation, Eisenhower Foundation, American Board of Family Practice, Independent Sector, and Rockefeller University Council.

JE: How would you assess the current state of black America?

JJ: Since the early 1970s, America has been battered by one recession after another. And the last one—the one that everyone says is now over—has left the black community in a continuing state of economic depression.

While white unemployment hovers around 7 percent, Blacks still face official unemployment of around 18 percent. We are half of the teenage unemployed, a third of the discouraged workers, and a third of the poor. Half of all black children are growing up in poor households. The typical black family earns less than the government itself says is an adequate minimal level.

All of this would be bad enough, but it is getting worse. Median real black income has actually dropped by almost 10 percent since 1971. Back in 1972, the typical black family earned 60 percent of the typical white family's income—today it is down to 55 percent.

I could cite scores of statistics, but they won't add to what we already know—that despite the gains of some, the bulk of black Americans are struggling to survive.

JE: To what extent are these problems attributable to government's indifference to the plight of the poor and minorities?

JJ: The government's own figures document that statement. The non-partisan Congressional Budget Office did a study of programs aimed at helping poor people. It found that the federal spending cuts in twenty-six human resource programs hit the poor the hardest. Families earning less than $10,000 a year lost twice as much income and services as higher-income families.

By 1985, spending for those programs will be $110 billion less than it would have been without the cuts. A fourth of that total was axed from key survival programs such as food stamps and welfare. Employment and training programs will be down by 60 percent, and training for the disadvantaged, including youth, will be off by over a third.

Child nutrition programs were cut by 28 percent, while compensatory education for disadvantaged children was reduced by 17 percent.

In human terms, those cuts are devastating. The elimination of public service jobs means that every seven months 600,000 jobless people who might have received temporary work and training will not. Some 325,000 families who received some welfare assistance now receive nothing. Another 350,000 families remained on the rolls, but their benefits were decreased. A million people who were eligible for food stamps no longer qualify for them. About 700,000 fewer students received guaranteed student loans. After cuts were made in the school lunch program, participation dropped by 3 million.

It is cruel to make such massive cuts while preaching that the private sector and a renewed work ethic will provide sufficient opportunities for all Americans. In truth, there isn't enough work to go around: Over 9 million people are jobless, and at least that many more are not counted as part of the labor force but are willing and able to work if the jobs were available.

Nor will the economic recovery change matters much. It certainly won't affect Blacks and Hispanics who are concentrated in the most vulnerable sectors of the economy and for whom recovery simply means moving from depression-level unemployment to recession-level unemployment.

Black people and poor people are caught between a rock and a hard place. They've been squeezed out of the job market at the same time that federal employment and social service programs have been cut to the bone. They've been forced to the edge of survival while the Pentagon has grown fat on bloated defense budgets and while the affluent enjoy tax cuts.

JE: What would you say to those who ask: Why should anyone—other than Blacks and poor people—care about this situation? What implications do these policies pose for the larger society?

JJ: There are two major reasons: First, fairness. Our society derives its legitimacy from the perception that it is fair—that all Americans are equal. When minorities, and most especially the largest minority—Blacks—are singled out for special treatment in the form of disadvantage and limited access to life's essentials, then the viability of our system is in question.

Second, economic self-interest. The millions locked into dependency and need will be unable to buy the homes, the automobiles, and the appliances necessary to keep our economy going. A consumer-based economy cannot thrive when millions of Americans can't afford to pay their rent, much less buy a new car.

Black Americans constitute 12 percent of the population, but their income last year was only 7.3 percent of total income. That's an income deficit of over $100 billion. If the black-white income gap were closed, black families could spend an extra $100 billion on goods and services.

When people earn, they spend. And that's good for business. When people don't earn, they need help. And even with the holes drilled in the federal safety net, that help amounts to many billions of dollars. And that means more people consuming tax dollars instead of more people paying taxes.

JE: The President contends that unemployment is down—that the unemployed number only 8½ million. Doesn't this represent significant progress?

JJ: The President's figures are misleading. The actual figure exceeds 18½ million jobless. There are two kinds of unemployment: the official figures and the real world figures. The official figures count as employed anyone who worked as little as a few hours in the month that the jobs survey was conducted. The official figures exclude from the labor force anyone who works part-time even if they want and need full-time work. The official figures don't count discouraged workers, even though they are willing to work but have given up hope of finding a job.

Underestimating unemployment is easy when officials cook the numbers that way. Simply add to the numbers of workers the involuntary part-timers and subtract from the total labor force the discouraged workers, and you can make the jobless figures look significantly better.

However, the National Urban League has devised a Hidden Unemployment Index drawn from official statistics that gives a different picture of the real world of the American worker. Our latest quarterly report on the social and economic conditions of black Americans—drawn, I remind you from official government statistics—shows that nearly 9½ million workers were officially unemployed in the first quarter of 1984. But there were an additional 2.6 million involuntary part-timers and 6.2 million discouraged workers. So, the real unemployment rate in America is double the official rate.

JE: Is unemployment, as administration proponents argue, color-blind?

JJ: No. Unemployment has a differential effect on the black community. Black workers are far more vulnerable to joblessness. This is not simply because Blacks are still in the last hired, first fired category, but because discrimination, lack of educational and training opportunities, and employer resistance to hiring Blacks are so strong.

Most of us would agree about the economic causes of unemployment and even about the solutions. But unless we take into account the special needs of the most vulnerable of the unemployed—the black Americans who are hit hardest by unemployment—then we aren't really dealing with the problem.

We can implement the Humphrey-Hawkins Act, create new jobs, and all the rest of it—and still find high black unemployment due to union barriers, employer discrimination, and educational and health handicaps traceable to poverty.

So, let's not assume that simply pushing the right buttons will automatically solve the unemployment problem. It won't unless we understand that the American nightmare of racism demands special efforts to overcome black disadvantage. And we should fully understand that black people are acutely aware of their special needs and of their special, negative status in the American scheme of things.

JE: Many experts believe that part of the solution to black unemployment lies in affirmative action. Do you agree?

JJ: Yes. It is the function of affirmative action to provide the temporary shift in priorities to help draw the people on the margin into the mainstream. However, instead of fighting for the primacy of equal opportunity, our government is actually undermining it. The administration is waging open war on affirmative action. It continues to label even the mildest steps to remedy past discrimination and its effects as "quotas." It has gone to court, not to ensure equal opportunity, but to ensure the principle of last hired, first fired. The same administration, for example, that consciously practiced affirmative action by placing a woman on the Supreme Court turned around and asked that same court to deny affirmative action in the hiring of black policemen in New Orleans and black firefighters in Boston.

This administration's philosophy is based on racial neutrality—something that has never existed in America and is impossible to implement without reinforcing minority disadvantage. Its definition of equal opportunity is based solely on individual rights, ensuring the perpetuation of group disadvantage. Blacks have never been discriminated against because of individual attributes but because of their blackness. America has been, and still is, a society that distributes its rewards and its responsibilities on the basis of group classification. Equal opportunity is meaningless if it does not take that into account. It is an empty phrase if it suggests that the power of the law is not needed to redress the balance. It is a hollow promise if it suggests we all can run the race from the same starting line.

This administration's concept of equal opportunity thus ignores history and economics as well as common sense. Affirmative action has become a dirty word in Ronald Reagan's America. But it is an inescapable mechanism to redress past wrongs, to remedy present inequities, and to move a mean-spirited society to a posture of decency and fairness. We cannot allow affirmative action to become lost in a fog of legal technicalities and debate. Strip away all the endless and ultimately meaningless formulations of the problem, and we confront the essence of what affirmative action is all about. President Lyndon Johnson put it well when he stated: "To be black in a white society is not to stand on level and equal ground. While the races may stand side by side, whites stand on history's mountain, and Blacks stand in history's hollow. Until we overcome unequal history, we cannot overcome unequal opportunity."

JE: Is it possible, as you see it, to overcome unequal opportunity? If so, how?

JJ: America will not be restored to greatness unless it comes to grips with the racial facts of life; unless it comes to understand that being poor is different from being rich; that equal opportunity can only come from extending a hand that helps people overcome the disadvantages of race and class.

As the National Urban League's advertising slogan puts it: "Everybody deserves a chance to make it on their own. Everybody!" And making it on your own means the operation of laws and customs to level the track to give everyone an equal chance. It means economic policies that provide jobs of all kinds in a growing economy. It means affirmative action that overcomes the factors that victimize and brutalize whole segments of society. It means that the groups shoved to the margin of our society are finally brought into the mainstream through conscious, deliberate policies to overcome their disadvantage.

Calling anything else "equal opportunity" amounts to mislabeled packaging. Worse, it leads to perpetuation of an America divided between white and black, rich and poor, suburban and urban, employed and unemployed. It leads to an America that discards millions of people along with its own best hopes for the future.

Our system is in peril if large numbers of Americans are excluded from it, if they are denied hope and opportunity, and if they are denied a stake in the future. If we give people opportunity, we give them a stake in our system. They become part of it; they contribute to it. Their lives are no longer desperate but hopeful. Their energies no longer focus on simple survival but on building for the future.

America was built on opportunity. Millions upon millions came to these shores—and are still coming—in search of opportunity. America's opportunities must include the black poor who have been left behind in every great wave that moved the rest of us forward. If America is to retain its greatness it must include those it has excluded; it must open windows of opportunity so that all of us have a stake in this land we have fought for and died for.

We must work together to help build an America that lives up to its ideals; an America that practices what it preaches; an America that truly is the land of opportunity. We must reject the dead voices of the past that preach resistance to affirmative action and distort the meaning of equal opportunity. Instead, we must fight for an America in which all of us—black, brown, yellow, red, and white—share America's bounties and her burdens, her joys and her sorrows, equally.

JE: To meet the challenge of black unemployment, the National Urban League has proposed a Universal Employment and Training system that guarantees productive work to the jobless and training to the unskilled. What are the major features of this program?

JJ: A Universal Employment and Training system would not be a make-work, token program to lower social tensions or to counter dips in the business cycle. Nor would it be just a government hiring program. Instead, a Universal Employment and Training system would be a joint public-private effort that rebuilds our decaying infrastructure, meets the manpower needs of the nation, and draws into the mainstream the millions who have been relegated to the margins of our society.

Just think of the tremendous amount of work to be done in an America where millions are idle. Our national infrastructure is falling apart. We need to repair and replace roads and bridges. We need to revitalize our rail system and ports. We need to build homes, sewer lines, and water systems. A decade of disinvestment forces us to strengthen the economic infrastructure of America if we wish to grow and prosper. And in the process we can clear the weeds from our steel plants and start producing again. We can revive our basic industries that are dying today. We can put millions to work—paying taxes and buying consumer goods.

Just think of the tremendous unmet manpower needs of our economy. There is a shortage of computer technicians, machinists, craftsmen, and a host of other occupations. While millions are jobless, positions are going unfilled because the skills they demand are in short supply. A training system that begins in the schools and extends to public support of private training for real jobs would answer the nation's manpower needs. Our changing economy demands such a system if we are not to lose the high-tech future to foreigners.

This nation cannot afford to waste its human capital. It cannot afford to discard millions of workers whose skills are outmoded. It cannot afford to write off millions of young people now denied the education, health care, and skills that could make them important contributors to a productive economy. And our nation can no longer afford to ignore the skills of its minority citizens. One of five Americans is black, Hispanic, or Asian. In less than 20 years, every fourth American will be non-white.

Can America hope to survive as an economic and world power without finally meeting the needs and aspirations of one-fourth of its population? Can such a large minority continue to be excluded from the mainstream without enormous negative results for the shrinking population?

Obviously not. Nor will tokenism take care of the problem. Even if white Hispanics, assimilated Asians, and the best educated Blacks are grudgingly granted equal opportunities, the numbers of those left behind will overwhelm the system.

The growth of America's minorities offers our nation a marvelous opportunity. Our Universal Employment and Training system will create jobs and bring skills and quality education to people at the margin, enabling America to tap enormous new human resources.

JE: Critics of your proposal cite the enormous costs associated with its implementation. Is this charge valid?

JJ: The Marshall Plan that rebuilt war-torn Europe took 10 percent of the federal budget; today that would come to $90 billion. Does that sound too large? Only to those who have been brainwashed into thinking that unemployment doesn't have its own costs.

For every percentage point of unemployment above 4 percent, we lose about $30 billion in lost taxes and higher social expenditures. So, today's unemployment presents the nation with a hidden bill of about $150 billion in addition to the terrible extra costs of crime, health, and emotional disorders caused by joblessness.

Whenever we talk about job creation or other programs with social implications, there is carping about costs. But what about the benefits? What about the added taxes paid by those who formerly consumed tax dollars? What about the savings to business through improvements in the infrastructure?

Our Universal Employment and Training system would be an investment in America's future, just as building a new plant is an investment in a corporation's future. Businessmen understand the nature of investments, even if politicians do not. That is why I am hopeful the business community will understand the need for this new investment program in America—an investment in human capital and productivity. Business knows it needs to retrain its work force. It knows it needs to recruit new workers with new skills. It knows that its future depends on investing in human capital to compete in the world's markets. Above all, the private sector knows that the free enterprise system cannot survive in a polarized society that keeps millions of minority citizens out of the mainstream.

A Universal Employment and Training system founded on a permanent partnership between government, business, labor, and the voluntary sector would renew America's economy. It would revive the American dream of equal opportunity and economic advancement. It would replace the despair of today with fresh hope for a sound future.

JE: How would you assess the impact of high unemployment on the black family?

JJ: Social scientists have long recognized the link between unemployment, crime, and illness. They've discovered that, long-term, a 1 percent rise in unemployment is associated with 36,000 deaths. The fact is, unemployment kills. We must recognize that. It kills people and it destroys families.

We've seen what unemployment has done to the black family. Twenty-five years ago, three out of four black men were working, and three out of four black families were intact. Today, just a little over half of all black men are working, and just a little over half of all black families are intact.

Anyone concerned about the rise of single-parent families in the black community doesn't have to look further for the reason. Unemployment is tearing black households apart. It prevents men from raising families. It drives women deeper into poverty. It tells young people they have no future.

JE: Many economists argue that full employment is impossible—that the system is incapable of providing sufficient jobs for all Americans. Do you agree?

JJ: No. Full employment is *not* an impossible dream. It is achievable. It must be achieved because the most precious human right is the right to work. Without work, human dignity is diminished, and civil rights becomes an abstraction. Full employment is necessary for stable, balanced economic growth shared by all. Achieving that kind of growth will require concerted action, including a reduction of a budget deficit caused by overspending and undertaxing. The deficit is an obstacle to passage of a full employment policy. Propose job creation and training programs, and you're told, "We can't afford it; the deficit is too high." Because of that deficit, the government's interest payments in 1984 amounted to far more than all of the cuts it made in social programs over the past four years.

We practice a neutron-bomb economic policy that preserves physical capital while destroying jobs. American jobs move offshore to countries where workers are fortunate to receive fifty cents an hour. And then we turn around and say that American labor is priced too high! Too high for what? For survival? Do we want an American labor force at Bangladesh wages? And if we do, who will buy the automobiles and computers rolling off the production lines?

As a result, macroeconomic policies that lower interest rates and enable the private sector to enjoy steady growth, instead of lurching from boom to bust, are part of the solution. But this works only if black workers get their fair share of the private sector's jobs—through increased affirmative action hiring and promotion, through a new emphasis on training the unskilled, and through a serious commitment to hire and train disadvantaged young people.

There must be an iron-clad commitment from the private sector to create opportunities for those it has neglected. But we also know that the private sector has never created enough jobs for all. The private sector needs partners if it is to create enough jobs.

Our partner is government. Full employment demands a clear federal commitment to a public-private program that rebuilds the infrastructure of the nation and provides the basis for future growth. Such a program would create jobs for unemployed skilled workers and for the unskilled. A training component would assure that people who lack skills would acquire them.

Another role for the government is a public service employment program—a good idea that was killed just at the point it was beginning to work well. There is no excuse for understaffed schools and hospitals, for closed libraries, and garbage-strewn parks and streets while millions of unskilled people could be put to useful work.

There's more to a full employment policy. It would include universal training programs for young people, school-to-work transition programs, an urban youth corps, supported work programs, and other targeted efforts.

The key to a successful full-employment policy is a voluntary sector that is an equal partner with government and the private sector. A tragic aspect of current national policy is the disruption of the cooperative bonds between government and the voluntary sector. Voluntary, community-based organizations are an indispensable mediating force between employers with jobs to offer and the unskilled with labor to offer.

Voluntary agencies perform an irreplaceable service as facilitators, administering federal projects to train people and to help them toward independence. Those programs generate more tax revenues than they cost.

JE: Can black America afford to rest its hopes solely on government? Are there things it must do to rectify the present situation?

JJ: A caring, activist government is clearly essential to black progress. But we make a big mistake if we look to government as our sole savior. Of course, government has to be a powerful ally. It has to follow constructive policies. It has to set the tone for national concern.

But we should learn from past experience that government is a weak reed. It can't do the job alone. It changes, and its policies change. Sometimes it makes problems worse as it tries to solve them.

So, government programs are only part of the solution—an essential part, but still just a part. Even as we look to government and to greater private sector action, we must also look to ourselves. For the black community has the strength and self-interest to do something about its own problems, and especially about the problems only Blacks can do something about. We have to get ourselves together—as a community—to cooperate to make our communities better and to help create opportunities for the black poor.

Black people have a strong network of community organizations we can use to work on our behalf. Just think of the good that could be done by our churches, our fraternities and sororities, our black colleges, our press, our social and fraternal organizations, our labor, business, and civil rights groups.

Those institutions are the infrastructure of the black community. Together, they represent the untapped volunteer power to help our communities combat crime, prepare young people for better lives, and help the needy among us. Together, we can work to further economic development in our communities, to help meet the human needs of the most vulnerable of our families—those headed by single women trying to survive in a hostile world. Together, we can work to prevent crime, to improve our schools, to meet community needs ranging from better street lighting to neighborhood health care clinics.

JE: Many critics maintain that the increase in poverty among women and children is attributable to the growth in female-headed households. Do you agree?

JJ: No. That's a description, but not an answer. Those families are poor, not because they are headed by women, but because jobs and training opportunities for disadvantaged single mothers barely exist. And female poverty has a racial dimension, too. Over two-thirds of black female heads of households with children are poor; only about two-fifths of similar white women and their families are poor.

But those female poverty rates are high enough for all groups to make the point that poverty is rapidly becoming feminized. In fact, the National Advisory Council on Economic Opportunity stated: "All other things being equal, if the proportion of the poor who are in female-headed families were to increase at the same rate it did from 1967 to 1977, the poverty population would be composed solely of women and their children by the year 2000."

Central to the issue of female-headed households is the related issue of teenage pregnancy and parenthood. Teenage pregnancy is a serious national problem. But policymakers and the public alike treat the issue in isolation and with a strong dose of morality. Realistic attempts to deal with the problem demand that we see it in the context of the needs and aspirations of young people themselves.

The black community is especially impacted by the problem of teenage pregnancy because of the disproportionate numbers of births to young black mothers. In the past, this problem has led to defensiveness, an understandable reaction, given the racism that permeates our society, and the smug, self-righteous, and condemnatory tone in which black teenage pregnancy has been discussed. But the black community must face this problem. And it is not a moral problem, but a socioeconomic one.

Children born to young mothers tend to be more susceptible to various birth disorders and to higher rates of infant mortality. They are more likely to grow up poor. And their mothers are less likely to acquire the skills to become economically independent.

The facts indicate why the black community is concerned. Nearly one-fourth of all black births occur to teenage mothers, and four-fifths of those occur outside marriage. The birth of a baby often means the end of schooling for adolescent mothers. Forty percent of black female school dropouts leave school because of pregnancy. That's about 45,000 young women per year or more than the number of black women who graduate from college each year. About half of those young mothers never receive their high school diplomas. So, it is not surprising that the majority of adolescent mothers are poor. The median income of households headed by young black women is under $4,000. However, far more white teenagers than black become pregnant, so this is an issue that transcends race. But in this, as in so much else, the impact on blacks is disproportionate.

We have to be concerned that out-of-wedlock births are becoming the norm in many communities. In New York City, one-third of all births are to unmarried mothers—that's triple the rate 20 years ago. In Harlem, four out of five births are to unmarried women. And an alarming proportion of those births are to teenagers. In other cities, the figures are even more disturbing. In Baltimore and in Newark, three out of five births are to unwed mothers. In almost all of our large cities, a similar situation exists.

It is important for us to realize that this is a relatively new situation for black people. Black family ties historically were strong, and families survived the most intense oppression intact. But today, the ravages of discrimination and big-city poverty combine to undermine the strengths of traditional family structures. To the extent that the black extended family continues to nurture its members, there is hope for survival.

But even the extended family is at risk if traditional two-parent families disappear. If that happens, ties of kinship may survive, but the basic family unit will weaken to the point where we will be threatened with becoming a mass of individuals alone in a hostile world.

Black people need the shelter of the family, the unity that brings blood and affection together to nurture and sustain. While individuals can find satisfying and supportive experiences within an extended family or a network of friends, a people needs an institutional structure, and the core of that structure—in every society—is the family.

JE: Do you see an answer to this problem? If so, what?

JJ: We must realize that we are in a race against time. We must marshal community institutions to deal with the crisis. And at the same time, we must make every effort possible to influence national, state, and local governments to respond to the problem.

At the national level, we have witnessed policies that create unemployment to control inflation. Those policies have had a devastating effect on the black community and have significantly harmed families through the loss of jobs and social programs that are so essential to survival.

Instead of helping poor families to climb out of poverty, a self-styled pro-family administration is cutting safety net programs dramatically. It cut $100 billion out of people programs over the past three years. It restructured the tax system to give the affluent tax breaks while the poor pay a higher share of their income in various forms of taxes. And it has concentrated its fire on programs that sustain families— programs that feed the hungry, improve the schools, and provide medical care for infants.

The failings of the federal government are all too familiar, but we make a big mistake if we think Washington is the only government in the country. State and local governments are just as crucial to issues affecting families. They run many of the programs we think of as "federal." They have enormous latitude to decide how to use federal funds under bloc grant regulations. Even without federal monies, they are responsible for programs and practices that have a primary impact on black family life.

For too long, many of us have been running to Washington to fight the fights that we should have fought at home at city hall or the state legislature. We must organize regionally and by state, in order to get local governments to focus on assuming their share of the burdens imposed on them by an uncaring federal government. And the national black organizations must keep up the pressure on Washington to save endangered programs and pass others that will help black families survive the present crisis.

JE: Are you suggesting the need for increased political action— the need to mobilize the political resources of black America?

JJ: Yes. We cannot talk about public policy or about government action without underscoring the importance of getting every eligible black person registered to vote. In fact, I suggest that the first priority on the agenda of anyone concerned with black children and black families is to get out the black vote.

The power of the black vote lies in numbers. If enough Blacks vote, whoever wins will have to relate to us. If we don't vote, both parties will feel free to treat us with their traditional indifference and hostility. We don't have to love the candidate or the party we decide to vote for. Perfection doesn't exist in politics. Compromise is the lifeblood of the political process. But if we don't vote, we won't be part of the decision-making that affects our lives. So, there's no excuse for not voting. Medgar (Evers), Martin (Luther King, Jr.), and the other heroes of the civil rights struggle did not die so that we could sit home and watch white folks vote and make the decisions for us.

We must view black political participation in terms of the long haul. We can't limit ourselves to an effort for just one candidate or just one year. Black empowerment requires a long, hard, painstaking effort in order to build a solid, grass-roots base of mass involvement in the political process.

We can't simply focus on the race for the presidency. We must get people excited about voting for the local candidates who run the schools, police the streets, and zone our neighborhoods. And we can't just get black people excited about voting. We must also get them excited about *running*.

Black political empowerment is a vital part of black efforts to save our families. If, as we have seen, those families are under extraordinary pressures because of the failures of government, then it is up to us to become involved in the political process and make government an instrument that saves families instead of destroying them.

Beyond what government can do, we must focus on what we can do, both as individuals and as members of community-based organizations. The network of black institutions must play a greater role both in advocacy on behalf of the black family and in concrete programmatic ways that provide aid to black families: assistance to help two-parent families stay intact, resources to help single-parent families survive, and programs that help our children to take their rightful place in society.

JE: Does the black community have the institutional and voluntary resources necessary to be effective?

JJ: Yes. Through our efforts, we can build on the existing strengths of black families and the traditions of extended families, mutual caring, and informal support mechanisms. I believe, too, that we can build on the black traditions of discipline, struggle, and concern for family stability.

Every element of our society must deal with that aspect of the problem for which it is best suited. That means government must be supportive, black institutions must marshal volunteer resources, and individual black people must accept responsibility for themselves and for preserving the family values that have helped us to survive. For among the strengths of black families is the strong interest we have in family stability, in acting responsibly, and in preserving the viability of the family unit.

We at the National Urban League have made family survival issues our major priority, focusing on crucial programmatic areas that directly impact black families and young people. Our national, regional, and local organizations have done the same. Together, we have the will and the wisdom to break the cycle of despair that encircles so many young black people today and destroys so many of our families. Together, we have the determination to devise community strategies that enable families to survive and our children to thrive. Together, we can recapture the spirit that has helped black people to overcome the chains of slavery and the bonds of oppression. For our lot has never been an easy one. In every generation black people have come together to work cooperatively to deal with the burdens society has placed on us.

JE: As you view it, how will the new high-tech era affect the fortunes of black America? Does it offer a special opportunity?

JJ: The high-tech future will belong to those who can work at computer terminals, be comfortable with advanced data processing and communications technologies, and have access to the techniques of an information-based economy.

This trend poses a major challenge to the black educational community. It means that black colleges and universities will have to retool. They will have to adjust curricula to the high-tech age and provide students in all disciplines with the fundamentals of technological literacy.

And that challenge is compounded by the financial squeeze most of our institutions face and by the traditional aversion to math, science, and other subjects that are fundamental to the high-tech era. Approximately six-hundred Blacks a year earn Ph.D.'s in education but only 20 to 30 in the physical sciences and engineering and only about half a dozen in math. In 1982, only one black person received a Ph.D. in computer science.

If you look at undergraduate degrees, similar percentages exist. Much as we need educators, social workers, and others skilled in the human and social services, the black future will be limited if we don't have our share of the skills that a high-tech society requires.

How to motivate people to obtain these specialized skills is a problem that has its roots in social disadvantage, inferior public education, and lack of opportunity in elementary and secondary schools. Future physicists and engineers come to college with sound backgrounds in math and the sciences. But most black students have been denied the access to those backgrounds and the encouragement to succeed in those fields.

One of the standard responses to all levels of education is to point the finger at the other guy. The colleges blame the high schools for not preparing students properly. The high schools blame the junior highs. The junior highs blame the elementary schools. And rather than take the blame themselves, the elementary schools blame the students and their parents.

Black educators clearly don't have that luxury. And the black higher education community especially has to forget about who is to blame and concentrate instead on remedying the damage. One way is to strengthen course offerings and the physical infrastructure in order to provide quality education in technology-based disciplines. Beyond that, I think we have the responsibility to work with the local schools to ensure that they provide their students with the capabilities they need to consider high-tech career options.

This challenge should cut across all fields. Not only does the engineering department have to become involved. The education department, also, must ensure that its graduates will be equipped to meet the high demand for technologically literate teachers to teach and to inspire our children.

The high-tech trend hits black people at a time when millions are still functionally illiterate in a society whose complexity demands more than minimal reading, writing, and math skills.

So we've got a lot of running to do simply to catch up. And the more our society changes with the advent of high-tech, the faster we'll have to run.

JE: What are the implications of your comments for higher education? What challenges do they pose?

JJ: In a changing economy, our educational institutions must change to meet the needs of their students. We need to produce individuals whose educations prepare them for a fast-changing world, individuals who are equipped not only with the technical skills, but with the adaptability to survive in a constantly changing economic landscape.

To do that, we must have a more flexible educational system concerned less with screening individuals out and more with developing the full potential latent in each individual. We must especially change the tracking system of post-secondary education. Despite the fact that black college attendance is slipping from earlier highs, Blacks are still heavily concentrated in the community colleges or two-year college programs. Many of those young people are unable to transfer credits to four-year colleges. In effect, the system has tracked them onto a vocational degree and placed barriers in their way if they decide to pursue a bachelor's degree.

Lowered educational expectations and achievements add up to a disadvantage in a restructured economy that places a premium on higher degrees and wider educational experiences. So we cannot speak of equal opportunity in higher education without finding ways that allow students to move freely among post-secondary institutions.

The danger in the trend of economic restructuring is that it takes place at a time when black equality is no longer a national concern. We've seen the effects of past restructuring on black people. We were restructured out of decent jobs when Jim Crow replaced black tradesmen and professionals with whites. We were restructured off the land when agriculture was restructured in the first half of this century. And we were restructured out of teaching and administrative jobs in the desegregation of the 1950s and 1960s.

White America sees restructuring as a step forward; for Blacks it is not so simple. Whether in fact it becomes a step forward for us will depend largely on whether black people have access to quality education at all levels.

JE: In what ways will a restructured economy—the kind that is presently developing—affect the future of black employment?

JJ: That goes back to high-tech, for changing technology has made some industries obsolete and has altered others beyond recognition. The same technological forces that are creating new opportunities for those that have mastered its essentials are changing the structure of the job market. These changes are polarizing the labor market—with some very good jobs at the top, many bad ones at the bottom, and fewer decent jobs in the middle.

The black economic future will be imperiled unless we get our share of the jobs at the top and don't lose ground on the middle-level jobs. Already, we see the effects of the change as lucrative, unionized manufacturing jobs are disappearing. Many black steel and auto workers who enjoyed middle-class incomes will never get back the jobs they lost in the past recession.

Black workers are disproportionately concentrated in the industries where jobs are hemorrhaging. And we are concentrated in the service jobs where we face two threats. First, those jobs may be automated out of existence. Second, Blacks may be squeezed out by displaced white workers or by arbitrary higher qualifications. It's happened before in our history. It may happen again.

So, high-tech is no salvation for Blacks. And it is no salvation for whites, either. If America loses its industrial base, many of those high-tech information jobs will ultimately go down the drain. Our economy is based on mass consumerism—on the premise that most people work, earn, and spend. But if they are not working or if they aren't earning enough, who will buy those goods? Robots don't buy automobiles.

JE: To what extent, if any, have the administration's cutbacks in education undermined black progress?

JJ: The cuts in education aid have tarnished the success story of the 1970s—the improvement in black reading and math scores on standardized tests. That improvement was due to Title I and to compensatory education programs the federal government funded—programs now being cut just as they are beginning to show a payoff.

Federal cuts in student aid impact black institutions and black students. It's no accident that there has been a decline in the proportion of Blacks attending college and in the black attrition rate at predominately white institutions.

Nineteen eighty-four was "The Year of Reports," and one report after another on the state of national education poured from the printing presses. Through all those reports ran one theme—we need to recapture excellence as a national educational goal.

But in spite of all the rhetoric about excellence, none of those reports demonstrated much concern with equity. The National Urban League stands for excellence in education—for all. Excellence and equity are not opposites. We believe that you can't have one without the other. An educational system can turn out more scientists and engineers than General Motors does cars. But if they are drawn from a favored elite while the rest of our students are doomed to semi-literacy, the system itself is far from excellent. In fact, it is a failure.

Equity is not an issue that America can sidestep. For Blacks, it is *the* central concern—equal access to quality education is the prime issue on the black educational agenda. I believe it has to be at the core of national educational policy as well. By pushing the equity issue aside, those reports have helped to encourage national policies that have undermined what little progress America has made toward greater equity.

Those national policies are widening the gap between black and white, rich and poor. The 1985 budget plans to make more cuts in education aid. The official response to the calls for excellence has been school prayer, rhetoric about discipline, and tuition tax credits that would undermine public education.

The government has already deeply slashed higher education funding for minority and low income students. Programs that helped disadvantaged young people succeed in college have been a prime target for the budget cutters. And the Department of Education's proposed restrictions on grants and loans to students will inevitably force many black people to abandon their hopes for higher education.

The programs that provide financial assistance to graduate and professional education have been a special target of the enemies of equal opportunity in higher education. And assistance to struggling black colleges has been confined to lip service: The resources made available to them are not at all proportionate to the needs.

JE: If President Reagan were to call you this morning and ask for your advice in resolving the problems you've delineated, what would you tell him?

JJ: I would tell him the following: "Mr. President, I respectfully submit to you that your policies are not working and have increased the misery in our land. I ask you to free yourself from the chains of ideology and begin again with fresh policies that free the energies and talents of our poor to contribute to a more productive America.

"Mr. President, it is not enough to condemn racism, to visit a black family whose home was attacked by racists, or even to sign the Voting Rights Act your Justice Department lobbied against.

"Mr. President, stop thinking of programs that feed the hungry, educate the young, and train the jobless as spending programs. They are investment programs that will pay off in a healthy, educated, and skilled people capable of restoring America's economic might.

"Finally, Mr. President, our call for a government that protects the weak, nourishes the springs of compassion, and fertilizes the American ideal of equality and justice is a call to leadership and to greatness."

JE: Finally, if you could make a similar plea to the chief executive of one of America's major corporations, what would you say?

JJ: I would say to him: "Mr. Chairman, you cannot be indifferent to the needs of a people dispossessed and in need, people who want to work and who want to give you an honest day's work for an honest day's pay."

"Mr. Chairman, in this time of hardship, re-examine your priorities and respond to the cries of pain from those most in need. Help your great company to go the extra mile to assist the people who don't have leaseback tax benefits, who don't have foreign earnings exemptions, who don't even have an idea of where tomorrow's meal will come from.

"Mr. Chairman, understand that bold words about voluntarism will be just meaningless babble unless our private sector responds to the urgent needs of the forgotten, invisible poor in our society.

"Finally, Mr. Chairman, keep working with us, with the National Urban League, to help move people off the mean streets and the back alleys of urban desperation into the jobs and the training programs they want and need."

Roy Innis

Truth, Lies, and Consequences

Roy Innis was born on June 6, 1934, in St. Croix, Virgin Islands, the second of nine children of Alexander and Georgiana Innis. His father died when Roy was six years old, and his mother completed the move of the family to Harlem in 1947. At sixteen, Innis, who was one of a handful of Blacks at Stuyvesant High School, one of the premier high schools in New York City at that time, lied about his age and joined the army. He attained the rank of sergeant by age seventeen and was honorably discharged at the age of eighteen. He then completed his high school education and entered a four-year baccalaureate program in chemistry at the City College of New York. He subsequently worked as a pharmaceutical chemist at Vick Chemical Company and as a medical chemist at Montefiore Hospital.

Innis became actively involved in the Harlem Chapter of the Congress of Racial Equality (CORE) in 1965, and though he continued to work as a chemist, this profession soon began to play a secondary role in his life. He observed tremendous energy and dedication in Harlem CORE but quickly realized that much of it was "misdirected" and that, if properly channeled, this energy could be a powerful liberating force for black people. He emerged as a strong proponent of black control of major social, political, and economic institutions within the black community and also revived and promoted the basic teachings of Marcus Garvey, the celebrated black nationalist. In an integrated organization unused to, unaware of, and unprepared for such a stand, Innis was viewed as an extremist.

In 1964, Innis was appointed chairman of Harlem CORE's Education Committee. In this post, he became a forceful proponent of community-controlled quality education. Elected chairman of Harlem

CORE in 1963, he campaigned for an independent Board of Education for Harlem, out of which came a proposition presented by CORE to the New York State Legislature.

In the spring of 1967, Innis left his position at Montefiore Hospital to become the first resident fellow at the Metropolitan Applied Research Center, headed by Dr. Kenneth B. Clark. From this point on, his influence and rank in CORE increased rapidly, and he was elected second national vice-chairman in the summer of 1967.

Seeking to turn the new CORE economic ideology into reality, Innis became one of the founders, the main organizer, and the first executive director of the Harlem Commonwealth Council, one of the first black power groups in the country. He served as executive director until his elevation to CORE's associate national directorship.

After Innis became national director in 1968, he attempted to centralize the organization and was solidly endorsed by CORE's National Convention when it adopted a new national constitution in September 1968.

This move reflected Innis's belief that the movement required a strong, unified philosophical commitment; that there was no place for the somewhat loose CORE structure of the past, wherein individual chapter efforts were not coordinated and chapters operated almost independently of the national office.

During the late 1960s and early 1970s, CORE's nationalistic program came into sharper focus. Innis argued that all black people are held together by a common bond—African ancestry—and that it was in the interest of both Africans and African Americans to recognize and utilize that bond. To that end, in 1971, Innis and a delegation of CORE officials undertook an official tour of seven countries in East and West Africa. During the tour, Innis met with several heads of state, including President Julius Nyerere of Tanzania and President Jomo Kenyatta of Kenya. The tour spurred Innis's desire to encourage Blacks in America and worldwide to become more attached to their homeland and to be more responsive to her problems and needs. In 1973, Innis was invited to Uganda, where he was the guest of the Ugandan government which was then headed by Idi Amin. The Ugandan government also invited Innis and the CORE delegation to be an official part of its delegation to the tenth anniversary meeting of the Organization of African Unity (OAU) in May of that year. Thus, Innis became the first black American, or any American, to attend the OAU in this capacity.

In 1978, a small group of ex-CORE officers, spearheaded by "crypto-governmental" agents, sought to oust Innis as national chairman, giving CORE the public appearance of great internal conflict and upheaval. Working in league with former CORE National Director James Farmer, the group brought a series of lawsuits in the New York State Supreme Court challenging Innis's election as head of CORE. These attempts proved unsuccessful. CORE's national membership rejected the group's claim at the National Convention held in September 1978. They retained Innis as national chairman by acclamation from the floor and gave him a mandate to purge the organization and to maintain its viability and goals on behalf of black America. In 1983, the New York Supreme Court handed down a ruling declaring Innis the legitimate head of CORE.

Also in 1978, the attorney general of the State of New York, in collusion with the dissident faction, instigated "a determined war of attrition" against Innis and CORE and nearly crippled the organization. Innis and his staff fought this "ill-disguised" attempt to shut down the organization and eventually won a momentous decision against the State of New York in March 1980. Still, this "war of attrition" against Innis and CORE with New York State and other governmental entities (city, state, and federal) in various guises has persisted. To date, their efforts have failed.

Hampered but undeterred by these challenges, Innis and CORE persevered in their attempts to protect the rights of black Americans. For example, CORE uncovered and pressed an investigation of a major cover-up involving high government officials in the death of a seventeen-year-old black male in Charleston, South Carolina. The United States Justice Department launched an investigation; the chief of police at the time of the killing committed suicide shortly before he was to be questioned by investigators (he was replaced by a black chief); two policemen involved resigned under pressure, one of whom has since disappeared from Charleston; and the youth's mother, with CORE's help, sued the city and won a cash settlement. During this same period, CORE, along with Herbert W. Armstrong and Stanley Rader of the World Wide Church of God, created the People's Self-Help program in the Liberty City area of Miami, Florida, a community ravaged by the rioting touched off by the police killing of Arthur McDuffie.

In 1981, Innis figured prominently in the investigation of the murders of twenty-eight Atlanta black children. Innis launched his own investigation after receiving information that an obscure cult was responsible for the majority of the killings. Based on the on-site data gathered by Innis and CORE staffers, many prominent individuals, including psychologists and private investigators, became convinced that the murders were the work of more than one person.

Setbacks and stumbling blocks notwithstanding, Innis and CORE have continued to "work for the liberation of black people." Some of CORE's many ongoing activities include: management training programs, job banks, a work program for former drug addicts, voter registration, and summer and after-school work programs. Additionally, under Innis's leadership, CORE continues to fight discrimination wherever it occurs—in housing, in the workplace, in the criminal justice system, and in education.

JE: Many political observers have described you as an "old-fashioned black nationalist." Would you describe your philosophy that way?

RI: Yes. Black nationalism is a philosophy which seeks to bind black people together through the creation of a feeling of group identity or peoplehood, which comes from an awareness and acceptance of a common culture, history, values, needs, and interests. Liberation from the oppression of the dominant white group and self-determination are the twin ultimate aims of black nationalism. Black power, which seeks black control of the economic, social, and political institutions operating in black communities, is the pragmatic ideology for the implementation of black nationalism. A lot of individuals call themselves "black nationalists," but they don't know what the word means. Generally, they use the movement as their own private hustles. They call themselves black nationalists; black nationalists call them "pork-chops."

JE: As a black nationalist, do you advocate racial separatism? If so, does this preclude working relationships with the white majority?

RI: No. Adherents of progressive black nationalism do not preclude from predominantly black communities the members of other ethnic groups. They do, however, insist that Blacks have the intrinsic right to full manhood in the American democratic republic. CORE has undertaken the task of creating those institutions through which black people can achieve that goal. Toward this end, the total thrust of CORE's endeavors to build a viable and positive black minority is directed toward self-help bootstrap efforts.

It seems to me that if our country continues on its present catastrophic course, then the vital interests of whites will be destroyed; they are the ones who will lose in the total Armageddon which looms before us.

I say this because I want all Americans to be aware of who will lose if and when black youth become kamikazes. We must clearly understand the difference between the man who commits suicide by hara-kiri—when one Japanese kills himself—and the kamikaze—when one Japanese pilot flies one *Zero* into one American battleship. One Japanese pilot dead; one battleship consisting of thousands of men destroyed. Interests must, of necessity, be bluntly calculated in those terms.

That is why it is in the interests of all black people *and* all white people to support black nationalism. It is the only rational and sane alternative to the racial collision course toward which we are now careening. We must remember that enlightened self-interest is the safest, the healthiest, the most honest, and the most pragmatic motivator of human behavior.

JE: Are you an advocate of racial integration? If not, why?

RI: No. I have never been committed to the philosophy of integration and shall never be committed to its concepts. The narrow and self-righteous interpretation of integration as the only social alternative by both the lower courts and the civil rights establishment has prolonged racial strife and has undermined black progress. An examination of major decisions on school desegration from *Brown* v. *Board of Education* (1954) to the present reveals, surprisingly, that the United States Supreme Court has ordered desegregation while assiduously avoiding reference to integration.

JE: Do you also oppose school integration? If so, on what basis?

RI: I do not oppose it per se. It's extremely important that the Supreme Court's rulings on school desegregation be clearly understood. Confusion on this point has abounded, aided and abetted by those who have fallen into the trap of viewing desegregation as synonymous with integration. Integration is only *one* possible way—not necessarily the best or most pragmatic way—of desegregating and creating a unitary school system. The Constitution mandates desegregation; it does not ordain integration.

In most cases where forced integration has been tried, the same white board of education that once ran the dual school system—one white, one black—is the same board that runs the integrated system. The superintendent of education under the old system becomes the superintendent of education in the new system. The policy makers and managers are therefore the same. Since their negative attitudes toward Blacks and favoritism toward whites remain the same, black parents can hardly expect that any attempt will be made to change the curriculum to reflect the needs of black pupils, or that they will have any say in the running of the school. In other words, even where integration has been tried, the schools remain white-controlled—a white power monopoly.

We must not assume that things will get better with time. The dynamics of *forced* integration are very different from those of *forced* desegregation of hotels, restaurants, buses, and other public facilities and services. These are what might be called transient settings of Blacks and whites sharing or functioning in the same approximate space.

Integrated schools, on the other hand, constitute an ongoing phenomenon that is seen as far more threatening. This is underscored by the fact that the relatively mild and short-lived resistance to the desegregation of public facilities and services was nothing compared to the massive resistance that has been mounted and continues to be mounted against integration of the schools.

Moreover, when integration does occur in the schools, the few strengths Blacks have had are rapidly eroded, so that with time they operate less and less from a position of strength.

Blacks who have supported integration have done so in search of dignity but have found humiliation at the end of the rainbow. They integrate for equality but find they are *together but still unequal*. They have less control and less influence, if that is possible, than ever before. In short, the integration that Blacks experience in most instances, North or South, has proven to be token equality, mere show and pure sham. Integration can be a desirable pathway to desegregation when it is a true and mutual "freedom of choice"—free of coercion from either group involved.

JE: Since you oppose forced school integration, how do you propose to achieve equal educational opportunity?

RI: Over the past few decades in many parts of the country, there has been structurally a movement toward consolidation, toward enlargement and centralization of school systems, rendering them less and less subject to the control of, and more and more removed from, the community and the family.

But a countertrend is now surfacing toward control of schools in relatively smaller districts by cohesive, concerned communities. Such communities must be self-defining, strictly on a voluntary basis, so that any family not wishing to form part of the community must be free to transfer its children to other schools without having to move physically. And, of course, they may not be coercively formed by the state along racial or ethnic or even socioeconomic lines. If they are to exist, they can rest only on the principle of voluntarism.

But a trend toward community control of schools under the conditions mentioned is clearly visible and, in the judgment of many qualified observers, may have highly beneficial educational results, as well as broader desirable consequences, by contributing to other self-reliant and constructive community activities. Some aspects of this trend are represented by voucher and tuition tax credit plans, which may represent positive steps forward.

JE: How do you view those who advocate integration? What are their motivations?

RI: There is the avowed integrationist; there is the romantic, naive, adventuristic revolutionary integrationist; and there is the mickey-mouse, psychedelic, boy-militant, superslick "pseudo-nationalist" closet integrationist. They are all misguided, but frankly, I have more respect for the avowed integrationist. At least he's honest.

JE: What do you see as the principal difference between liberation and revolution? Which point of view do you advocate?

RI: I advocate liberation. There is a great difference between liberation and revolution, revolution being a homogeneous phenomenon—the overthrow of an established government subsequently replaced by another. In essence, it is the effort of a racially or ethnically *similar* people to alter their form of government among themselves as did the French bourgeoisie when they guillotined the French aristocracy during the French Revolution.

Liberation, on the other hand, is a heterogeneous phenomenon; it is a struggle between two racially or ethnically *different* people, with one group casting out or extricating itself from the other.

Recent examples of successful struggles for liberation include the ousting of the British from Kenya and Ghana and the expulsion of the French from Guinea. These three independent nations of Africa are not now politically dominated by any outside power. At this time, black Americans are seeking their salvation through the latter form, liberation, by extricating themselves from the racist social, political, and economic oppression of the United States.

JE: In your view, is black oppression more attributable to race or class?

RI: The order of oppression in America for the black man is race first, class second. Thus, the primary struggle in America is race. Struggle is most effective when it is homogeneous (unmixed); even when conditions compel it to be heterogeneous (mixed), it is still best conducted from a homogeneous base.

The black nationalist's primary commitment is to the struggle for social, political, and economic liberation of black people by any means possible and pragmatic.

The black nationalist may have other important commitments, such as resolving class antagonism through revolutionary struggles within and outside of his group. But while conditions may dictate that he pursue them simultaneously, these struggles must be secondary and tertiary to the main goal of racial liberation.

The romantic revolutionary has an illicit and immature love affair with violence, with the gun as his phallic symbol. He is often irrelevant, but sometimes dangerous, especially to himself. We must teach him that the so-called revolutionary is not the only one who uses a gun in his struggle. We must teach him the meaning of the principle "liberation by any means possible and pragmatic"!

JE: What do you see as the major cause of black oppression?

RI: There is a unique problem concerning the existence of black people in America that requires a unique solution. Clearly, no other people in the history of mankind have been so distributed within the widespread boundaries of such a vast country as America or under such extreme conditions of oppression wielded by a majority group at the height of its military power.

While other people have been and are being oppressed in the land of their oppressors, usually foreign oppression takes place in the homeland of the oppressed. In other words, the British army in India oppressed the Indians in India, the French army oppressed the Algerians in Algeria, and the British army in North America oppressed the English colonists. But we (black people in America) are oppressed in the land of the oppressor, with the oppressor being the premier military power in the world. That is a different problem; it requires a very special solution, because the normal solution to oppression is to boot out the oppressor. Unless we have plans to ship the Europeans home, the alternative and unique solution—and the one that black people hope to achieve—must be mutually satisfactory to both sides—black and white. It requires that both sides understand that black people cannot enjoy political power without an economic base; conversely, it must be recognized that there can be no economic development without a political base; and that neither group can exist without social, educational, and cultural foundations. It should be remembered that all other attempts to solve the racial problem in this country have thus far failed.

JE: Under your leadership, CORE has taken a number of controversial stands, one of which was your support of Edwin Meese as attorney general. Why did you testify in favor of the Meese nomination?

RI: Few offices in the executive branch of government demand the imperatives of sensitivity and understanding of the diverse sets of realities in America today like the office of attorney general. This office requires an unswerving and courageous dedication to principle, basic fairness, human decency, and justice. More than any other office, it interacts directly with people of all strata of society—from the very poor to the super rich. It can be aptly called the guardian of the Fourteenth Amendment of the Constitution.

Edwin Meese is viewed as a conservative, a Republican, insensitive to the poor, a hard-liner on crime, and a close associate of President Reagan. According to many black leaders, this automatically disqualifies him for this important position. But I am not a conservative, nor am I a Republican, nor am I a Democrat, nor am I a liberal. I am an *independent*.

I do not know the President personally, nor am I a close associate of his. But I am very hard-nosed on crime. And while I do not agree with Mr. Meese's statement that "there is no hunger in America," I do believe that there are abuses in America's hunger program. It is the careless administration of social programs and the exploitation of them by the greedy that expose the needy to attack.

As to his close association with the President, it appears to me that this is one of the key qualifications Mr. Meese brings to the job. I want the President's closest associate to be in charge of this critical area of government—if he is intelligent, fundamentally decent, competent, accessible, and open to dialogue with people of all points of view.

I have broken with the traditional approach of many civil rights leaders; on this issue, I march to a different drummer. I am familiar with the popularly accepted rhetorical characterizations of Mr. Meese, and I reject the way many of my colleagues relate to someone so defined. I have met personally with Mr. Meese, and I have discussed with him issues of critical importance to my people. I have found him to be accessible, affable, and open to discussion. It is this openness to dialogue that most influenced my opinion of Mr. Meese. There were several points of agreement in our discussion. In fact, the most important one was his commitment to continued dialogue with the black community.

JE: As far as Blacks are concerned, what recommendations did you make to Mr. Meese?

RI: I made several key recommendations concerning civil rights enforcement. First, I recommended that he examine and refocus the civil rights division of the Justice Department and restore the Community Relations component to its former prominence. Second, although the black community is not wedded to forced busing as the only method to desegregate schools, I stressed the fact that the Justice Department should not advocate its elimination without proposing adequate alternatives so that those affected have a choice. Third, I underscored the fact that affirmative action has been upheld by the United States Supreme Court and that the attorney general must police its implementation.

JE: Under your leadership, CORE recently endorsed the Simpson-Mazzoli immigration bill, a position that was opposed by most civil rights organizations. Why?

RI: I have witnessed with great sadness and disappointment the strenuous opposition of some black political and civil rights leaders and the unresponsiveness of many others to the Simpson-Mazzoli immigration bill which is presently before the Congress. This bill could grant legal residency or amnesty to the more than one million-plus Blacks from Africa and the Caribbean now residing in the United States without proper papers. Simpson-Mazzoli is far from perfect; in fact, it contains several questionable provisions, such as the sanctions against employers of illegal aliens. But with all its shortcomings, when pragmatically weighed against the existing immigration laws, it is clearly an improvement. The present immigration statutes are based on racist quotas which invidiously discriminate against our black brothers and sisters abroad. This fact is well known, and it has been amply documented.

I have worked closely with our Caribbean and African brothers and sisters, who contact our office daily for help with their immigration problems and with those problems stemming from their lack of proper residency status, such as employment, housing, legal, training, and so forth. I am personally aware of their pain and suffering and of the penalty that is paid by their families—especially their children. Because of their status, they are exploited by unscrupulous lawyers, employers, landlords, and training schools.

I believe that other civil rights leaders have followed a faulty strategy in reference to this bill. Their strategy, where it existed, was devoid of pragmatism and an understanding of the immigration issue. The unfocused total opposition and simultaneous inaction around the bill by black leaders has robbed Blacks of a meaningful role in the development of the legislation. Even more unfortunate, black leaders pliantly followed the lead of certain Hispanic and labor leaders. Our allies in big labor were naturally pursuing their own self-interest. Our good friends and allies in the Hispanic community were also guided by their own self-interest. And that is as it should be. But where was the self-interest of black Americans?

We must do for ourselves first; we must think of our people first— like everyone else. We should have first pursued the interests of the million or more of our less fortunate African and Caribbean brothers and sisters who are in this country without legal status. After we have given full consideration to the vital needs of our people on this issue, we can attempt to reconcile our position with our Hispanic brothers and sisters and with our friends and allies in big labor.

JE: Not long ago, CORE provoked widespread controversy when it questioned the selections of Miss Vanessa Williams as the first black Miss America and Miss Suzette Charles as the first black runner-up, describing the action as a "bittersweet victory" which was "a small step forward, but a giant step backward." Why did you oppose their selections?

RI: At the outset, let me state that we laud their talents and beauty. We do not wish to take away from their personal triumphs. The fact is, however, that the features of these attractive and talented young ladies are far closer to Mediterranean or Latino types than to classic black features.

From our perspective, the entire event reeked of irony. The Miss

America Pageant officials allegedly set out to break the color barrier. (According to media reports, Miss Williams was actively recruited by pageant representatives.) It would have been laudable (and daring) if they had selected Blacks who were at least recognizable as black in color, if nothing else. Many people who saw Miss Williams on television that evening either had no idea she was black or were not sure.

The Miss America contest is one in which ideals of beauty and conduct are projected and reinforced to the nation, particularly its young. As such, we are pessimistic about the long-term damaging effects of these ironic selections on the self-image of beautiful and talented black women with typical Africanoid features, hair, and skin color.

During the 1960s, CORE helped to lead the campaign to get Blacks recognizable as Blacks in television commercials. We are not among those who are happy with a thrown bone and half a loaf, particularly when it comes to standards of beauty and aesthetic values. In one broad, insidious, and far from accidental blow, the Miss America Pageant denigrated and attempted to cancel out many of the gains of the 1960s "Black is Beautiful" movement.

To repeat, our criticism of pageant officials was not intended as an indictment of Miss Williams but rather as a recognition of a generations-old color caste system that has wreaked havoc on the lives of black people. That system has been used by our oppressors to divide us by giving positions and privileges to our lighter-skinned brothers and sisters while devaluing and demoralizing our darker ones.

We must forever reject and bury the American and South African racist principle that for Blacks to make progress, the ones with the *highest percentage of white blood* must succeed first. That is the Shockley theory which has long since been discredited.

JE: In recent months, CORE broke ranks with other civil rights organizations and endorsed President Reagan's defensive energy-beam initiative. Why did you support this proposal?

RI: This new high-technology system to destroy incoming Soviet nuclear missiles will provide opportunities to Blacks that will create a new economic revolution in black people's lives.

I think it is important that Blacks separate the idea from the presenter. The idea must not be lost because people identify it with Reaganomics.

The energy-beam idea is not new. CORE embraced the idea well before it was proposed by President Reagan. Indeed, Lyndon H. LaRouche, a leading economist and spokesman for the National Democratic Policy Committee, has long advocated its development and implementation.

I think it's vital that black institutions of higher learning like Tuskegee Institute, Fisk University, and Howard University inaugurate crash programs to produce more black scientists and engineers to help meet the imminent demand. We cannot remain in the "six-shooter" era while others are developing lasers and engaging in beam-weapons technology. Blacks must get in on the ground floor of twenty-first-century technology now—in the twentieth century. We must participate in the science to prevent nuclear war.

JE: Over the past year, you've expressed open criticism of Jesse Jackson's presidential campaign. In one interview, you stated: "I am disturbed by the anti-intellectual reign of terror that exudes from the Jackson campaign that discourages any criticism of him or his associates. The messianic nature of his candidacy breeds an intolerance that inhibits or intimidates even those who are willing to make a constructive critique of the campaign." What are your main objections to Jackson's candidacy?

RI: A leader must "know thyself, and to thyself be true." He must possess the qualities of honesty, sensitivity, decisiveness, and consistency. Jesse Jackson, a brother of tremendous leadership potential and good fortune, must learn these things—if he is presumptuous enough to lead. The sponsors and mentors of Jesse—those who would make him king, those who have chosen him to be the *capo-di-capi* (boss of bosses) of black Americans—must teach him. Jackson's sin is not his Middle East position, nor is it his taking of Arab money. He has a right to his opinions and associations. His "Hymie" statement was wrong, silly, and idle, but that is not his greatest sin. His greatest sin is the way he dealt with these discretions and indiscretions.

JE: To what extent does Jackson speak for black America? Does he represent the views and aspirations of black people?

RI: Jesse Jackson does not speak for black America. I will say that categorically. He is, however, the symbol of black aspirations. The two are quite different things. Jesse is a creation of the media. He was chosen by the media to serve as the spokesman for black America. But Jackson's agenda is not the agenda of black people.

Look at the issues which he champions. He has called for a united Ireland. Black people are not interested in the war in Ireland. He has demanded the creation of a Palestinian state. Black people have no interest in the establishment of a Palestinian homeland. He has championed the cause of the guerillas in Latin America. Blacks have no interest in the plight of the leftists in El Salvador or Nicaragua. Jackson has endorsed school busing. Blacks are not interested in cross-town busing. These issues are not at the top of black folks' agenda. I'm not saying that these issues are unimportant. They *are* important. But they do not speak

to the goals and aspirations of black America. The media, without critique, debate, or research, credits Jackson with all kinds of accomplishments—whether he had actual or tangential involvement in the project,
whether the assumed positive results were real or imagined. Brief examples of Jesse receiving unchallenged media attributions are: 1) the
PUSH education program—the achievements of which are never questioned; and 2) the voter registration campaign that has involved almost
every major group in black America, the credit for which the media
fortuitously gave Jesse—doing so before and after he became a candidate. No. Jesse is a conscious artificial creation of the white media. The
press has dubbed him the spokesman for black America. As a result,
they shower him with attention and importance. No one can convince
me that Jackson, operating on his own steam, could generate the amount
of press he receives without some kind of manipulation. There's no way
that anyone can convince me that Jackson can lie the way he does and
get away with it without the acquiescence of powerful elements in the
media. He is the voice of the media, not the voice of black America.

JE: During the past year, America has witnessed the rise of Louis
Farrakhan, the leader of the Nation of Islam. Can Farrakhan lay claim
to the title of leader? Does he represent the popular thinking of black
America?

RI: No. Farrakhan, like Jesse, is a symbol of the aspirations of a
segment of black America. In his case, he appeals to the lower socioeconomic strata. Like Jesse, he's a media event. He personifies the mulatto
image. He dresses impeccably, drives a fancy car, and espouses a crude
dogma. He does so, however, with style.

Farrakhan was once a professional entertainer, a Calypso singer. As
such, he knows how to entertain an audience. Farrakhan and Jesse are
both master entertainers. Farrakhan represents the masses in the
streets—more in terms of their aspirations than their views. He ex-
presses their frustrations. He curses out Whitey the way the guy in the
street would if he only could. When Farrakhan curses out the white
man, he's cursing for him.

Farrakhan is simply doing what the demagogues in Athens and
Rome used to do—that's nothing new. The street rabble-rouser dates
back to the French Revolution and before. Farrakhan understands that
well. He knows what he's doing. Farrakhan appeals to the basest instincts in people: hate, fear, anger, and revenge.

Does Farrakhan speak for black America? Show me one program
that Farrakhan speaks to that represents the agenda of black America.
He doesn't speak about community control, or tuition tax credits, or
high unemployment, or political power. Farrakhan doesn't speak to the

real problems of the black community. He curses the policeman, but he doesn't do what we in CORE do, which is to prevent that policeman from stopping and frisking black folks on the street—which occurred when the Supreme Court modified the exclusionary rule.

Farrakhan doesn't call the chief of police and accuse the department of violating the First Amendment by preventing folks from talking and congregating on the public sidewalks. Yes, Farrakhan is expressing the feelings of the oppressed, the pent-up frustrations of the masses, but he's not speaking to the real needs of the oppressed. He is not saying anything that will result in improved conditions or greater power for the masses. Farrakhan is an agitator; he fires up and entertains his audience.

JE: Why has Farrakhan singled out the Jews as the target for his criticism? What makes this group such a prime target?

RI: Historically, the Jews have been a convenient scapegoat. However, I don't think that Farrakhan picked the Jews; the Jews were picked for him. I believe that the Louis and Jesse sideshow is exactly that—it was manufactured out of whole cloth. Someone (or some group) created a two-headed dragon: Jesse on one side, Louis on the other. Between the two, it was assumed that they could co-opt the full spectrum of black America. This is the first time since Booker T. Washington that anyone—in this case, two people—has co-opted such a large spectrum of the black community.

No previous leader (or partnership of leaders)—be he Farmer, Wilkins, Young, Randolph, Rustin, or even King, Elijah Muhammed, or Malcolm X—has co-opted the full spectrum of black America. I've deliberately left out Marcus Garvey, since his movement was unique. In doing so, Louis and Jesse owe their success to the media. The media muffled serious critique of them. They were projected as the new mass leaders of black America.

Look at the Jesse-Louis phenomenon. Here are two suave guys, with relatively crude messages, appealing to the basest instincts in people. Jesse's message is slightly more polished, more sophisticated. His appeal is to middle-class and even some upper-class Blacks.

Jesse deals with issues that, even when irrelevant or just plain wrong, are intoxicating to them. He's allegedly a serious presidential candidate. Jesse and Louis go to Syria and talk with the head of state, Assad. Jesse travels to Cuba and talks with Castro. They are seen regularly on "ABC News Nightline" and are featured prominently in *Time/Life* publications. The middle and upper classes are impressed by that. And the press in general accepts that also. However, they didn't universally accept Jesse prior to the start of the "silly season"—the presidential nominating game. The perfidy of the media pyrotechnics around Jackson and Farrakhan ignites the passions of the masses as did the spectacles of imperial Rome.

Jesse is the darling of the black press. They love him. There's hardly an issue of *Ebony* or *Jet* that doesn't feature his name or picture. But it was only when the white media legitimized him, with positive (or sometimes seemingly negative) coverage, that he was taken seriously. Jackson and Farrakhan symbolize the image of the charismatic black religious leader: Their looks, their style, their sardonic manner, their superficial and demagogic issues, and their programs (or lack thereof) satisfy the agenda of certain powerful interests who control much of major media. But their interests are not those of black folks.

JE: What explains the fact that most black leaders view you as a political radical? Do you see yourself this way?

RI: No. I think that that characterization stems from confusion. Some black leaders view me as an extreme radical; others see me as an extreme conservative. What they're really saying is that I am the furthest away from the kind of knee-jerk responses that they represent. For example, take the educational issue. I'm not part of the busing clique. I don't interpret or misinterpret the *Brown* decision to mean that America must employ school busing in order to bring about quality education.

Moreover, I differ from most other black leaders on the issue of private education. I have studied America's educational system. America has two educational systems—one public and one private. That system has worked very well for the majority of Americans. The Kennedys were not hurt by attending private schools. They did not suffer from racial isolation. They learned and prospered. I cannot accept the fact that Blacks cannot learn and prosper in a similar environment—that is, if they have access to quality private institutions, comparable to the ones the Kennedys attended. No, I can't buy the simplistic analyses that are made by black leaders on these and other issues. Because of that fact, some leaders view me as a radical; others, as a conservative.

In truth, I'm not doctrinaire about anything, except, perhaps, in my steadfast commitment to my people and to truth. But I'm not doctrinaire when it comes to ideas or programs or policies. My views are not easily predictable. I evaluate ideas, issues, legislation, people. I do not point my finger to the wind to check where the liberals or left-wingers are going, where the Democrats or Republicans are going, where big labor or big business is going. I check to see what makes sense for black people, and if it goes against big labor, then I'm against big labor on that particular issue. If it goes against white liberals, then I'm against white liberals on that issue. And so on. My approach is truly independent. I'm not beholden to or dependent upon any group or interest. My sole interest is the welfare of my people.

JE: Why do you think you've been the target of so much criticism by other black leaders? What explains their blatant hostility?

RI: It's due to several factors. First, of course, is the color question—the intraracial discrimination, the hidden monster, the most retarding factor in black development. There's tremendous prejudice against dark-skinned Blacks in the black community. In the United States, there's great dishonesty around this fact. The culture of slavery and its aftermath has produced a unique and unpleasant phenomenon in the African diaspora—the phenomenon of a racial caste. Usually mulattos, quadroons, and octoroons intermarry among themselves or with whites. With time, a hardened caste evolves, creating a special group with mixed loyalties, mixed interests, and mixed aspirations—clearly different aspirations from those of the black masses. Most African-American leaders come from this group. And everyone knows it. Most leaders would prefer to lie about it; but I will not! I have a deep commitment to the truth.

Truth is the most powerful weapon for our liberation. I will talk about unpleasant things even when it hurts. And it *does* hurt black people to talk honestly about this psychologically most damaging type of racism—intraracial prejudice and discrimination. Americans (Blacks, coloreds, and whites) discriminate invidiously against a person in direct proportion to the assumed percentage of that person's "African blood."

Another factor is my independence. I'm a relatively independent person. It's quite natural that other leaders could be jealous of that fact. I have to account to the kind of individuals who surround me—individuals who came up in the movement with me. We're not beholden to foundations. We're not beholden to government. We're not beholden to fat-cat donors. I am *one* black leader who is truly independent. I can say what I want to say, when I want to say it, and how I want to say it. This doesn't mean, of course, that I should talk nonsense, saying silly, useless, insulting things about other people. But in the policy arena, I can talk very straight and say what I mean. I don't have to bite my tongue.

Then there's the ideological factor. I'm a black nationalist, which means that I believe in self-determination. I accept America as it now exists and as it relates to the rest of the world. America is the modern Roman Empire. I have to define my nationalism within the reality of that world—of an Etruscan living in the midst of the Roman Empire, or a Greek or Egyptian living at the height of Roman imperial power.

But I'm still a black nationalist. Therefore, I seek economic and political power for my people.

Unlike most black leaders, I'm not an integrationist. That doesn't mean I don't like whites. I do; I like people. It has to do with the fact that people exist as discrete factions in society. At times these factions have divergent interests. In order for a minority in a democracy to maximize its interests, it must be able to form a majority somewhere. But to do that, it must be able to define itself as a political entity when necessary and pragmatic.

Most black leaders have different aspirations than the masses of black people. They have attempted to align themselves, involve themselves, and submerge themselves into institutions and political entities of other groups, contrary to the nature of man, contrary to the nature of most animals. The media projects the integrationist as one who loves humanity, cherishes noble virtues, and embraces the goodness of man. On the other hand, the black nationalist is depicted as a chauvinist: a mean, race-hating, inflexible separatist. Of course, this is not true; neither group has a monopoly on decency.

Finally, my main problem with most black leaders is the question of honesty. Most black leaders are cruel, cowardly, and coarse liars. I don't flatter them. I don't seek acceptance from them. I seek only respect. Most black leaders would never enter into a serious discussion with me. They certainly wouldn't debate me publicly. I've had few if any discussions of the kind we're having here with known black leaders in the more than twenty-plus years I've been in the movement.

When it comes to Roy Innis, there's a kind of pathological fear on the part of most black leaders. They will not deal with me on an intellectual level. Instead they deal with me in a disparaging way, from a distance—like a thief in the night, a knife in the back—that kind of thing. They're not willing to confront me directly, face-to-face. They much prefer to operate concealed in the dark. I'm not going to assault or abuse them (physically or verbally) in any way, although that image of me has been projected by the media. I'm one of the few gentlemen in the movement.

They know, for instance, that if I invite them to my house or to a CORE activity, they are completely free from attack by me or anyone in the organization. They know I will never dishonor myself or the organization to break a flag of truce or a gentleman's agreement. So, it's not a matter of fear even if they accepted the media image. The media, at one time, projected me as some kind of black Mafia chieftain. That image was similarly projected by some ex-CORE hoodlums—interestingly enough, these guys were true-blue hoodlums that were expelled from the organization. As part of their scheme, they went to Mike Wallace and Jack Anderson, claiming that I was the Idi Amin of black America, that I had used intimidation to win the chairmanship of CORE. Fortunately, their lies were exposed. I am a man of honor; I would never discredit myself or CORE.

JE: Some of the fiercest criticism you've received has come from the black press. How do you explain their criticism?

RI: Who is the black press? Who are these black reporters? In general, the black press is owned, run, or disproportionally influenced by the mulatto aristocracy in America. The black press is one of the most selfish, provincial, schizophrenic institutions in this nation.

While they profess integration, they understand the meaning of black nationalism enough to be a separate black press; they have no desire to integrate the black press. I don't see them trying to merge with white newspapers or magazines. I don't see black editors or publishers trying to get jobs with the dominant white media in their area. My friend John Johnson, the editor and publisher of *Ebony* and *Jet* magazines, is not about to look for a job as an assistant publisher or editor at *Time/Life*. He doesn't want to merge *Ebony* and *Jet* with the *Chicago Tribune* or *Chicago Sun/Times*. Not at all. These guys are very nationalistic when it comes to their own black institutions, from which they derive tremendous profits.

The people and issues that are projected most favorably and flatteringly are those of their own caste and class. The civil rights (integrationists) aristocracy is given the most exposure—quantitatively and qualitatively. This outlook reflects the mulatto syndrome which is reflected in the pages of most black publications. That can be proven very easily. If you examine the centerfolds and pin-ups in most African-American newspapers and magazines over the last fifty-two weeks, you'll see very few Africanoid girls on those pages. And when one is displayed, if she's very black skinned, she's likely to have very straight (Caucasian or Indian) hair, or she's likely to have very Caucasian features.

Now, let me move to the black reporter. Who is the black reporter? There are two kinds of black reporters. There's the black reporter who writes for the black media, and the black reporter who writes for the white media. In the case of the former, his position on Roy Innis is very simple. He mirrors the views of his publisher. He suffers from a total lack of honesty. He will write whatever kind of article he's asked to write by his boss. There's very little original research or writing in the black media.

The black media is a carbon copy of the white media. And not even a good copy. If you're popular with the white media, you'll be published in the black media. That is certainly the case. If you're discovered by *Time/Life*, as was Jesse Jackson, then you've got it made in the black media. Nobody in the black press will take you on. So, in the end, the powers that be at *Time/Life* become the greatest creators of black leaders. If Ted Koppel on "ABC News Nightline," Phil Donahue, the "Today Show," or any major network show discovers you, then the black media will adopt you overnight as one of its own.

Now, the other fellow is a strange bird—that is, the black writer who works for the white media. These writers typically come out of two modes. In the late 1950s and early 1960s, such writers were virtually non-existent. They were expected to be very reserved, very distant from the black community. They were supposed to write in a more antiseptic way about Blacks than even white writers. As a result, they tended to be rather sterile, reserved, even hostile—afraid to really deal with and report accurately about Blacks.

This changed following the emergence of the black power movement. The new black writer adopted a left-wing orientation. It became acceptable, even fashionable, to espouse a left-leaning Third World perspective. Unfortunately, it proved to be very superficial. There is no honest intellectual commitment to these ideas nor real understanding of them. Neither Roy Innis nor CORE are part of the Third World left-wing syndrome. We are true nationalists, true Pan Africanists. Our commitment is based upon careful study and research. That gives us the unique perspective that is sorely lacking in such journalists.

This left-wing commitment poses another problem. There has always been a tension between the Marxist and the nationalist. For example, Marcus Garvey experienced a similar problem with the left-wing. The left-wing deals with Blacks with a kind of arrogance, which derives from a basic racist mentality. They use Blacks and black crises as instruments for their causes—as cannon fodder in their wars. The nationalist believes that the primary struggle centers on race; the Marxist disagrees, contending that the real problem is class. If the nationalist were to concede that class is also part of the problem, the Marxist would still refuse to relinquish the exclusive primacy of class struggle over race antagonism.

Left-wing black reporters suffer from the herd mentality. They espouse whatever is the popular or prevailing Marxist dogma at the time. They have a very superficial understanding of history. I will not let them define the agenda for black people. We will not subordinate our agenda to theirs. I will not let them pretend that their falsely assumed "superior intellect" gives them the right to define the problem and to propose the solution. I find that kind of paternalism most unacceptable.

JE: Over the years, you've been the subject of many charges and criticisms, one of which is that you've exploited CORE for your own financial aggrandizement. How would you respond to this charge?

RI: I've heard this charge many times, although it often goes unspoken. It was projected on "60 Minutes" in front of 60 million people, for eighteen tortuous minutes, by Mike Wallace, who should have known better. It was repeated in the black and white press under banner headlines. The charge is without foundation. It cannot stand up to close scrutiny. When it was challenged in the courts, we emerged with resounding legal victories. News of the verdicts was buried on the obituary pages of some newspapers. The media was quite willing to repeat the charges to anyone who would listen, but they were unwilling to report the verdicts when we were vindicated. That's quite typical of the media. They're wedded to the big lie. When that lie (or error) is exposed, they refuse to admit their mistake.

The truth is: My involvement in CORE has led to my personal financial ruin. Compare my circumstances with those of other national civil rights leaders. I don't drive a Rolls Royce or a Mercedes. I don't live in a fancy penthouse apartment. I don't wear expensive designer clothes. I don't have any foreign bank accounts. In short, I am a man of modest means, who lives very modestly.

Let me be more specific. Instead of Roy Innis bilking CORE, CORE has drained me financially. What is my bank credit line? Citibank holds a $50,000 note signed by Roy Innis that was used to rescue CORE and has since been defaulted on. As a result, I am at least $50,000 in debt. There is another $5,000 that I drew on my own personal bank account and line of credit, which was used by CORE during the war with government-sponsored black traitors that began in 1978. My credit rating is not good. And all this is attributable directly to CORE. CORE owes me thousands of dollars, with no possible way of paying it back. Forget the debt, what about all the salary that I am owed that is years in arrears? Check the record: Roy Innis was the lowest paid civil rights leader from 1968 to 1980. During those twelve years, my salary was $25,000. My salary did not increase one penny during that entire period. Can any other civil rights leader make that same claim? Still, many black leaders, as well as the media, continue to repeat these palpably false charges.

JE: Another criticism that has been leveled against you, particularly by several ex-CORE leaders, is that you are an undemocratic, autocratic, ruthless dictator who runs the organization with an iron hand. Is there any truth to this charge?

RI: This charge was leveled during the court proceedings against us by several disgruntled ex-CORE officials. They used this allegation to argue that either I be removed as national chairman or, failing that, that CORE be dissolved. Like the other charges, this charge is totally baseless. These same people will also tell you, in the same breath, how they hate the way I run the organization—especially the long meetings and the all-night sessions. Well, I don't know any absolute dictator who takes all night to make a decision on anything. I don't know any absolute dictator who debates the issues with his own lieutenants. Obviously, I need to take a dictatorship course.

Perhaps I should take Dictatorship 101 under Professor Idi Amin, Professor Anastasio Somoza, Professor Carlo Gambino, or better still, Professor Fidel Castro. These individuals knew what they were doing. Their meetings were very short. And their dissenters never seemed to show up at the next meeting. Now, which one of my critics is missing? These individuals are very present—too present. You can see them on "60 Minutes" or spilling their imaginary tales to Jack Anderson. I must be a very incompetent dictator to engage in all-night meetings and permit my enemies to run hither and yon attacking me to anybody who will listen.

I do think I am guilty of one thing—namely, boring my top officers and staff to death with long discussions and debates in order to reach consensus. We operate on the basis of consensus. There's no more democratic process in the world than consensus. We try to achieve near one hundred percent agreement on policy decisions. That's why the meetings take all night. I don't dictate policy. I don't impose my will on the organization. At times, it's extremely difficult to reach consensus. After all, how many leaders can claim one hundred percent agreement with their actions? Let President Regan see if he can do it. Let Congress see if it can? Obviously, they can't.

It was ironic to see James Farmer, who was projected as the super-democrat, the super-liberal, the super-non-dictator—that man who would suspend democratic procedures at the drop of a hat—condemn me for failing to follow such procedures. The charge was total hypocrisy.

JE: Another charge is that you inherited a thriving organization and transformed it into a mere shadow of its former self; that under your leadership, CORE's reputation declined, membership dropped, contributions fell off, and the influence of the organization evaporated. How do you view such allegations?

RI: I've heard these allegations many times. If there's any truth to them, then when did the decline supposedly begin? I could show you statements in the press about CORE's membership decline, the collapse of the organization, the loss of influence, almost immediately after I succeeded to the national leadership. These criticisms were instantaneous. How is that possible? How did all this occur within hours? I'd like to know. It defies all logic. The facts are quite different. Now, it's true that once it became clear that the young nationalists, the young Turks, were about to take over the organization, many of the whites (who controlled fund-raising) quit the organization. The old guard knew that we were rapidly approaching the goal line. They knew that we couldn't be stopped. The thumping feet of nationalism were at the door. So they began to run.

One of the culprits in this regard was Marvin Rich who was CORE's chief fund-raiser. When Rich and his crowd left, they gutted the fund-raising department. The fund-raising list and contacts are the only capital you have in a civil rights organization. Overnight, we were without an effective fund-raising operation. Needless to say, we faced one financial crisis after another—especially when we realized that James Farmer and his cohorts left CORE over a million dollars in debt, including many thousands owed to the Internal Revenue Service. I spent the first few years of my administration struggling to retire that debt and doing so without an effective fund-raising mechanism.

Then there was the exodus of the Jews. Again, this began before I was elected national chairman of the organization. A fellow in Mount Vernon, New York, by the name of Clifford Brown made an outrageous statement about Hitler and the Jews. This cost CORE millions of dollars in contributions. (We nicknamed him Million Dollar Cliff!)

Instead of condemning the statement, forthrightly, the Farmer team proved equivocal, incompetent, and bungling. The Jews were outraged at the way in which the matter was handled. They never forgave CORE for what happened. I inherited that too; and as detailed memory of the incident faded, I was blamed for it, not James Farmer—although I was without national rank and not part of the national leadership cabal.

As for the decline in membership, that also began before my election. I didn't force anybody out of CORE. But the fact is, the whites left the organization. They were scared. We didn't throw them out; we simply made it clear that Blacks had to control CORE. This was our organization. We felt that it should be run by Blacks. This didn't mean that whites couldn't remain as members or even in some leadership positions. It simply meant that they couldn't run the organization. And that made many whites angry. So they left in droves. At the same time, black membership increased dramatically. In the 1950s and early 1960s, most CORE members were white. That changed when I took over. For the first time in its history, CORE became a predominantly black organization. I view that as a good thing.

JE: Finally, as you look back over the past decade and consider the many battles you've waged, how would you assess their impact on the organization and on you personally?

RI: It has done irreparable damage to my family, my wife and my kids, in particular. I simply cannot explain to my kids what's happened. It's difficult to convince them that their dad is a good guy, when they hear such pernicious things about me from the media. I sense some disbelief in them. It must be tiresome for them to have to defend me and CORE to their colleagues. And that makes me sad.

It has also done irreparable damage to the families of my lieutenants, my staff, who have stuck by me through this war of words and charges. Things were not particularly good before the war, and things deteriorated hideously after it began. What's worse is that it appears, much of the time, like a dark tunnel with no light at the end. Each time we think we've won, the government or the media hits us with a new phony charge. So, when I tell my staff that there's light, boom, we're back on the battlefield!

I don't even try to tell them anymore that it's going to be over soon. I can't. I've told them that too many times before. How can I tell them that it's going to be over soon, when every year, usually around Christmas, we're faced with a new war? Still, we're in this to win. We won't throw in the towel. We won't give up. There's too much at stake.

When I was in junior high school, I was the kid who won the algebra award and the Spanish award, and yet the kids in the class picked the mulatto kid, who looked very white, as the boy who was most likely to succeed. That hurt me a great deal. I think that was the incident that guaranteed my moving up in life. I had to show those kids, even though I hardly see them anymore, that I was a winner—that I could defy the odds and win. That's how I felt then, and that's how I feel now.

One final comment about the role of government entities (and other "crypto-entities") that have impacted negatively on CORE's operations and on my image: A secret government document fell into my hands that outlined in some detail how to disrupt and destroy independent black organizations and how to *discredit* independent black nationalist leaders.

In addition, the document, known as the "Brzezinski memo," detailed how to create a new black political leader, fashioned, of course, to replace Dr. Martin Luther King, Jr. This memo was said to be issued by Zbigniew Brzezinski, President Carter's National Security Advisor; and it was to signal the re-creation of the old discredited J. Edgar Hoover counterintelligence program. One cannot understand what has happened to CORE and me (and others) without reading and understanding the import of that document.

Mary Hatwood Futrell

The Assault on Public Education

Mary Hatwood Futrell was born May 24, 1940, in Altavista, Virginia. She received a bachelor's degree in business education from Virginia State College in Petersburg, Virginia, and a master's degree from George Washington University in Washington, D.C. She has completed graduate work at the University of Maryland and Virginia Polytechnic Institute and State University.

In Alexandria, Virginia, where she taught high school business education, Futrell was president of the Education Association of Alexandria, the local National Education Association (NEA) affiliate, from 1973 to 1975. Futrell later became president of the NEA-affiliated Virginia Education Association (VEA), serving two terms between 1976 and 1978. Earlier, she had served on the state association's Program and Budget Committee, the Virginia Minority Caucus, and numerous other state-level panels. She was also an elected delegate to the VEA Assembly between 1968 and 1980.

Throughout these years, Futrell also devoted considerable energy to national NEA affairs. She served on the NEA Board of Directors, chaired the NEA Human Relations Commission, and participated actively in a wide variety of national association projects.

Futrell became the NEA secretary-treasurer in 1980 and then, in 1983, was elected the association's president. As president, Futrell leads the nation's largest (1.7 million members) organization of teachers, professors, and allied school employees.

Futrell has been extremely active outside the NEA in organizations dedicated to educational and social progress. She has worked closely with the National Assessment of Educational Progress and serves on the Carnegie Foundation's Panel on the Study of the American High School. Futrell was co-convener of the August 27, 1983, observance of the 20th anniversary celebration of the historic March on Washington led by Dr. Martin Luther King, Jr.

Futrell has also served on a number of official boards and panels in her native state. Virginia Governor Charles Robb named her as a state representative to the Education Commission of the States in 1982.

Internationally, Futrell has been equally active. She served as a member of the NEA's delegation to the 1980 International Teacher's Conference to Combat Racism, Anti-Semitism, and Violations of Human Rights in Tel Aviv, Israel. Futrell visited Israel again in 1982, at the invitation of the Israeli Teachers Union, to survey that nation's schools and educational methods.

In 1981, under the sponsorship of the Ford Foundation and the National Committee on U.S.-China Relations, Futrell travelled to the People's Republic of China with a delegation of women leaders invited by the All-China Women's Federation. Also in 1981, Secretary of State Alexander M. Haig, Jr. appointed Futrell to the U.S. National Commission for the United Nations Education, Scientific, and Cultural Organization (UNESCO).

Futrell headed a 1982 NEA delegation to study the French education system and has been a delegate to the 1982 and 1984 biennial conventions of the World Confederation of Organizations of the Teaching Profession.

Futrell has won numerous honors and has been featured frequently in the national media. She has appeared on many major network television programs, including "Good Morning America" and the "Today Show." In 1983, *The Ladies' Home Journal* named Futrell one of the nation's 100 top women. *Ms.* magazine named Futrell one of its 10 most outstanding women in 1984, and *Ebony* magazine named her its 1984 black professional and business person of the year.

JE: How did your childhood upbringing shape your educational philosophy and your view of the educational system?

MF: I was born in Altavista, Virginia, which is approximately 30 miles from Lynchburg. My mother worked for a furniture company. My father was a construction worker. In the very early days of my life, I recall us being a very happy, very close-knit family. At the time, we were in the process of purchasing a home. We had a little land and raised a garden. And then my father became ill. He developed a kidney condition, and the hospital in Altavista was too small to treat him. We had to take him to a hospital in Lynchburg.

In those days, we didn't have a car. We had to commute by train back and forth to the hospital in Lynchburg. Eventually, we decided to move to Lynchburg to be closer to my father. That was when our lives turned upside down. We had to give up our home in Altavista since we couldn't afford to maintain two homes. We lost everything. My father didn't have insurance, so the bills kept mounting up. It was a terrible situation.

Back then, there were no day-care centers or nurseries. School officials allowed me to start school at age three—not as a regular student, but in order to help my mother. It was a black school, in a black community. I wasn't allowed to participate in all the classroom activities, but the school assigned me projects of a developmental nature.

My father died just prior to my sixth birthday. I can vividly recall the funeral. I also remember how stubborn my mother was about not accepting welfare. She made ends meet by doing domestic work. We spent the next seven or eight years, after my father's death, paying off the medical bills.

My mother put a great deal of emphasis on school. "You go to school, you get an education," she would say. Once, I remember, school officials told my sister and me that we had to wear shoes to class. We simply couldn't afford shoes, so we played hooky for one day. When the school told my mother, she was very angry. She told us, "It doesn't matter what you wear or what you have, that's not what's important. What *is* important is that you get a good education."

I was raised in a family that placed tremendous emphasis on hard work—on not being afraid to work. At an early age, we learned how to take care of the house while Mother was at work. We did all the washing, ironing, cleaning, and cooking. We were poor, but we were a happy family. My mother used to have spelling bees with us. We would always try to outspell her.

My mother had dropped out of school in the sixth grade when her parents died. She didn't want her children to drop out. She used to sit up in bed at night when she came home. We would come into her room, and she would read to us, or we would read to her. We didn't know it then, but that was her way of encouraging us to do our homework, her way of instilling in us a love of learning.

You never knew when my mother would show up at school. She wouldn't just show up at a PTA meeting or a special event; she was likely to show up at any time. Our teachers knew that if they had a problem with us—discipline or homework or anything else—all they had to do was call home. My mother checked our report cards every grading period. She knew exactly when the report cards were supposed to arrive.

My mother didn't want me to simply slide by or do average work. I could never understand why she was so hard on me. If I received a "C," for example, and she thought I should have received a "B," then I was punished for the next grading period. Or if I had received a "B" and I dropped to a "C," then I was punished. She made sure that I did my work. I was the first one in my family to graduate from high school, as well as the first one to graduate from college.

My mother's encouragement helped me develop a keen appreciation of education and a deep love of teaching. She was my role model. She taught me to value education and to respect my teachers. She put teachers on a pedestal. In her view, nothing was more important than school. Her views were contagious. I grew up with the same values. As a result, it was only natural that I should pursue a career in education.

JE: As a student, you attended segregated elementary and secondary schools. What do you recall of the experience? How did it shape your view of the world?

MF: It instilled in me a deep sense of pride and a sense of, "If you try, you can do it." I attended segregated schools through undergraduate school. I did not attend an integrated school until I enrolled at George Washington University, and I did not teach in an integrated school until 1965.

My schools were segregated, but my teachers taught us personal pride as well as the importance of education. My teachers cared about me. They wanted me to succeed. They spent a lot of time working with me, encouraging me to try new things. When I failed, they wouldn't chastise me. I remember, for example, when I tried out for the chorus, I didn't make it because I couldn't sing. But I recall the chorus director saying, "It's okay. You'll make it at something else."

Both my schooling and my background emphasized the importance of community involvement, be it in the church, the YWCA, or whatever. I was taught to help people and to share, and I learned that I had a responsibility to give something back. I was taught not to sit around and complain. If you're unhappy with things, try to change them. You can always do something to make things better. That's the way I was raised. I was taught to believe that life is not an easy road—that it's full of hard knocks. I was taught that I would get knocked down but that every time I got knocked down, I should pick myself up and start over. And I was taught to be ready for opportunity. In short, I was taught to survive and to meet life's challenges head-on.

JE: Did you experience feelings of frustration or anger at being forced to attend segregated schools? Did your experience cause you to question yourself or society?

MF: I never really experienced the anger until I entered college. I did, however, experience frustration at the world around me. We lived on Pearl Street. One half of Pearl Street was black; the other half was white. The children on the street played together. But when it came time to go to school, I walked to school and they rode the bus. We would pass each other going to school. I remember days when it was very hot or cold or rainy, and we had to walk to school while the white kids rode the bus.

I remember several other things that seemed small at the time, but which later proved important. For example, the city built a swimming pool at the white high school but refused to build us a new library at our school and claimed they couldn't afford it. I also recall when they built a YWCA in our neighborhood. At the time, we thought it was a fantastic building. And then a year or so later, they built a Y in the white neighborhood that was really fabulous—it had everything. Our Y was a modest two-story building. The white Y was a four-story building, replete with a pool, billiards, tennis courts, everything. I also remember the time they closed the city pool, because Blacks wanted to use it.

So I grew up quite frustrated—but not really angry. To understand my feelings, you have to understand my mother. She would never let us go to the Y or use the pool. We were never permitted to use those facilities. But we would read about them in the newspaper or hear rumblings in the community.

When I went to college, my frustration increased. That's when I became involved in the civil rights movement. I remember when we marched on Petersburg to integrate the lunch counters and when we marched to demand better facilities at Virginia State College. In the latter instance, I recall us trying to tell officials of the State Department of Education: "This building should be condemned. It is so old and in such bad shape that we should not be forced to attend classes in this building." And that's when I felt the anger. Before that experience, I was aware of things that were happening, but I didn't understand the full meaning of them. When I became involved in the civil rights movement, I began to understand what I had lived through at home.

JE: What impact did segregation have on your education? Do you think you received an inferior education?

MF: It depends on how you define "inferior." We missed out on many things. For example, we lacked access to needed facilities and equipment. This was especially true in health and physical education. I also recall that we wanted to introduce French and Russian in my high school, but we were told that we couldn't do it because of lack of funds. Yet they expanded the foreign language program at the white school. The lack of programs limited our access to many different kinds of learning. At the same time, our teachers tried to do everything possible to open up the doors of learning. By being denied the opportunity to attend school with white children, we were also denied the opportunity to learn from them and have them learn from us. Clearly, that limited our education and theirs.

JE: Upon graduation from college, you became a classroom teacher. How would you describe your teaching style? What would your students say about you today?

MF: My kids would probably say that I had a nice way of being nasty. And I must say, I've changed my style over the last 20 years. When I started out, I was very rigid. I've learned how to be a little more flexible. My students would probably say that I was a no-nonsense kind of teacher—that I demanded a lot from them, but that I was also very caring. I believed that every child I had could achieve. And I wanted them to know I felt that way. I also wanted them to know that I would do everything within my power to help them achieve. I was the kind of teacher who would give up my afternoons to stay after school to work with a student, even if it meant staying until 5:00 or 6:00, and then probably give the child a ride home.

I was the kind of teacher who would give up my lunch period to work with a student. I was the kind of teacher who would try to help a child who was having difficulty and be very patient in the process. When my students did a good job, they would know it by the look on my face. I might even give them a handshake or a hug.

At the same time, I was also the kind of teacher who would let them know when I didn't like something they were doing. If a child was misbehaving, or not paying attention, or not trying, he or she would know that, too. I took a lot of time with my students.

I remember one young girl in class who said to me: "Why do you take so much time? Kids from the ghetto aren't supposed to learn." That broke my heart. Maybe the reason why I felt as strongly as I did was because I came from the ghetto. To say that these kids can't learn is, in my opinion, a terrible indictment. You're really sending them a very negative message. A teacher has to take the time to work with students on an individual basis. So many children come to school believing that they can't learn. They're convinced that they can't succeed. They've been told, over and over again, "What's the value of an education? What can you do with it? Where's it going to get you?" My job, as a teacher, was to convince students that they were important, that they could learn, and that education is important.

I'd often use myself as an example. I'd frequently tell them about my own background and how I made it. That's the kind of teacher I was. I didn't accept failure. I didn't like students to say, "I can't do it."

You never know what you can do until you try. That's the way I worked with my students. I'm sure that some of them thought I was too hard, too demanding. I would say to a child, "You're supposed to be in my class at 9:00. I expect you to be here on time. I also expect you to come with paper, pencil, and book, and be prepared to do the day's work." That was my attitude. But I was not the kind of teacher who was afraid to have a child question me. Sometimes, I would deliberately say something wrong to see if they were listening and to see if they would question what I said. If they didn't, I would say, "Why didn't you question that?"

JE: Did you find being a classroom teacher frustrating? If so, how did you deal with it?

MF: Oh yes, particularly during the 1970s, when we were experiencing desegregation. Those were difficult times. There were days when I questioned whether I had made the correct choice—whether I should have done something else with my life. Inevitably, I came to the conclusion that I *did* make the right decision—that education was where I should be.

There were many days when I was frustrated. I knew that a particular child could learn, but for some reason he or she did not. And I would ask myself: "Am I imparting the knowledge in such a way that the child understands?"

I also experienced frustration when the parents didn't seem to care—when I'd call them or ask them to see me and then they wouldn't show up or would show very little interest in their child.

Sometimes, I would become frustrated because I wouldn't receive the proper support from administrators. One of my most frustrating moments occurred one year in the late 1960s when the administration forgot to order enough books for my ninth grade general business class. I was six weeks into the semester, and I didn't have books. That was the first time I ever became angry with an administrator—angry enough to raise my voice. I told the assistant principal that I didn't care what she did, I was going to get books for my kids. And when the books finally came, she told me I could give books only to those children who had saved their slips. After waiting seven or eight weeks for books, how many ninth graders would still have their slips? I told her, "Look, I am giving out the books. We'll worry about the slips later." I was certain that I would lose my job.

As a teacher, you have countless frustrations, including frustrations over the way the public perceives how you're doing your job, particularly when you know you're doing everything humanly possible. You get constant criticism. Yes, I've had lots of disappointments. But I've had far more good days than bad ones. I'm pleased when I go shopping in Alexandria, where I live, and a young man or woman comes up to me and says, "Do you remember me? I'm a nurse now," or "I'm studying to be a teacher," or "I'm in computer science." Those are the same children whom everyone thought would never make it—who would be on the streets, on welfare, or even in jail. It's that kind of experience that makes you feel that teaching is worthwhile—that you can stick it out.

JE: How did you become involved in the NEA? What did you hope to accomplish?

MF: I attended my first NEA Convention in 1969. When I walked onto the convention floor, more than 10,000 teachers were there. As I sat and listened to them, I said to myself, "More teachers are in this room than there are people in the town in which I was born. And not only are there more, but they're of the same vein as Mary—we're all teachers, and we're all here to talk about education."

I was particularly impressed with the democratic way in which the convention was conducted—anyone could get up and speak. It was that convention which really motivated my interest in the organization. I liked NEA's commitment to education and civil rights.

I was one of the first individuals to form the NEA's Black Caucus. I was also an officer within the caucus for several years. We said to the NEA: "You've got to open up the process to include minorities. You can't expect us to be members and not allow us to be involved in the governing structure of the organization." We challenged the NEA in many areas. For example, we said: "Many black teachers have been dismissed or demoted in many parts of the South where desegregation has occurred. We must speak out about what's happening to these black children who are attending desegregated schools."

So I became very involved in the organization. I also became more involved in my local and state affiliates, but my first real love affair with NEA came at the national level. Interestingly, I was only able to attend that convention because of a fluke—one of the delegates couldn't go. I'd been a member of the NEA, and the delegate happened to be in my school. She asked me if I would like to go to the convention. In those days, you could make such an arrangement. Today, you must be elected. When she asked, I said, "I don't have anything else to do—sure, I'll go." And that was the beginning of my association with the NEA.

JE: Can you summarize your involvement in the NEA? What events led to your election as president?

MF: I began as a delegate. Then I became deeply involved in the Association of Classroom Teachers (ACT). I served as the secretary of its Minority Forum—which really was an organizational training program.

Then I was appointed to several committees: The Human and Civil Rights Committee, the Committee to Study Campaign Expenditures, the Committee on Revenue and Structure. I was elected local president for 1973–1975, and state president for 1976–1978. Those two offices allowed me to remain active at the national level. In 1978, I ran for an at-large seat on the NEA Board of Directors, and was elected. In 1980, I decided to run for secretary-treasurer of the NEA. The campaign was interesting, mainly because of the hurdles I had to overcome. A major hurdle was my being a woman. My opponents said I wouldn't be able to do the job—that women couldn't perform such work. They raised the same arguments about my being black. People said that all I would care about would be minority issues—that I wouldn't really support all members. But I overcame those objections, and I was elected. I served as secretary-treasurer for three years. In 1983, I ran for and was elected president of the NEA.

JE: How would you describe the mission of the NEA? Has it changed under your leadership?

MF: No, not really. The mission has not changed. But the focus may have changed. The mission has been, and continues to be, to improve the quality of education for all children and to improve the conditions under which our members work. I've simply tried to refocus the activities of the NEA. For ten years, we concentrated on collective bargaining and political action. Since becoming president, I've argued that collective bargaining and political action are simply the means to achieve our end. The end must be quality public education for all students.

JE: How would you compare and contrast your approach with that of your chief counterpart, the American Federation of Teachers (AFT)? How do the two organizations differ? Why are the two groups often at odds?

MF: I think we're different in a variety of ways. First, consider size. The NEA comprises 1.7 million members—and all our members are part of the education community. The AFT consists of around 400,000 members, and many of these members have nothing to do with education. The AFT organizes sheriffs, nurses, noneducational public employees. We don't.

The NEA and AFT also differ in terms of governing structures. I am a classroom teacher, and the membership elected me for a two-year term. At most, I can only serve for four years—or two terms. At the end of four years, I will go back to the classroom. An AFT president can serve in that position for an indefinite period of time.

The 7,000 NEA elected delegates who attend a Representative Assembly every year make the policies, and, as NEA president, I am bound by those decisions. I might feel a certain way about a particular issue, but if my position is in opposition to the majority view of the membership, then I cannot go against that policy. On the other hand, the AFT president is not accountable to the membership and can espouse views that differ significantly from the policy of the organization. Let me give you an example. I've read the AFT's position on merit pay. Its policy is far more negative toward merit pay and more rigid than ours. Yet Albert Shanker, the current AFT president, will stand up at public forums and say, "We support certain merit pay plans"—a statement that totally ignores the official AFT position on merit pay. So, yes, there are significant differences between the two organizations. I believe ours is more democratic, more accountable to the membership, more committed to quality education.

JE: On several occasions, Mr. Shanker has described the NEA, under your leadership, as being radical, militant, and out-of-step with the views of America's teachers. What do you think motivates such charges?

MF: It boils down to a question of competition. Shanker will say whatever he thinks will help recruit new members for his union. Let me give you an example. When Tennessee Governor Lamar Alexander put forward his merit pay plan in 1983, Shanker immediately went to Tennessee and embraced the governor and his plan before the plan had really been fleshed out. We in the NEA said that we could not support the governor's plan, because, in our view, it violated many teacher rights basic to a quality school environment. Shanker thought his support for the governor's plan would gain AFT members. He even opened up a special organizing office in Tennessee. What has happened? The NEA membership in Tennessee is up, and the AFT has closed its organizing office. Who speaks for teachers? I think the answer in Tennessee and all around the country is fairly clear.

JE: How would you assess the state of American education?

MF: Nearly 20 years ago, President Lyndon Johnson, in his Inaugural Address, quoted one of his most illustrious predecessors: "Thomas Jefferson said that no nation can be both ignorant and free," said Johnson. "Today," he continued, "no nation can be both ignorant and great." How curiously outdated Johnson's words seem to us now.

Few people today speak of education and national greatness. We speak instead of education and national survival. We are a "nation at risk," contends the National Commission on Excellence in Education. "We are guilty," it says, "of a dangerous educational disarmament . . . Rising tides of mediocrity are threatening to sweep us away."

I agree. We are at risk. We stand only fifteen years from the year

2000. Some futurists speculate that technological wonders will transform our lives and ease our daily burdens. Unfortunately, what I see ahead are demographic nightmares. I see a society splitting deeper and deeper into two very unequal parts—one part comfortable and content, the other frustrated and falling behind. Not long ago, the Census Bureau reported that there are over 34 million poor people in America. Of these, over 13 million are children. Let me put that another way. More than one American child in five lived in poverty last year.

These figures are alarming—and they are rising. In each of the last four years, the Census Bureau has officially reported at least one million *new* poor children. Over half live in single-parent households headed by women. This may be the most significant statistic of all because, demographically, households headed by women are rising most rapidly. Since 1966, the number of Americans in such households has risen by over 67 percent.

Some experts maintain that this rising poverty cannot last. The high-tech revolution, they contend, will fuel a new epoch of economic growth, in much the same way as the automobile recharged a sputtering economy at the turn of the century. I see little evidence to support this optimism. The Department of Labor does indeed predict 150,000 new jobs for computer programmers by 1990. But the department also predicts that there will be far more of a demand—three times more—for janitors. Most jobs in the decade ahead will be distinctly *low*-tech and low-paying.

Between now and 1990, the economy will generate three times as many nurses aides as licensed practical nurses, three times as many sales clerks as skilled carpenters, twice as many fast-food workers as well-paid automobile mechanics. Low-paying jobs are squeezing out high-paying jobs—and, for far too many Americans, there is simply *no* pay, period. One out of every four teenagers who wants a job can't find one. Two million 16–19 year-olds are wasting their fundamentally important young adulthoods. We are building a permanent underclass of despair.

JE: Are the schools addressing these harsh realities? If so, how?

MF: Those of us who teach often reflect upon these saddening facts. How we would love to shut our schools off from the problems of society! How we would love to make our classrooms a refuge where teachers and students could chase the joys of pure learning!

But our schools are no refuge. They are very much part of our society and always will be. The problems that plague our nation enter—and disrupt—our classrooms every day. The child who comes to school hungry cannot learn. Young teens who *have* to work every night after school don't have time for homework. High school juniors, whose older siblings can't find decent jobs, have little incentive to study. "Why should I bother to get an education," they argue, "when there's no job out there for me?"

I am not an economist. I am not a sociologist. I have no economic game plan or social scheme that is likely to reverse the trends that increasingly divide this nation into two nations. But I am a teacher, and, as a teacher, I know that the classroom alone cannot solve society's problems. Every sector has to do what it can.

Do business and industry want well-educated students graduating from our schools? If so, then they will have to provide sufficient jobs for graduating students—*all* graduating students. Our students need that incentive. They need to be able to see that pot of gold at the end of the rainbow. Knowing that the pot of gold is waiting for them is a powerful incentive to achieve educational excellence. If the pot of gold is not there, then our schools will not succeed. And our society will not succeed.

As a teacher, I know that the prerequisite for meaningful social and economic progress is an educated citizenry, a nation of men and women who can democratically debate and resolve the problems that face them. This faith, I admit, is an old-fashioned one. But teachers truly believe that strong public education is fundamental to democracy. The stronger our educational system is, the more capable, the more effective, the more lasting our democracy will be.

JE: How serious an educational problem is the lack of discipline in the classroom?

MF: I strongly believe in the right of children to learn in an orderly classroom. The teacher must not permit an unruly student to disrupt the learning process for 20 or 30 other students. But, as a teacher, I resent the fact that some people have tried to paint a picture of America's public schools as a blackboard jungle. Our research shows that we are making considerable progress against discipline problems. In 1979, over 74 percent of teachers said that discipline problems impaired their teaching effectiveness. By 1983, the figure had dropped to 45 percent.

I would urge the media and the public to visit the nation's classrooms to see for themselves what is occurring in the public schools. Obviously, problems exist. And where problems do exist, educators and citizens should take strong action. At the same time, many schools are orderly, and many students can and do learn.

JE: Do most minority youngsters, in your view, understand the long struggle for freedom and justice in America? If not, why?

MF: No. Most minority students have little or no understanding of the struggle to achieve civil and human rights. They don't know that just 30 years ago they could not have attended school with whites. They don't know that 20 years ago many of them could not vote. And they don't know that today some people would still deny all Americans those two most basic of rights: education and voting rights.

JE: What is wrong with competency tests? Why shouldn't teachers be required to pass basic subject-matter tests?

MF: I want to see a quality teacher in every classroom. Forcing practicing teachers to take a paper-and-pencil test is not going to guarantee students a quality teacher. *All* teachers must be evaluated, not by multiple-choice tests, but in person, by trained evaluators who go right into the classroom and examine how a teacher actually teaches. Teachers who don't pass these evaluations should receive the special help and training they need to improve. If they don't improve, they shouldn't remain in the classroom and teach.

JE: In your view, what remains to be done to achieve equal educational opportunity?

MF: I believe that we in the educational community must assume part of the blame for the present situation. For years, we fought to desegregate schools, businesses, lunch counters, restrooms, and other public facilities—and then we let our guard down.

We at the NEA have fought to open the doors of opportunity for women and minorities—only to see today these groups continually passed by and passed over and to hear those words, "We're only interested in 'qualified' people to fill vacancies." I've often wondered why the word "qualified" is only used when it's our turn to walk through the door.

Today, we hear the old familiar voice of regression. We're told that school desegregation and the achievement of educational equity were gained at the expense of excellence. This is hogwash! We must stand firm in our belief that equity and excellence are not mutually exclusive. Equity and excellence are mutually dependent. Both must be vital national priorities if our public schools are to live up to this nation's time-honored ideals.

JE: Finally, what steps would you recommend to reverse the present situation?

MF: We must continue to espouse our ideals and work to improve the quality of education for *all* children! And, yes, we must insist that every child receives the maximum opportunity to achieve his or her highest, greatest potential. We must insist that schools encourage minority and female students to enroll in academic, as well as vocational, courses. We must insist that educators design programs to help children in elementary and secondary grades who fall behind in reading and math. We must insist that educators develop programs to identify potential school dropouts and find ways to encourage them to stay in school. And we must not allow—no, we must insist—that affirmative action not be blamed for the faults in teacher education programs. Affirmative action has not produced a drop in standards. Programmatic quality declined when the emphasis was placed on filling beds instead of filling heads. Affirmative action, instead, opened doors to higher education institutions for thousands of academically talented minorities and women. It is vital that we do make our teacher education programs as strong as possible. Generations of teachers yet to enter the profession will be hurt by programs that fail to prepare them to succeed in the classroom. We must change that situation!

I wish that we could separate human rights and education from politics. But I know that no area of public life is immune to politics. We must become actively involved in the political process. We must stand up for what is right. This will not be an easy fight. Nothing important ever is. But it is an *important* fight—a fight we must win. We have an opportunity to reverse our present course. Indeed, we have a challenge before us. For our children, for our nation, we must triumph over the enemies of equal opportunity and political access. We cannot—and must not—allow these enemies to stand in the way of the future.

Floyd B. McKissick

Making Black Capitalism Work

Floyd B. McKissick was born March 9, 1922, in Asheville, North Carolina. By December 1942, at age twenty, McKissick was struggling hard to put himself through Morehouse College, in Atlanta, Georgia. By January he had volunteered for the United States Army. World War II took McKissick to Europe for three years. He earned five Battle Stars and the Purple Heart for heroism in combat. And in the rubble of Europe, he witnessed engineers, planners, and scores of other technicians rebuilding cities out of ashes.

When McKissick returned from the war, he received a Bachelor of Arts degree from North Carolina College at Durham (now North Carolina Central University) in 1950. There he spearheaded the first group of law students before the state legislature to demand accreditation of the North Carolina Central University Law School.

McKissick was a staunch advocate of the elimination of trespass statutes which were often used to confuse and deter non-violent action campaigns against segregation. His strong advocacy and steel-like determination propelled the issue to the United States Supreme Court, and resulted in a decision that voided hundreds of trespass convictions.

In 1951 McKissick became the first Black to attend the University of North Carolina Law School. After completing his Bachelor of Laws degree in 1952, he was admitted to the North Carolina Bar and to the United States Supreme Court. A specialist in constitutional law, he is licensed to practice law in both the District of Columbia and North Carolina and before the Federal Communications Commission, the Federal District Court of Appeals, the United States Court of Appeals, and the United States Customs Courts. During his career, he has handled a record number of civil rights cases. His clients have also included businessmen, labor unions, and individuals of all races.

In 1963 McKissick was elected the national chairman of the Congress of Racial Equality (CORE) by acclamation. He was then appointed national director of CORE in 1966, when the organization's debt exceeded $4 million and morale was extremely low.

As national director, McKissick assumed the responsibility for reorganizing CORE, both from a financial and philosophical point of view. He raised morale to a new high. He also raised more than $3 million in two and one-half years.

For more than twenty-five years, McKissick has advocated black enterprise as the spearhead of racial equality. As a result, in the summer of 1968 he resigned as CORE's national director to form Floyd B. McKissick Enterprises, Inc. and to put into practice his advocacy of black capitalism.

From his memories of the rebuilding of Europe's great cities after World War II, McKissick launched what was to become the most ambitious development plan ever attempted by a black American: the creation of a new town: Soul City, North Carolina.

As envisaged by McKissick, Soul City was to be a $73 million prototype new town located in the heart of North Carolina's tobacco and textile producing country, a free-standing community of 5,076 acres of rolling fields and woodlands in Warren County. Soul City was conceived as a multi-racial community—a place for people of all races, ages, and religions to work together, play together, and learn together.

McKissick drew heavily on his own resources to launch Soul City. From the time the new town was announced in 1969 until the project agreement was signed with the Department of Housing and Urban Development (HUD), most of the costs of the project were borne by Floyd B. McKissick Enterprises, Inc.; McKissick himself invested, borrowed, and/or guaranteed loans of more than $1 million.

To McKissick, this is what the civil rights struggle of the 1960s was all about—an opportunity for Blacks to emerge as an economic force and to take their place in the free enterprise system. As McKissick saw it, Soul City was a grand experiment to prove the efficacy of black capitalism, to provide an alternative for the victims of a deteriorating agricultural economy who might otherwise drift off to a jobless existence in the cities, and to demonstrate that free-standing new towns could be a means to solve an increasingly worrisome national problem—namely, the maldistribution of population.

Sadly, the dream came to an abrupt halt. In March 1975, North Carolina Senator Jesse Helms accused the Soul City Company of misappropriating funds and lagging behind in development. A General Accounting Office audit was requested; after spending $500,000 and stopping further development at Soul City until December 1975, Soul City was given a clean bill of health. However, hostile publicity and widespread misinformation doomed the project to failure. Additional pressures were brought to bear, and proposals to bar further loans to Soul City were made in 1979, causing HUD to foreclose on the project.

Despite setbacks, restrictions, investigations, and insinuations, McKissick has not wavered in his efforts to make black capitalism work. Although Soul City is dead, McKissick's dream lives on. Throughout his life, McKissick has been more than a dreamer. He has been a doer. And he is hard at work today on new projects—projects which are designed to test the viability of black capitalism and the resourcefulness of black people.

JE: In 1969, you dedicated your book, *Three-Fifths of a Man*, to "... all the young people I have known and worked with who are seeking to bring about change in their society and who can see very clearly that changes must be made." Do you see in today's young people this same commitment to social change? If not, why?

FM: Well, I certainly see it in some of them. I run across a few students—a very few—who are strongly committed to eradicating injustice, but the desire to do something about injustice is, of course, not uppermost in most students' minds, as it was when I wrote the book. Generally speaking, they are concerned about everything *but* injustice— jobs, money, status. . . . They simply lack the commitment and/or understanding necessary to analyze what is happening and take action to change it. I recently attended a conference at North Carolina State University, in which the theme was human rights. I didn't see ten people there who were under thirty years of age. And there were more than 300 people in attendance. Most of the people there knew each other, and most of them were active in the 1960s. I don't understand why more effort wasn't exerted to attract young people. Certainly, there are young people out there who are committed. Many of them are involved with some of the more radical or newer organizations, as opposed to the more established ones. These groups tend to be fairly limited in their scope, as opposed to the organizations from which they sprang. So while I do see some committed young people, I'm just not sure whether we'll ever recapture the commitment which existed in the 1960s.

JE: What do you think explains this generation's lack of interest and/or commitment to the kinds of issues which concerned your generation?

FM: There are any number of reasons. First, the times have changed. The average high school student today wasn't even born in 1960. Therefore, most of them have little or no knowledge of what took place in the 1960s and why it took place. These kids never experienced segregation. Sadly, most black students have no knowledge of their own history. This, I think, contributes significantly to their preoccupation with drugs. My generation was very proud of its history. We wanted to understand our roots. You don't find that among today's young Blacks. They've been brainwashed into believing that they're secure—that history will never repeat itself. Many of them think that history began with their own birth.

Second, there has been a great decline in church attendance. For my generation, the civil rights struggle originated in, and was sustained by, the church. There was a strong commitment to the Judeo-Christian ethic—one which united us religiously and tied us to a philosophy that carried over from the Torah to the New Testament. It was a philosophy of service and sacrifice. It emboldened us to demonstrate in the streets knowing full well that there would be casualties. And there were casualties, many of which went unnoticed. Many of the young demonstrators developed mental disorders, some so severe that they had to be institutionalized. There were times, for example, when you went to a demonstration knowing that you might not make it back, but you went anyway. And oftentimes we made provisions just in case we didn't make it back.

JE: Over the years, you've placed great emphasis on the importance of education as a means of advancement. How well are America's schools preparing young people, particularly Blacks, for the challenges which await them?

FM: Not too well, I'm afraid. We don't teach ethics in the public schools, and that is unfortunate. We no longer even espouse ethical values in our schools. Moreover, we don't teach about the positive contributions that Blacks have made to our society, only about those who could sing or dance. That's a poor image. And promoting poor images will not prepare young Blacks for the challenges ahead.

JE: In what ways have you changed or matured since your early days in the civil rights movement? Are you the same person today that you were back then?

FM: I suppose I've changed some, but not too much. In fact, the only thing that's changed is my strategy, not my philosophy. It's basically the same today as it was then. It's necessary, however, to adapt to changing circumstances. One's approach must fit the times. That's critical in order to survive the long haul. My philosophy has always been long range. As a result, I've had to modify my approach. But fundamentally, I haven't changed. I'm just as radical today as I ever was.

JE: As you look back over your life and what you've been able to accomplish, what gives you the greatest satisfaction?

FM: I think I've made a number of contributions to the struggle. I led the first march down Fifth Avenue on behalf of women's rights. I was one of the people who initiated the National Conference of Black Lawyers. I worked with the Fellowship of Reconciliation, the War Resister's League, and nearly every major leftist cause. I issued the call to go down to Mississippi to help James Meredith, at a time when few people understood the significance of what he was doing. I played a role in the establishment of the Congress of Racial Equality (CORE) and helped to reshape its direction. CORE has made a vital contribution to the struggle, although it has received little recognition. And I launched Soul City, one of the early experiments in black capitalism. This area is a very different place because of what we did in Warren County. I spent a great deal of time, effort, and money trying to make it work, because I believed deeply in what I was doing. I gave up a great many things in the process. But the foundation has been laid. And now that that has been done, others can learn from our experience and initiate similar projects of their own.

JE: Are you still active in the civil rights struggle? If so, how?

FM: Although Soul City is ostensibly dead, I've not lost interest in the concept. Nor have I lost interest in the area in general. I work with a host of groups in this part of the state. I'm active in the National Association of Black Manufacturers, a group which I founded. I'm vice-president of the North Carolina Black Leadership Caucus. I'm active in the National Conference of Black Lawyers. I also work with many community groups, some of which I represent in legal matters. I speak before as many of these groups as possible, sharing with them my concerns about the future. Lately, I've worked closely with the North Carolina Black Political Party. I've also turned my attention to writing, which is quite difficult, what with my many interests and commitments.

JE: Are today's leaders, from your perspective, raising the correct issues? Do they appear to understand the direction in which the country is headed?

FM: Obviously, we're not living in the 1960s any longer. That's quite evident. Some leaders, however, seem preoccupied with the past. Their criticisms reflect the past rather than the present. And their strategies are rooted in the past. I understand their concerns, although I don't necessarily agree with them. In fact, I've always disagreed with the leadership in terms of where we should go. I've argued and will continue to argue that America is built on economics. I think we should have put greater emphasis on economics back in the 1960s, when the momentum was strong. Blacks must have an economic stake in America. And they must demand a share of the economic pie. I preached that message throughout the 1960s. However, the media chose to ignore it and focused instead on Dr. King and his approach to the issues. Black kids must be taught economics. Indeed, economics should be mandatory in the schools. Moreover, they must learn to read and write and compute. They must be able to develop an idea, value it, and keep others from stealing it. And they must learn more about themselves and their people, their culture and traditions. If not, these things will be lost. When I look at the Jews, for example, I marvel at what they've accomplished, how they've been able to preserve their rites and customs. They continue to struggle for the same things that blacks should be struggling for today. I admire their fortitude. I only wish we had it.

JE: How do you assess the record of the Reagan Administration, particularly in the area of civil rights?

FM: I think Reagan's election was a blessing in disguise. It proves how far this country has swung to the right. It shows that the coalition of the past—Blacks, liberal whites, and Jews—has broken down. And it underscores the fact that we need to come together again—that we need to reorganize and develop a program to reverse this trend. More important is the question: How did it happen? How did Reagan and his cohorts pull it off? I think we have to assume part of the responsibility because we permitted it to happen. We failed to see what was occurring. The biggest part of the blame, though, rests with the media. The press made Ronald Reagan, Jesse Helms, and Jerry Falwell. In the 1960s, the media exhibited high moral courage. They tried to be fair. Now, they seem to have retreated from that position. Today, the big thing is to get the story—at any cost, regardless of who's hurt. And they're rewarded for it, be it with money, status, recognition . . . For a long time, we believed that the government consisted of three branches: the legislative, executive, and judicial. Now, we must add a fourth one to the list: the media. It has the power to make or break someone or something.

JE: Does it concern you that several black leaders, some of them quite prominent, endorsed President Reagan and his program?

FM: Yes, very much so. It doesn't concern me, however, that Blacks are joining the Republican Party. I'm a political maverick. I believe in participating in both political parties. I think that's good for black people. What does trouble me, though, is what these people are saying and how they're saying it. Clearly, Reagan's rhetoric is vastly different from his actions. He talks a good game. But his policies are very dangerous. Those black leaders who support Reagan have urged our people to take hemlock in the guise of candy. It's like giving ExLax to children and telling them that it's chocolate. So yes, we must participate in both parties. That's a good thing. Our voices need to be heard. We should not allow ourselves to be taken for granted. But truth is truth. And the Reagan Administration is a Trojan Horse. Its goal is to keep the rich, rich and the poor, poor. His constituency is very clear. But it's not mine. And it does not speak to the needs of Blacks.

JE: Did you ever think the day would come when men like Jesse Helms and John East would be elected to the United States Senate? Did their victories surprise you?

FM: No, not at all. I was born in Asheville in 1922. I have relatives all over the state. I know all about lynch mobs. I've seen them in action. I've studied the politics of this state for years. Helms, for instance, opposed my admission to the University of North Carolina. He spoke out against it. Later he tried to get me disbarred. So, in an atmosphere where the pendulum has swung to the far right, I wasn't surprised to see either Helms or East elected to the Senate. That's why I favor a strong two-party system. The people must have a choice. A two-party system gives them that choice. While Helms and East may speak for the Republican Party, they are vigorously opposed by the Democratic Party, which has campaigned strongly against them. Not all political leaders in North Carolina are of the Helms-East stripe. There are great leaders, like former Governor Terry Sanford, who is now the president of Duke University. Through his efforts, many things in the state were changed for the better. He is the person most directly responsible for bringing about integration in this state. In fact, he nearly integrated the state before the Civil Rights Act was enacted into law. That's the kind of man he is. He knew what the state was, and he could relate to all elements within it. He wanted to be governor of all the people—and he was. Were it not for him, serious riots would have broken out in the state on a number of occasions. Although he represented the voice of moderation, he did not compromise himself in the process. Terry Sanford led the way. And the progress that has been made is directly attributable to his efforts.

JE: Do you view politicians like Helms and East as the new prototype of southern politicians? Are there many Helms-East types waiting in the wings?

FM: History teaches us that one man is always seeking to move up the ladder at the expense of another. It's like Hitler's rise from a paperhanger to a world leader. What's scary is that it can happen again. Helms, East, and others studied the civil rights movement—learned from it. And they've adopted some of the same tactics that we used so successfully. What's more, they have the organizational skill and financial resources necessary to reach millions of people. Interestingly, Helms receives an enormous amount of money from right-wingers through-out the country. He receives much more from outside the state than from within. So, to answer your question more directly, yes, Helms and East represent a new breed of politician. And yes, there are more like them out there. But there are also many who disagree with them and are willing to take them on. They're just as dedicated and determined, though not as well organized or financed.

JE: Are you concerned about the resurgence of the Ku Klux Klan and other hate groups in the country? Do you think they pose a serious threat to the political fabric of our nation?

FM: Yes, they pose a threat. It's become fashionable to speak of the "new" Klan. That's rubbish. The Klan's not new. It's the same Klan. What's different is the wrapping. The message is the same. They're still the enemy. Just because they wear Brooks Brothers suits instead of sheets doesn't mean they've changed. Groups like the Klan feed on hate. They prey on ignorance and fear. They always have and they always will. Unfortunately, they've proven quite adept at organizing and raising funds. And that makes them a formidable threat. It's important to take them seriously. They're dead serious.

JE: There are those who argue that the struggle for freedom and justice has been won—that the evils of the past have been eliminated. Would you agree?

FM: No, not at all. The struggle has *not* been won. There's no evidence to prove it. The civil rights acts are very much needed. Integration is still not a reality. You only have to look at the courthouses to see that. There are still very few black judges and attorneys. Justice is not meted out equally. The court system uses Blacks to bear the cost of running the country by arresting them at alarmingly high rates. Whites, on the other hand, are largely left alone. And I'm not exaggerating. Just look at the record. Fifty percent of the people in prison shouldn't be there. They're there for the wrong reason. They're the symptom, not the problem. If law and justice were administered fairly, we'd have a very different prison system from the one that exists. And the answer to the problem is not more prisons. That won't solve the problem. The problem is *injustice*—at all levels of society. So, no, the struggle has not been won—not by a long shot. In fact, many of the gains made in the 1950s and 1960s are now being systematically eroded. I think, for instance, that Attorney General William French Smith was expressly appointed by President Reagan to shut down the Justice Department, particularly those divisions charged with enforcing civil rights laws.

JE: Are you satisfied with the increasing numbers of Blacks who have been elected to public office? Do you see this as a sign of real progress?

FM: Well, yes, it represents progress—certainly, that was not the case before. And I'm glad that more and more Blacks are getting elected. Still, this does not mean, in and of itself, that there's any real sharing of power—which is, after all, the name of the game. Real power, you must understand, is economic power. It's not some game that's exercised or played before the public. The people with the money control the system. They have power by virtue of their economic muscle. This whole process of electing people, really, is a game. And we all know the game. They let a black person on the city council, the board of education, or whatever. But because that particular Black represents a minority, he can only express one person's opinion. After that, the others simply vote around him. The Black is never invited to the luncheon meeting where the real decisions are made. And at the public meeting, which is largely for show, issues are dispensed with in a matter of minutes or seconds. So, no, I don't see the election of a few Blacks as, in itself, particularly significant. Instead, we need sophisticated leadership at all levels of society, including the political arena, the church, and the streets. But we've never been allowed to develop that kind of sophistication. We're denied the opportunity to participate in those areas where we could learn the political ropes—something which would allow us to advance as a people.

JE: What will it take to bring about the economic sharing of power that you advocate?

FM: First, government must be committed to taking action on this front. Second, Blacks must believe in themselves and be willing to work hard to bring it about. To date, I see little evidence of either.

JE: Can these changes be made within the system, or is it necessary, in your view, to change the system itself?

FM: I'm not sure. The system has many defects. However, we must deal with the situation as it is. And capitalism, at least in some form, is here to stay. This means that we must seek to change the system from within. I believe this can be done. It is still possible to bring about reform. The system can be made to work better. It has to.

JE: What changes would you like to see made in the capitalist system?

FM: In America, capitalism and racism are intertwined. So much so, in fact, that they appear as one piece of cloth. Capitalism rewards ideas. Racist doctrine tells us, however, that "niggers" are not supposed to have ideas. As a result, society frequently takes our ideas and dreams away from us. Without ideas, people are lost; they stay at the bottom of the economic ladder. A good example of what I'm talking about is the music industry. American music owes a great debt to Blacks—indeed, American music derives from black music. But because of a lack of knowledge of copyright laws, Blacks benefit the least from the industry. You don't have lawyers to protect the interests of Blacks when it comes to copyright violations. Instead, they look out for their own interests. The only thing that Blacks can depend on is that maybe, just maybe, someone on Capitol Hill will protect their interests. But if that someone on Capitol Hill is in the hip pocket of some special interest group, then Blacks are left out in the cold. The music industry is not an isolated example. You can find other such examples throughout society. Another good one is land ownership. The old idea was not to allow Blacks to achieve power through owning land. As a follow-up to that idea, today the cost of homes has risen so high that Blacks are finding it next to impossible to purchase homes. The price of a house today is around $80,000. Even in rural areas, prices have soared to more than $40,000. These days, a three-room bungalow will sell for more than $50,000. Owning a home is no longer within the reach of most Blacks. For them, the American Dream is just that—a dream. Not long ago, I happened to read the list of black entrepreneurs put out by *Black Enterprise* magazine. Each time it comes out, there are fewer and fewer names on it. Because of a general disdain for black enterprise, financial institutions are quick to foreclose on black businesses at the first hint of trouble. It's similar to what happened at Soul City. Instead of our senators working to bring industry to Soul City, they fought us every step of the way and used the power of their office to destroy us. It was rumored that one of them remarked: "Hell will freeze over before I help that nigger. First, get the niggers out of the project; then we'll bring in all the industry you want." There was an active campaign to keep industry from locating in Soul City as long as I and other Blacks were involved in its operation. These are just some of the reasons why I'm critical of capitalism. What's the answer? We need a heightened understanding of the capitalist system. We've got to go through a re-education process. And we must become more adept at raising our own capital.

JE: As you see it, what can Blacks do to overcome the forces you've just mentioned?

FM: That question is both interesting and complicated. It requires more than an accusatory analysis. We must examine the methods we've used in the struggle and see whether they're applicable today. Some are, some aren't. Can groups like the NAACP, CORE, and SCLC be the forces they once were, or are the days of the civil rights organizations gone forever? Should we look to the political arena or to some new prophet for our salvation? Clearly, the situation requires a new approach—a new coalition. We must have an organized plan with clearly defined goals. This will enable us to take stock of our situation at any given time. Such a strategy is vital to our success.

JE: You've spoken of a "new coalition." What are the key elements of such a coalition?

FM: First, it must consist of a variety of individuals and groups. It should include the kinds of people who were active in the 1960s. The coalition should be committed to working within the system—reform as opposed to revolution—but the approach should be more broadly based than it was back then. The coalition would have to agree on common goals and objectives. And each element within it would have to recognize the significance of the desires of every other element. Also, it would have to be much more localized than simply a national center with a figurehead leader. The coalition would have to speak to the great masses of urban Blacks. Most of all, it would need a skillful public relations network. This was one of the failings of the civil rights movement of the 1960s. We desperately need that now. The coalition would have to devote considerable attention to establishing such an apparatus which, of course, brings us back to economics—the headpin of the whole system.

JE: As you look down the road, are you hopeful about America's future, particularly as it relates to the race issue?

FM: While I do see several hopeful signs, I am probably more doubtful today than I've ever been. The coalition I've proposed must be a partnership between two groups of people who come together because of some common purpose—each having something of equal value to contribute, in order to solve their problems. By that, I mean that a strong coalition must always be based on a sound economic footing. Unless Blacks are encouraged to participate fully in the economic system, we will continue to exist as an appendage of society. We must face facts, however unpleasant they may be. We live in an economic society, and unless we are part of that system, we will always remain on the fringes of society.

JE: In *Three-fifths of a Man* you wrote: "It may be too late now to reverse the great tides of racism and the sickening righteousness that has cloaked those forces." That statement was written in 1969. Are your feelings the same today?

FM: I still feel the same way. Very little has changed. It may just be too late.

JE: If you're correct, what does the future hold? Is there any reason for hope?

FM: Perhaps. What was right two million years ago is still right today. And by the same token, what was wrong then is still wrong today. Moral values are eternal. They do not change with the times. They are true for the ages. I can see a new wave of righteousness sweeping this country. The time will come, I think, when men of goodwill—of all races—will rise up and demand that we live up to our ideals. That has to happen. The future of America depends on it.

JE: Speaking of Soul City, what have you learned as a result of your experience? Has it made you wiser in terms of the political process?

FM: No, not really. I knew what the system was capable of doing. I knew how Blacks were destroyed by the system when they reached a certain point—not necessarily because they did anything that whites didn't do, but because of their color. I've seen many men sentenced to prison who never should have been. I saw Adam Clayton Powell (D-N.Y.)—a black congressman—fall. Like those before him, he was a victim of the white power structure. I saw what they did to Charles Diggs (D-Mich.). I watched them hound him out of the Congress. I knew that in a racist society, a similar fate could easily befall me. Caste and class still exist in this country. It makes no difference how high a black man goes in this country—there are still places he cannot go. There are still places in America—in this day and age—which exclude Blacks. We're excluded today by a system of private membership and economic deprivation. So, in that sense, I did not learn anything from what happened at Soul City. But to observe how it was done—and by whom—was a learning process. I really learned the value of public relations in shaping public opinion. It was public opinion—and the poisoning and control of that opinion—which ultimately doomed Soul City. It's things such as these that I'm more cognizant of today.

JE: At what point did you know, deep down, that Soul City was in trouble—that forces existed which were determined to destroy you?

FM: It started when the government failed to follow up on its scheduled activities. There were two major reasons for that—Rockefeller's death and Nixon's resignation. With Rockefeller's help, we were supposed to get support from private industry. When Rockefeller died, that support didn't materialize. Nixon's resignation served to divide the political establishment, which subsequently lost interest in the project. The Small Business Administration had promised to bring industry to Soul City. That never took place. The Department of Housing and Urban Development (HUD) made a commitment to provide housing but never financed a single house. They said it wasn't feasible after they had already agreed to do so. Unfortunately, most of the things we had agreed on never materialized. It was one broken promise after another. Another problem arose when we joined the League of Cities and requested higher staff salaries. Prior to joining, we had no idea of what people administering other community development projects were making. When we found out they were making three to four times what we were, we demanded—yes, demanded—that we be given similar salaries. That action infuriated the establishment. They thought we, as Blacks, should have been willing to do the job with a smaller staff and less money. Yes, we *were* doing more with less, but that's not how it should have been. Still another factor was this country's basic attitude toward black people. They started calling Soul City—and projects like it— "black capitalism" and "give away programs." They weren't giving anything away, but they used the label nonetheless. Such labels pave the way for the destruction of projects like ours.

JE: In terms of what ultimately occurred, how significant was Senator Helms's opposition?

FM: It was extremely critical. During that period, there was a great internal fight taking place between Senator Helms, Governor Hunt, and President Carter. And despite the fact that there was a Democrat in the White House, Helms, a Republican, was able to control HUD's office in Greensboro. He had the power to reach out and do a great many things. For example, more than once he introduced legislation to halt development at Soul City. In those instances, we were able to stop him, thanks to a bipartisan coalition of Democrats and Republicans who joined forces to defeat him. But he didn't give up. He used his influence to get the government to place all kinds of unrealistic requirements on the project. For example, HUD required that we use interlocking boards. But when they were quizzed about it, they denied it. They required a management plan but gave us little time to develop one. They told us that we would have to recruit industry after they had promised to do so. They asked us to replace the person who was serving as the project's general manager for no apparent reason. They established a line budget, whereby six people came down from Harvard, the Massachusetts Institute of Technology, and George Washington University and formulated most of the criteria—the budget, the goals, and the procedures of the project. All of this was done as part of the New Communities Program. We told them repeatedly that several of their goals were unrealistic. But they said, "No, they're *very* realistic, and if you want the money, you'd better do what we ask." Those are just several things they hit us with. I could go on and on. That's the way the government works, though. I gave up many years of my life to develop Soul City. I hustled and raised the money, and I bought the land long before the government became involved in the project. You might ask: Why did the government do what it did? The answer is fairly obvious. There were just too damned many intelligent Blacks congregated in one small area. And that frightened them.

JE: Toward the end of the project, you were subjected to several personal attacks, particularly in the media, where it was charged that you had misappropriated funds and engaged in nepotistic hiring practices. How did these charges affect you?

FM: Obviously, they hurt. They hurt me as well as my family. Those charges, of course, were never proven. Several audits were made—and are still being made—and we were given a clean bill of health. The General Accounting Office, in fact, did an exhaustive investigation of the charges. They found no basis to them. The newspapers had a field day. They knew the charges were unfounded. They had the facts in hand. But they refused to print them. I think their campaign was carefully orchestrated. As a public figure, I was fair game. I had to stand there and take it. I thought about suing. But you have to prove malicious intent, which is next to impossible. But, as I said, none of us took one penny of government money. We kept very accurate records. But since we didn't have a public relations firm and had no access to the media, we weren't able to fight back. And a large segment of the public believed what they read. What the public does not know, however, is how much money we had to raise to get the project off the ground. We had to raise more than $1.5 million just to get started. I spent a lot of years—and a lot of my own money—because I believed in Soul City. I still do. And to think that they accused me of misappropriating funds. Why, I lost money—and a lot of money—as a result of my involvement in the project.

JE: Finally, you recently enrolled as a divinity student at Shaw University. What motivated you to go back to school? And why religion? What appeal does it hold?

FM: It's something I had always wanted to do. I promised my father, my grandfather, and myself that I would do it one day. And the time seemed right. I've always felt that religion gives you the best of mankind and the world. It seems to me that it's the best way to understand society and human relationships. You might ask: What's next for Floyd McKissick? Well, I've been approached by some people who want me to help them build another Soul City. I've been offered several jobs with prominent law firms. But I'm committed to staying in the area. I've also been approached about running for office, but I'm not inclined to do that. I am inclined, however, to help others do so. And there's another role to play, I think. I'll probably become an elder statesman. And then there's writing. I'm going to write on topics of special interest. In fact, I've already started doing so. So, I figure I'll have plenty of things to keep me busy for a while.

Benjamin F. Chavis, Jr.

Blessed Are the Freedom Fighters

Benjamin F. Chavis, Jr. was born January 22, 1948, in Oxford, North Carolina, the direct descendant of the Reverend John Chavis, one of the first ordained black ministers in the United States. He holds a Bachelor of Arts degree in chemistry from the University of North Carolina; a Master of Divinity degree from the Divinity School of Duke University; a Doctor of Ministry degree from the Divinity School of Howard University; and is presently a candidate for the Doctor of Philosophy degree at Union Theological Seminary.

A former school teacher, Chavis is an experienced civil rights leader who has worked closely with Dr. Martin Luther King, Jr., the Southern Christian Leadership Conference, and the National Association for the Advancement of Colored People. He is the co-chairman of the Southern Organizing Committee for Economic and Social Justice and is currently attempting to organize the National Black Political Party.

In 1972, Chavis and nine other civil rights activists garnered national headlines when they were convicted of firebombing a grocery store during a series of race riots in Wilmington, North Carolina, in 1971. Although the case was tainted by evidence of repeated prosecutorial misconduct, the "Wilmington Ten," as they were called, were sentenced to a combined total of 282 years in prison. After nearly a decade—and legal expenses totalling over $1 million—the Wilmington Ten were freed. Chavis, who spent four and a half years in prison, was described by Amnesty International, the 1978 Nobel Peace Prize recipient, as one of America's political prisoners. On December 4, 1980, the Fourth Circuit U.S. Court of Appeals overturned the convictions of the Wilmington Ten and cleared their records and names.

An ordained minister of the United Church of Christ, Chavis presently serves as deputy director of the United Church of Christ

Commission for Racial Justice. A veteran of more than twenty years in the civil rights movement, Chavis has received numerous national and international awards. Among them are the National Community Service Award—Congressional Black Caucus (1977); the Paul Robeson National Freedom Medal—German Democratic Republic (1977); the Letelier-Moffitt International Human Rights Award—National Institute for Policy Sciences (1978); the National Courage Award—Southern Christian Leadership Conference (1979); the National Award—National Conference of Black Political Scientists (1980); the International Human Rights Award—Howard University Law School (1980); the Marcus Garvey/Steve Biko Memorial Award—University of Colorado (1981); and the William Spofford Human Rights Award—the Episcopal Church Publishing Company (1982). In addition, he is the recipient of Distinguished Public Service Awards from such cities as Detroit, Michigan; Dayton, Ohio; Louisville, Kentucky; Washington, D.C.; and Los Angeles, California. Chavis is the author of *Psalms From Prison* (Pilgrim Press, 1983).

JE: Can you describe the racial climate in Wilmington, North Carolina, prior to the celebrated firebombing of Mike's Grocery in 1971?

BC: Yes. From 1968 to 1971, during the height of the Nixon Administration's repression against civil rights workers and anti-Vietnam War peace activists, many school districts in the United States actively resisted the integration of black and white students. This was the case in Wilmington. However, through a successful civil rights suit filed by the National Association for the Advancement of Colored People, the schools in Wilmington were forced to desegregate. Reactionary forces including the Ku Klux Klan, the Rights of White People, and other paramilitary organizations violently protested the orderly desegregation of the schools.

JE: Why did the United Church of Christ dispatch you to Wilmington? What was your stated assignment?

BC: After receiving several requests for assistance from local community leaders, I went to Wilmington in February 1971 as a community and civil rights organizer for the United Church of Christ Commission for Racial Justice. I organized and led two nonviolent marches and demonstrations in support of the black students' requests for fair and equal treatment in the school system.

Owing to the possibility of violence and the intimidation of the black community by the Rights of White People, the Ku Klux Klan, and others who opposed school integration, I requested that city and state officials impose an official curfew to prevent the "night riders" from terrorizing black residents. However, Wilmington city officials refused to impose a curfew to prevent racial violence and refused to protect black citizens in their homes and churches from the vigilantes who were roaming the streets and terrorizing the black community.

Gregory Congregational United Church of Christ, the focal religious worship and meeting place of the local civil rights movement, came under intense armed attack by the vigilantes. Both within and in the vicinity of Gregory Church, black people were simply attempting to exercise their basic human rights and fundamental freedoms—including freedom of speech, religion, and conscience.

One year later, in March 1972, eight young black student leaders, a local white woman supporter of the civil rights movement, and I were arrested and charged with a long series of felony offenses that had allegedly occurred in February 1971. We became known as the "Wilmington Ten." From the moment of our arrest, until our exoneration, we repeatedly and steadfastly declared our complete innocence of these charges.

JE: Prior to the trial, did you have hopes that the charges would be dismissed? If not, why?

BC: On June 5, 1972, when we were first brought to trial in Burgaw, North Carolina, we all entered pleas of "not guilty" to the Superior Court of Pender County. During the jury selection process, we accepted a jury composed of ten black jurors and two white jurors. However, the state prosecutor, James T. Stroud (J. Stroud), prevented the trial from proceeding by demanding a mistrial on the grounds that he had (conveniently) become suddenly ill. It became obvious that the state prosecutor was determined to prevent the Wilmington Ten from receiving a fair trial before a jury composed of a majority of black jurors.

In spite of legal objections raised by our defense attorneys, the judge granted the mistrial and thus denied the Wilmington Ten (in violation of the Constitution of the United States and the Universal Declaration of Human Rights) the right to a fair trial before an impartial jury of our peers.

JE: Were the events significantly different when your case was brought to trial the second time? If so, how?

BC: On September 11, 1972, the Wilmington Ten were brought to trial for the second time in Burgaw, North Carolina. During the jury selection process, the local state prosecutor, aided by the North Carolina Attorney General's office, employed all but one of the forty "preemptory challenges" to prevent in sequence thirty-nine black jurors from being selected to serve on the jury. The presiding judge refused to excuse white jurors for "cause," although several admitted to being members of the Ku Klux Klan.

Consequently, the Wilmington Ten went on trial before a prejudiced and hostile judge and before a jury composed of ten white jurors and two elderly black jurors (the composition exactly the opposite of the first jury accepted by the defense). The wanton power of racist forces, acting in concert with the state judicial apparatus and the agents of racial injustice and political repression, conspired and set the stage for the unjust conviction of the Wilmington Ten.

JE: In your view, how damaging was the state's case? Who were the principal witnesses against you?

BC: Only three state witnesses gave incriminating testimony against us at the trial: Allen Hall, Jerome Mitchell, and Eric Junious. At the time of the trial, all three young men had previously been victimized by the vicious cycle of growing up in the United States in absolute poverty; running afoul of the law at an early age, only to "graduate" eventually to the adult prison system; and living the life of "street" and "ghetto" survival. Hall, Mitchell, and Junious were each under the detention and supervision of the state juvenile system initially and later of the adult prison system prior to their trial testimony.

JE: Do you believe that the state conspired to harass and silence the Wilmington Ten prior to the fire-bombing incident itself?

BC: Yes. For example, in February 1972, Allen Hall was taken by law enforcement officers from Lumberton, North Carolina, where he was incarcerated, to the Cherry Mental Hospital in Goldsboro, North Carolina, to meet with Jerome Mitchell who was undergoing psychiatric observation. Hall himself had been confined for psychiatric examination and observation in the fall of 1971. Hall and Mitchell, together, met at Cherry Mental Hospital for several hours with J. Stroud, state prosecutor in charge of the Wilmington Ten case; local law enforcement officers; and William Walden, an agent of the Alcohol, Tobacco, and Firearms Division of the U.S. Treasury Department. Hall and Mitchell testified that at several other meetings between Hall, Mitchell, and Stroud, law enforcement agents not only plotted the frame-up but made numerous attempts to coerce Hall and Mitchell into lying against the Wilmington Ten. At the Cherry Mental Hospital meeting, Hall and Mitchell were shown photographs of each of us so that they could identify us in court. Following the meeting, Treasury Agent Walden prepared separate typewritten statements incriminating the Wilmington Ten, which Hall and Mitchell signed later.

Eric Junious has since publicly admitted in sworn statements that he was shown marked photographs of the Wilmington Ten and instructed by the state prosecutor as to how to identify us prior to Junious's testimony in court.

The actions of the prosecutor in exhibiting marked photographs of the Wilmington Ten to the state witnesses Hall, Mitchell, and Junious to enable them to identify us at the trial constituted an illegal, coercive, and impermissibly suggestive identification procedure. This was in violation of our rights under the North Carolina Constitution, the United States Constitution, and the Universal Declaration of Human Rights.

JE: It is your view, then, that the state deliberately set out to prejudice the trial?

BC: Yes. The prosecution knew before and during the trial that the testimonies of Hall, Mitchell, and Junious were completely false. These fabricated testimonies facilitated the political persecution of ten innocent civil rights activists. In using testimony they knew was false, the state prosecutors denied the Wilmington Ten the right to a fair trial, due process, and equal protection of the law, confrontation, cross-examination, and effective assistance of counsel. This was in violation of the Constitution of the State of North Carolina, the Constitution of the United States, and the Universal Declaration of Human Rights.

JE: At what point in the proceedings did it become apparent that something was wrong—that the facts were not as presented by the state?

BC: In August 1976, the facts and truth about the Wilmington Ten frame-up became publicly known throughout the nation and world. The chief state prosecution witness, Allen Hall, signed a sworn, notarized statement declaring that his testimony against the Wilmington Ten in 1972 was completely false. He swore that he had testified because of false information given to him by the state prosecutor and police officers and because he had been promised that he would be released from jail within six months after he testified. Interestingly, although Hall received a twelve-year prison sentence in January 1972, that sentence was unlawfully amended in October 1972 (after Hall had lied in court against the Wilmington Ten), to make it possible for him to be eligible for immediate release. The amendment of Hall's sentence was made by Judge Marvin Blount at the insistence of state prosecutor Stroud.

In March 1977, Hall testified before a federal grand jury in Raleigh, North Carolina: He again acknowledged that his testimony was false and that he had been induced to give that false testimony by the state prosecutor and by the investigating officers. Hall testified that he had in fact been coached in giving his false testimony. Mitchell also appeared before the same grand jury and testified that his trial testimony was likewise false and that he too had been coached by the same person. He had also been promised by the state prosecutor that he would be released from jail within six months' time. Mitchell, in a letter received by the North Carolina Parole Commission on June 10, 1974, had already notified the commission that his testimony was false. However, this letter was not revealed to our defense counsel until its contents were reported by the news media in April 1977.

In January 1977, Eric Junious stated in a sworn, notarized statement that he had been promised a job and a mini-bike motorcycle for his trial testimony against the Wilmington Ten. In 1972, at the time of his trial testimony, Junious was only thirteen years old. In April 1977, Junious swore that his testimony at the trial was false and that he had been led to give such testimony because he had been told he would receive the mini-bike motorcycle. It should be noted that the state prosecutor, J. Stroud, did in fact give Junious the mini-bike a month after the Wilmington Ten trial in 1972.

JE: Can you describe the events surrounding the post-conviction hearing? Did these events prove significant?

BC: In May 1977, a post-conviction hearing for the Wilmington Ten was held in the Superior Court of Pender County in Burgaw, North Carolina. The hearing lasted for two weeks (the longest post-conviction hearing in the history of North Carolina). However, we were not allowed to be present at the hearing: We were kept locked in prison cells hundreds of miles from the Pender County Courthouse.

The denial of the fundamental human right to be present at our trial hearing was another deliberate and flagrant violation of the Helsinki Act, the Universal Declaration of Human Rights, and the International Covenant on Civil and Political Rights.

At the post-conviction hearing in May 1977, Allen Hall, Jerome Mitchell, and Eric Junious all testified under oath that their trial testimony against the Wilmington Ten had been false and that they had all received promises from the prosecutor which caused them to give the false testimony. For example, Mitchell testified: "They told me to cooperate or I could face life in prison . . . . They reminded me I had a brother who had just been convicted and that he also faced life in prison."

JE: What role, if any, did the Ku Klux Klan play in the case?

BC: Jerome Mitchell testified that the state prosecutor, J. Stroud, as well as other law enforcement officers, had kept him and Hall, both before and during the Wilmington Ten Trial in 1972, at a Carolina beach cottage, where they were visited by Tex Gross, a local Klan leader. The close relationship between Klan members and law enforcement officials in the Wilmington area simply confirms the racist intentions of the judicial and law enforcement system at its base. Clearly, it was impossible for the Wilmington Ten to receive a fair trial in eastern North Carolina because of the close ties between the police, the courts, and the Klan.

JE: Did the defense call witnesses who contradicted the testimony of the three young men? If so, why do you think you were convicted?

BC: On May 12, 1977, Reverend Eugene Templeton and his wife, Donna, testified at the post-conviction hearing in the Pender County Superior Court that Marvin Patrick, Connie Tindall, James McKoy, and I were actually inside their Wilmington home at the time Mike's Grocery was burned in February 1971.

In 1971, Reverend Templeton was the pastor of the Gregory Congregational United Church of Christ. At the May 1977 post-conviction hearing, Reverend Templeton testified that he had asked United Church of Christ officials to send me to Wilmington to help organize the local civil rights movement, particularly in terms of the rights of black students struggling against racism in the school system.

Assistant North Carolina Attorney General Al Cole, when he cross-examined Reverend Templeton, asked, "Why didn't you just tell them to leave?" (Cole was referring to those people present in the church during the violence: the students, their parents, and church members.) Reverend Templeton replied, "The feeling in the black community at that time was that they would not be intimidated by radical conservative whites . . . . It seemed at the time necessary to stay and defend the right to assemble."

Mrs. Donna Templeton testified: "After the church received bomb threats, whites in pickup trucks, members of the Klan, began riding by and shooting at the church and our home . . . . I was shot at twice."

John and Stephanie Green both testified at the post-conviction hearing that Wayne Moore could not have been at Mike's Grocery on the night that it was burned because Wayne was at their house at that time. Mrs. Slaton likewise testified that Joe Wright could not have been at Mike's Grocery at the time it was burned because Joe was at Mrs. Slaton's home.

At the post-conviction hearing when our chief defense counsel, James Ferguson, attempted to question the chief state prosecutor, J. Stroud, about the illegal coercion of the state's three principal witnesses —Hall, Mitchell, and Junious—Stroud repeatedly responded, "I do not recall."

Despite the fact that the state's major witnesses recanted their testimony and alibi witnesses testified that members of the Wilmington Ten were not present at the scene of the alleged crime, at the conclusion of the post-conviction hearing Superior Court Judge George Fountain refused to grant the Wilmington Ten a new trial. On May 20, 1977, Judge Fountain ruled: "I find no violations of constitutional rights." Thus, the conspiracy to persecute, to deny basic human rights, and to silence the Wilmington Ten continued unabated.

JE: Can you describe your experience in prison? Was it a difficult ordeal?

BC: Yes, very much so. The essential aim of the American penal system is punishment—not reformation or social rehabilitation. During the four and one-half years I was in prison, I personally saw the physical brutality of many inmates by prison officers. I saw prisoners who were physically forced to take dangerous behavior modification drugs such as thorazine and prolixin. I spoke to prisoners who were forced to submit to electric-shock treatment on their brains. I saw prisoners "watered down" in their cells with a 200-pound-pressure water hose by prison officers. And I saw elderly prisoners made to slave in plantation fields until their limbs gave out (often resulting in amputation of their legs).

On March 18, 1976, at Caledonia State Prison, as punishment for reading the Bible to fellow prisoners and speaking to them about prisoners' human rights, I was put into leg irons and chains, lifted up and placed on the back of a prison truck, and transferred 200 miles to McCain State Prison. While I was incarcerated at McCain Prison for three months, state prison officials refused to let me physically touch my children and family when they came to visit.

In May 1976, because of the cruel and inhuman treatment, I went on a 131-day "fast" and hunger strike to protest the unjust treatment and imprisonment of the Wilmington Ten and to protest the feculent conditions of the prison system.

JE: In 1980, after nearly a decade, your conviction was overturned, and the Wilmington Ten were freed. Who was most responsible for the reversal?

BC: On December 4, 1980, the Fourth Circuit U.S. Court of Appeals in Richmond, Virginia, overturned the unjust conviction of the Wilmington Ten. The Wilmington Ten were freed and vindicated as a result of both personal struggle and an active praxis-faith in God. In the end, our fate was not decided by the courts, but by public opinion. A legion of concerned Americans and others throughout the world—both black and white—raised their voices on our behalf. In the end, justice triumphed and righteousness prevailed.

JE: As deputy director of the Commission for Racial Justice, you have waged a personal war against racially motivated violence in America. How serious is the problem? Are there signs that it is abating?

BC: In recent years, America has witnessed unprecedented numbers of black people victimized by racially motivated violence. But I would like to expand my definition of the victims of racially motivated violence. There are literally entire black communities behind bars: men, women, and children. To me, this is an institutionalized example and manifestation of the increase in racially motivated violence.

The so-called criminal justice system is appropriately named. It is a *criminal* system. It is antithetical to talk about criminal justice, even though many people are attempting to reform the criminal justice system. As we try to reform that system and to make that system just for non-criminals, we find that it is very difficult in the absence of being involved in the overall struggle to transform society at large. This is why we must talk about the struggle for black liberation, the struggle to transform America from an unjust society to a just society, from an exploitive society to a nonexploitive society.

History will bear out that as soon as those who are oppressed, particularly in this society, organize themselves and attempt to stand up for what is right, somehow the powers that be will come down on them. More than ever, I believe that we need lawyers, experts in the legal field who are committed to being freedom fighters and who are committed to using their skills and resources to transform the system.

JE: Do you believe that the political system can be reformed? If not, why?

BC: I do not believe you can reform a racist system. Those of us who understand the system must transform it progressively. It is not enough to condemn Klan violence. We must condemn all racially motivated violence. In doing so, we must transform this nation. This can only be achieved through a protracted struggle, and that involves adopting a non-traditional approach.

To eliminate racially motivated violence, we must identify its causes. Certainly, the racism that has persisted over the years is a primary factor. Reaganism is another primary factor. I don't like to use the term "Reaganomics" because that term suggests the existence of a worked-out economic theory. In fact, there is no such thing as Reaganomics. There is "Reaganism," which is synonymous with racism. I think that the massive buildup in America's nuclear arsenal represents an increase in racially motivated violence. The Supreme Court is no longer a place where people can look to the judicial branch of government to intervene when the executive and the legislative branches exceed their authority. Today, the legislative, executive, and judicial branches of government belong to the same camp. They have always belonged to the same camp, but that fact has not always been manifest in the past. There exists as much of a Ku Klux Klan mentality operating in my hometown in Oxford, North Carolina, as is operating in the White House, in Congress, and in the Supreme Court.

Very often people ask me, what's the number-one problem facing our people? Nine times out of ten, someone who belongs to the black middle class will respond with "inflation" or "balancing the budget." We must reduce inflation. And we must balance the budget. However, I think that if the budget were balanced, even more racially motivated violence would exist. I believe that the system is dysfunctional and that we must admit that fact. I think it is vital that we—those of us in the middle class—accept the role of organizing those who are oppressed. We must become the organizers of the poor and rejected, because only when we build a mass-based movement in this country will we really convince those in power to stop their policies. In fact, the issue goes beyond stopping their policies. We must remove them from public office. The two-party system will not accomplish that objective. We must build alternative political structures in this society—an independent political party and other organizations that can apply pressure on those who enforce Reaganism and racism and those who permit racially motivated violence to continue unabated.

JE: Do you believe that high public officials either support or condone racially motivated violence? If so, who?

BC: Let me cite a specific example. Why is it that at no time in American history has a prosecutor ever been arrested and indicted for the abuse of the prosecutorial office? One of the things we learned in the Wilmington Ten case was that a prosecutor in this country not only enjoys immunity but has unbridled power. In fact, the criminal justice system has been used and continues to be used violently against those who would transform this unjust system into a just system. You might remember that in 1970 and 1971, during the height of the Nixon Administration, there were calls for law and order. Nixon and Spiro Agnew (the vice-president) campaigned across the country demanding law and order. In fact, law and order was a code phrase for keeping the movement in check—keeping the civil rights movement in check, the freedom movement in check, the peace movement in check. This assured that those who advocated progressive change in the 1960s would dare not advocate such changes in the 1970s; if they did, then the full arm of so-called law and order would come down upon them.

Racially motivated violence was committed against the Wilmington Ten and the Charlotte Three. It was committed against Angela Davis, Fred Hampton, and Mark Clark. Why? It was not because they were breaking the law; it was because these brothers and sisters were actually organizing people to transform society. And the full arm of the so-called law came down upon them to maintain the status quo.

So when we talk about preventing an increase in racially motivated violence, I hope we dare to go to the real core; I hope we dare to penetrate the surface areas in terms of what might be the causes, the factors; and I hope we go to the root of the problem. America is the problem. Let us not talk about a decrease in racially motivated violence inside the United States if we are not also willing to talk about decreasing racially motivated violence outside the United States in the Third World. So much of the violence to Third World people emanates from this country. American foreign policy emanates out of its domestic policy. The reason why this nation is in favor of moving closer to the racist apartheid regime in South Africa—if you listen to the speeches that Prime Minister (Pieter William) Botha makes—is that Botha intends to subjugate the rising masses by establishing a pseudo-middle class in South Africa. In doing so, Botha is looking to the American experience to try to discover a way to suppress the great masses of African people.

Therefore, let us be mindful that this problem of racially motivated violence is not simply a local problem or a national problem but a world problem. The Third World, the poor, and the oppressed are riding the tide of liberation. We must celebrate this fact because they too have been the victims of racially motivated violence. Those of us who support black liberation in America cannot talk seriously without supporting black liberation in the Caribbean, in Latin America, in the Middle East, in South Africa, and throughout the world. I'm not saying that these are the only important liberation struggles. But out of my own history and culture, I must say that these have to be my particular priorities. We know that we must build coalitions. However, coalitions must be built from a position of strength and not weakness. Too often in the 1970s, people tried to build coalitions from a position of weakness. Folks thought, well, if we join together, although we may be weak in our community, then we will have strength. It never happened. But if you bring strength to a coalition, then that coalition will in fact be strong.

JE: What specific strategies would you propose, both short- and long-term, to eliminate racially motivated violence?

BC: First, we must accurately assess those parts of the country where an effective struggle against racially motivated violence exists. If I didn't learn anything else from the Wilmington Ten case, I learned that if you are going to struggle against the system, you must employ both legal and extra-legal means. These means must be linked and must be planned. We need a long-range plan. We can't simply react every time the Ku Klux Klan burns a cross. We can't let the Klan and other hate groups determine the momentum of the struggle against the increase in racially motivated violence. Instead, we must have a long-range plan of action and strategy and carry it out.

I think the handwriting is on the wall. We must not only read, understand, and make an analysis of the times in which we live, but we must also be bold enough and courageous enough to go back into our communities and organize people who share our views to bring about this transformation. The struggle involves sacrifice, the struggle involves pain. But the truth of the matter is that a lot of brothers and sisters are experiencing great pain and suffering, anyway. I would much prefer to catch difficulty in life because I'm struggling for my freedom than to catch it while lying back, aloof to what's happening in my community.

JE: Do you foresee any dangers in this struggle? If so, what?

BC: Unfortunately, too many middle-class Blacks think that they have outgrown the struggle, and that in itself is a major danger. As a minister, I know that God is with us in this struggle, whether a person believes in Him or not. We must be clear as to where we wish to go and how we plan to get there, and then have a vision of the kind of society we would like to see. Racially motivated violence must not only be viewed as an unacceptable proposition, but it must be eliminated through our struggle to transform this society into a just society for all Americans, regardless of race or socioeconomic status. If we do our homework in this country, then the whole world will benefit. People around the world will realize that their ability to struggle in their own geographical context will be greatly aided if we build a struggle here.

The struggle for black liberation is alive and well. To the extent that we make progressive movements forward, we will help others in the process. Every gain that we have made as Blacks in this country has also benefitted other people. This is something that must continuously be taught. One of the things that a racist atmosphere does is to try to pit individuals against one another so that they will be blind to the real enemy. We must forge ahead and hope that those in the progressive community will support that struggle but grant us the self-determination to develop our own leadership, our own goals, and our own methodology.

JE: In recent years, you have written and spoken extensively about what is called "rainbow theology." What is rainbow theology?

BC: "Rainbow theology" is, first and foremost, a liberation theology. It is a theology that seeks to involve people of faith in the liberation of the oppressed. In the United States, rainbow theology represents an attempt to cross racial lines to bring together Blacks, Hispanics, Asians, native Americans, and progressive whites in a spiritual and political movement that seeks to effect social change.

The term "rainbow" underscores the rainbow promise to encourage both group identity and inter-group cooperation. Our goal is not to merge the colors of the rainbow into a new tint, a new color, but to say to the Hispanic community, for example, that we appreciate your culture, your traditions, your heritage. We understand your struggle because of our own oppression, and we must join forces against our common enemy.

Rainbow theology is an ecumenical theology. It encompasses all major religious denominations. It provides the religious community an opportunity to work together to bring about a more humane world. It derives from the historical struggle for freedom and justice. It is not an abstract theology. It is rooted in real-world realities. It is a practical theology. I think the church movement can learn much from the advent of rainbow theology. It has succeeded in building a broad-based movement—one which cuts across racial, class, and religious lines.

JE: How would you describe your view of God? What role does God play in your life?

BC: I believe that God is God of the universe. I also believe that God is the judge of what He has created. We, as human beings—along with the rest of God's creations—have a special responsibility to the creator. I don't think that God created us only to turn us loose to live our lives as we please. I believe that God personifies justice. I see God as the ultimate power, separated in time and place from everyday life. At the same time, I think that God has already appeared among us—that He has and does intervene in life. However, I do not believe in the Apocalypse. I do not expect God to singlehandedly purge the world of its sins. We must do God's work here on earth.

I believe that God has revealed Himself in many different ways, to many different people, at many different times. I do not think that any one religion has a monopoly on the truth. The story of religion—all religions—is the pursuit of justice. Clearly, the world boasts riches enough for everyone. But because of greed, racism, and exploitation, there exist hunger, illiteracy, ignorance, and deprivation. These conditions exist because we, as human beings, have allowed them to exist. I don't think, for example, that God wishes or likes for people to go to bed hungry at night. There is nothing noble about poverty. I believe that the church must take the side of the poor. The church must stand with the oppressed. But the church must do more than "stand" with the poor: It must seek to eliminate the causes of poverty. In other words, the church must serve as liberator. For me, God is God of the oppressed—not the oppressor.

Most political leaders, including President Reagan, profess a belief in God. However, I do not believe that Mr. Reagan believes in God. I believe that one's faith in God is determined by how one lives, not by what one says, or writes, or proclaims. As a Christian, I think we must stand with the poor—that we must use whatever means we have at our disposal to eliminate the causes of poverty. President Reagan talks a good game, but his actions contradict his faith. He has embraced the oppressor, not the oppressed.

JE: The church has always played a major role in the black community. Why?

BC: First, the black church originated as a protest church. It originated as a gathering place where the slaves, the descendants of slaves, and those who had escaped from slavery could gather and pray for help in their difficult struggle. Second, the black church has provided a vehicle for the development of leadership. Under its tutelage, the mantle of leadership has been passed down from one generation to another. Third, the black church is one of the few bastions of independence. It has been the only institution where black people, independent of the majority population, could maintain economic control. And because of that economic independence, the black church could serve as a forum for the discussion of controversial issues without fear that the members would lose their jobs. Fourth, the black church has always placed a high premium on the family. The black church resembles an extended family—at least it has in the past. It symbolizes unity, togetherness, solidarity. Those values are extremely important to the black church. The black church has always inspired hope in times of darkness. Whenever a crisis arose in the black community, the first place Blacks would go to was the church. They didn't flock to the church because they believed the minister had a miracle cure, but they came together in the presence of God and hoped that somehow, someway, they could together find a solution. This explains why the black church was such an excellent spawning ground for the civil rights movement. The church was the ideal place for Blacks to congregate in the spirit of unity and purpose to join forces to do common battle against injustice.

JE: Does the black church serve a similar purpose today? Is it still the moral conscience of the black community?

BC: Yes. In fact, the church is the only institution which speaks for black America. As you know, I worked closely with Reverend Jesse Jackson during his 1984 presidential campaign. I travelled across the country with Jesse, visiting countless black churches. The church has not only brought Blacks together, but it has instilled in them a personal responsibility to effect change. The black church has always possessed the ability to sound the alarm when the alarm needed to be sounded. It possesses the ability to advance specific strategies for specific problems. And it is not afraid to tackle the problem of social or economic injustice.

I do not think, however, that the black church is without criticism. It is our role, as black clergy, to be self-critical and to develop mechanisms to improve our effectiveness and our ability to respond to social wrongs. The black church has great potential. As black clergy, we must use our position to improve and enhance the quality of life for our people. We must stand united. In doing so, we must avoid interdenominational rivalry. The stakes are too high to permit petty squabbling to deter us from our overall purpose—which is the total emancipation of our people. We must never lose sight of that objective.

JE: You've described Reverend Jackson's decision to run for president not only as a political decision, but also as a moral one. What did you mean?

BC: I believe that Jesse's decision was *more* of a moral decision than a political one. Let me explain why. I spent several months with Jesse prior to his 1983 presidential announcement. Although tremendous grass-roots support for his candidacy existed, many black leaders were opposed to his running. Clearly, his decision to run was a liability in terms of the black leadership. Second, the threats on Jesse's life increased tenfold as the time grew closer for him to announce his decision. This was true not only of Jesse personally, but also of his family. Third, Jesse's decision to run was not universally applauded by Operation PUSH, the organization which he presently heads. PUSH is vitally dependent on Jesse. It was built around Jesse the man. When Jesse suggested that he would have to take a leave from PUSH, it caused serious reverberations within the organization. For Jesse, it was an organizational liability to leave PUSH to run for president. Fourth, Jesse recognized that he had to do more than wage a symbolic campaign: It had to be a competitive effort. This meant that he would have to make whatever sacrifices the campaign required—and they were many.

Jesse *did* decide to run. And he ran as the spokesperson for the poor, the despised, the rejected. If you read his announcement speech, you will see that it reads very much like a church sermon. Jesse said that he decided to run for president in order to give voice to America's dispossessed. He told his supporters that he decided to run so that they would have a voice in national politics—so that they would no longer be ignored by those seeking the highest office in the land. In other words, Jesse's decision to run was a *moral* decision—it was the correct thing to do if one was serious about eliminating poverty and injustice. Jesse did not run out of political expediency. In fact, most of the quasi-politicians around Jesse urged him *not* to run. They said it would be political suicide.

I was with Jesse when he decided to go to Syria. We were at a minister's meeting in Memphis, Tennessee. At that meeting, Jesse said, "I think we should do something about Lieutenant (Robert) Goodman." Many of Jesse's lieutenants said, "Look, Jesse. You're running for president. If you go to Syria and come back empty-handed, you're through politically." And Jesse said: "What about Goodman? What will happen in the Middle East if something happens to him? Everyone will lose: the Syrians will lose, the Israelis will lose, the United States will lose, and certainly Goodman will lose." Then Jesse said: "I want us to pray about this." And so we prayed. Jesse appointed Reverend Wendall Howard, as well as several other ministers, to form a delegation. Later, Jesse publicly stated that his decision to go to Syria was to make a *moral* appeal to President (Hafez al-Assad) Assad—not a political appeal, but a moral one.

Jesse's trip to Syria was a moral pilgrimage. That is why it was so successful. He wouldn't have gotten to first base if the Syrians had thought that he had come there to talk politics as a tool of the United States government. The Syrians viewed him as an authentic voice of the powerless in the United States. Therefore, what he said took on greater meaning in the international arena. That is why Jesse proved so successful in negotiating the release of Lieutenant Goodman.

I also accompanied Jesse when he went to Cuba. He did not go to Cuba to protest our government's immoral blockade of Cuba. He went to forge a closer relationship between the black church in this country and the church in Cuba. Indeed, both Jesse and President Fidel Castro met at the same church, at the same time, and spoke from the same pulpit. It was a historic moment. It proved extremely significant. Once again, Jesse was able to bring home the captives. He didn't go to Cuba to make a political appeal to Castro; he went there to make a *moral* appeal. In fact, he said: "Mr. President, you should take the moral initiative. Release the prisoners with no strings attached." It worked. Castro bought it. Once again, Jesse's was a moral pilgrimage.

JE: How do you view the relationship between politics and religion? Do you support Reverend Jerry Falwell's intrusion into the political process?

BC: Reverend Falwell and the Moral Majority have had a profound impact on American society. But the Moral Majority is nothing new. We've always had a so-called Moral Majority. In fact, during the slavery era, there were those in the church who sought to sanctify that evil institution. Citing biblical authority, they argued that blacks were the descendants of Ham and thus should be enslaved. They cited scripture from the New Testament, which extolled the virtues of obedience to one's master. So, Falwell's Moral Majority is not new; it has deep historical antecedents.

However, the existence of the Moral Majority does not upset me; it's perfectly proper for those in the church to speak out on social issues. It would upset me greatly, however, if there were no counterpoint—that is, if there were no Jesse Jackson or rainbow coalition. It's not enough to condemn the Moral Majority. We must articulate our own vision of America. We must be proactive, not simply reactive.

We must propose our own critique—the Moral Majority critique must not be allowed to stand unchallenged. I also think that Falwell's support is thin. We could win over many of the Moral Majority if we attempted to do so. If we ignore this group, then their ranks will continue to grow. The black church, as well as progressive white churches, have enormous potential, but too many of them remain silent on the great issues of our time. Why is it, for example, that Riverside Church (in New York City) is always viewed as the great peace church? Why shouldn't every church in America be a peace church? Every community ought to boast a Jesse Jackson, a Martin Luther King, Jr., a Malcolm X, a Fanny Lou Hamer, a Rosa Parks. Today's black leadership must till the ground for the next generation of black leaders. We must honor yesterday's heroes, but we must also pave the way for tomorrow's heroes.

JE: Do you think that the Moral Majority will enjoy greater influence in the future? Do you view the Moral Majority as a threat to black America?

BC: If the Moral Majority were to enjoy real influence, then I would certainly fear for the future of black people. Clearly, America would be an inhospitable place for Blacks. Although the situation is far from good today, it would be considerably worse were Falwell to have his way. Now, at least, we can work to transform America into a more hospitable place in which to live. Falwell symbolizes regression—he is a throwback to the days of Jim Crow. Were he to achieve real power, the very foundations of free expression would be challenged, if not eliminated. The Moral Majority's influence is attributable, in large measure, to their skills in organization. We on the left, however, have failed miserably in this regard. We are unorganized and disunited. This must change if we are to successfully counter the growing influence of groups like the Moral Majority.

JE: Like Reverend Falwell, Minister Louis Farrakhan, the leader of the Black Muslims, has sparked enormous public controversy. Does Farrakhan speak for black America? Has he made a positive contribution?

BC: Minister Farrakhan is a *great* leader. And like most great leaders, his greatness will probably not be recognized until his death. Farrakhan possesses a certain audacity, which I think is extremely important to the movement. But it doesn't actually matter what I think of Farrakhan. In terms of the black community, Farrakhan is welcomed and cheered wherever he goes. He shatters the myth that in order to be an effective black leader, you must accommodate the interests of the ruling class. To some extent, Farrakhan derives from the Malcolm X tradition, while Jackson derives from the Martin Luther King, Jr. tradition. I do not mean to suggest that Jesse is a carbon copy of Martin or that Louis is a carbon copy of Malcolm. But, I do believe that in the black community, we need both traditions. As an oppressed community, we must reserve the right to be audacious—the right to say what may be unpopular, but what may also be the truth. I believe that much of what Farrakhan says is true. It is unpopular, yes, but it's true.

Has Farrakhan made a contribution to the moral debate? Yes, very much so. However, his contribution has been both positive and negative. Still, I would rather have him make *a* contribution than *no* contribution, even if I may occasionally disagree with what he says. Farrakhan speaks not only for himself but for large numbers of Blacks who share his moral outrage. Not all Blacks agree with him on everything—for example, his views on the Middle East—but I think that most Blacks recognize that there exists the need for leaders who represent his point of view. As far as the rainbow coalition is concerned, I think that Farrakhan has done much to give meaning to the theology of the movement. He brings to the dialogue the insights of the Islamic religion, which I think are extremely important.

JE: Do you think that Reverend Jackson's campaign will significantly affect the way in which Blacks view the political process? If so, how?

BC: The Jackson campaign will affect the political process in two major ways. First, it will heighten black involvement and participation, as well as serve as an inspiration and encouragement to large numbers of black Americans. I think that is healthy. Second, Jesse's campaign has heightened the contradictions in American society, which is also healthy. In running for president, Jesse has forced the Democratic Party to rethink its approach to black America. He has said to the party, in no uncertain terms, "Let us in, make room for us, give us a chance." I do not believe that the rejected and locked out will stop participating simply because Jesse lost his bid for president. The Jackson campaign has made a monumental contribution. The future will depend, to a large extent, on whether the leadership of the Democratic Party will make way for this large group of forgotten Americans. If not, we may well see a new political party in 1988.

JE: How would you respond to those who argue that it is inappropriate for a clergyman to become actively involved in politics—that such involvement threatens the very principle of separation of church and state?

BC: Political advocacy is part of our calling. Our calling requires that we teach as well as lead. And we must not be apologetic about it. Unfortunately, the church has allowed itself to be pushed up against the wall. It has been too quick to apologize for using its position to effect social change. That is why I disagree with the Pope. The Pope's position is replete with contradictions. He will tell the church of Poland, as well as Solidarity, to do battle against poverty and injustice. At the same time, he will go to Latin America and warn the clergy to stay clear of politics. The Pope denounces the evils of communism but refuses to advocate militant action to rectify the conditions which breed communism. I think the Catholic Church would be better served if it was both anti-communist *and* anti-capitalist. But the Pope has chosen to be only anti-communist. I disagree with that position. The Pope has a right to extol the virtues of capitalism if he views it as an expression of the Kingdom of God. But if he feels that way, he ought to say so. But I would disagree with him on that point. I believe that capitalism is the antithesis of the Kingdom of God. For me, God is a God of justice, and the church should be a justice church. I don't think the church should embrace an economic system which reinforces disadvantage and oppression.

JE: Many critics of the left argue that Christian clergy are frequently apologists for leftist dictators who deny religious freedom in their own countries. How can a clergyman embrace a Marxist leader who actively opposes religious freedom?

BC: That's an interesting question. That objection is often raised, for example, when speaking of Fidel Castro. I have been to Cuba. Religious freedom is alive and well in Cuba. In fact, I preached in a Baptist church in Havana. When Castro visited the church, the people celebrated both the Cuban Revolution and Jesus. They shouted the names of Fidel and Jesus. It was an extraordinary moment!

Many people are critical of Cuba because of what the Cuban Revolution did to the Catholic Church. Keep in mind, however, that at the time of the Cuban Revolution, the major part of the church was Catholic. At the same time, the majority of the priests came from Spain. There were very few Cuban priests. In addition, the Catholic Church had become a counterrevolutionary force in Cuba. Castro did not close the churches, but he did round up the Catholic priests and send them back to Spain. In the process, a new class of Cuban priests emerged—one which believes in Catholicism as well as the importance of revolutionary change. Today, the church is actively involved in the struggle. It accepts its responsibility to help effect meaningful change. It identifies with the common man, as opposed to the wealthy land barons.

JE: Finally, do black clergy have a special responsibility to black America? If so, what?

BC: Yes. Black ministers have a responsibility to articulate unapologetically the issues which affect our people. They have a responsibility to provide moral leadership to help rectify the problems which affect our communities. They have a responsibility to preach love, respect, and pride. The black church must never forget its mission. It must speak out on the great issues of the day. It must lead the battle for racial justice. It must denounce the evils of oppression, discrimination, and bigotry. It must mobilize the black masses. And it must never forget that its responsibility extends beyond the pulpit. It must be a community-based church. And that community must be defined in the broadest possible terms. It must champion justice everywhere—and it must condemn oppression wherever it rears its head.

PART FIVE

State and Local Government

Carl B. Stokes

Causes Lost, Causes Won

Carl B. Stokes was born on June 21, 1927, in Cleveland, Ohio. The great-grandson of a slave, Stokes was only two years old when his father, Charles, a laundry worker, died. His widowed mother, Louise Stokes, supported her two sons by working as a domestic but found supporting her family exceedingly difficult. As a consequence, the family was forced, at times, to live on public assistance. Carl and his older brother, Louis, augmented the family income as newspaper carriers for the *Cleveland News*.

Stokes dropped out of high school (East Technical High School) in 1944 and went to work in a foundry. Shortly after his eighteenth birthday he entered the army. While serving with the Army of Occupation in Germany, he resolved to complete his education. When he returned to Cleveland following his discharge, Stokes re-enrolled at East Technical and received his high school diploma in June 1947. He then attended West Virginia State College and Cleveland College of Western Reserve University. In 1954, he received a Bachelor of Science in Law degree from the University of Minnesota. Two years later he earned a Doctor of Laws degree from Cleveland Marshall Law School.

In 1957, Stokes entered private law practice with his brother Louis in the firm of Stokes and Stokes. The following year he was appointed assistant city prosecutor and served in that position until 1962 when he became the first black Democrat in the history of Ohio to be elected to the Ohio General Assembly. He was re-elected in 1964 and 1966. At that time members of the assembly were elected county-wide. Cuyahoga County's population was only 14 percent black. Stokes remains the only black Democrat ever elected county-wide to the Ohio State Legislature.

In 1967, Stokes attracted international attention when he was elected mayor of the City of Cleveland—the first black mayor of a major American city. Since Cleveland was only 38 percent black at the time, it also marked the first time a black person had been elected mayor of a predominantly white major American city. In that election, Clevelanders selected the great-grandson of a slave over the great-grandson of a United States president. Following his victory, the White House asked Stokes to represent the United States on several goodwill trips to Europe as well as to the Caribbean.

Stokes continued to score a series of "firsts" during his tenure as mayor. In 1970, the 15,000-member National League of Cities, composed of mayors and city and county officials from throughout the nation, unanimously elected him president of that organization—the first black official to ever hold that office. He also served on the Advisory Board of the U.S. Conference of Mayors, as well as on the Steering Committee of Urban America, Inc.

Stokes served two two-year terms as mayor and won re-election in 1969 by a margin that was more than double his previous vote count two years earlier. In 1971, he announced that he would not seek re-election to a third term but, rather, would expand his efforts beyond the Cleveland area to assist others, particularly black Americans, to better understand their role in politics and government.

In 1972, Stokes became the first black anchorman to appear daily on a television news program (NBC's flagship station, WNBC-TV) in New York City. He also served as urban affairs editor and United Nations correspondent where he interviewed many heads of state and other foreign dignitaries. Additionally, as a correspondent, he traveled on assignment to several African nations, including The Gambia, Zambia, Kenya, and Mozambique.

In 1980, after eight years as an award-winning broadcast journalist, Stokes returned to Cleveland and to the practice of law and became the first black lawyer to serve as general counsel to a major American labor union—the United Auto Workers, Regions 2 and 2A. He also represented Cleveland's largest labor union—Laborer's Local 1099—among others.

In 1983, Stokes was elected judge of the Cleveland Municipal Court. Within weeks of his election, his colleagues voted him administrative judge of the court. Shortly thereafter, his fellow judges elected him presiding judge. Never before had a freshman judge been elected administrative presiding judge of the Cleveland Municipal Court, which retains thirteen judges. Judge Stokes's election was a benchmark in American history, since few Americans—and no other black American—have ever been elected to the legislative, executive, and judicial branches of government.

JE: In your autobiography, *Promises of Power*, you state: "For a brief time in Cleveland, I was the man of power. I had what no black man in this country has had before or since: direct control of the government of a predominantly white population." As you look back on your tenure as mayor, how would you assess the power you had? Were you able to use it to full advantage?

cs: At the time I wrote that comment (1973), I believed it to be the case, even with the racially motivated checks and balances that the city council exercised. My experience was quite similar to that of Mayor Harold Washington, who is presently experiencing similar problems in Chicago. Still, despite the fact that I was elected mayor seventeen years ago, I suspect that I was able to exercise more power proportionately than Washington has been able to exercise in these so-called more enlightened times. In Chicago, the city council has attempted to downplay the race issue, while in Cleveland, the city council proved unable to do so. This made it easier for me to take advantage of the strong-mayor form of government.

je: To what extent did your experiences as a jailhouse lawyer prepare you for the rough and tumble world of politics? What did it teach you about the political system?

cs: My experiences at the 21st Street Police Court, both with the police and those accused of crimes, represented perhaps the sharpest definition of basic politics that one could find. The judges were totally dependent on the voters and those who financed their campaigns, which caused most of them to dispense justice with an eye to the next election or a potential campaign contribution. I observed police officers close up—not as abstract figures, but as human beings—subject to all the warts and foibles and ambitions and yearnings that typically accompany power, including corruption. The police station was the center for ward politics. It mirrored the worst aspects of machine politics. What I observed, and for that matter experienced, contradicted virtually everything I had learned in school about our judicial and criminal justice systems. Ethics was notable in its absence.

je: What was the personal lure of politics? Why didn't you pursue a career as a lawyer or a judge?

cs: Quite simply, black lawyers had few alternatives. I was associated with the most active black law firm in Cleveland, a firm headed by Norman Minor, a former county prosecutor, and Merle McCurdy who, in 1961, became the first black United States attorney. Together with my brother Louis, we controlled nearly 70 percent of the criminal trial docket of Cuyahoga County. This necessitated a 12–18 hour work day. In those days, we were unable to rent an office downtown (owing to racial discrimination), let alone belong to one of the white law firms. So, like most white lawyers at that time, if a black lawyer had an aptitude for politics, it was an excellent way to build a career. Far more opportunities were available in politics than in law. Back then, it was extremely difficult to make ends meet, let alone achieve financial security. Nearly half the city council was lawyers (black and white); lawyers dominated the state legislature. That's no longer true today. So, for economic reasons, I thought the political arena offered the most promise.

JE: You've been described as "a hardheaded realist"—as one who took to politics as a duck does to water. In what sense did politics mesh with your personality?

CS: In the first place, I was exposed to politics at an earlier age than most people. Moreover, I was motivated by certain economic considerations. When I was twenty, I was a driver for John O. Holly, a local politician. He masterminded what became the only statewide black political organization then or since—the Federated County Democrats of Ohio. That experience afforded me an opportunity to closely observe this veteran politician forge an organization throughout Ohio that resulted in the election of Frank J. Lausche as governor. Following Governor Lausche's inauguration, I was one of his first appointees to the state liquor department. That was a patronage position. It sealed the ready advantages in politics for me. I enjoyed watching Holly interact with people and observing the approaches he employed, and I was intrigued by the prospect of organizing individuals toward a common goal—in this instance, the election of Frank J. Lausche.

Throughout my educational career, I always had a deep interest in history. Although I was a good all-around student, I had a particular love for history, which matched only my general love for reading of all kinds. I was especially interested in political biographies. Books of this kind fascinated me. As a result, I had an intellectual curiosity about politics and politicians.

Moreover, I was always very gregarious, so my personality lent itself to politics. As early as elementary school, I acted in plays and organized small bands—show business, in other words. And, of course, show business is a fundamental part of politics. I remained interested in similar things through junior high school, where I participated in the glee club and the theater club. As a college student, I was extremely active in Karamu, the black theater in Cleveland. A rather unique community theater, Karamu has produced a number of well-known black actors and actresses—many of them now on Broadway. The theater fascinated me. That theatrical part of my personality, I suspect, lent itself to politics as I moved from community theater to the theater of politics.

Then, I suppose, another key factor was my competitive nature. I was a product of the slums of one of America's oldest industrial cities. I was determined to escape the hopelessness of the streets. In this regard, my mother was an important influence. She had a dream about America that I never really understood and perhaps don't even understand today. She was an immigrant from the South, as much as the Poles, Italians, and Yugoslavs were immigrants from Europe. My mother loved this country. She believed in the promise of success. Although she never tasted great success, she yearned for it. And she passed her yearning on to her children. Most of these Southern immigrants never became rich themselves or held high office, but they lived out their confidence in America through their children's successes. My mother was fueled by the same dreams that inspired the offspring of the European immigrant—namely, that if you received a good education, you could climb any mountain.

In the end, she proved correct. She instilled in me a basic confidence in myself and my future. I can only attribute my own success to her influence. My willingness to take on new challenges and to defy what seemed like overwhelming odds flowed from her faith in America's potential. For that reason, I guess, I've never really questioned the capacity of America to respond to any challenge. For instance, consider the battle cry of the Jackson campaign: "If not Jesse, then who? If not now, then when?" That refrain was reduced to rhetoric, and that's too bad because if I had decided, as Jesse did, that I wanted to run for president, I would have done so with a consummate confidence in the ability of this nation to respond. Still, I may be wrong about that. I *was* wrong in 1958 when I ran for the Ohio State Senate. I *was* wrong in 1960 when I ran for the Ohio General Assembly. But I was *right* in 1962 when I ran a second time and was elected to the Ohio General Assembly. I *was* wrong in 1965 when I ran for mayor of Cleveland. But I was *right* in 1967 when I took a second stab at that office and was elected. And in 1983, after not having run for office for thirteen years and being away from the city for eight years, I defeated an incumbent white judge for a seat on the Cleveland Municipal Court. It never occurred to me that I could lose.

JE: Did you grow up with your mother's vision—that America is a land of opportunity and promise?

CS: Yes. But I must say I've had my moments of disillusionment. Still, I feel that way today and, whenever possible, attempt to convey my optimism to young people. Although there is a gap between the rhetoric and the reality, America does represent the hopes and aspirations of the struggling masses, both in this country and abroad. Black Americans believe strongly in the American dream, which is why they feel betrayed by being excluded from full participation in American life. If they didn't believe in this nation, their exclusion would be less painful. But the fact is, black Americans, like all Americans, believe in the ideals upon which this nation was built: liberty, equality, opportunity, and acceptance of diversity. Those ideals speak as powerfully to black America as they do to the rest of America. Our task, yours and mine, is to make them come true for the millions of Americans who value freedom, but who, for a variety of reasons, have been denied basic human rights.

JE: Although you've always enjoyed the political game, are there aspects of electoral politics that you find disagreeable?

CS: I've never been a "good" politician in the sense that I've never fully accepted the old maxim "You scratch my back, and I'll scratch yours." There are some backs I just won't scratch. But I recognize and accept the fact that if I'm not willing to scratch John Doe's back, then I can't expect him to scratch mine. As a consequence, I've missed out on several opportunities—good opportunities—because I found it difficult to scratch certain backs.

In addition, I've always been a very private person. I've never been a totally public person. That has produced certain problems, particularly with people from the media, who feel, as Justice Hugo L. Black did in the case of *New York Times* v. *Sullivan* (1964), that it's virtually impossible to libel a public official. Well, I don't believe that. I'm willing to make certain sacrifices. I'm willing to spend less time with my family. I'm willing to forego a five-day week. I'm willing to sacrifice playing golf and tennis. But I'm not willing to sacrifice my privacy. After all, in the end, I only own two things: my name and my right to privacy.

As a consequence, I suppose I've filed more libel actions against the media than any other political figure in this country. Obviously, that does not endear me to the press. This is particularly important today, as the media stands at the cornerstone of politics, especially with the declining importance of political parties. When I ran for judge, the newspapers supported the incumbent; organized labor supported the incumbent; and the Democratic Party, while it did not formally support any candidate, informally supported the incumbent. And yet, despite their opposition, I won.

But that's only part of the story. Each time I've run, I've had a difficult race. If I had accepted the traditional wisdom—namely, "To get along, go along"—I would have been able to win much more easily. For example, in terms of my recent race for judge, I might have been appointed, instead of having to run for election. But that's been the story of my life. And yet, I consider it a very proud part of my life. But, no, I'm not a "good" politician. I've never had a good relationship with the Democratic Party. I've never wanted to be a part of the party structure, which invariably means that a politician has to accept the party's ground rules in order to win its backing. I'm not prepared to place the party's interests above my own interests, particularly if they clash with my beliefs.

Mayor Harold Washington faces a similar problem in Chicago. And I grieve for him. Alderman Edward R. Vrdolyak isn't really interested in supplanting Washington as mayor. He much prefers his present role as protector of the Cook County Democratic political machine which has, for decades, been a steady source of income, jobs, and power. Many people depend on Vrdolyak, and, as such, they must maintain his favor. This, of course, has posed problems for Washington, who opposes the party machine and has been caught in the crossfire ever since becoming mayor.

I much prefer to be independent. And my independence has paid off at least in terms of my relationship with the community. I don't have to carry the baggage of corrupt politicians. Instead, I've proved able to enlist the support of non-political people, and there are certainly more non-political individuals and groups than there are political ones. Instead of attempting to court the favor of old guard politicians, I've tried to build solid working relationships with civic, fraternal, church, and charitable organizations: the Boy Scouts, Mothers Against Drunk Driving, the Muscular Dystrophy Fund, the Baptist and Inter-Denominational Alliances, etc. Most politicians ignore these groups because the politicians do not realize that they represent the political pulse of the community.

JE: Do you have a "thick skin" when it comes to criticism? Are you particularly sensitive to criticism?

CS: Only when I feel it's undeserved. In such cases, I strike out against it when it occurs. I do, however, accept general criticism, which I view as a legitimate part of the political game. For instance, if I'm involved in a project with a group of hack politicians—who are there to advance their own selfish interests—and they criticize me, well, then I can accept that. However, I have not and will not accept criticism which seeks to cast unwarranted aspersions on my character. If the criticism is particularly vicious, I will, as I stated earlier, pursue the matter in court. I will not allow anyone to build a reputation at my expense.

JE: You once stated: "Politicians are, for the most part, primarily interested in perpetuating their own privileged positions." If so, how are you different?

CS: A politician's primary motive is to win re-election. That's really what that statement means. And it's true even of the best of them, and there have been some great public officials. For instance, Senator Birch Bayh (D-Ind.) destroyed his political career in Indiana by adopting a liberal stance. On the basis of principle, Bayh tried his best to sell his liberalism to Indiana's voters but proved unsuccessful. He was not re-elected.

For most politicians, the bottom line, when it comes to how to vote, is: "How will it affect my re-election prospects?" Obviously, if you're a professional politician, you want to be re-elected, just as an engineer wants to win new contracts for his firm, a school teacher wants to receive tenure, and a newspaper reporter wants to become a feature columnist and/or a contributing editor. That motivation is no different from that of any other profession. It's simply a reality of the job, one which is seen as particularly important in politics because of the great influence which politicians wield. But, like Birch Bayh, I've never subverted a principle for the sake of re-election.

JE: What would you say to a politician who confessed, "I'd like to support you, but I can't. It could cost me the election"?

CS: I really don't know because if I have to tell him, then, obviously, we're not on the same wavelength. All I could say is, "Look, I've never compromised my personal beliefs, and I've fared pretty well." I've never based a vote or an action on how it might affect my re-election prospects. Now, I've made many decisions—and perhaps many wrong decisions—but never on the basis of how they might affect my political career.

For instance, never in the history of the municipal court has the clerk been held in contempt. But I held him in contempt—and I hadn't been on the job for six months. I received numerous dire warnings about what would happen if I took such an action. Well, nothing has happened, except that the clerk found out that he has to obey me. As a white man, he may not like having a black judge tell him what to do, but that's too bad. He took the case to the court of appeals, and the court told him that he'd have to do what the administrative judge said, which is what I tried to tell him in private conversation. And when he wouldn't, I did what I had to do.

Let me give you another example. For years, people have told me that it's dangerous to sue newspapers. Well, I *do* sue newspapers. I'm preparing to sue one now. But I won't sue a newspaper unless I'm confident that I'm going to win. I've never lost a libel action. Whenever I bring a suit, it's because I believe the press has committed a verifiable wrong.

One final example. On July 23, 1968, as mayor of Cleveland, I was faced with a crisis with which no mayor has ever been faced—namely, a literal war in the streets between the black nationalists and the police. Both sides had a long running battle, and each had their own cache of weapons. On one occasion, three policemen were shot dead in the street by several black nationalists, who used them as target practice. The police, in turn, fired on the house in which the black nationalists were holed up. The building burned to the ground, and eleven people were killed in the fire. I had to take action. The police department requested that all officers be pulled from the rest of the city and sent in to "clean out" the area. I felt that such an action could result in mass extermination. However, a great many people, both black and white, were virtually unanimous in wanting the police to be sent in. I knew that if I let the police go in, they would seek revenge. And so, one year into a two-year term, I took an unprecedented step: I removed all the white officers from the area and asked the county sheriff to loan me his black deputies and black policemen. I then put together a cadre of black community leaders whom I sent into the area to quell the disturbance.

Well, it *did* quell the disturbance, but it also wreaked hell with my political career. It didn't prevent my re-election in 1969, but it did undermine the support I had in the white community and among the black middle class. But I didn't care. My main concern was to prevent further bloodshed. Fortunately, no additional lives were lost once I pulled the white policemen out of the area. Moreover, we were able to diffuse the anger in the community. Now, that damaged me politically, but if I had to do it over again, I'd do precisely the same thing.

JE: Throughout your career, you've eschewed political compromise. What is it about you, and your makeup which makes compromise so difficult?

CS: I don't know. I suppose it goes back to my mother again. She instilled in us the importance of principle. My brother Louis, for example, served as chairman of the House Ethics Committee. He was selected for that post by Speaker Thomas P. "Tip" O'Neill who knew that he was one of the few members who had no skeletons in his closet. Because of that, he enjoys the respect of his colleagues.

I really can't answer your question, however, because neither Louis nor I have ever believed otherwise. The only real blemish on the family name occurred when Louis was stopped for drunk driving in Maryland. But that incident had no bearing on his official duties. I guess it's just the way our mother raised us. I was a street type, much more so than Louis. But even in the streets, I had my own morality. I balanced my reputation as a "schoolboy"—which is what they used to call me on the streets—with the fact that I was tough. I suppose that my worst decision was quitting school because of the streets. Whenever my street buddies would talk about committing a heavy crime, I would refuse. On the street, the main thing was to be one of the boys. But I wasn't one of the boys when it came to participating in any criminal action for which I could go to jail.

The same attitude carried through in politics. As mayor, I had many attractive offers that would have made me quite wealthy. I would listen to the proposal, and then ask the person: "Let me understand this. If this matter becomes public, can we go to jail?" Of course, the person would always say that there was no way that it could become public. And I'd ask again, "But if it did, could we go to jail?" As soon as they'd say, "Well, if it did come out, sure, we could go to jail," that was the end of the conversation.

I wasn't as much concerned with morality as I was with common sense. As a result, neither Louis nor I have any money today, but we've survived the Nixon probes, the Internal Revenue Service, the Justice Department, numerous media investigations, the county prosecutor, and countless rumor-mongers. For twenty-five years, I've been the subject of these and every other conceivable kind of investigation. They've all proven fruitless. And, you know, I'm able, at any time, to leave my home or office and take a vacation without worrying. The guy who never takes a vacation is the one you've got to worry about.

When I assumed my present position as administrative and presiding judge, I did so with the realization that, for five years prior to my becoming a judge, the Federal Bureau of Investigation (FBI) had been investigating this court. Since becoming presiding judge, I've done several things that no previous judge had done. The major problem focused on the clerk's office. When the FBI investigated the situation, they found evidence that a number of cases had been fixed. However, the files were either missing or destroyed. I told the clerk to reorganize his system. He refused, and I cited him for contempt. We have since changed the system. We had the locks on his doors changed. All files must now be signed for. Judges no longer dispense justice on brown index cards, as a substitute for missing files. If a file is missing, we won't hear the case.

Now, my predecessors could have done this. But they didn't. I shouldn't have had to go through a tortuous public trial when I cited the clerk for contempt. But I did. And although I took some blows from the appellate court, the system has changed. The FBI is welcome here anytime, as long as they base their investigation on the existence of missing files.

JE: Have you always found it easy to relate to people of different backgrounds, cultures, and races, or have you had to learn how to over the years?

CS: I suppose I had to learn because I grew up in Cleveland's black ghetto. No white kids ever went to school with me. And yet, whites have always played a significant role in my political life. When I hear about the problems that black children have in white schools, I can readily understand what they're experiencing. For two years, I was the only black student in the University of Minnesota law school. But I've never had a problem with whites. I've always been able to build good relationships. I've never viewed whites as ogres. To me, they're just like everybody else. I've had some good white friends, as well as some bad ones.

At the outset of my involvement in the civil rights movement, I had several close Jewish friends, who were closely allied with the black freedom movement. In fact, from the time I quit the army and became active in politics, I've always been heavily involved in the Jewish community. We've always shared mutual political interests. My association with my Jewish friends marked my first relationship with whites which has steadily broadened over the years.

JE: And yet, in your autobiography, you state that during your service in the army, you developed "a clean-edged unadulterated hatred for whites." What experiences produced that feeling? Was it difficult to overcome?

CS: After leaving the service in 1946, I went to West Virginia State College. A professor friend there, Dr. Herman G. Canady, told me: "You won't get a good education down here. You've got to go up where those white boys are. That's where the real teaching is taking place." So, I went to Western Reserve University and became involved in the Young Progressives, which was actively supporting Henry Wallace for president. It was dominated, for the most part, by liberal Jews—both young and old—some of whom had been communists. Also, it was there that I met Paul Robeson, who introduced me to organized labor and strengthened my commitment to working-class people. At the time, it wouldn't have made any difference to me whether the people I was working with were WASPs or Jews, except that the WASPs I knew weren't out walking the picket lines or out demonstrating. From that time on, my attitudes changed from being anti-white to pro-people. My anti-white feelings were, in a very real sense, a reaction to the system—which I saw then as unjust—as well as to my lack of contact with whites.

JE: In your view, what explains the present schism which exists between Blacks and Jews? Is this rift permanent?

CS: I think that most Jews no longer see the need for social change. Today, they're sufficiently integrated in white society, particularly in the business world. It's difficult for young Jews to relate to the social problems which plagued earlier generations of Jews. And that's sad. Like Blacks, Jews were the beneficiaries of the 1964 Civil Rights Act and the sundry affirmative action programs which were passed. Today, many Jews oppose the quota system, but it was the quota system which made it possible for some of them to attend certain universities and take advantage of many government programs. Historically, there were no quotas for Blacks. They were totally excluded. Today, things have changed, and many Jews find it unnecessary to relate to Blacks. This has served to distance many Jews and Blacks.

As a consequence of their newly found security, Jews can afford to focus their attention more on Israel than on the day-to-day survival of the American-Jewish community. That's because Jews no longer face the overt problems they did several years ago.

JE: What are your feelings when you hear someone like Louis Farrakhan, the well-known Muslim leader, utter what many have described as blatantly anti-Semitic remarks?

CS: I view Farrakhan as I do Meir Kahane (the founder and spiritual leader of the Jewish Defense League). They're both demagogues. Neither really gives a damn about the inter-racial or inter-faith relationships of their people. Both act with absolute impunity and disregard for the impact of their acts on black and Jewish people.

Farrakhan has no influence upon me, and I certainly can't affect him. He couldn't care less what impact his statements may have on my life because he's blinded by his own shortsighted personal goals. I would describe Meir Kahane as the Jewish people's Louis Farrakhan. His goals may be more publicly acceptable—because of his expressed concern about Israel—but he is, nonetheless, a demagogue and a disgrace to the Jewish people's legitimate quest for a secure Israel.

Farrakhan's statements have done tremendous damage. I recognize, however, that I can do little to prevent his outbursts. Instead, I prefer to work in my own way to forge closer black-Jewish relations. Separatism is not the answer. The answer lies in understanding, which is something both men seem to have forgotten or consciously disregard.

JE: How do you feel when you hear younger, more militant Blacks condemn you as an Uncle Tom? Do these attacks hurt?

CS: Fortunately, they haven't said these things to my face. I would not, however, have put myself in the position that Andrew Young and Coretta Scott King did at the 1984 Democratic National Convention when they spoke openly against the elimination of run-off primaries. This made it convenient for Blacks to level such charges at them. Don't misunderstand, I have heard such comments—but from other people. That kind of criticism doesn't bother me. I know the truth. The fact is, I've always enjoyed a close relationship with members of the black community—they are the mainstay of my political base.

Over the years, I've learned that you can't please everybody. You just can't. And you don't have to. If you can secure 50 percent plus one of the vote—and do it consistently—that is ample proof of broad-based acceptance. Obviously, I must be doing something right. I've won the almost unanimous support of the black community in every race I've ever run. Their support is a demonstration of public approval. And that's what matters. The rest is merely rhetoric.

JE: In a speech several years ago, you stated: "Politics, especially local politics, tends to draw second-raters." What did you mean? Why is this so?

CS: It's more true today than it was when I made the statement. During the time I was growing up, many talented people lived in the cities. Politics was considered a status occupation. All major ethnic groups—the Irish, Italians, Jews, Eastern Europeans—depended on politics. In those days, many politicians were willing to subordinate their own principles, desires, goals, and ambitions to those of the party. As a result, I always viewed them with a mixed contempt.

Today, the vacuum in politics is even worse. This was evident in the 1984 Democratic presidential race. All of the candidates, with the exception of Jesse Jackson, were pedestrian politicians. Gary Hart (D-Colo.) had previously failed to make a name for himself in the Senate. Senator Ernest Hollings (D-S.C.) was best known for the dirty jokes he told. Former Governor Reuben Askew (D-Fla.) was a good governor but lacked vision. None of the candidates approached the stature of an Edward Kennedy, who, due to the Chappaquiddick incident, in 1969, limited his political effectiveness. This, I believe, is a tragic loss to this country. He would have been a great president, far greater than his brother John.

Compare these candidates to the political giants who preceded them. President Harry Truman, for example, appealed to a broad cross section of the nation. He had enormous courage, the kind I tried to marshal when, as mayor, I had to fire three police chiefs. Truman had the courage to fire General Douglas MacArthur, one of the most popular war-time generals of all time. Or Senator Wayne Morse (D-Oreg.), whom few would have expected to become the giant on the world stage that he became. Or Senator Thomas Kuchel (R-Calif.), a man of integrity and courage, who won the respect of friends and foes alike in the Senate. Or Senator Hubert Humphrey (D-Minn.), the paragon of conscience in the United States Senate.

Where are these kinds of leaders today? They're still being born, but today they're in business, in law, in medicine, in academe. They just don't have that civic consciousness. Look at the United States Senate. Where's a Robert Taft? I don't give a damn that our philosophies differed. He was a conservative but a tower of principle. There's nobody there today who can match his stature. Among our governors, where are the Nelson Rockefellers? And where are the remarkable women— women like Eleanor Roosevelt? What woman dominates the political and intellectual scene today like Mrs. Roosevelt? Or take the United States Supreme Court. Where are the Benjamin Cardozos or Felix Frankfurters? Who do we have today? The Warren Burgers and William Rehnquists. Part of the problem, of course, is the pay. Supreme Court justices receive only $80,000. Imagine the kind of money Frankfurter could make today with his mind. I repeat, it's not that persons of ability don't exist. They do. It's just that they're not in government.

JE: Has your own idealism waned with the years? Do you still believe that government can make a major difference in people's lives?

CS: I do. Look at the negative impact that Ronald Reagan has had on America over the past four years. And that's not partisanship. It's a fact. Today, there are more than a half million more identifiable people who are in poverty than there were four years ago. And the major support systems—which people have necessarily grown to depend upon—have broken down since Reagan took office. You can prove the positive by citing the negative. Obviously, if government can have such a profoundly negative impact on people's lives, then it only goes to prove the positive impact it could have in the reverse. It's fashionable to talk about getting government out of people's lives, but the result of this action would be cataclysmic. Given the consequences, I think most people would prefer an active, caring, involved government.

Why, for example, have there been no serious challenges by Blacks for the United States Senate? If Edward Brooke (R-Mass.) could do it, why can't others? Is Brooke such a unique individual? Sure, he's a good lawyer, and a good man, but he's also black, and the baggage that he carried—both personally and politically—was substantial. I don't know why other Blacks haven't taken a serious shot at the Senate. I certainly haven't discounted a race for the Senate. If I should tire of the judicial branch, then I might have a go at it.

JE: When you were first elected mayor, you stated: "I knew I had to be, in that horrible racist phrase, a 'credit to my race.'" Why did you feel that way? What pressures did it impose?

CS: I was keenly conscious of it. I knew, as the first black mayor of a major American city, that I would be judged by white America and that they, in turn, would judge black America by my success or failure. I knew it wasn't fair, but it was a reality. As a consequence, it meant that I could not do many of the things that my predecessors had done. I could not ignore one area of the city because of my political strength in another. Whenever we had a snowstorm, I had to make it a priority that the white streets were plowed before turning my attention to making sure that the black east-side was served. Instead of being able to select a cabinet of friends and cronies, I had to select one which reflected the racial diversity of the city and, at the same time, one of unassailable character. In making appointments, I was always conscious of the possible white reaction, particularly if it involved a black appointee. For example, in my relationship with the police, I always understood that I was vulnerable because the white community saw the police as their last line of resistance to a possible black insurrection. I knew that I couldn't invest in the stock market like my white predecessors. And I couldn't purchase land in Florida. I couldn't take advantage of advance information on the sale of city property—not because I found it morally repugnant, but because, as a black man, I could not do it and get away with it.

Therefore, if I wanted to serve as mayor, I'd have to serve with the understanding that I could not do as my white predecessors had done. I impressed that upon the people I appointed. I tried to explain to them that they would be faced with many temptations in their new positions—after all, there had never been a black mayor before—and that they would be amazed at the opportunities that would come their way. I told them to refuse such offers, however, because the city's white establishment would not permit a black administrator to get away with the things they had traditionally let white administrators get away with.

Some appointees did not believe me. They wound up being indicted, their professional lives wrecked—which would have been fine if it was just them. But unlike Reagan's sleazy characters, their dishonesty rubbed off on me. I was seen as responsible for whatever happened to black people, particularly those in my administration. And some outrageous things happened. For example, I had a very bright engineer—trained at the Massachusetts Institute of Technology—who bought a home on my street, four doors down from me. Damn, if I didn't wake up one morning and read in the newspaper that he had built an addition to his home with city labor and city materials—right there on my street. If this guy thought he could get away with it—because he was a commissioner or a head of a department—he was wrong. After all, if he could get away with it, what about all the little guys down below from whom you could not expect the same level of moral and intellectual understanding as you would from an engineering graduate from MIT? The one thing I could do, however, was to make sure that they never found the mayor, the black mayor, in such a position. In the end, I left city hall, despite the media's constant efforts to tarnish my reputation, unblemished.

I suppose my lowest point as mayor occurred when I finally came to the realization that what had happened to me was the result of a determined onslaught by the major white forces in the city. This occurred, I suppose, because I was functioning at a level where no black man—particularly, an activist black man—had functioned before. When you're an activist, you have to expect a reaction. I could have functioned like Mayor Tom Bradley of Los Angeles and still be mayor today. As a result, the black-white tension was further exacerbated by the fact that I was an activist.

Unfortunately, I lacked an experienced staff, individuals with proven experience in government. The people I appointed would do anything I asked of them, but no more. They didn't know how. For example, Mayor Andrew Young can take a trip to Africa and not have to worry about the city of Atlanta. He has an experienced cadre of seasoned professionals from the Maynard Jackson era and individuals who had worked with him while he was a congressman or at the United Nations. The same is true of Mayor Coleman Young of Detroit. When a crisis develops, the agency head who is responsible for that area handles it. The administrator doesn't contact Young unless everything else has failed. I didn't have that luxury. I had to personally fight every fight. And it drained me. Although I enjoy combat, ultimately, it exhausted me, and the cumulative effect of the racial animosity and the lack of money to operate the city convinced me that it was time to move on. I reluctantly reached the point where I found it increasingly difficult to govern the city. There's a difference between getting re-elected and governing. When my efforts to increase the city income tax failed twice and I realized that the white business community and the press were committed to denying me the needed revenues, I knew it was time to get out. I had learned long before that money isn't everything, but it's much more than whatever is second. There was no need for me to get re-elected, only to have to preside over a city plagued by problems that were insoluble without the necessary funding. After all, city hall would not be the last step in my life. I concluded that it was best to step aside and let someone else try to run the city—someone who did not have my negative baggage—baggage either that had been heaped on me or that I had created for myself.

But I must admit, it was a low point. I was disillusioned. I knew I had done a lot, but I wanted to do so much more. I only wish that I had had the luxury of a four-year term. But the fact is, I didn't. Back then, my major priority was an income tax increase. I knew that, given the situation with which we were faced, I would not be able to win such an increase. If I were really concerned about the welfare of the people of this city, then, I felt, I should content myself with the thought that I had done the best I could but that it was time to move on. I've seen public officials outlive their usefulness too many times.

JE: As mayor, you became an overnight celebrity. Was being a celebrity a two-edged sword? How did you avoid getting swept away by it?

CS: I never succumbed to it. Other than the increased attention, my private life has never really changed. In fact, people don't know anything about my private life because I've kept it that way. Being a celebrity proved to be both a positive and negative experience. It was, of course, deliriously ego-satisfying to have people visit the city just to see this phenomenon—this black mayor. At the same time, this attention conflicted with my ability to run the city. You can't run a government when you're forced to hold two press conferences a day. You just can't. You can't run a city where the media are working full-time trying to outdo one another to unearth the latest failure of the black mayor. For example, in one story, the media charged that the sanitation department only worked four hours a day. Well, the fact is, it always has and does so today. In 1967, the media made a big thing of it. And who was to blame? The mayor. This showed, they said, an inability to manage the city. And then there was the time they discovered that the rubbish collectors charged businessmen $5 a week to pick up their trash (under the code, they're not supposed to pick up their rubbish). Who did they blame? The mayor. Well, the rubbish collectors have always charged businessmen $5 a week to pick up the trash. They still do. It wasn't a big deal. But they made it one in my administration.

However, my celebrity status gave me an opportunity to take part in several influential mayor's groups, which meant that I had clout with my colleagues not only on the local level but also at a national level. For example, in 1968, President-elect Richard Nixon asked me to meet with him to discuss the crisis of the cities. That came as a result of the efforts of Senator Daniel Patrick Moynihan (D-N.Y.), who told Mr. Nixon about my efforts on behalf of general revenue sharing and my support for one of Moynihan's pet proposals, "minimum income assistance."

Another thing I hated, in addition to the constant media attention, was the fact that everybody wanted a piece of me. At the time, I had an untrained group of people around me. And, of course, I had never before run a business with 11,000 employees and a $120 million budget. I was learning myself, and everybody around me was learning as well. All the while, they were taking bits and pieces of me for this and that. I was expected to attend everybody's luncheon, dinner, birthday party, or bar mitzvah. Such distractions filled up a hell of a lot of clippings books, but they proved extremely distracting. Fortunately, I could still get away—go to my old neighborhood hangouts, play tennis, and shoot pool. I only went to the obligatory social affairs—such as the Urban League and the NAACP—when they'd have an official affair or dinner. But I wouldn't go to the dinner and eat; I'd find out when I was scheduled to speak, arrive at that time, make my speech, and leave. I always found it uncomfortable to have to spend an evening with Urban League types—middle-class Blacks. I have no tolerance for gossip or "chitchat." But if a street club asked me, I'd stay all afternoon with them. They were genuine people. They were part of my roots. And that's why, for example, I was able to win election to the bench. Few middle-class Blacks live in Cleveland. My kind of people live in Cleveland—working-class types. They know I'm a judge, they know I've been mayor, but they still call me Carl. That's not only a big compliment, but a big success, too, because I've never let them down. I've always fought for them—publicly and privately. My fighting embarrasses middle-class Blacks. They'd rather have me talk things out behind closed doors. My circle of friends has remained ostensibly the same—it hasn't widened much over the years. I think I've stayed pretty much the same Carl Stokes. And I've fought zealously to prevent my family from becoming involved in the glare of the publicity.

JE: What explains the long-standing antagonism between you and the press? What is the root cause of the conflict?

CS: It's the result of several factors. First, I've always been an independent black man. Second, public officials and the media are natural adversaries. Third, the media believe that, over the long haul, they can beat down a public official because they have daily access to large numbers of readers. I compounded the problem by not pandering to members of the press. I refused to be at their beck and call. Many reporters were, I discovered, quite envious of my position. They would have liked to be a legislator or the mayor, but they lacked the ability to be elected. Many of them had a police mentality—that is, they enjoyed exercising power over people. As a result, some insignificant wimp of a newspaperman could, by his pen, cause mayors, councilmen, and legislators to fear him. I do not fear anybody. I've made that clear at every stage of my career. I may bow to certain political realities, but I will never bow to oppression by anyone, particularly the media or the white power structure. As the city's first black mayor, I owed my primary allegiance to the 93 percent of the Blacks who supported me, not to the 23 percent of the whites who voted for me. As a consequence, I did what I felt had to be done.

When I became mayor, there were no Blacks in high-level government positions—despite the fact that Cleveland was then the eighth largest city in the United States. In two years, I appointed the first thoroughly integrated cabinet, including the first black law director, black chief police prosecutor, black safety director, black service director, black woman appointed to commissioner rank, black city treasurer, black purchasing commissioner, black parks commissioner, black public utilities commissioner, and on and on. I put Blacks into middle management and locked them in with civil service status where they still are today. But, as I've said many times, every time I appointed a Black, it meant I had to fire, force to resign, or otherwise replace a white person, which the media always publicized widely. I steered city contracts which had been exclusively those of whites to black businessmen. The whites raised hell, and the media exploited it.

In truth, what I did was what everybody says to do today and what the Kerner Commission said in its 1968 report. I placed Blacks throughout city government. Well, the white community didn't like it. But the whites didn't elect me mayor. The Blacks did. But I paid a price. My satisfaction today derives from the fact that I did everything possible to develop black power in this city. So when some guy comes up to me and says, "Jack, you ain't up with the times; you've joined with the folks," I can say I didn't know anybody on the scene at that time who would have done what I did.

I did it despite the fact that the press picked apart every person I appointed in a way that they never did white appointees. The newspapers assigned a reporter to the day-to-day activities of each department. They expected us to do, in each department, in two years what white mayors had not done since the beginning of this century—namely, to turn around the failures of the past in less than eighteen months. These were impossible goals—racially motivated goals. And I made that clear then—and I make it clear today. If the media doesn't like it, damn the media. The media didn't elect me. My being in office is not dependent on the media. It never has been and never will be. If I run for the Senate, I won't run with the support of the media. If I run for the Ohio Supreme Court, I won't run with the support of the media. If I decide to run for either office, I'll do it with a broad-based coalition. The media doesn't like that kind of independence on the part of any politician, white or black, but particularly on the part of a black politician.

The media also abhors the fact that I'll sue them. They view that as outrageous because they harbor the ridiculous notion that they're fair—that they're balanced. That's ludicrous! If they were fair and balanced, their employee and management practices would reflect it. There's not a white newspaper, television network, or radio station that is fully integrated. Just watch the evening news. Not one network has a black anchorman.

JE: Once you left the mayor's office, you became a television anchorman. Were your preconceptions well founded? Did you face any racial problems?

CS: I must admit that the only reason I was chosen to be a television anchorman was because I *am* black. As a white man with no previous journalistic experience, I never would have been picked up out of Cleveland, Ohio, and showcased on the weekly news hour of NBC's flagship station in New York (WNBC). If I'd been white, they would have sent me to somewhere in upstate New York—some little station—and told me to get some experience. So I got the benefit of starting at the top without having to pay any dues, because I am black. WNBC thought that it would serve them well by me being an oddity, the first black mayor of a major American city—a person who was known nationally. They had had six anchormen in nine years and were still number three in the ratings. They figured that if they brought me in, given the large black population in New York, I'd help to pull in the black audience. Well, I did, for about a week. And then, with their curiosity satisfied, viewers went back to the better news stations they had been watching. After about 18–20 months, the network acknowledged that they had made a mistake. At that point, they did what they should have done in the first place—which would have been better for both of us. They made me a reporter, which does not exactly require a great mind but does require a knowledge of the business. I proceeded to learn my craft and wound up as the only NBC reporter to win an Emmy in 1979.

I never experienced any overt racism while working as either an anchorman or a news reporter. And I must admit, WNBC didn't treat me as a simple reporter. I was molded into a kind of urban affairs editor, with a personal segment of my own called the "Urban Journal." It really didn't deal with explicit race-related issues; rather, it dealt with stories about urban decay, poverty, energy, and housing. However, I always reported on these issues evenhandedly. Oh, you're always going to get critical letters and calls when you're doing stories five days a week, but the complaints weren't really racially motivated. I spent the last two years at the United Nations and covered stories which most viewers couldn't comprehend anyway, except perhaps when I reported on tensions in the Middle East or the Iranian crisis. But few racial factors were involved in audience reaction to those reports.

So, I must say that, inside NBC, I had no major problems. I really didn't spend much time in the office. I'd edit my tape, and I'd split. That was perhaps the happiest time in my life. For the first time since I was twenty years old, I had a private life. I was getting my ego stroked and making more money than I'd ever dreamed I would make. But the one thing that does not excite a New Yorker is a celebrity. They see celebrities every day. As a result, my wife and I could go skating, dancing, out to eat, and no one would hassle us. I guess if you got to Michael Jackson's stage, privacy would be a problem. But someone who happens to be on television or in politics or something doesn't faze New Yorkers. In Cleveland, the mayor can't move around without a swarm of bodyguards to keep people off him.

JE: Finally, after leaving city hall, you wrote: "I often felt that I was alone and that most of the people didn't give a damn whether the city lived or died and certainly didn't care if the poor, the elderly, the unemployed, the sick, and all those who needed help lived or died." Did this realization come as a surprise? Did it cause you much anguish?

cs: Most people didn't give a damn about the city, but they did give a damn about their own turf. That was what infuriated me about those thirty-three city councilmen who divided up the city into thirty-three little fiefdoms: They constantly asserted their own domain at the expense of the others. As a result, it was always a battle to get anything done, because you couldn't satisfy all thirty-three of them or even a consistent majority of them.

Helping people to help themselves was also a constant battle. And, of course, there were those white councilmen who did not want to be helped if the help might look as though the mayor was responsible for it. That used to infuriate me, because I believed then and believe now that our cities are governable. I may have concluded, when I left office, that I was no longer the man to govern the city at that time, but that didn't mean the city wasn't governable. And for a highly sustained period of time, I showed them that I could run this city; that this city could be productive; that it could be attractive; that people could be housed; and that jobs could be found. But I faced no end of resistance.

No one makes a great issue of crime today, but they did 15 or 20 years ago when the riots were taking place. Then, citizens were almost obsessively preoccupied with the incidence of crime. People had to attribute it to somebody, so they attributed it to the Blacks. And, frankly, the statistics supported that conclusion. Unfortunately, citizens viewed the problem as all-inclusive—that is, if you contained the Blacks, you could contain crime. That's ridiculous! Black people are already contained, and most of the crimes they commit are against other Blacks. Sometimes when you understand the prejudices of white people, you almost get to the point of saying, "Well, damn it, if the whites really want to wreck this city, let 'em do it." But you just can't. If you're concerned about people and about government and you love government, as obviously I do—I must have, to come back as I have—then you can't let anyone wreck the city. And you have to have my kind of faith, which is based on the fact that man has continually progressed. The knowledge that we've amassed over the past fifty years is greater than mankind has amassed since we first came upon this earth. I've been lucky enough to have lived to witness the progress we've made from the Works Progress Administration days to the present. We've made major strides. And, in my own way, I've tried to help make those strides count—for all those people who've believed in me and trusted in me. Hopefully, their faith has been well founded. Hopefully, I've been able to make a small difference.

Ernest N. Morial

At Odds with the Past

Ernest N. Morial was born October 9, 1929, in New Orleans, Louisiana. He attended parochial and public schools in New Orleans before attending Xavier University, where in 1951, he received a Bachelor of Science degree in business administration. In 1954, Morial became the first black graduate of the Louisiana State University School of Law, receiving a Juris Doctor degree. He is also a graduate of the National College of Juvenile Justice of the University of Nevada, a fellow of the Institute of Politics at the John F. Kennedy School of Government at Harvard University, and a recipient of an honorary Doctor of Laws degree from Xavier University. Morial has been an instructor for the Orleans Parish Public School System and has served on the faculties of Southern University, Tulane University School of Law, University of Louisiana, and Harvard University.

Morial was elected mayor of New Orleans in 1977. On May 1, 1978, he took office as the first black mayor in the history of New Orleans. In 1982, the people of New Orleans voted to return Morial for a second term as mayor. His election marks the latest in a series of the many "firsts" Morial has achieved in his career: 1965–1967, the first black United States attorney in the State of Louisiana; 1967–1970, the first Black to serve in the state legislature since Reconstruction; and 1974–1977, the first Black elected to the Louisiana Fourth Circuit Court of Appeals.

Morial boasts an impressive background in the area of civil rights. Together with noted attorney A.P. Tureaud, he successfully entered suits to eliminate segregation in the City of New Orleans and the State of Louisiana. When Louisiana law prohibited teachers from holding membership in civil rights organizations, he successfully challenged the law under the First Amendment, his wife Sybil serving as the plaintiff.

While a member of the state legislature, Morial continued his leadership by sponsoring legislation in such areas as welfare reform, civil service employment, consumer credit protection, housing reform, and voter registration. He successfully advocated lowering the voting age to eighteen.

Morial has served on numerous boards and organizations and has been president of the New Orleans Branch of the National Association for the Advancement of Colored People (NAACP), the American Bar Association, and the United States Conference of Mayors. He is a founder and was the first president of the New Orleans Legal Assistance Corporation and has been a member of the Board of Directors of Loyola University, the Tulane University Medical Center Board of Directors, Xavier University Board of Trustees, and the National Urban Coalition. He also served as national president of Alpha Phi Alpha, the oldest black social service fraternity of college men. He serves on the National Board of Directors of the NAACP and is a founder of the Lawyer's Committee for Civil Rights Under Law, organized at the request of President John F. Kennedy.

JE: Throughout your public and private life, you've demonstrated an unusual ability to overcome the handicaps of prejudice and discrimination. What is it about you or your approach to life that has enabled you to turn political defeat into victory?

EM: It's difficult to answer the question, "Why me?" I suspect it has to do with the conditions and the times, the environment, the individuals with whom I came in contact during the formative stages of my life, and their influence upon me. My parents brought us up in terms of the Judeo-Christian ethic. That kind of upbringing, coupled with the opportunities of the times, served as a powerful motivating factor. Over the years, I've devoted myself to personal growth and self-improvement. I've always had a very positive attitude. I grew up believing that I would succeed, that there was very little I could not do if I invested the necessary time, effort, and energy. I've never viewed my life in terms of limits. Certainly, I've never permitted race to dictate what I could or could not do. While prejudice is a fact of life, I've never used it as a crutch. The problem lies not with me but with others. I've never permitted others to define my life on the basis of race.

JE: As a youngster, did you aspire to success? Did you have a sense that you would succeed in your chosen endeavors?

EM: Really, I simply applied myself to the task at hand. I had no real sense of what I would become or what would become of me. My goal was not power but excellence. I wanted to be the best at whatever I did. I strongly believed in the work ethic. I knew that my future would depend, to a large extent, upon hard work. And so I worked hard.

I never expected to be the mayor of New Orleans. Back then, no Black had ever held the city's highest office. I had no reason to believe that I would be the first. I never thought in those terms. My goals were more general. I knew that a political career was dependent upon many factors, many of which were beyond my control. As a youngster, my goals were many and varied. It wasn't until much later that I gave thought to a political career.

JE: When did you first conclude that a Black could be elected mayor of New Orleans? Did you think that you could be the first?

EM: No, not really. I never saw myself as the first black mayor. In 1968, while running for an at-large seat on the city council, I appeared before the New Orleans Press Club. In my remarks, I noted that the chances were good that New Orleans would elect a black mayor within ten years. That made sense, given the demographics. After I was elected to the city council, the newspapers reprinted my comment, implying that I harbored mayoral aspirations.

It never dawned on me that I would be the first elected black mayor until my election to the state legislature. Later, I became a judge on the Fourth Circuit Court of Appeals. I surmised that I would probably retire as a judge, never again to run for elective office. However, as an activist—and a longtime catalyst for change—I felt frustrated on the bench. It became clear that I could not function as a change agent because of the nature of the litigation with which the court dealt. At that point, I decided to run for mayor.

JE: When you announced your candidacy for mayor in 1977, did you believe you could win? Did your close friends and political associates encourage you to enter the race?

EM: No. They had deep doubts. Most believed that the time was not right. I expected this response, as several had made previous commitments to other candidates. Some politicians felt uncomfortable about my candidacy. It forced them to take a stand at a time when they did not wish to do so. This was true of several liberal politicians who felt that they were being backed into a corner.

To be fair, I also harbored certain doubts. But I felt that, regardless of the odds, I should give it my best effort. After all, the worst I could do was lose. I ran because I felt I could make a difference. I believed that I could provide the city with new leadership. And I felt that I could give voice to certain of those issues which I felt strongly about. Even if I lost, I felt that my candidacy would serve an important purpose. It would afford me an opportunity to speak directly to people about those issues which I considered critical to the future of our city.

Actually, the situation was not too different from when I ran for the city council. I spoke before many groups, knowing full well that I might not receive their support. But it gave me an opportunity to present my point of view on the issues. A political candidate with good credentials will at least receive a hearing. And that's all I really wanted. I felt sure that if people heard me out, I would do well.

JE: To what extent was race a salient factor in the election? Was it difficult to overcome?

EM: The other candidates did not really inject race into the election. However, the media exploited the issue, stirring up passions on both sides of the question. Their influence was extremely negative. Instead of encouraging a debate on the issues, they made race *the* issue. Fortunately, the people rose above it, which is a testimonial to the progress we have made as a city.

Some whites will always vote for black candidates; however, it's always a very small segment of the electorate. Blacks, on the other hand, have been conditioned historically to vote for white candidates—often because they had no choice. White voters have not been conditioned to vote for black candidates, and there are some who, under no circumstances, would vote for a black candidate. If Jesus Christ reappeared—and he were black—they wouldn't vote for him. That's why I think excellence in performance is such an unfair burden to place upon black officials. Despite a candidate's excellent track record, many whites—owing to race alone—will not support a black candidate.

At the same time, black candidates can win, as my election proved. Black candidates must continue to run. The fact that nonbelievers and naysayers—both black and white—exist should not dissuade serious black candidates. Times change and so do attitudes. It's quite possible to overcome the race barrier, but it requires a unique kind of candidate—one who believes in himself and believes that people will respond favorably if they are approached in the proper manner.

JE: Was it difficult to walk the racial tightrope—that is, to appeal to black voters while courting the city's white establishment?

EM: Yes. It's difficult because, quite frankly, you're misunderstood by both groups. There are those who demand performance, but who expect the politics of personal treatment as well. I've often said that the level of expectations is geometric, while the capacity to deliver is not even arithmetic. That's true for both Blacks and whites. Blacks expect a black candidate to be a redeemer. They've been deprived so long, excluded from the system so long, that they expect a black candidate to work miracles. Miracles are few and far between. When you can't pull one out of a hat, Blacks become disillusioned. They expect much more from a black candidate than they do from a white candidate. Unfortunately, it's not always possible to produce miracles.

JE: Was it more difficult to convince Blacks—and black political organizations—than whites and the city's business leadership that you could govern intelligently and effectively?

EM: It depends upon which group you're speaking about—and its goals, interests, constituencies. These groups never argue in terms of race. They always speak in terms of policy—that is, what is good for the city. Race is a subtle factor. White groups never raise the race issue directly. However, it underlies many of their fears and doubts. They're frightened by the possibility of black power. They don't know how to deal with it. Many don't object to a black mayor, but they do object to a black mayor with power. It's all right to be mayor, but don't upset the economic applecart. Don't push for minority set-asides. Don't push for black capitalism.

JE: When you first ran for mayor, you were described as an "outsider"—a maverick who was independent of the regular party machinery. Did this prove to be an asset as well as a liability?

EM: Yes. But it depends upon whom you're talking to. If you're talking to those who made up the old political order—many of whom were very critical of my candidacy—I'm sure they would say it was a liability. But they won't describe it that way. Rather, they'll attribute it to my personality; they'll say that I'm abrasive, arrogant, feisty. Members of the old guard have repeated that line time and time again. They opposed my election then—and they oppose my administration now. Many of these people don't want reform; they like things the way they are. An outsider is seen as a threat. They're afraid he'll upset the old order. And they're right—at least, in my case. I don't identify with the past; I identify with the future. My goal is not to preserve the old order—which was often unfair and discriminatory—but to establish a new one based on justice and equity. That frightens them. And I can understand why.

JE: Iris Kelso, a political reporter for the *Times-Picayune*, once wrote: "His [Morial's] political philosophy is probably closer to that of the conservative white business leaders he courts than to the political leanings of his black constituency. Morial may be the only conservative black mayor in the United States." How accurate is this comment?

EM: My philosophy is very simple: I wear my heart on the left and my pocketbook on the right. In fiscal matters, I suppose, I'm a conservative; I believe in strict accountability. Given today's circumstances, I think that's absolutely critical. Cities like ours simply do not have the revenues they once had. And federal-state relations have changed for the worse. New Orleans faces severe economic problems. Historically, this city has not been treated like many big cities, owing to rural domination of the state legislature. Times are changing but very slowly. We can't spend what we don't have. If that makes me a conservative, then I'm a conservative.

However, when it comes to social issues, I'm as liberal as anyone else. But labels don't really tell you much about a person. You can be conservative on some issues, while being liberal on others. You have to look at the entire gamut of issues—not just one. A one-issue analysis won't tell you very much about me. You have to look at my record in its entirety. Overall, I'm a political moderate. My philosophy reflects the views of the rank and file of this city.

JE: To what extent has the fact that you're black, for example, affected your relationship with the city council and the state legislature? Has the race factor hindered your effectiveness?

EM: To some extent these relationships reflect racial considerations, perhaps more with the state legislature than the city council. The city council better reflects the population diversity of New Orleans than does the state legislature. The two black members of the city council frequently join forces with three of the white members. With the white members, race may be a factor in their response to initiatives from the mayor's office. Very often these members will use the Blacks to accomplish their own political objectives. The attitudes of the white members reflect hard political realities. Their relationship with the black members is best described by the old cliche, "You scratch my back, and I'll scratch yours." City council members are most interested in political survival. They attempt to accommodate every group—and every political whim or caprice—in order to win re-election.

As a result of having served in the state legislature, I've always thought that there are some issues that you should support on grounds of principle. If it's good and right, then you should vote for it. I can cite several instances. For example, when the state legislature passed a half-cent sales tax for the city and the schools, we attempted to put it into effect before the end of the year because it would have meant $2 million to the city. Several members of the state legislature opposed it and were successful in defeating it. Later, one member told a reporter: "We opposed it because the mayor proposed it." We tried to eliminate a home-state exemption recently. One member of the city council told the press: "It's a good idea, but I'm against it because the administration is part of it." We proposed a development across the street from city hall. A city councilman told a spokesman for the group: "The project is good, but you can expect some trouble because it's the mayor's project."

So, yes, race is a factor. Many black politicians are apathetic to the situation, partially because they aspire to sit in this office. If they succeed, they will discover what I have discovered. Moreover, many groups have requested favors or asked for preferential treatment, which I refused. They became angry and joined with the opposition in spearheading attacks against my administration. They're not retaliating against me personally, though they think they are. I view it quite differently. The mayor is transitory. Mayors come and go. But the city is going to be here. Some of their actions will backfire on them if and when they ever become mayor.

JE: Since becoming mayor, you've devoted considerable attention to minority enterprise. How successful have your efforts proven in this area?

EM: Since I took office in May 1978, I have made it my personal goal and the goal of my administration to begin to include in the economic mainstream of New Orleans that segment of our community to which 56 percent of our people belong. I am referring, of course, to the minority community. This is not an area to which we have merely paid lip service.

When I became mayor, we discovered that the business climate was such that minority businessmen and women did not find it conducive to do business with the city. There were only a handful of people within the community who held any contracts with the city, and most of those were contracts with funding from the federal government. They provided for very little employment within the community and were restricted to a very small, tightly controlled group of persons.

We immediately began to take steps to change this situation. We hired the city's first-ever minority business counselor and created the Minority Business Enterprise Unit. The purpose of this unit is to provide a place within city hall where minority businessmen can receive assistance in just about any area of their operation. Through this unit minority businessmen can find out what they have to do in order to bid on contracts with the city, as well as obtain advice on how to establish their corporate structure. The unit sponsors minority business seminars each year which bring together leading businessmen and speakers on a wide variety of subjects of special interest.

Once we established the Minority Business Enterprise Unit, we took several other important steps in this area. In one of the most difficult efforts of this administration, we received authorization from the city council, in the form of an ordinance, to create a Minority Business Set-Aside Program. This met opposition—very strong opposition—almost from the moment it was proposed. It required giving up a pint of blood and a pound of flesh for us to get the measure passed.

Many persons who had held the economic reins in the city for a number of years immediately felt that they were being asked to relinquish some of their power. They failed to realize at the time that the minority businesses not only can, but must, stand side by side with established businesses if our city is to survive and grow. Our set-aside program requires that certain procurements of goods and services by the city be set aside for awarding to minority firms and individuals. This does not mean that minorities may not bid on other projects and contracts. On the contrary, we encourage minorities to bid on all projects with city government. But in an effort to create the type of atmosphere and climate that had been non-existent for a number of years in the city, we designated certain areas where only minorities may bid.

It is important to understand that the set-aside program is consistent with the principles of a free enterprise system. It is not a program that is favorable to any particular individual or company. Under the set-aside program, minority firms are bidding against other minority firms for the awarding of a contract. This is consistent with the highest principles of our democracy.

As a result of our efforts, both in the set-aside program and in our normal purchasing procedures, we have been able to identify more than 300 individuals and firms in the minority community that are now doing business with the City of New Orleans. We have created a climate where minorities no longer feel threatened when they do business with the city. They know that they will receive the same support and commitment from the city that other entrepreneurs have enjoyed throughout the years.

JE: Are there signs that the black community is developing a new sense of political sophistication?

EM: Yes. But I think it will require a major educational effort. It's too great a challenge to place on a single individual, be he the mayor or sheriff or whoever. In the end, it will require the combined efforts of interested individuals and groups, all working toward one goal—namely, the maximization of political power. It will also require certain improvements in the educational system over which the mayor has no control. It will require that public officials join forces to promote political interest and awareness among Blacks. In a sense, New Orleans is not too different from cities like Baltimore where, for example, there are more than 100 black political organizations. Some of these are localized.

One or two have city-wide influence, but most are localized. Many of these groups do little to increase voter registration, preferring instead to run candidates for public office. To my knowledge, they never sponsored a voter registration drive, nor did they participate actively as a group in the efforts of organizations such as the Urban League or the NAACP. I do think, however, that these various groups, working cooperatively together for a common goal, can prove immensely effective.

JE: As mayor, you've been the subject of fierce criticism by the local media—specifically, the *Times-Picayune*. What explains your running battle with the press?

EM: You're right, of course. Our relationship has been marked by considerable conflict. From my perspective, the press has not been as fair as I would like it to be nor as fair as I think it should be, based upon our performance in office and the things we've accomplished. I suppose there are some underlying reasons for that—most notable the relationships that existed prior to my administration, in which the press enjoyed greater power and influence. It's only natural that they would want to preserve that advantage. To do so, they have attempted to discredit my administration in the hopes of persuading the public that we have failed to solve the great problems of this city. At times, I've found it extremely frustrating to break through the information stranglehold which they have on the city. Still, we keep trying. Eventually, the voters will realize that they've been sold a bill of goods.

JE: Like many black mayors, you inherited a city debilitated by decades of neglect. How have you attempted to reverse this trend?

EM: Although we've been able to piece together balanced budgets over the past several years, we have not solved the fundamental problem of generating sufficient revenue to fund what could reasonably be considered an adequate level of public services. If anything, the problem that confronts us now is even greater than in years past because we have already made every cut possible to eliminate waste and inefficiency. Every department has been cut to the bone.

It would be foolish to assume in these times that additional financial aid will be forthcoming from the state or from the federal government. With the federal deficit now topping $200 billion and estimates of a state budget shortfall of more than $100 million this year, it is very probable that state and federal aid to cities will face further cuts.

It is clear that the only course available to us is to seek additional local revenues if we are going to fulfill our responsibility to provide adequate public services for our citizens. The only perfect tax measure would be one that raises large amounts of revenue that no one has to pay. Unfortunately, no one has yet devised such a tax.

JE: Today, many cities face similar problems. Indeed, several mayors have called for increased taxes in order to offset the loss of federal funds. Do you favor increased taxes and, if so, what type?

EM: In determining what type of revenue measure we should adopt, I believe that we should consider the following criteria: First, any revenue measure must raise enough revenue to meet not only our immediate needs but also the projected needs for the years ahead. Second, it should be assessed fairly on our citizens. It should take into consideration the ability to pay and avoid placing a disproportionate burden upon the poor. Third, it should take into account regional considerations. It should be adaptable to and promote a regional approach to taxation because suburban areas are facing fiscal problems similar to ours. Fourth, it should help to promote economic development and jobs by providing sufficient revenues to enable us to make our city a more attractive location for business and industry. And fifth, it should be a measure that can be implemented quickly with the fewest procedural delays.

There are several possible options. After long and careful consideration, we have recommended that the city council adopt a 1 percent tax on all earnings in New Orleans with an exemption for those persons who earn less than the minimum wage. In considering the advantages and disadvantages of all the alternatives, the earnings tax is the only reasonable and responsible choice.

The earnings tax is the only alternative that can generate sufficient revenue to stabilize our city's finances and give us the latitude to address many serious problems that have been deferred for years. It is a fair tax because it does not place an inequitable burden upon the poor as does the sales tax. It ensures that everyone pays in proportion to their ability to pay.

Moreover, an earnings tax provides for regional considerations. It recognizes that many of the people who work in our city, who drive on our streets, who receive our police protection, and who benefit from city services should help to support those services. For decades, public officials and other community leaders have spoken of the need for a regional approach to our common problems. Public officials have long vowed to seek new and innovative ways to promote regional solutions. Today, the time has come to do more than simply talk about regional cooperation. It is time to act.

The fiscal problems of local government are not unique to the city of New Orleans. The city of Kenner is facing a continuing crisis in meeting its payroll. Jefferson Parish has been struggling for years to deal with its drainage problems, and the parish is beginning to encounter problems similar to ours in funding its transit deficit. I do not believe that any local government in the New Orleans area can claim that it is providing an adequate and acceptable level of services to its citizens.

Recognizing the problems of our neighborhood parishes and wanting to take a major, unique step toward regional cooperation, we have recommended that an earnings tax be adopted in New Orleans with a provision to share a portion of the revenues it will generate with the surrounding parishes.

We propose to redistribute or share 25 percent of the revenues collected from non-residents with the local authority where the taxpayer resides. We believe that the earnings tax should eventually be adopted throughout the metropolitan area. If any neighborhood parish were to adopt an earnings tax, we would, of course, expect an agreement of reciprocity in which New Orleans would also share in their revenues collected from our residents.

JE: Over the years, you have spoken out loudly and vigorously concerning the need to develop America's cities; you have argued that in our zeal to cut taxes and reduce waste, we have dealt a severe blow to the future of America's urban areas. How would you define the challenge that we face today? What can and should be done to remedy this situation?

EM: When we speak of the "urban core," we are speaking of *ourselves*. We are speaking of ourselves working with the establishment in our nation's cities. And we are speaking of ourselves becoming part of that establishment. In order to preserve ourselves, we must take steps now to ensure that we are part and parcel of determining our own future, both politically and economically. While we wonder about our future, we must begin to do something about it.

While being confronted with a private sector economy that is in dire straits, we find ourselves being abandoned by a federal government to whom we have turned in the past for assistance. Indeed, Blacks today own less than 3 percent of the businesses in America. And our businesses are failing in greater numbers than ever before. Unfortunately, many of them are being helped toward their demise by the Reagan Administration.

One of the cornerstones of the urban core is minority enterprise. If we in the cities are to survive, we *must* assure both the survival and the growth of minority business. These businesses are endemic to our communities which make up the core of our cities. Indeed, as white-owned businesses flee the urban centers of this country, seeking the protective umbrella of the suburbs, it is the responsibility of minority businesses to fill the gaps that remain behind. The first step to preserving the urban core is to take whatever measures and enact whatever programs are necessary to guarantee the survival of minority businesses.

The second step in preserving the core of urban America goes hand in hand with the survival of minority businesses. We must ensure that every citizen who is able and who wants to work is able to find a job. To do that, there is no doubt in my mind or in the minds of those who have been involved in the struggle for equality over the years that the federal, state, and local governments must work together. But the Reagan Administration stands on the brink of abdicating its responsibility in the areas of job training and employment. This abdication takes the form of the so-called New Federalism proposed by the administration.

JE: As you understand it, what is the New Federalism? Has it accomplished its stated aims?

EM: No. The real New Federalism arose two decades ago as a solution to urban problems. The Great Society and measures such as revenue sharing were exciting proposals that for the first time opened up a dialogue between the federal government and America's cities. The hunger and poverty of millions of urban dwellers became heard throughout the land and were no longer cries in the wilderness of legislatures with primarily rural concerns. The federal government reached out its mighty arms to help America's cities, and over the last two decades, we worked to rebuild America. This is the New Federalism I know.

But the New Federalism proposed by the Reagan Administration is a sham. It is an insult to those who worked so hard and to those who gave their lives in the struggle for equality. The real New Federalism was a friend to urban America. The Reagan Federalism is a flimsy cover for a program designed to abdicate the federal government's role as protector of the underprivileged and the needy.

I think that the President's desire to maintain a strong defense posture is admirable. But it is only admirable to a certain point. Once that posture begins to be financed on the backs of the poor and the needy, I say we have gone too far. Everywhere we turn cuts are being made in assistance to urban America, and we are being told that the President is intransigent on his stand for massive increases in funds for the Department of Defense.

The two goals are not incompatible. It is possible to have a defense second to none in the world and still provide for the defense of home and hearth against the enemies of hunger and disease. We are told that a high unemployment society is acceptable to those who would bring inflation down. Whether or not the economic dreams of the administration come true, President Reagan is well on his way to leaving America with one fundamental and disastrous legacy: the wreckage of five decades of public policy aimed at creating a more equitable society. Our hopes for opportunity and advancement which were raised in those decades are being destroyed as we watch the executioner wield his economic instrument of death. Our nation badly needs a successful presidency in 1984. All of us, Democrat and Republican, black and white, would have rejoiced had this president led our nation wisely and ably toward our shared goals of prosperity, social justice, and peace. But he has not.

JE: What concrete political steps should be taken to preserve the urban core?

EM: Probably the most important step we need to take now is to recommit ourselves to ensuring that every young man and woman, when he and she reach the age of eighteen, exercise the franchise and vote. Let me tell you a story. You know, being the good, practicing Catholic that I am, I am the proud father of five children! Three of them are now over the age of eighteen. My wife and I made it a family practice that when we went to vote, our children went with us, no matter how young they were. So, from the time they were very young, they got a lesson in civics—a lesson in how to exercise the most fundamental, the most important of all rights we have.

We must do everything within our power to encourage every black person in America to register to vote. Then and only then will we be able to exert the kind of political pressure necessary to move forward in our struggle for freedom and justice.

JE: Are you hopeful that Americans can and will reverse the present policies of the Reagan Administration?

EM: Many pundits have reported that we are in a recession. But for our community, we are in a depression. I wonder if the damage that has been done to our nation's cities can be repaired. This is not alarmist thinking. I am not an alarmist. I am, however, a realist.

Not long ago, the Reagan Administration released figures showing that unemployment in our country had fallen to around 8 percent. But this statistic is deceptive. The Labor Department has begun to include members of the armed forces in the unemployment statistics. How many people in the military are unemployed? And, of course, there is no change in the staggering figures that reflect the unemployment picture in minority communities.

And yet there seems to be a willingness on the part of the Reagan Administration to accept unemployment figures above the 8 percent level. Well, we cannot and will not accept that. A figure of 8.3 percent—and that is what the *real* unemployment figure is when you remove the military—is an unacceptable level of unemployment in urban America.

Using the guise of economic necessity, the social philosophy of the Reagan Administration has pushed us back to a time that we thought we had moved beyond decades ago. For twenty years prior to 1980, the percentage of people living below the poverty line in this nation declined at a steady rate. But under the Reagan Administration, that percentage has risen significantly.

JE: How do you view the President's decision to reduce federal aid to education and tighten the eligibility requirements for student loans?

EM: I think it's tragic. At the very time when we're reaching the point where jobs are becoming more and more complex and require a much greater degree of education and training, the doors to a better education are being slammed shut in the faces of our youth by the Reagan Administration.

This administration is responsible for tightening the eligibility requirements for student loans. This has been coupled with a dramatic reduction in the level of state aid to public institutions and a deluge of new applicants to those public institutions who can no longer afford to attend private colleges. These two factors have left educators wondering about their futures as well.

JE: Finally, as you look at New Orleans today—in light of where it has been and where it is headed—what do you see? Are you optimistic about the future?

EM: Yes. At any given time, you can walk down Bourbon Street and hear the sound of New Orleans. At any given instant the beat of New Orleans is being heard somewhere in the world, so universal has the cultural legacy of this city been. All the exquisite joys of living—music, dining, leisure, and love—have been shaped by this historic old city.

Because of this unique fame, few people think of New Orleans as anything but tempestuous and fun-loving and, perhaps, a trifle indifferent to progress. Sometimes you can hear it said, perhaps with a trace of wistfulness, that in the 1840s and 1850s—those tranquil antebellum days with the distant air of tragedy—New Orleans was a glorious commercial city, bursting with vitality, with banks high in the nation's financial ranks and commerce that made it a rich city of the South and golden city of the nation. It is anything but a tattered legend.

The eventual hostilities changed New Orleans, shattering the city's sense of grand economic destiny, if not its great and boisterous spirit, for more than 100 years. In the eventful post-World War II years, New Orleans's economy remained comparatively unnewsworthy.

While the city appeared seemingly unconcerned and satisfied with a way of life that enchanted visitors, economists were busy issuing forecasts. The day was inevitable, they said, when New Orleans would finally get its act together. And they were right. It has. When we wonder when it all began to move forward, we look back to the latter part of the last decade, when little changes began to grow into big changes. The unmistakable sense of progress truly came upon the city before it acquired general credibility.

It is this other New Orleans, the tale of the other city where the sound of the trumpet grows louder, but the sound of the hammer even louder, that I see. It is both epic and historic, comparable only to the 1850s. Indeed, New Orleans may well be the new city of the South in the 1980s. I certainly hope so. And I would like to think that I played some small part in making that a reality.

Marion S. Barry, Jr.

A Time to Act

Marion S. Barry, Jr., the son of sharecroppers, was born March 6, 1936, in Itta Bena, Mississippi. When Barry was two years old, his father died, and he, his mother, and two sisters moved to Memphis, Tennessee. His mother worked as a domestic and remarried. As a student in the Memphis public school system, Barry became one of the first black Eagle Scouts in the nation. He was the first in his family to attend college and received a Bachelor of Science degree in chemistry from LeMoyne College. He later earned a Master of Science degree in chemistry from Fisk University and entered a doctoral program in chemistry at the University of Tennessee. He was one of the few black students enrolled in a doctoral program in this field at that time.

While he attended college and graduate school, the civil rights movement became increasingly important in Barry's life, and he eventually left the University of Tennessee to devote himself full time to voter registration and organization. He helped found the Student Non-Violent Coordinating committee (SNCC) and became SNCC's national chairman in 1960.

Barry came to Washington in 1965 as the director of the Washington SNCC office. He immediately joined with other civil rights activists in organizing and leading a successful anti-fare-increase bus boycott that significantly benefitted low-income and elderly residents of the District of Columbia (D.C.). From this success, he established the Free D.C. Movement. This movement sought to overturn the district's "colonial status," which subjected district residents to the whims of congressmen elected from other parts of the country. Next, Barry helped to establish a major job-training program for the unemployed youth of the city. Youth Pride trained and placed 15,000 of the roughest, toughest, hard-core unemployed youngsters in the District of Columbia.

In 1969, Barry was elected to serve on the Pilot District Project—his first elected position. The Pilot District Project was an experimental police-community relations project established in the aftermath of the turmoil and unrest following the assassination of Dr. Martin Luther King, Jr. Later, as chairman, Barry helped to lead the police and community to a better understanding of each other's needs and rights.

Deeply involved in community-based activities, Barry ran for an at-large seat on the Washington, D.C. Board of Education in 1971. He won and was subsequently elected president. He served as president for two and one-half years and was able to unite a factionalized and contentious school board and demonstrated his ability to bring together people with diverse views and opinions.

In 1974, Barry was elected to an at-large seat in the first city council election in the District of Columbia in nearly 100 years. He served as chairperson of the Committee on Finance and Revenue, where he compiled a long list of impressive legislative accomplishments, among them: property tax relief and credits for homeowners, renters, the elderly, and the handicapped; increased funding for all levels of public education; the Minority Contracting Act, which set aside 25 percent of all contracts with the city for minority firms; and the Office on Aging, which assists the city's senior citizens. From this post, Barry led the way in streamlining the D.C. government, slashing $50 million annually from the executive branch's budget and tax requests. In 1976, Barry ran for re-election, receiving 73 percent of the vote, after which he continued his efforts on behalf of job creation and training, senior citizen programs, and sound budget management.

In January 1978, Barry announced his candidacy for mayor, pledging to bring "competent and compassionate government to the people." He ran in a strong field of three, with most political pundits predicting a last-place finish. Barry, however, forged a broad-based coalition, known as "Barry's Army," comprised of the District's labor unions, community activists, women's rights groups, gays and lesbians, small businesspersons, the poor, Blacks, and progressive whites. He was endorsed by the *Washington Post*, numerous civic associations, unions, and many community leaders. Barry won the crucial Democratic Party primary and went on to sweep the general election in November 1978.

On January 2, 1979, Barry was sworn in by Supreme Court Justice Thurgood Marshall as the second elected mayor of the District of Columbia. Barry worked tirelessly to fulfill the promises he made during the campaign. In the four years that followed, he translated many of those promises into specific legislative and executive proposals, ranging from crime prevention, to public housing, to job creation, to private sector investment, to governmental reorganization, to bal-

anced budgets, to governmental efficiency. Barry ran for and was elected to a second term in November 1982, and has since concentrated on making further strides in these and other areas.

JE: Many Americans believe that the present conservative climate, coupled with the re-election of President Reagan, makes social change impossible. Do you agree? If not, why?

MB: No. It always amazes me when I hear defeatist attitudes among people who have no right or reason to feel that way. The fact is, there are far too few people who are seriously working to achieve social change at any level. No one says it is easy. But I do believe that those of us whose eyes are open to the social and economic problems facing us today have a responsibility to develop alternative proposals—at all levels of government—to help solve problems. And because so few others are attempting to make policy changes at *any* level of government, we do have a chance to have policy changes implemented. It takes a deep commitment, but it can and must be done.

As Vernon Jordan has said, "In a few brief years, our nation has moved from We Shall Overcome to We Don't Care." In the late 1960s, somebody, somewhere, played a soft lullaby, and everyone went off to Dreamland. In their dreams, the majority of citizens saw an America which was slowly, although painfully, recovering from the strife of the 1960s. People no longer had to take to the streets, and the cities no longer had to be burned.

In their dreams, things were improving for the nation's disadvantaged. Americans dreamt we had jobs programs so successful that even they went too far. Qualified members of the majority community could scarcely find work because minorities were getting all the plum jobs. While members of the middle class were having trouble finding homes, the poor were receiving subsidized housing.

In their dreams, free health care for low-income people was universal, even though the poor might occasionally have to wait in long lines. It was difficult for the average person to buy gas for their car. But in their dreams, Americans believed the poor could always hail a cab to their local social service center or cooperative food store and submit a voucher for reimbursement. While the rest of America could scarcely afford hamburger, the poor could simply cash in their food stamps for a juicy porterhouse steak.

Our society reasoned that after America had tolerated this favoritism for a while, it could always swing back again to the right and end the luxuries. I honestly do not know how so many millions of Americans could have accepted such myths. But in actuality, America has been swinging to the right for several years now, and this trend, under the leadership of President Reagan, has been accelerating.

Despite claims of progress, we are retrogressing. There exists no national leadership to solve the problems which confront us. The Reagan Administration has turned its back on the poor, the powerless, the helpless, and the oppressed. Still, I think there is reason for hope. I discern, even in the midst of the present national meanness which grips the nation, signs of optimism.

Those of us who advocate social change are better educated and more sophisticated than ever before. We have the tools to effect change. And we know better than to depend on the goodwill of the American people. We must do the job ourselves. In my view, the future rests, to a large extent, on the private sector. The present realities may seem grim: Minorities are presently receiving only a small share of the new jobs created in the private sector. In addition, many young people do not even wish to work in the private sector. Yet, we must be alert enough to recognize that much of the anti-government fever is the direct result of affirmative action employment practices in the public sector. If we achieve employment successes in the private sector, it is unlikely that the nation will turn on its corporations and cut back private sector resources. People aren't anxious to jeopardize their own dividend checks.

We must ensure that our cities are not excluded from future federal budgets. And we need a national housing policy, now. How much low, moderate, and middle income housing stock should this nation have? How should we get it? Where should it be located? What will happen to those who are displaced? Sadly, we have no national answers to these crucial questions.

Obviously, we need national health insurance and improved health care to eliminate the discrimination which presently poisons the lives of poor people and minorities. The facts are clear: In 1984, the infant mortality rate for minorities was nearly double the white rate, while life expectancy for whites was approximately six years longer than for minorities.

Tax reform must be a reality. And I don't just mean tax breaks for the relatively well-off homeowner. We need those. But we also need substantial income redistribution by implementing our stated taxation goals and eliminating tax loopholes.

Above all, as far as I am concerned, we need to develop—for the first time in this nation's history—a comprehensive national urban policy. And I am not referring to a position paper, written by a few federal officials in their spare time, on the plight of the cities. That has been our approach in the past. We need a comprehensive urban policy with specific goals and timetables, as well as specific well-thought-out strategies to accomplish those goals. This policy should be complete with legislation and a budget—and backed by a president and a Congress who are sincere about reducing this nation's enormous social and economic burdens.

JE: Since becoming mayor, you have spearheaded the fight for the District's Voting Rights Amendment. Why is this amendment necessary?

MB: District residents believe strongly in full voting representation and the need to control our own destiny. This need is not peculiar to the District. All Americans want greater control over their own lives. The public must recognize that our fight is their fight—that they will not be free until we are free.

The right to self-government and representation in Congress is central to a democratic society. We sometimes feel that people outside the District cannot understand our frustrations over not being able to act in the interests of our own people. We feel particularly frustrated when we witness the visible signs of everyone else's voting rights occurring on our home ground, and yet we are forever on the outside looking in. As we have gained limited home rule step by step over the past twenty years, we have harbored the hope that this situation will change.

The realization of home rule has been a slow process, but we now feel as if it might be within our grasp. However, we will need the support of the entire nation to bring this about. It was not until the 1964 presidential election that District residents could vote for president and vice-president. Until 1967, the District was administered by three commissioners appointed by the President, who also appointed all local judges. In 1967, we changed to an appointed mayor-commissioner and council system, which also was appointed by the President. Our right to elect local officials came with an elected school board in 1968, replacing a board appointed by federal judges. In 1971, we were granted a nonvoting delegate in Congress. Can you imagine how frustrating it is to operate on Capitol Hill without a vote to give teeth to your actions! A limited form of home rule was enacted in 1973, and the first elected mayor and council took office in January 1975.

But that is only the beginning of our story. With that limited home rule, we acquired the right to pass our own legislation, carry out local planning authority, and set our own taxes. All of our legislation and much of our planning is subject to lengthy federal review, increasing greatly the amount of time required to implement any measure desired by our citizens.

Our entire budget is reviewed, line by line, by Congress. Aside from the obvious frustrations of having our priorities take a backseat to those of others, this creates a budget process so cumbersome that we often lag far behind in meeting citizen needs. The entire budget approval process takes anywhere from two to three years, since the budget often isn't approved until the end of the fiscal year in which we are operating. We often not only don't know what we will have to spend the following year but cannot even determine how much we will have to spend during the current year. This makes sound financial planning a nightmare.

In addition, we are prohibited from taxing persons who work in the District and use our services but who live elsewhere. This right to tax non-residents—often called "commuters"—is enjoyed and practiced by all fifty states, as well as by many large cities across the nation. Further, while we receive a federal payment to compensate for the services we provide the federal government, and to make up for the fact that we cannot tax the more than half of our land (55 percent) which is either used by the government or exempt from use, this payment is considerably lower than it should be. Further, this payment is made at the whim of the President and those in Congress who review the budget, so that we have no way of planning or predicting the size of that payment. The net effect of all this, and the harsh reality for the residents of the District, is that we must tax our own citizens more heavily than forty-nine of the fifty states, in order to subsidize the presence of the federal government. That is the truth, and I think it is a truth which is little known across the nation.

JE: What would voting representation mean to the District, both symbolically and as a practical matter?

MB: If we had voting representatives in Congress, we would gain the advantage not only of our votes, which would be substantial, but the psychological advantage of being on an equal footing with the other members. No longer would we be the beggars who must take what we can get. Instead, we would be able to interact with the rest of the nation and its representatives as equals. That is very important to us, just as it is to all Americans. It would afford us an opportunity for the first time to participate in shaping the collective destiny of this nation, along with the residents of the fifty states. For the first time, we would have a full voice in the legislative process upon which the lawmaking of this nation is based. This is vitally important to us both as a practical matter and as a basic right of citizenship.

JE: Given its importance, why has the amendment failed to win ratification?

MB: There are those who fear that we would somehow tip the balance of power away from the interests of citizens in other parts of the nation. I believe that these individuals have nothing to fear, anymore than they had to fear the same thing from occurring with the passage of the Voting Rights Act. Our sense and sensibilities on important national issues will, as always, be based on the same careful judgments as those of representatives of any state in the Union, and the positions we will take in the interests of the people of the District will surely coincide with the interests of the entire nation.

In my view, we are not naturally at odds with the people of any state in the Union. Our deep interest in peace and freedom is a more important and binding tie than any interest which might separate us on one or two issues at any particular point in time. Further, I know that the people of this nation would not deny us the right to participate in the democratic process on the chance that we might differ on some issues. If that were the case, it is doubtful that the United States would have grown beyond the original thirteen states. This has always been a nation which has welcomed diversity and extended voting rights to its citizens without questioning their position on a particular issue or issues. We are asking to be treated no differently.

JE: How would you respond to the argument that the District's voting rights could best be provided by retrocession of the District to the states of Maryland or Virginia?

MB: There are serious problems with this position. It's simply not a viable alternative. The Twenty-third Amendment recognized that there was no practical purpose for linking the District to Maryland for the purpose of electing a president, and there is similarly no justification today for linking it for purposes of voting in Congress. In fact, Maryland has made it clear that it opposes retrocession and instead favors voting representation—a statement backed up by its vote in favor of the Voting Rights Amendment. The retrocession argument raises a number of legal and constitutional questions. In fact, under retrocession, the federal government would have been subject to the powers of the state of Maryland, which would contradict the federal provisions that established the District as a federal entity. And if the District were linked to Maryland for voting rights purposes, would not the residents of the District also have the right to vote for state officials in Maryland? Clearly, this is not a reasonable alternative, and no one has recognized this more strongly than the state of Maryland itself.

JE: Would you be willing to support a compromise, in which the

District would be granted voting representation in the House but not in the Senate?

MB: No. Some critics of the amendment are willing to grant the District a vote in the House, with population being the basis of representation, but not in the Senate, where they argue that only states can be represented. In fact, however, since the ratification of the Seventeenth Amendment, which established the election of senators by popular vote, senators have been elected by the people of the states and not the states as such. To deny the residents of the District the right to representation in the Senate would be to continue to deny the District residents the full rights of American citizenship. House representation alone would not achieve the purpose of this amendment or meet our needs.

JE: Did Jesse Jackson's 1984 presidential campaign produce a sharp increase in black registration in the District? Are you satisfied with the progress that has been made in this area?

MB: Yes, the Jackson campaign had an enormous impact on black registration. But I am concerned that only 60 percent of the District's residents are registered to vote. We must boost that figure by 20 percent, 30 percent, and more. As one who has devoted his life and career to the struggle for civil rights and as one who was arrested many times in the course of this struggle, I know just how important and how basic voting rights are to achieving human rights and personal freedom. Being able to go to the ballot box and express and enforce our views is the best means of assuring that our civil rights will be maintained, that our hard-won progress will not slip away, and that equal opportunity will become a reality in our society. Without voting rights, any other right or liberty we have in this society can be taken away without recourse.

That is why it is so important that we wage a strong voter registration drive in the District. Each and every person eighteen years and over should register and vote. We must provide leadership for the nation in this regard, because we in the District have the advantage of being able to focus national attention on this effort. Also, we should show members of Congress, who argue that we are not interested, just how much we do care by registering and voting.

It is significant that many of the leaders and many residents of the District have joined forces in this effort. It is a demonstration that, when it comes to the issues which really count—which are basic to the lives and dignity and liberty of our citizens—we in the District can and will come together in unity of spirit and purpose.

It is vital that Blacks register to vote. The job begun with the Voting Rights Act is far from complete. It is more important than ever because of the focus on economics in these difficult times, making it easy to forget how important this freedom is to economic security and personal dignity. It is more important than ever, in order that Blacks and other minorities can make their voices heard and can make further progress in sharing the benefits of this society. When it comes to solving the crushing urban problems of joblessness, inadequate housing, poverty, and hunger, I believe that there is a leadership gap which must be filled through widespread voter participation.

JE: Many Americans believe that the struggle for civil rights has long since been won—that the Supreme Court decision in *Brown* v. *Board of Education* (1954) eliminated the last vestiges of segregation and discrimination. Do you agree?

MB: No. The nation recently celebrated the thirtieth anniversary of the *Brown* decision—a monumental event in the lives of black Americans. The Supreme Court's landmark ruling, handed down in 1954, outlawed racially segregated education in America's public schools. For millions of Blacks at the time, the decision promised to open the doors to educational opportunities which the republic had denied us for more than 200 years.

Black Americans hoped and expected that access to equal education would now be ours and that this decision would herald significant changes in the lives of millions of our young people. Well, they were both right *and* wrong. They were right in that in the South, the federal government began, however slowly, to enforce the court's decision. Southern states, counties, and cities were threatened with government lawsuits and cut-offs of federal dollars for non-compliance with the *Brown* decision.

Heartened and energized by this gesture of the court, the then fledgling civil rights movement pressed into action, wary of the effectiveness of the new law, but determined to test its strength. In many ways, the *Brown* decision was the catalyst for the era of twenty years of progressive social change witnessed by this country. For example, had it not been for the *Brown* decision, the milestones of voting rights and civil rights of the mid- and late-1960s might not have been realized.

In the South, integrated education moved forward, and the rewards of the twin instruments of litigation and agitation are everywhere to be seen. Today, Blacks hold positions in the public and private sectors which were unthinkable thirty years ago. Indeed, the success of today's corps of black elected officials, of which I am proudly one, is partly attributable to the gallant efforts of such dedicated souls as Justice Thurgood Marshall, Dr. Kenneth B. Clark, Dr. James N. Nabritt, Judge Constance Baker Motley, Dr. Herbert Reid, and the cadre of NAACP attorneys who carried the day thirty years ago.

Yes, *Brown* was truly a landmark decision and a cause for great rejoicing and optimism in those early years. But the optimism of thirty years ago is not justified today, for we have witnessed during the past decade both the procrastination and outright refusal of the northern cities and states to carry out the mandate of school desegregation. Today, we need only consider the *Bakke* decision; recent budget cuts in social programs; the re-emergence of a national conservative movement; the influence of the New Right; the shift in the Supreme Court; the assault on civil rights gains; and the callous treatment of Blacks, the poor, and other minorities, to see that the battle is far from won.

While there appears to be a retrenchment in the area of civil rights, new frontiers call for the imaginative and creative skills of the legal profession, as well as others, to press the fight for the continued advancement of America's forgotten. The task before us is immense. Look at Ronald Reagan's America, an America which bears witness to the erosion of affirmative action, equal education, public housing, and employment opportunity. Witness the infirm and ominous condition of our economy and the devastating effect it has had on the survival and dignity of the poor and less fortunate. Witness the disenchantment with the law as an instrument for social progress and social justice. Witness the misery, degradation, and hopelessness wrought by the developing drug culture. Witness the continuing festering threats to world peace and the hopelessness it breeds. Witness the international disregard for human rights and self-determination, both at home and abroad. These are but a few of the myriad social problems which confront our society and operate directly to adversely affect the plight and decline of the poor, the black, and the forgotten.

So, no, the job is far from complete. We Blacks who are the beneficiaries of the sacrifices and toil of others would be remiss if we contented ourselves with complacency, noble pronouncements, and financial success. Instead, we must dedicate ourselves to a goal which has as its sole object keeping the doors of opportunity, hope, and freedom wide and forever open for all our people The future of our people, indeed of all who are oppressed, will be determined in large measure by the degree to which we will answer the urgent call of our times to keep alive the struggle for freedom and justice.

JE: There have been many heroes in the civil rights movement— both famous and little known. Few figures, however, stand taller than Dr. Martin Luther King, Jr. How would you assess his contribution to the movement? What role has he played in your life and work?

MB: Dr. King taught us to come together—people of cause, concern, and commitment. He taught us to look beyond who we are or who we perceive ourselves to be and to work until we are weary; to give of ourselves until it *helps*; to tear down real or imagined barriers—racial, cultural, social, or economic; to build a strong foundation for our cities—cities firmly placed on the goodwill, thoughts, and deeds of all citizens.

Dr. King helped us to understand the value of a significant message, "Together we can," and "If it is to be, we must make it be." For clearly, then as now, it is the time for us! He impressed upon us a sense of knowing that in the best of us, there is better.

He insisted on a timetable that kept the nation fixed at the clock on the wall, so that we would never forget that the hour has grown late for those who have for too long been denied; for those who have competed in life's hard ball game, only to hear the umpire shout, "You're out!" Dr. King caused each of us, all of us, to focus acutely on who we are and who we are not, what we have done and what remains to be done, and where we have been and where we must go.

JE: If Dr. King were alive today, what message do you think he would preach to black America?

MB: If Dr. King were here, surely he would look at our condition and know as we must know that now is the time when we must put ourselves on the side of right; then put destiny before politics and principle before power; bind our heads, hearts, and hands in one accord; and in these times serve as the guiding light to the nation and know that because of who we are, we will rise.

Dr. King would tell us to reach down within ourselves to find the strength and courage to face the harsh realities which invade our lives as needed services vanish and the listening ears of the federal government fall deaf. Today's priorities are defense and missiles, not day care and milk for our babies. Our imprint is measured by our inscription on our communities, our neighborhoods, our block clubs, our individual families, and our children—who, in generations following, will stand ready to take our place on the next leg of life's marathon.

Dr. King would remind us that our greatest resource is ourselves. We are best suited for the task to direct us towards where we are going and how we will get there. We determine whether we help or hinder, encourage or oppose, lift or limit—whether we walk towards rather than walk away from.

We must be power brokers to go to the extraordinary lengths and to learn the lessons of Dr. King. In this regard, we must use education as an instrument of economic, social, and political development. We must be analytical in thought, articulate in the spoken word, and reflective while we listen to others. Education can afford us the *know how* to build on the bridges built by our churches, fraternities and sororities, banks and insurance companies; bridges built by entrepreneurs and investors who have enabled us to travel a safe, if not secure, passage into the twentieth century. It is for us to build on those bridges; for it is our requirement to secure our tomorrow—*today, not tomorrow!*

JE: Do you view education then as the key to black progress? If so, why?

MB: Yes. I am reminded of Booker T. Washington's observation, in *Up From Slavery*, in which he said: "Education is meant to make us give satisfaction and to get satisfaction out of giving it. It is meant to make us get happiness out of service to our fellows. And until we get to the point where we can get happiness and supreme satisfaction out of helping our fellows, we are not truly educated."

An educated person may achieve some happiness—in fact, one may seek to become educated in order to become happy. But the key point is that one cannot achieve either education or happiness in a vacuum or solely within oneself. To me, this means that education inherently possesses a value realized only through interaction with others. Further, the means for that interaction is *service*. Service provides the structure for meaningful relationships. It provides the possibility for caring for others. Service elevates us and those we serve. In other words, we educate ourselves and bring happiness into our lives through work, through the act of helping others. At a very basic level, education and the development of a moral sensitivity are one. An education which ignores the moral imperative of service somehow remains incomplete because it fails to provide for the means to achieve happiness, as well as the means to expand our consciousness of human nature.

Washington demanded maximum performance and tested students against that measure. But in order to require so much from students, Washington himself had to set the example. Only when we maintain high standards for ourselves can we expect them from others. It is perhaps a comment on the educational system today that educators test for minimum competency. As former Secretary of Education Terrel Bell stated, before the Education Commission of the States: "If you test for minimum competency, that's what you get."

Educators ought to demand the best of themselves; they ought to perform as they expect their students to perform. Inner city children perform best when teacher and administrator expectations are highest. We ought to expect maximum competency of both ourselves and our students. We can no longer be satisfied with minimum competency, either for our students or for ourselves. We must expand our outreach. We must expand our service to students. We must recognize the essence of Dr. King's statement that "All men are bound together in a single garment of destiny," and thus band together with each other and with our young people. We must work, as Washington admonished, ten hours a day at the job and an additional two hours after that, if need be. We must work together, we must cooperate, because that is the only way we can achieve our goals. The future of our cities, of our youth, and of our nation depends on it.

JE: Since becoming mayor, you have spoken out against President Reagan's New Federalism. Why?

MB: President Reagan has enunciated his philosophy on numerous occasions and has stated: "I've always believed that the best government is no government." And as if to prove it, he dragged out what he called the "New Federalism." He offered the states a massive swap of programs, suggesting that everything will come out even. As part of his crusade to, as he said, get the federal government off our backs, Reagan proposed turning over an increasing number of responsibilities to state and local governments. He argued that they are clearly more responsive to the will of the people.

In his 1982 State of the Union Address, the President proposed to do this with a giant swap of programs and dollars: The federal government will take Medicaid, while the states will take Aid for Families with Dependent Children and food stamps. Meanwhile, the federal government will turn over nearly forty categorical programs to the states—programs for health care, highways, social services, and education—and establish a temporary trust fund to finance them. But the states can eliminate any or all of these programs and use the trust fund money for anything they choose. The President said that the whole package was an even-steven deal.

All in all, the New Federalism is a cynical piece of work. It's a return to states' rights—just states' rights, with a fancy new label. But the New Federalism doesn't stand alone. It's just one thread in the burial cloth that this administration has woven for justice, equity, and fairness in America.

JE: Given what you've said, what explains President Reagan's overwhelming 1984 re-election victory?

MB: I don't really have an answer except that this nation seems to be cursed with historical amnesia. People think that Reagan's ideas are something new—and thus they are something attractive—only because most of us have forgotten that these ideas have all been tried before.

The last time we witnessed them in action was immediately prior to the economic stroke this nation suffered in 1929. This administration is operating on a set of false premises that resulted in economic disaster a half-century ago. The first is that the rich and powerful are naturally superior. Ronald Reagan, like Calvin Coolidge, appears bound to the assumption that people who achieve or maintain wealth are somehow wiser, somehow nobler in spirit, somehow more deserving of society's benefits than thee or me.

This view of America derives from country club cocktail parties and Norman Rockwell magazine covers. In it, all the bankers are round-faced and friendly, the doctors take care of sick puppies, and the millionaires shake hands with newsboys.

According to this view, the aristocracy of wealth is good, and government is bad. Why? Because government can commit mortal sins against the orthodoxy of wealth: It can tax; it can say no to those crimes committed in the pursuit of self-interest; and it can attempt to promote the general well-being—the good of all versus privilege for the few.

To free us from this ungodly nonsense, the Reagan Administration has abandoned the basic responsibilities of government—to protect health and safety on the job, to protect the economic security of the elderly, to help maintain some minimum dignity for the poor, the deprived, and the handicapped, to preserve our land and earth and water, and so much else. If the administration had its way, it would entrust these responsibilities to the noble impulses of the great charitable institutions—institutions such as Mobil Oil, Hooker Chemical, and their kind.

In short, God created the marketplace for America, so let the marketplace solve our problems. Every major action of this administration—in its budget cuts, in its tax excesses, in its mugging of regulations, in its monetary policies—has furthered the lopsided unfairness between the rich and the rest.

Who pays for those helicopters for El Salvador? Who pays for those new nuclear, biological, and chemical weapons? And now corporations not only pay no taxes but also receive big bucks back from Uncle Sam. Who pays for that? The people do.

This administration shows every sign of what you might call a "political genetic defect," a political logic that is as twisted as a strand of DNA. This administration is against the greedy—but only those greedy who depend on welfare to stay alive. It is against "waste, fraud, and abuse," but only if it involves five-and-ten-cent crimes and not those gross corruptions bred by Pentagon stupidity or corporate cupidity. It is against the free lunch, but only if it involves the thirty-cent meal served to a hungry kid and not the $100 feast of a defense industry lobbyist.

So, what are members of this administration for? They are for the needy. Not those needy who found that the safety net was woven out of cheesecloth, but the truly needy—the individual millionaires and multi-billion-dollar corporations.

And worst of all, this administration's program does something more than destroy our economy. It is working to destroy the faith that poor people and working people have had that their government would protect them against the excesses and the tyranny of the few and the wealthy.

Under the Reagan Administration, basic rights are up for grabs: human rights, worker rights, women's rights, consumer rights, and certainly civil rights. In the area of civil rights, this administration's record is an unremitting insult. The White House attacks those laws that protect minorities while seeking to reward bigotry. It cripples programs that provide an escape from the economic ghetto and increase political access. If you need any further demonstration of intent, all you need do is to look at the list of White House nominees to the Civil Rights Commission or the Equal Employment Opportunity Commission.

JE: Do you sense, among black Americans, a firm commitment to reversing the present situation? If not, why?

MB: As I survey the American landscape today, it is clear that there are hundreds, if not thousands, of black Americans who are geared to do battle against social injustice. We need these freedom fighters as never before. As we sit here today, millions of poor people and minorities are hungry and unemployed because of the misguided policies of a national government that has determined that the cure for social ills is to feed the *truly needy* by first feeding the *truly greedy*.

Those who died to secure the vote and civil rights cry up in *outrage* from the grave because a national government has enforced civil rights with indifference and actively sought to reverse the sacrifice of thousands by attacking affirmative action, busing, and rewarding those who practice discrimination with tax credits. Sadly, the apostles of hate have risen from their dark slumber. Once again, we can hear the crackling of burning crosses and see the stain of swastikas upon the walls of temples and holy places.

Despite the discord of the moment, I still have hope, for I am reminded that if we dare to stand up like Medgar Evers, Martin Luther King, Jr., Rosa Parks, and countless others who bore the battle in the heat of the day, even though *dark be the night—joy will come in the morning*!

But the *morning* will only come when we develop the resolve to turn *to* each other rather than *on* each other. The *morning* will only come when the residents of the Gold Coast recognize that their destiny is inextricably linked with the residents of America's poorest neighborhoods. The *morning* will only come when every person, irrespective of intellect, wealth, or position *understands* that the supreme duty of life is to have romance with the rejected and fellowship with the dispossessed.

JE: What specific strategies would you recommend to counteract the growing ground swell of conservatism that is sweeping the nation?

MB: There are a large number of bewildered and befuddled politicians all over this land who claim that no solutions exist for America's social and economic problems—solutions to problems which oppress cities and oppress low income people. I think we still have a problem of *basic values*. The problems are still with us—and they are magnified—simply because the vast majority of those who are in charge do not care enough to seek out the answers and commit themselves and the resources they control to solving those problems.

There is widespread national discontent with the progress we've made in these areas. We have no comprehensive urban policy, no comprehensive housing policy, no comprehensive energy policy, and no comprehensive health and social services policy in this nation.

I am not disillusioned. I know it will be a battle to achieve even the smallest victories in 1986, just as it was in previous years. Being discouraged, alienated, or disheartened will serve little purpose. Ronald Reagan's America is *not* my America—nor the America of black people. Nor is it the America of the poor, the elderly, the minorities, the women, and all the diverse groups outside of America's economic mainstream. Ronald Reagan's America means fewer jobs, lower incomes, less housing, and reduced day care and other social services—all at the expense of greater well-being for those who are already well-off.

JE: What do you mean, for example, when you say that that America lacks a "comprehensive housing policy"? Isn't the Department of Housing and Urban Development spearheading a national effort to build low income housing?

MB: No. As of 1985, we still have no plan as to how many housing units we plan to construct, how low income people will be housed, where people will be settled, and how we plan to cope with the enormous influx of wealth which is destroying neighborhoods for the sake of profit. The policy makers in the legislative and executive branches have never attempted to develop a master plan to adequately house our citizens because they would then have to set a price tag on the costs involved in sheltering America's poor. From their perspective, it's better not to know; that way they can proceed with business as usual, without reordering our national priorities. On the other hand, our leaders know *exactly* how many nuclear weapons we should have in our arsenal, but we *hope for the best* when it comes to providing decent, safe, and sanitary housing.

We should *demand* a plan from our "leaders"—whom we will house, where, and at what cost, and whom we will *not* house, and *why*. We should demand a displacement policy, as well as a national policy for rental housing. Little if any new rental housing is being built in many American cities. We should demand a national policy concerning condominium conversion and co-ops. Many people blame rent control, but their only response is to lift the present controls so they can double their rents and attract a whole new income class to replace their present tenants. We should demand a progressive policy on rent control and the preservation and expansion of rental housing. The need is surely there—people need only open their eyes to see it.

JE: Would you also characterize the administration's approach to social services as one of callous neglect?

MB: Yes. However, before discussing the present human services crisis, let me indicate that over 30 percent of black Americans live in poverty, compared to less than 10 percent of white America. Therefore, nationwide, nearly one out of every three Blacks lives in poverty. Every black person I know can easily cite a friend or family member who is living in poverty or close to poverty. Yet, many Americans do not know a single poor person. It is this lack of personal contact and basic understanding which is directly responsible for the callous policies of this administration.

Now, as far as your question is concerned, we need a national public assistance program, *administered by the federal government*, which brings everyone who is below the poverty line to at least the poverty line. This should be our first priority. Why should a state or city which actively shuns low income people be rewarded with reduced budgetary pressures? On the other hand, a city which provides compassion and support for low income persons is penalized by severe budgetary pressures, tax increases, and service cutbacks because it accepts the social and economic burdens of its metropolitan region.

No jurisdiction should be able to rezone or otherwise avoid the burdens of caring for America's poor. Like national defense, poverty is a national concern, and we all must share in the solution equally. We desperately need a comprehensive social services policy which provides such support services as child care, adoption, foster care, and other forms of residential placement, homemaker services, counseling, senior citizen centers, food banks, and health care. The relatively affluent presently enjoy the necessary human support services and, therefore, find it difficult to identify with those who must do without.

As pervasive as poverty is in America, we need a national health and social services policy to cope with poverty's debilitating personal effects. How many people are presently being served and in what ways? How many people have we chosen not to serve and why? We should at least know what we are doing and not doing and carefully plan our actions accordingly.

The late A. Phillip Randolph once proposed a "Freedom Budget" for the American people. This budget was designed to eliminate poverty in our nation—to bring dependable health services, a first-rate education, and decent, affordable housing to every citizen. In addition, it guaranteed a job and an above-poverty income to all our people.

Radical? Yes. Expensive? Yes. The cost was projected to be $185 billion over a ten-year period (during the 1970s). Yet, Randolph demonstrated that, given a national commitment, it could be done. By comparison, the Vietnam War cost our nation $275 billion. In 1914, for example, Henry Ford found that by more than doubling worker pay to $5 per day, he could expand consumer buying power and create an entire new market for his automobile.

Similarly, Randolph's Freedom Budget, by wiping out the poverty which consumes more than 35 million Americans, would expand buying power enormously and create a new national prosperity. We must begin to realize that the cost to perpetuate class and racial disadvantage—in terms of public assistance, crime, incarceration, mental illness, drug addiction, alcoholism, and so forth—far outweighs the cost of a Freedom Budget.

JE: As mayor, you have taken a number of controversial stands, including proposing strict handgun legislation. Why do you support gun control? Is this a serious problem in the District?

MB: Yes. The handgun is the favorite weapon of the street thug, the tool of the assassin. In too many American homes, it is the time bomb just waiting to go off and claim a loved one. Every thirteen seconds another handgun is produced and sold and adds to the domestic arsenal of over 50 million handguns. Pistols and revolvers—concealable weapons—have helped turn our city streets into battlefields and our homes into jails. Handgun-toters have made us afraid to walk our own neighborhoods. They have caused us to wall our homes with bars and locks. And this is America, the home of the free?

Several years ago, President Reagan nearly died because of a handgun attack. Many commentators shrugged their shoulders. Nothing would change, they lamented, in the handgun control battle. The handgun forces would continue to prevail. Well, these pundits were wrong. Something has happened and is happening throughout America. From

Morton Grove to Maryland, from Chicago to California, from Washington, D.C., to Ohio, people are rising up to demand legislative action to combat the handgun cancer. They are proclaiming enough is enough! Enough of the National Rifle Association's (NRA) grip on our legislators! Enough of this handgun fear which is shaping the way we go about our daily lives! Enough of the handgun body counts! Enough handgun funerals! Enough is enough!

We know from national surveys that 90 percent of the American people favor stricter handgun laws. And this handgun control majority is beginning to stir in America. Its political power is awakening. And politicians had better wake up to this fact, or soon they will be without jobs.

In the District, we long ago decided that we needed a stricter handgun law. The city council adopted a law prohibiting the sale of handguns by a wide margin. As you might imagine, the NRA was outraged. They had lost at their place of residence. They tried to persuade their friends in Congress to kill our handgun measure. But we were too strong. The NRA lost. Then they turned to the courts in an effort to have our law overturned on constitutional grounds. But again, they lost.

When President Reagan was shot, they seized upon the incident, claiming that it proved that our handgun law was a failure. But they failed to point out that the assassin did not purchase his handgun in Washington. In fact, he bought it at a pawn shop in Texas, a state with one of the weakest laws in the country.

We need stricter local handgun laws. We need stricter state handgun laws. But above all, we need a strict national handgun control law. Can you imagine how many Americans would be alive today had Congress passed a stricter handgun law years ago? Can you imagine how many Americans today would not be paralyzed because of handgun wounds? Can you imagine what kind of society we would now have? We cannot change the past. But we can shape the future. We must rededicate ourselves to the cause of handgun control. We must not give up until we have strict handgun control laws across America. We must and will prevail.

JE: As mayor, you have spoken out vigorously on behalf of tough alcohol and drug abuse legislation. Why?

MB: Drug abuse is among the most destructive and most pervasive negative forces in our communities, and alcohol abuse has similar serious effects. Drug abuse not only destroys young lives, as recent data demonstrate but also affects older, former users who have been able to kick the habit. Today, many people are abusing *both* drugs and alcohol.

Drug abuse destroys the promise and talent and service to society which such persons could have contributed. And it destroys their families, too. Further, drug and alcohol abuse, along with drug traffic, has a deleterious impact on entire communities—an impact of fear, violence, and crime—which reduces the quality of life for all our citizens. The young, the old, the handicapped—those who are least able to defend themselves—are the principal victims. As responsible citizens, we cannot ignore these destructive forces.

The increase in drug abuse—which is largely an increase in heroin abuse—is a national problem caused by the importation of increasing quantities of heroin, typically from the Southwest Asian countries. The supply is plentiful. The product is pure. And the cost in terms of human life is very, very high. What is happening in the District closely mirrors what is happening elsewhere.

The fact is that heroin is flooding into the United States and into our cities with a deadly effect on our people. Unfortunately, federal enforcement efforts to curtail the illegal importation of heroin have not been strong enough and fail to provide adequate protection for our people and for local jurisdictions from this deadly menace.

The net result of these facts is that state and local governments must vastly increase their efforts to fight the local effects of this epidemic—for enforcement, for treatment, and for all of the hidden and related costs to society. The cost in terms of human lives cannot be measured. It is ironic that this is occurring at a time when inflation and shrinking tax bases of local jurisdictions—especially in the older northeastern cities—have created severe difficulties in maintaining even current levels of basic services, to say nothing of providing the kind of resources we need to combat this problem.

Despite these difficulties, the District is forging a strong cooperative effort. This cooperative community network is critical if our cities are to be mutually supportive. We also need added support from the federal government. Present enforcement efforts must be strengthened and expanded so that the flow of heroin can be cut off, and health and treatment programs must be ready to assist in this effort. We cannot get heroin off our streets if it is flowing down our highways and waterways and dropping from the skies. We must have a strong and effective cooperative law enforcement network at all levels if we are to reduce the supply. In fact, effective law enforcement at the national level could prevent the flow of heroin into our country and into our cities. Law enforcement efforts at the national level could solve the problem. By the same token, we must have increased national funding for treatment and prevention, because heroin addiction has fast become a national, as well as a local, problem.

JE: During your tenure as mayor, you've worked hard to eliminate discrimination against women. Have you made significant progress in this area?

MB: Yes. The District has a strong record in recent years in the area of women's rights. We have one of the broadest and most progressive human rights laws in the nation, and we have strong enforcement policies. Recently, we initiated an investigation into the patterns of systemic discrimination which affects groups or categories of residents, in addition to responding to individual complaints filed under our law.

As mayor, I have placed a strong focus on the appointment and promotion of women to the highest positions within District government, as well as to leadership positions throughout the District. This continues to be a major focus of my administration, along with strengthening our entire human rights system. Under our new independent personnel system, for example, most District employees who previously have not been represented by unions will be in the future. The unions will be able to bargain for wages, as well as other employment benefits, so that the District government will have a highly unionized work force under our home rule system.

It is time for the unions, which helped to lead the fight for human rights and worker rights, to take a united stand for the inclusion of women and minorities under their banner. We must encourage the union movement to stand squarely behind equal rights for women and minority members, including the right of entry and apprenticeship into unions.

JE: Unlike most politicians, you have strongly endorsed gay and lesbian rights. Why?

MB: I believe that gays and lesbians are entitled to full and equal protection of the law. Until they are free, none of us will be free. My experience with gays in politics derives from fifteen years of involvement in the political life of the District. In this regard, the District is the most hospitable city in the United States for gay people. Gay rights are better protected in Washington than in any other city in the country, and gays are more fully integrated into the political life of the District than anywhere else.

None of this occurred by accident. It is a combination of a humane and tolerant electorate—most of whom have known discrimination themselves—and of a politically sophisticated and well-organized gay community, and, I would add with all modesty, of scores of elected officials who have recognized that gays are an integral part of the political, social, cultural, and economic fabric of the city and must be able to fully participate in all aspects of District life.

We have in Washington, I am proud to say, the strongest human rights laws in the country. Discrimination on the basis of sexual orientation is prohibited in housing, employment, and public accommodations, and these restrictions are vigorously enforced. And we have made this protection a part of our city charter to protect it against shifts in the political winds. Today, virtually every elected officeholder in this city is supportive of gay rights, and that includes every member of the city council. It is politically unacceptable to be opposed to civil rights for gay people in the District.

JE: Finally, if you were asked to summarize your vision for America, how would you do so?

MB: Today, we share an opportunity to lead ourselves into a future shaped by our own struggles and our own dreams. If we have the courage to follow our vision, we can discover a new vitality of spirit and commitment to change. If we find opportunities where others have found obstacles, we can build our lives upon a new foundation. If we value cooperation over conflict, neighborhood stability over chaos and disruption, compassion over complacency, economic justice over blind greed, and human decency over the destruction of humanity, we can accomplish what others have only promised and forgotten.

Let it be said of our generation that we met the new challenge, that we forged ahead the cause of social justice for all, that we turned decaying cities into citadels of new life and new freedom in this democracy. To achieve this goal in the District, we must protect, defend, and expand home rule. We must be vigilant that this community does not fracture itself in the years ahead, so as to jeopardize the civil rights gains we have won. Our legal institutions, though a long way from being perfect, nevertheless remain the goals of civilized nations. We must remain vigilant. We must not take freedom for granted. And we must never forget that no one is free until we are all free. That is what I want for my city— and for America.

Johnny L. Ford

The Politics of Pragmatism

Johnny L. Ford was born August 23, 1942, in Tuskegee, Alabama. Ford left Tuskegee in 1960 to attend Knoxville College in Knoxville, Tennessee, where he received a Bachelor of Arts degree in 1964. In 1965, he studied public administration at the National Executive Institute in Mendlam, New Jersey. From 1967 to 1968, Ford majored in journalism at the New York School of Announcing and Speech in New York City. In 1977, he received a Master of Arts degree in public administration from Auburn University, in Montgomery, Alabama.

Ford first became active in politics in 1968 when he served as political campaign strategist for the late Senator Robert F. Kennedy. Following Senator Kennedy's assassination, he returned to Tuskegee to become executive coordinator of the Tuskegee Model Cities Program from 1969 to 1970. He then served as vice-president of the Multi-racial Cooperation Model Cities Consulting Firm in New Orleans, Louisiana, from 1970 to 1971. In 1971, Ford was appointed state supervisor for the Community Relations Service, United States Department of Justice, in Montgomery, Alabama. In 1972, Ford was elected the first black mayor in the history of Tuskegee, Alabama. He was re-elected in 1976, 1980, and 1984.

Ford boasts a long and distinguished record of public service. He organized the Alabama Coordinating Council of Minority Economic Development and is secretary of the Executive Committee of the South Central Economic Development District. Ford is a board member of the Alabama League of Municipalities; vice-chairman of the Municipal Electric Association (Alabama); and a member of the Governor's Manpower Ancillary Committee, Environmental Committee, Tourism Council, Advisory Committee, and State Law Enforcement Supervisory Committee—Juvenile Justice Committee.

Since 1979, Ford has served as chairman of the Alabama Southern

Christian Leadership Conference (SCLC), as well as a member of the National Board of Directors of SCLC. He is co-chairman of the National Committee for a Two-Party System. In 1972, he organized and founded the Alabama Conference of Black Mayors, which later became the National Conference of Black Mayors. He has served as chairman of the Alabama Conference of Black Mayors and as vice-president of the National Conference of Black Mayors (NCBM). In 1982, NCBM unanimously elected him president for 1982-1984, and in 1984, he was elected president of the World Conference of Mayors.

Ford has received numerous awards and citations. He has been profiled in *Personalities of the South, Outstanding Young Men of America, Who's Who in America,* and *The Dictionary of International Biography.* He is the recipient of the Freedom-Humanitarian Award, National Law and Social Justice Leadership Award, and SCLC Presidential Award. He has been made an "Honorary Citizen" of Banjul, The Gambia, West Africa, the ancestral home of Alex Haley and sister city to Tuskegee, Alabama, and he has been awarded the keys to over fifty American and foreign cities.

JE: Throughout your life, the church has played a major role. How has it shaped your life and philosophy?

JF: Before I speak or take any action, before I get up in the morning or lie down at night, I first acknowledge Jesus Christ, the Lord and Savior of our universe. I have been taught this all my life. My mama and papa taught it to me as a young boy, and I'm not going to forget it or deny it.

When I first started attending church, my papa taught me that Jesus is our Master and that I should put Him first, and that philosophy has stuck with me throughout my life. As a young boy, I grew up in the church, believing in the power of God. When I was very young, I became desperately ill and lay near death. I almost drowned after catching a cramp, fought to stay above the water's surface, went down two or three times, and swallowed a great deal of water. I finally gave up and said, "Lord, if this is the end, then let it be." It's a terrible feeling to be near death.

I can also recall, when I was fourteen, being desperately ill in a hospital bed in Columbus, Georgia. It was then, I suppose, when I really rededicated myself to Jesus and promised my God that if He would let me live, I would live for Him and rededicate my life to service in His name. That was a long time ago. And every day since, I have been working for my Jesus. It may sometimes appear that I'm working for

Tuskegee, or my people, or my fellow man, but deep down I'm working for my Jesus. As a young man, there were many times when I did not know which way to turn or what to do, which road to take or what decision to make. I was at an impasse. It was beyond my human capacity to know what tomorrow would bring. On such occasions, I would go into my room, fall upon my knees, and ask my Master for guidance to show me the way.

JE: Your first foray into electoral politics occurred in 1968, when you served as a campaign strategist for Senator Robert F. Kennedy. Did your experience in his presidential campaign strengthen your call to service?

JF: Yes. It was a tremendous experience, one which enabled me to travel the length and breadth of this country. I met thousands of people and witnessed firsthand the problems which faced our nation. I can vividly recall the primaries in Indiana, Nebraska, Oregon, and finally California. I revered Senator Kennedy, whom I saw as a prophet of a new and better world. I will always remember that rainy April night in Minneapolis, Minnesota, following the assassination of Martin Luther King, Jr., when Senator Kennedy addressed a large crowd of Blacks. Speaking out of aching memory, he said: "Martin Luther King dedicated his life to love and to justice for his fellow human beings, and he died because of that effort. . . . For those of you who are black and are tempted to be filled with hatred and disgust at the injustice of such an act, against all white people, I can only say that I feel in my own heart the same kind of feeling. I had a member of my family killed, but he was killed by a white man. But we have to make an effort in the United States, we have to make an effort to understand, to go beyond these rather difficult times. . . . What we need in the United States is not division; what we need in the United States is not hatred; what we need in the United States is not violence or lawlessness, but love and wisdom and compassion toward one another and a feeling of justice toward those who still suffer within our country, whether they be white or they be black. . . . Let us dedicate ourselves to that, and say a prayer for our country and for our people." His words proved to be prophetic. That night in Los Angeles, California, while standing in the Embassy Room of the Ambassador Hotel, after a triumphant victory earlier that evening in the California primary, I was convinced, more than ever, that America was ready for a change. I believed that the best way to change our policy was to change the men and women who made it. For the first time, I felt this new world was within our grasp.

Later that night, owing to the illness of his wife, Ethel, Senator

Kennedy decided to change his route and go back through the hotel kitchen. The rest is history. As he lay there, in a pool of his own blood, he inquired about the welfare of those around him—even then, at that terrible moment, he was more concerned about his fellow man than about his own life, which was slowly drifting away.

On the airplane flight back, I remained fixed on that moment and wondered where our country was headed. When we arrived in New York, we made preparations for the funeral and for the train ride from New York to Washington, D.C., where he would be buried. I can still recall the Mass at St. Patrick's Cathedral in New York City, listening to his brother Edward tearfully deliver the eulogy: "My brother need not be idolized today beyond what he was in life, but be remembered as a good and decent man who saw wrong and tried to right it, who saw war and tried to stop it, who saw suffering and tried to heal it. Those of us who take him to his final rest today pray that what he was to us will some day come to pass for all the world. As he said many times, in many places across this country, to those who sought to touch him and to those whom he sought to touch: 'Some men see things as they are and ask why. I dream things that never were and ask why not.'"

At the time, I didn't know what to do. Senator Kennedy had given me a sense of direction. But he was gone now. I decided it was time to go home—to go back to my roots. My thoughts went back to 1963 when Dr. King said, in his now-famous speech before 250,000 Americans in Washington, D.C.: "This is our hope. This is the faith with which I return to the South. With this faith we will be able to transform the jangling discords of our nation into a beautiful symphony of brotherhood. With this faith we will be able to work together, to pray together, to struggle together, to go to jail together, to stand up for freedom together, knowing that we will be free one day."

This is the faith with which I went back to my hometown of Tuskegee in 1969, convinced that if I wanted to do my God's will, then I ought to do it at home and among my own people. Since that time, we've worked hard in Tuskegee to try to improve living conditions for our people. We've tried to take our people out of the shacks and shanties and put them into decent, clean, sanitary housing—housing where they can live in dignity and health. We've tried to put our people into jobs and take them off the welfare rolls. I don't want my people to be on welfare. I want them to have jobs, because there is pride in work. A person who is able to earn his own money can stand up on his own two feet and meet his responsibilities. He can hold up his head with pride and know that his children will not want for food or clothes. That's what we're trying to do in our city. We're trying to heal the sick and make decent health care a reality for all our people. We in Tuskegee will never forget that nearly forty years ago the federal government perpetrated a vicious study to determine the effects of syphilis on the human body. They selected 400 black men as subjects, and even after they discovered that penicillin would cure syphilis, they refused to administer it. As for the men, all they received was a $25 bond and a decent burial. As long as I am mayor, no one will come into our city—be it the federal government, state government, or anyone else—and take advantage of our people again.

We're also working very hard to make our city a safe place in which to live. The Lord said, "Thou Shalt Not Kill," and "Thou Shalt Not Steal." These are the laws of the Bible, as well as the laws of our community. In Tuskegee, everyone must obey the law: black and white, rich and poor, young and old. Everybody. No one is above the law. Once in a while, you'll see a brother wearing a big hat, fancy clothes, and talking nonsense. Well, if he's selling drugs to our young people, he's not our brother. He's our enemy in Tuskegee. I don't care how black or white you are. If you break the law in our city, you're going to jail.

We're also creating an environment in which all our children— black and white—can play together in our parks and playgrounds throughout the city. I can recall that when I was a child, we had to peep through the fence to see the white children play. That's not the case today. All of our youngsters play together. And it's a beautiful thing to see. They don't have any of the hatreds or prejudices of their elders. I can only hope that we will learn from them.

We've also developed programs for our elderly—our senior citizens. We have a bad habit, in this country, of casting aside our old folks when they're no longer useful. I won't ever forget my mama or my papa and how they scuffled to help me get where I am today. My mama worked in white folks' kitchens while my papa worked two or three jobs just to make sure I had clean clothes to wear and food to eat. I love my parents for that. All of us have a responsibility to take care of our older people. In our city, we're trying to do just that.

So, as I go forth to do God's will, I go content, singing the same song my mama used to sing. As a young boy, I'd often come into the kitchen and ask her, "Mama, why are you singing that song?" And she'd turn to me and say, "Son, I sing this song because I'm happy. I sing this song because I'm free. I sing this song because there's a little wheel turning. I sing this song because my heart is yearning. I sing this song because there's a little fire burning. Amazing Grace. How sweet the sound, that saved a wretch like me! I once was lost but now am found, was blind, but now I see. My country 'tis of thee, sweet land of liberty, of thee I sing. Land where my fathers died, land of the pilgrim's pride, from every mountainside, let freedom ring."

JE: In recent years, much has been said and written about the "New South." To what extent, if any, is race still an issue in the South?

JF: In the South, bigotry has become increasingly less acceptable. Blacks are now voting for white candidates and whites are voting for black candidates. This demonstrates, I think, that people in the South are now beginning to vote for candidates on the basis of their platforms rather than the color of their skin. This certainly is a good sign.

In the South, Blacks and whites—for a longer period of time than in the North—have shared a close physical and social proximity. As a result, once Blacks realize that they're equal to whites and whites realize that they're no better than Blacks, I think we'll be better able to accept one another from a racial, social, and political point of view.

As I see it, the South is characterized by what I would call "bi-racial politics." I often tell politicians from other parts of the country that, in the South, some of us are black and some of us are white, but in the final analysis, we're all southerners.

I believe that the South will rise again—but this time, as part of the American mainstream. Blacks and whites will stand on an equal basis, armed with the realization that they must work together in peace and harmony. In 1895, Booker T. Washington, in his now-famous Atlanta Exposition Address, told his black brothers and sisters in the South: "To those of my race who depend on bettering their condition in a foreign land or who underestimate the importance of cultivating friendly relations with the southern white man, who is their next-door neighbor, I would say: 'Cast down your bucket where you are'—cast it down in making friends in every manly way of the people of all races by whom we are surrounded." In the same breath, he said to those of the white race: "I would repeat what I said to my own race: 'Cast down your bucket where you are.' Cast down your bucket among my people, helping and encouraging them as you are doing on these grounds, and to education of head, hand, and heart . . . . I pledge that in your effort to work out the great and intricate problem which God has laid at the doors of the South, you shall have at all times the patient, sympathetic help of my race." That dream is fast becoming a reality in the South.

JE: What factors have contributed to the rise of bi-racial politics?

JF: There are several key factors. Blacks recognize that political power is one of the most effective ways to bring about systemic change. We have proven extremely successful in winning local office throughout this country and, as such, are fast becoming part of the political mainstream. In order to best serve their communities, black politicians recognize the importance of joining hands with other political leaders, be they black or white. We realize that politics is the art of compromise, negotiation, and coalition-building. Blacks understand that in order to win an election, they must secure an electoral majority. We've learned that whites *will* vote for black candidates but only for those black candidates who promise to represent all the people, including whites. Whites have always recognized this fact, but Blacks have only recently begun to realize that this principle applies equally to us.

In addition, many people—both black and white—have played bi-racial politics, because of the social changes which have occurred in the South. Both races now go to school together, pray together, play together, and do many other things together. In other words, in the South, bi-racial relations are now a fact of life, both in terms of social interaction and political activity.

Finally, many political candidates are actively soliciting the support of both black and white voters. When I ran for mayor of Tuskegee, I ran against a white incumbent—an elderly gentleman who had been mayor for eight years. I waged an aggressive campaign, promising to stimulate economic and commercial growth in Tuskegee. We ran a progressive campaign and, as a result, were able not only to win the black vote, but to attract the votes of many whites—especially in the business community. Business-oriented whites are far more concerned with economic progress than they are with the color of a person's skin. In the end, green power (economic power) proved more important than black power.

JE: Did you find it difficult to court the white vote, given your growing-up years in the South?

JF: As a black man, I experienced a strange sensation when walking up a long pathway leading to an old antebellum columned mansion appearing out of a scene from *Gone with the Wind*. I grew up in a very different Tuskegee. I was now asking the same whites for their support—the very people for whom my mother had worked as a domestic. As a youngster, I worked as a yard boy. The only words I ever spoke to those whites were, "Yes, Sah" and "Yes, Mam." But times have changed. I walked up to those same elderly whites, introduced myself as Johnny Ford, a candidate for mayor, and asked for their support. Of course, the response ranged from shock to amazement to resentment to a very cordial and warm acceptance. But the point is, both black and white candidates are now actively courting the votes of both races.

JE: Is Governor George Wallace an apt example of bi-racial politics?

JF: Yes. In the late 1970s, for the first time, Governor Wallace and many other white candidates began meeting regularly with black leaders. This was the same George Wallace who, only ten years earlier, stood in the doorway of the University of Alabama. Today, he's back at the University of Alabama but this time to crown a lovely young black woman as the University Queen. The same George Wallace who bitterly opposed integration for decades now actively attends and participates in meetings of the Southern Conference of Black Mayors, an organization which represents millions of black voters throughout the State of Alabama and the South.

For me, it's easy to play bi-racial politics, because I view politics as a tool to be used to help solve the problems facing my community. As a result, I am willing to work with any political leader, be he black or white, who possesses integrity, dignity, and a willingness to help the people of my city, particularly those who are poor and disadvantaged.

JE: You were roundly criticized, both by Blacks and whites, for supporting Governor Wallace in his re-election bid. Why did you endorse his candidacy?

JF: I've been asked this question many times. I supported Governor Wallace for several reasons: First, I endorsed the governor after I was asked whom I was supporting by a local newscaster. Of the candidates running, I thought that Governor Wallace was the best qualified. In this particular race, there was no black candidate. I have a very simple rule in such cases: I ask myself which candidate is best qualified to serve and who, once elected, will best represent the interests of my people.

Second, after I was elected mayor of Tuskegee, I went to Governor Wallace and asked if he would help us to solve some of the problems facing our community—specifically those of attracting new industry and jobs. Over the past decade, I've worked closely with Governor Wallace and his staff. They've kept their word, and they've been fair. That's all I can ask of any governor, be he black or white.

Third, I endorsed Governor Wallace because I felt that, under his leadership, the State of Alabama would receive a larger share of public and private assistance. And if Alabama received more, then Tuskegee would likely receive more, too.

Fourth, I believed that poor people—black and white—should have someone in a leadership position who can relate to the governor of the state, regardless of who he or she is. That person must serve as a catalyst—be willing and able to pressure the governor to better represent the diverse interests of the state. I thought I could play that role with Governor Wallace.

In the past, many people have asked me how I could support Governor Wallace, given his actions ten years earlier. After all, wasn't he the same person who had preached a policy of segregation now and forever? Well, ten years ago, I was marching and picketing, and the governor was standing in the schoolhouse door. We were both on different sides of the fence. And we're occasionally on different sides of the fence today. But the point is, times have changed. And so has Governor Wallace. If Governor Wallace is willing to put aside his past prejudices, then we, as Blacks, should be willing to put aside our past differences and work together for the common good.

JE: In the past, you've characterized your philosophy as one of "pragmatic politics." Is this why, for example, you endorsed President Richard Nixon over George McGovern in 1972?

JF: Yes. Politics and economics go hand in hand. They go together like love and marriage. When a young man says to his sweetheart, "I love you. Will you marry me?," and she says, "I will," then from that moment on it's economics. He's got to pay for the marriage license, the preacher, the honeymoon . . . . Let's face it, that's the reality of life in this country.

And that's why we, as black people, must realize that political power controls the economic strings in this country. My goal is to serve my people. I'm not talking about playing games. I wasn't elected to play games. I've got a job to do. I didn't create the political system in this country. And like it or not, the system is here to stay. My job is to use that system to benefit my people. That's why I'm pleased to be the co-chairman of the National Committee for a Two-Party System, along with Floyd McKissick, the well-known civil rights activist and founder of Soul City in North Carolina.

The main purpose of the National Committee for a Two-Party System is to bring together black Democrats and black Republicans and, yes, those whites who are concerned about the problems facing black people and poor people in this country. After all, the major problems we face—housing, health care, education, jobs—cut across racial lines. It doesn't make sense to get hung up over party labels. We must concentrate on the business at hand—and that business is being able to deal with whoever is in the White House.

Under the Reagan Administration, the National Committee for a

Two-Party System provides an opportunity for black Democrats to work through black Republicans who might have rapport with the Republican administration. Four years from now, should the Democrats regain the White House, the committee will provide a vehicle for black Republicans to work through black Democrats who might have rapport with a Democratic administration. In other words, we must be able to deal with whoever is in power. Keep in mind, politics is power. We shouldn't vote for political candidates just for the sake of it, or just because they're Democrats or Republicans, or because our mamas or papas voted for them.

My message to my people is very simple: Don't vote for anybody for nothing. Hell, this is a business! Never vote for a political candidate unless he or she makes a firm commitment to help you and your people. In the last election, I supported all winners. As black folks, that's part of our problem. We've supported too many losers. Some time back, a man asked me, "Why didn't you support George McGovern in 1972?" In the first place, I knew McGovern wasn't going to win. How would he help me in Alabama, when he can't even solve the problems of the Indians in South Dakota? Yes, I supported President Nixon, as well as a number of Democratic congressmen. After all, as mayor, I have to work with these people. During the Nixon Administration, Macon County (in which Tuskegee is located) received approximately $60 million a year in federal assistance, thereby giving us the highest federal support per capita of any county in the country. And that's not by accident.

Not long ago, someone asked me an equally silly question, namely, "Why do you cooperate with the Reagan Administration?" It's business with me. I won't support anybody for nothing. In Tuskegee, we're not asking anybody for anything. We're only asking that you be fair. And if you're fair, we're going to get our fair share.

My folks are counting on me to deliver, but I won't compromise my principles in the process. But, you see, all of this, as far as I am concerned, is a game. Politics is a game. You either win, or you lose. And if I'm going to help my people, I must win. I've learned that white people never lose, no matter who is elected president, or which party is in power, because they go both ways.

JE: Like other cities, Tuskegee faces severe economic problems. Is it possible, in your view, to revitalize America's cities? If so, how?

JF: It's easy to throw in the towel, but that's not the answer, for America's greatest resource is still her cities. After all, cities are made up of people. And people are our greatest resource. Yes, we can revitalize America's cities through sound planning and sensible business practices.

How do Blacks fit into this scenario? Very simply, if Blacks become a part of the economic mainstream of America, then we will also become a part of the political mainstream of this country. For where there is economic power, there is also political power. You can't separate the two.

But what of the cities? What is the problem? I have often stated, when testifying before Congress, that I believe the best way for America to solve her urban problems is by solving her rural problems. As I see it, the South is the new frontier in this country. But like other cities, southern cities face many of the same problems as their northern counterparts.

America's cities face enormous problems. The first is immigration. Immigration has placed a severe strain on housing, schools, recreation, services, and jobs. In turn, these problems have bred additional problems: crime, unemployment, poverty, frustration, and despair.

Second, immigration has encouraged the emigration of business and industry. Many businesses and industries have moved to the suburbs, where there is less congestion, less crime, less regulation, lower taxes, and more people with money and skills. America is becoming one giant suburb. And the cities are paying the price.

The third problem is a declining tax base. When business and industry relocate, they take their tax dollars with them. Cities must have sufficient revenue to operate. As business and industry have relocated, the cities have been left with fewer and fewer tax dollars. This has necessitated a cutback in services. Cities can only provide those services which they can pay for. With a declining tax base, we simply cannot continue to provide the same level of services that people have come to expect.

The fourth problem is that many urban areas and infrastructures are fast decaying. They are simply inadequate to serve the influx of new people. This has affected such city services as streets, lights, water, sewers, pollution, airports, sanitation, and housing. The old infrastructure is at the point of collapse; it must be either repaired or rebuilt. Unfortunately, this costs money—which is something most cities don't have.

Given these facts, can we revitalize our cities? Hopefully so, for it will assure Blacks a political-economic base. Clearly, the strength of black America is in our cities. As I see it, revitalization depends on the will of the people. Our communities must look inward; they must ask themselves whether they are prepared to pay the price of revitalization.

If the answer is yes, then the next step is to wage an aggressive campaign to attract those who left the cities for greener pastures: investors, taxpayers, skilled workers, and consumers. People represent money. We can't operate our cities unless they return. In addition, we must develop industry and commerce. And Blacks must have an economic stake in the existing businesses. We must encourage new businesses and industries to relocate in our cities. And Blacks must own and manage some of them. Their decision to return to our cities will mean greater tax dollars and increased job opportunities.

We must also revitalize the infrastructure. Greater attention must be paid to such city services as water, sewage, streets, parks, and airports. These services are crucial to the survival of any city and are essential if new businesses and industries are to relocate. To pay for these services, cities must press for greater assistance—federal, state, and local.

JE: In the past, you've proposed a Black Economic Common Market as a means of strengthening the economic base of black America. What are its principal components?

JF: I would liken a Black Economic Common Market to the anatomy of the human body. The common market represents the body. Financial capital is the blood that runs through our veins. Black education represents the head. Black workers symbolize the hands. The foundation of the common market can be likened to the feet: the left foot stands for black votes; the right foot represents black businesses. The black church stands for the soul and conscience of the common market. Black organizations—social, cultural, civic, fraternal, and athletic—represent the outer garments which adorn the body. The agitator, the motivator, the generator, symbolizes the heart—a role which Jesse Jackson has performed so well.

JE: Over the years, you've been extremely critical of the two-party system. Do you favor the development of a new third party?

JF: As I've stated, I serve as the co-chairman of the National Committee for a Two-Party System. In my view, both major parties have failed to keep their promises to black America. Instead, both parties must aggressively support voter registration, minority rights, women's issues, and economic justice. As Blacks, we must not blindly follow any *one* political party—we must become more selective and support only that party which best represents our interests.

America is moving toward a three-party system: Democrat, Republican, and Independent. I think that's a healthy development. When the two major parties fail to keep their promises, we should pursue a third party or independent route. More and more, special interest groups and wealthy fat cats are exerting their influence to prevent the nomination of qualified black and female candidates. The two major parties have a clear choice: They can listen to the rich and powerful, or they can listen to the tens of millions of minorities and poor people upon whom they depend for support. If they choose the former, we should then seriously consider the third option, remembering that in a three-way race, it only takes 34 percent to win—not 51 percent.

In the future, I expect to see more and more blacks run as non-partisans for office. After all, how do you think we elected 260 black mayors? If Blacks had run strictly as Democrats or Republicans—as a party's official nominee—then we never would have succeeded. True, most of us are either Democrats or Republicans, but we ran as independents in nonpartisan contests. After all, people, not parties, decide elections. And so we must run on whatever ticket promises us the greatest chance of victory. Winning elective office or exercising the vote is very much like going to the grocery store. If you wish to purchase some groceries, show the clerk the right ID, and he will honor cash, checks, or food stamps. Similarly, if you present the right ID to the voters, they will accept a Democrat, Republican, or Independent. Party labels are irrelevant—that is, if you are the right candidate at the right time.

JE: From your perspective, how can Blacks best effect political change?

JF: With the landslide re-election victory of President Reagan, Blacks face difficult times ahead—but not so difficult that we need throw up our hands and give up. The administration has adopted a very simple approach—that is, to return many existing programs and policy decisions to state and local governments. That's the game to be played. And we, as Blacks, must learn to play that game—and play it well. That's why I tell my people all across the country: Our number-one priority should be the election of Blacks and sensitive whites to key positions in city, county, and state government. After all, that's where the decisions will be made in the future. That's where elected officials will decide how our money should be spent. Unless we become good at that game, Blacks will be left out in the cold. The fact is, we presently lack adequate or equal representation in the decision-making process at the local level.

What about political protest? Hell, marching, picketing, and demonstrating are fine. They're a good form of exercise. And they were certainly effective in the 1960s. But, let's face it, we're in a whole new ball game now. In order to change the system, we must become part of the system. And we must change it from within. Blacks must penetrate the system. We must make sure that we're present at every level of government and that our interests are represented. Power is the name of the game. And we've got to use our power wisely. After all, political decisions will be made with or without us. It's in our interest to use the system effectively.

JE: As you survey America today, are you optimistic about the future?

JF: Yes. I envision a new America—one which represents the interests of all Americans: black and white, rich and poor, young and old, male and female. To a large extent, the future will be determined by the South. And, as I've said, I foresee a new South—one which eschews the politics of division and embraces the politics of brotherhood.

As black Americans, we must stand up and demand a piece of the action. We must demonstrate that we can take our rightful place along-side other groups in this country. Face it, no one in this country is better than anyone else. Black folk aren't any better than white folk; and white folk aren't any better than black folk. We're all God's children. Equal. There it is! I know that some people—both black and white—won't like what I've said. But that's too bad. This is America—1985! It's later than you think. And, in the words of the late, great Sam Cooke, "A change is going to come."

So, as Blacks, we'd better get smart. We've got to stop giving away our vote! This is a serious business. We not only have a responsibility to ourselves but to our people, too. Consider my case, for example. As long as I was Johnny Ford, it didn't make any difference who I supported. But the minute I became the mayor of Tuskegee, I accepted a respon-sibility to deliver services to my people. When the sanitation workers get off on Friday night, after a long week's work, they want their checks. I can't scratch my head and say, "Ah, ah . . . ." My people elected me to do a job—not because I'm black and proud but because I promised to produce.

As a people, we must rethink our approach to politics. In many cases, we've been our own worst enemies. We either failed to vote, or we voted for politicians who didn't give a damn about us. That must change. My advice to Blacks is simple: Find a brother whom the com-munity can support. Then go out and work like hell to elect him. If a brother can't win, choose the best white candidate in the race. Support him, as you would a Black, but make sure you get a commitment from him. Don't ever give your vote away. Politics is deadly serious. We must act as if our future depends on it.

As a black leader, I have a job to do. My job is to help feed my people and help them to become self-supporting. Today, people want action, not rhetoric. The old platitudes won't cut it. People want re-sults. Talk won't put food on the table, but power will—if we use it intelligently.

I'm sure that some black people disagree with me—with my pragmatic approach. That's all right. I can't please everyone. I don't have to.
I've got a job to do, and I know that by being a Deep South politician,
there may be some difficult and dangerous days ahead. But I'm not
worried about that now. Because, you see, I've been to the mountain
top, and no one is going to stop me from serving my God through
serving my people. And even if I must lay down my life, while standing
up for my principles, then let it be. No price is too great for the people
of my city. Like Robert Kennedy, I believe in the words of Tennyson,
who wrote in *Ulysses*:

> The lights begin to twinkle from the rocks:
> The long day wanes: the slow moon climbs: the deep
> Moans round with many voices. Come, my friends,
> 'Tis not too late to seek a newer world.

Wilson Riles

The Good Fight

Wilson Riles was born on June 27, 1917, in rural Louisiana, near Alexandria. Orphaned at an early age, he worked his way through junior and senior high school by laboring in sawmills and delivering milk from 2:00 to 7:00 o'clock every morning. Following high school, he moved with his foster parents to Arizona. Riles received a Bachelor of Arts degree from Northern Arizona University in 1940 and, after three years in the Army Air Corps, completed a Master of Arts degree in school administration at Northern Arizona University in 1947.

Riles began his educational career as a teacher in a one-room school on Apache Indian Reservation near Pistol Creek, Arizona. After working in other Arizona public schools as a teacher and principal, he moved to California in 1954 to take a position as Pacific Coast Secretary of the Fellowship of Reconciliation. He joined the California Department of Education in 1958. In 1965, he became director of compensatory education, administering a $100 million program for disadvantaged children that became a model for similar programs throughout the nation. Riles was appointed deputy superintendent for programs and legislation in 1969.

Riles was elected superintendent of public instruction for the State of California in 1970 and was re-elected twice—serving as superintendent for twelve years, from 1971 to 1982. He provided leadership in California's public school system during twelve years of unprecedented challenges to the nation's resources and programs. As superintendent, he faced such awesome challenges as declining enrollment, the *Serrano* v. *Priest* (1971) decision, imposed revenue limits, and mandatory basic competency legislation. During the same period, he provided leadership in the development of early childhood education programs, special education programs, gifted and talented education programs, programs for limited and non-English-speaking youngsters, and general programs designed to improve education for all students. As superintendent, he served as an ex-officio regent of the University of California and a trustee of the California State Universities and Colleges.

Riles earned national recognition during his service as state superintendent. He was elected president of the Council of Chief State School Officers, was an advisor to four American presidents on educational issues, and served on numerous national boards and commissions concerned with school-related matters.

Honored by a variety of groups and organizations, Riles has received nine honorary doctoral degrees and a variety of citations and medals. He has been recognized by the University of California, the National Association for the Advancement of Colored People, and Columbia University, among others. In 1978, he received the Robert Maynard Hutchins Award.

As state superintendent, Riles became a vital link between education and the world of business and industry. He is a member of the Industry Education Council of California, the Foundation for Teaching Economics, the Joint Council on Economic Education, the Advisory Board for the Stanford University School of Business, and is a director of the Wells Fargo Bank and Pacific Gas and Electric Company.

Today, Riles is president of Wilson Riles and Associates, Inc., an educational consulting firm with headquarters in Sacramento, California. Although no longer state superintendent, he remains interested and involved in public education. Riles serves in an advisory capacity to several school districts; does consultative work for an executive search firm, a book publisher, and a computer company; and speaks regularly at schools and colleges on issues of current interest.

JE: At what point in life did you first give thought to becoming a teacher? What appeal did teaching hold?

WR: As a young man, I had little interest in teaching. My goal was to become an artist. As a student in elementary school and high school, I had a special fondness for art. I can recall quite vividly having illustrated a number of school publications.

Upon entering Northern Arizona University, I discovered that the art department was quite limited. The faculty consisted of only two or three professors. I learned quite early that I was not cut out to be an artist. I could draw fairly well, but art was not what I wanted. Since Northern Arizona was primarily a teachers' college—at least, that was the largest academic program—I gravitated toward teaching. I majored in elementary education with a minor in history.

I never set out to become a teacher. I made that decision after enrolling in college. There was a time when I flirted with the idea of becoming a lawyer. And, believe it or not, at that time, there was not a single law school in Arizona. You became a lawyer by what they called "reading law," which you did under the tutelage of a lawyer. Looking back, I have no regrets. I think I made the correct choice, at least for me. Education has proven to be a wonderful career. It has made possible a host of exciting possibilities. I could not have asked for a more satisfying career.

JE: What was your first teaching job? How did it come about?

WR: Teaching jobs in Arizona were scarce in those days. Some schools were segregated while others were not. The elementary schools were required to be segregated, whereas the high schools had the option to segregate or not. Flagstaff, for example, had a segregated elementary school, which in reality affected Mexican-Americans more than Blacks. The high school, however, was integrated; everyone went to the same high school. At the time, there were so few Blacks in Arizona that it was not economically feasible, in every case, to maintain segregated schools.

My first teaching job was near McNary, a sawmill town in Apache County. It had a segregated elementary school. There was also a logging camp, some thirty miles in the mountains, which had a one-room schoolhouse. I heard from a friend that the schoolhouse had an opening, and I applied. I asked one of my professors, Mildred Kiefer, if I could borrow her car so that I could drive to the school for an interview. She offered to drive me to the school, which was about 175 miles away. And she not only drove me to the interview, but she recommended me for the position. So my first job was at a one-room schoolhouse on an Apache Indian Reservation with nine kids ranging from grades one through seven.

JE: Did your academic training prepare you well for this position? Was teaching as easy or as difficult as you had imagined?

WR: It was a difficult job, but no more difficult than I had imagined. As a student, I had been exposed to a variety of teaching styles. And, as a teacher, I taught as I had been taught. While I benefitted from my classroom experiences, I learned more by observing those teachers I most admired. They were the ones who were most interested in my growth and welfare. Likewise, I attempted to transmit their love and concern once I became a teacher.

JE: Were you a good teacher? Did you possess the necessary skills and temperament?

WR: I suspect that only my students could answer that question.

I worked very hard, because I knew those kids needed a good start. I gave them everything I had. I wanted them to understand the problems they would face, both as young people and as adults. And I tried to understand their true feelings. In the end, I suppose, a teacher remembers the successes and forgets the failures. But a good percentage of those kids went on to finish college. Many carved out productive careers. And that makes me feel good. It makes me feel that my time and effort were well spent.

JE: What kinds of individuals make the best teachers? What are the "right" reasons for becoming a teacher?

WR: In the first place, no one goes into teaching to become rich. If you're going into teaching for that reason, you've picked the wrong profession. Moreover, you have to possess a missionary-type attitude if you're going to succeed. The primary rewards of teaching are intrinsic—that is, you must have the inner knowledge that you have contributed to your students' growth and development.

Now the problem is, as I have watched the schools evolve and change, that they have become more impersonal and less concerned with the individual welfare of students. Part of the problem, I suspect, is attributable to public attitudes towards the schools. At one time, although the pay was low—ridiculously low—teachers were held in high regard. The teacher was viewed as a community leader. He was the object of respect. And his efforts were appreciated.

That's no longer true. In all too many cases, the teacher is the object of blame and derision. He is unappreciated and underpaid. And he no longer enjoys the admiration of the community. Sadly, there are few psychological payoffs associated with teaching. The positive reinforcement which I received is non-existent. And the press doesn't help. The media plays up every problem. So, consequently, it's no surprise that fewer and fewer people are choosing to become teachers. One has to ask the question: Why should a bright, sensitive, caring person want to take such a beating?

JE: Can you discuss your career in public education? How did you become state superintendent?

WR: As I've said, I started out as a teacher near McNary where I landed a job teaching the children of black loggers. The following year, I was made a teaching principal at the school in town. During the summer, I went to work at an ordnance depot in Flagstaff for the unheard-of sum of $40 a week. And I enjoyed the work. When school opened in the fall, I went back to McNary, spent another year there, and decided to move to California in the summer of 1943. It was during World War II, and I wanted to support the war effort.

After scouring the job market, I was hired by North American Aviation in Inglewood as a shipping clerk and moved to Santa Monica. Shortly thereafter, I was drafted and left for the Army Air Corps on the day my eldest son Michael was born. While I was in the service, my wife decided to return to Flagstaff where she secured a teaching position. After the war, I joined her in Flagstaff where I was hired as a teacher at Dunbar Elementary School and became involved in the school desegregation battle. We were able to change the law in 1953 just prior to the Supreme Court's historic desegregation decision. I enrolled in a master's program at night and taught during the day. I also became actively involved in several Indian-related programs and worked closely with the American Friends Service Committee, a group composed largely of Quakers. Through them I became acquainted with the Fellowship of Reconciliation, a non-denominational pacifist organization. This association would change my life.

Although I had not seen combat duty, I was at a point in life where I was disheartened by much of the hypocrisy that was connected with religion. I couldn't understand how religious people could mistreat people and take human life and, at the same time, read the Sermon on the Mount. Then I met the Quakers, many of whom were pacifists and whose ancestors during the slavery period were the backbone of the underground railroad. Indeed, these people practiced what they preached. They lived the ideals which they espoused in church. This came as quite a shock. I came to admire them greatly. And I participated in a number of their programs. Not long thereafter, I took a job in Los Angeles as Pacific Coast Secretary of the Fellowship of Reconciliation and worked with the group from 1954 until 1958.

Then one day a friend of mine who had seen a civil service announcement called and told me that there was a position available with the State Department of Education in Sacramento. The job called for a person who possessed school administrative experience, a background in intergroup relations, and a commitment to community service. He said I would be perfect for the job. I remember telling him, "I'm satisfied with what I'm doing. I've never been to Sacramento. And, moreover, what makes you think they would hire a Black for the position?" I asked him how many black professionals they had in the department. He told me he didn't know of any. And I said, "Well, that's your answer." About two weeks later, I saw him again. He again urged me to apply for the position, and I gave him the same answer. But when I got home, I told my wife about the job. She told me I should apply—that I had nothing to lose. I took a civil service test, passed it, and eventually was hired.

At the time, the state legislature had recently passed a law which established, within the Department of Education, an office to assist and advise school districts on the elimination of discrimination in teacher employment. It was a nebulously written piece of legislation, but the department established the office. I was assigned to the chief deputy, George Hogan, who proved extremely helpful. He said, "Look, I don't know anything about discrimination, at least as it relates to Blacks. I was born in Humboldt County, where we had few Blacks. I know the Irish are discriminated against, because I'm Irish. So, I'm going to have to rely on you in this area." However, Hogan did know the administrative side, and he had a wide circle of contacts. He told me to take my time, to become familiar with the people who were doing the hiring. He said that he would introduce them to me. As I became more knowledgeable, he said, I could exert influence. And he was right. My message was simple: "Any time you fail to hire the best qualified person, it is the children who suffer."

I can remember the first person I visited. He had hired a black teacher who happened to come from Flagstaff. It was in Covina, California. I went down there to build a case. I wanted to know why he had hired her, how she had worked out, and that kind of thing. I knew that people feared the unfamiliar. I thought that if I looked at cases which had worked out, then I could point to tangible successes and encourage others to follow suit in their hiring practices. That was the beginning.

From there, I expanded my efforts to include intergroup relations on a broader scale and pushed through legislation to establish a Bureau of Intergroup Relations. Following that, I worked to ensure passage of the Elementary and Secondary Education Act, which was signed by President Lyndon Johnson in September 1965 and which provided federal funds to states to raise the achievement level of children from low-income families.

At that point, the Department of Education appointed me director of compensatory education, which carried with it the title of associate superintendent. I was assigned the responsibility of managing that part of the program which dealt with disadvantaged kids. I started out with nothing but a secretary and a desk. But the moment President Johnson signed the bill, I was responsible for administering a budget of $70 million.

I worked extremely hard in that post—in fact, I don't recall ever working any harder. I derived tremendous satisfaction from developing a comprehensive program to raise the achievement level of disadvantaged kids.

I held that position until 1969, at which point I became deputy superintendent for programs. By this time, Max Rafferty had become state superintendent. I got along well with Max on a personal level, but, God, was he a character. He was an extremely negative influence on education. Many talented people quit the department, disgusted with Max and his policies. I had always felt that I could work with anyone so long as they permitted me to do my job and maintain my integrity. I didn't want to become involved in all of the conflicts that were taking place in the department. I realized that I just couldn't work under Rafferty—we differed on too many important issues. So I began to look around for a new position. I received a number of offers from all over the country. And then I thought, why not run for state superintendent? Why run away from the situation? If I won, I could turn things around. So in 1970 I decided to challenge Rafferty for the job of superintendent of public instruction.

JE: At the time, did you really believe you could defeat Rafferty? If so, why?

WR: I thought it was doubtful. However, it wasn't an impulsive decision. At the time, I had never run for any public office. One year earlier, Dorman Commons, who, at the time, was vice-president of the Occidental Oil Company—and a very caring and sensitive individual—had urged me to run. And I said, "Man, you must be out of your mind."

At any rate, I gave serious thought to challenging Rafferty. In addition, I spoke to a number of people whom I respected and who had experience in the political arena. One was Marion Joseph, a member of the Compensatory Education Commission. And what I said to them was that I wanted them to analyze the situation. I said, "Don't tell me that it will be a cinch or that I will win hands down. I just want to know if it's possible. If so, I'll run. If not, I don't want to waste my time. I'll do something else."

Well, Marion Joseph introduced me to several seasoned politicians, including veteran campaign manager Sandy Weiner. I can recall that meeting quite vividly. Weiner asked me several personal questions. Then, he asked if I had an honorable discharge. And I said yes. Then he asked if I had a clean record. And I told him yes. Then he asked if I really wanted to become state superintendent. And I said yes. Then he said to me, "You can win. It will be tough, but you can do it."

I talked to one other person who had considerable influence. He was Dr. Henry Paul, a black physician who was a member of the Compensatory Education Commission. I asked him to meet me one morning for breakfast. I said to him, "Look, I'm trying to decide whether or not to run. I don't want to run unless I have a chance. I don't want to waste my time if I can't win. But if there's even the remotest chance, I'll run." Then I said, "I want you to be square with me. You live in Los Angeles. You understand the situation." He told me I ought to run. I said, "Why do you think I can win?" I reminded him that Tom Bradley, a Black, had recently been defeated for mayor of Los Angeles by Sam Yorty. Tom was ahead in the polls, ran ahead in the primary, but lost in the general. And I asked him, "If Tom couldn't win, what makes you think I could? Everybody knows Tom was the best person. But he lost. And it was the white hard hats who beat him. What makes you think I could win?"

He said, "Wilson, in my practice, I have a number of clients, many of whom are lower middle-class whites. You're right, they were frightened into voting for Yorty. Yorty ran a racist campaign. He frightened people into believing that if Bradley won, the city would fall apart." And then he said something that really turned me around. "But, Wilson, I've noticed something interesting. Talking to these people, I sense a different attitude. Many of them now realize [this was one year later] that they voted against Tom for the wrong reason." He said, "Let me tell you something else. I was born in Mississippi, in the heart of the Bible Belt. I came to observe the lower middle-class white mentality. They may have been prejudiced or even racist, but they were honest about it. But there was also a counterstrain which ran through their philosophy which said, 'You may not like this guy, but you must be fair and straightforward.'" And then he said, "Wilson, my guess is that many of the same people who voted for Yorty have since come to regret their decision. I think many of them feel that they did the wrong thing. It may just be that they need redemption. You ought to give them the chance to redeem themselves." I don't know if he was right. I'll never know. But I do know I won 54 percent of the vote to become state superintendent.

JE: How would you characterize Rafferty's political philosophy? Why did he provoke such strong emotions, both positive and negative?

WR: Rafferty was an enigma. As I've said, we got along well on a one-to-one basis. Max wanted to be liked. He wanted to relate to you. But whenever he got before a microphone, it was like someone had waved a wand, and he became a demagogue. And that brought him a lot of notoriety. He represented the extreme right. And, I guess, philosophically, Max and I were 180 degrees apart. But I had the feeling that this was a tactic on his part—a way to get attention. And he parlayed that to full advantage. His ultimate dream, of course, was not to become state superintendent, but to become a United States Senator or even higher. And he almost made it.

As you recall, two years earlier he challenged Senator Alan Cranston and lost. He lost, but not by much. I read where several pollsters said that if the election had lasted another two weeks, he could have won. We'll never know. But we do know that his ultimate goal went well beyond that of state superintendent.

Max was an extremist. Educationally speaking, he championed views that even made many conservatives angry. He wasn't satisfied urging a return to basics in the schools; he wanted to go back to the McGuffey readers. That pretty much sums up his educational philosophy.

On a personal level, I felt pity for him. He was a torn man. But what really convinced me to run against him was not Max; it was the people around him. Some of his top advisors were awful. One, in particular, was hated by everybody. You could never depend on his word. He would tell you one thing and then do another. And he had a major influence on Rafferty.

Max was a master manipulator. He understood the media and how to use it to full advantage. He was made to order for the press. He knew that he could make an outrageous statement and that the media would print it. The more ridiculous the statement, the more coverage he received. The board meetings were never dull when Max was there: Press people were everywhere, hounding him for a quote. He refined the process to an art. It got to the point where, for example, he would say to a reporter, "Do you want thirty seconds, a minute, what?"

Max was a disaster for education. He was extremely divisive. He polarized people. He liked to make waves. I don't think Max ever expected to see his ideas implemented. I think he viewed himself as a commentator on the sorry state of things. As state superintendent, he could not point to a single accomplishment that grew out of his right wing agenda for the schools. He was totally ineffective when it came to implementing his ideas. And I think he knew it. As a result, he was content simply to make philosophical pronouncements, knowing that they wouldn't go anywhere.

JE: Did you find it difficult to convince California's white voters that you could solve the state's educational problems?

WR: I believed that as a public official—one who was in a responsible position of leadership—it was incumbent upon me to treat everyone fairly. I think that's a *must* for any public official. You must serve the people—meaning, all of the people. That's why they elected you. It would have been wrong for me to employ the same discriminatory practices for which I blamed others.

As a black person—one who had experienced firsthand the evils of discrimination—it was incumbent upon me to demonstrate that I could rise above such pettiness. My goal was not to fire all the whites and replace them with Blacks. Instead, it was to make the school system work. To make it work, I had to bring together talented people—both black and white—in order to make that a reality.

Now maybe I'm being too idealistic. And I say this with all sincerity. But if we're going to change things in this country, particularly in terms of race, then someone has to step forward and say, "Come hell or high water, I'm going to be fair and just." And who is better able to do that than a person who has come from the oppressed, black minority.

Having said that, how did I do it? First, I developed a broad-based coalition of concerned people. I did not—I repeat—I did not aim my campaign at any one group. I made sure that every campaign committee reflected the diverse interests of the population. My platform was one that stressed educational excellence. And when you talk about education, you're talking about a subject that everyone can relate to, be they white or black or whatever.

Second, my record, insofar as raising the achievement level of the disadvantaged, was clear. But what most people don't understand, I'm afraid, is that achievement is related to socioeconomic status. Many people thought that compensatory education was a black program. As a matter of fact, when the state distributed the funds in California, most of the money went to white children.

Third, our platform reflected the diverse needs of students. For example, we called for programs that would meet the special needs of such students as the gifted and the physically impaired. We wanted to upgrade education at every level. And we wanted every child to feel that the state superintendent cared about the schools and the quality of education. I wasn't interested in black kids or white kids. I was interested in *kids*. My goal was to represent the kids.

JE: To what extent did Rafferty attempt to infuse race into the campaign?

WR: He did not attempt to do it overtly, because, after all, I had been at the education department before he was elected superintendent and had moved up the ladder afterward with his support. So it would have been difficult for him to argue that I was unqualified or that I lacked experience.

He did, however, on occasion, resort to smear tactics. Let me give you an example. And this was one of the things that turned the campaign in my direction. During the race, a mailing was sent out which painted me as a communist or one who had communist connections. It was a real scandal sheet. Harry Farrell, the political editor of the *San Jose Mercury*, obtained a copy of the mailing and called me. He wanted to know about the Fellowship of Reconciliation and the nature of my association with the group. I told him that I had worked with the organization for four years, but that they were not communists; they were religious pacifists who had a strong moral objection to war. I told him that I hadn't worked with them for several years, but that if he wanted to check out my story, he could call them. They were located in Nyack, New York. And I gave him the number. Evidently, Farrell was satisfied. He realized that the statement was part of a smear campaign against me. Then he called Max, and said, "Why are you distributing this thing on Wilson Riles?" And Max said, "Oh, no, I haven't put out anything like that." He disclaimed everything. And the editor said, "Well, I have it right in front of me." And Max said, "Oh, it might have been put out by some over-anxious supporters." He said that he disassociated himself from it. He told Farrell that it had no connection with his office or his campaign.

Now this guy did something that I'd never heard of before; he went to the post office and traced the markings on the envelope. Sure enough, it was mailed from Max's headquarters in Sacramento. In the primary, the *San Jose Mercury* had endorsed Max. With that information, however, they reversed their endorsement and supported me. And that endorsement, coming from a major paper, made headlines all over the state.

JE: What were the key factors that proved most decisive in your victory?

WR: I think Max had run his course. He had been elected with a great deal of fanfare, but by this time, people were disgusted with him. He had run for the United States Senate and lost. In doing so, he took on a fellow Republican, Thomas Kuchel who was extremely influential in the Senate and well liked throughout the state. He knocked Kuchel off in the Republican primary. And then he committed the unpardonable sin of losing the seat to his Democratic opponent, Alan Cranston, in the general election. That served to turn off every moderate Republican in the state. And they were looking around for someone to get even with Max. I've had several of them tell me so personally.

So, it was a combination of things that just came together at the right time. And I was there, able to take advantage of the situation. In reality, a lot of what happens in politics can be attributed to being in the right place at the right time—there's no doubt about it. Had it been earlier, I probably wouldn't have run in the first place. I was the first black to be elected to statewide office. And my election paved the way for others. For example, two years later, Bradley challenged Yorty again, and this time he won. And two years after that, Mervyn Dymally was elected lieutenant governor.

JE: In your first four years you served under then Governor Ronald Reagan and in the last eight under Governor Edmund G. Brown, Jr. To the surprise of many, you stated in one interview that you preferred Reagan to Brown. Why?

WR: It was largely due to the personalities of the two individuals. In the case of Reagan, he was accessible. I think he was embarrassed by Max, too. Once I was elected, the first thing I did was to make an appointment to talk to Reagan because he had endorsed Max. When we met, I said to him, "Governor, the election is over. I want you to know that I will not play partisan politics as state superintendent. I will be political, but I will not be partisan. My job is to represent the children of this state. I think that the state's founding fathers knew what they were doing when they made this the only nonpartisan statewide office." That appealed to him. I went on to say, "I know you endorsed my opponent. But the election is over now. I want to work with you in the interest of the kids. And I want to have access to you when there's a problem or a potential problem, because I've discovered that elected officials frequently find themselves at odds, not because they necessarily are at odds, but because the people around them are at odds. I don't want that to happen. I want to establish a relationship where, when you have a problem, you can pick up the phone and call me, and I'll be honest with you." He liked that. And then he said to me, "You said that I endorsed Max. I had some political debts to pay and, you're right, I *did* endorse Max. But the endorsement was limited to responding to a direct question, one time, from a newsman." And then he added, "You may be surprised, Wilson, how we voted."

Reagan kept his word. I got $25 million to launch the Early Childhood Education Program with his endorsement. I got another $35 million to expand it the next year. In fact, he supported most of the programs that I proposed. For example, I was able to set up a grants office in Washington because of his endorsement. I served on the National Council on Educational Research because he picked up the telephone and asked that I be appointed to the council.

You had to frame things in a way that did not clash with his philosophical beliefs. For example, I knew that he opposed federal aid to education. But, I went to him and said, "Look, we have all these federal programs. People from my department are flying back and forth to Washington every day of the week. Federal aid is not a gift from Uncle

Sam. California represents 10 percent of the nation's population. That's our tax money. If we don't get it, someone else will. We should get 10 percent of the action for our kids." I went on to say, "Listen, it's not cost-effective to have people fly back and forth this often. If we had a small office back there, we could interact more closely with the United States Office of Education and ensure that we receive our fair share." He said, "Wilson, that makes sense. Go ahead and set it up." Do you think I could have got that from Jerry Brown? Hell, no!

Jerry Brown? In the first place, you couldn't get to him. When you did get to him, you couldn't get an answer. I suspect it goes back to his Jesuit training, where a discussion consists of an endless series of questions and answers. A friend of mine once joked that, in Jerry's case, he never completed the training. So, that was a problem. You'd ask him a question, and he'd respond by asking you one. You would never get a yes or a no answer. I liked the guy, but he was impossible to work with. I don't think he really thought you could make a difference in government. He just let things boil up and percolate, and then hopefully something would come out. That was his style.

JE: Do you hold Brown partly responsible for the passage of Proposition 13? If so, why?

WR: I hate to say this, again, because I like Jerry, but from my perspective, if he had exerted the kind of leadership that a governor could exert, we wouldn't have had a Proposition 13. Now, let me tell you why. Everyone knew that the property tax situation was out of control and that it needed to be addressed. Indeed, the state legislature was grappling with a half-dozen bills to do just that. This was the year before Proposition 13 qualified for the ballot. The state legislature debated, argued, fought. They just couldn't reach a consensus. And Jerry just sat on the sidelines and watched it happen. He failed to provide *any* leadership whatsoever. He didn't have a bill. He didn't bring the sides together. And he didn't demand that they act. He just sat there.

I recall that, on May 1, 1978, the Field Poll was released. At that time, 41 percent of the voters favored Proposition 13; 39 percent opposed it; and 20 percent were undecided. I had to fly to Washington to speak to several state superintendents, and they were anxious to know how the vote would go. My prediction was that it was going to lose narrowly, because I knew that the organization against Proposition 13 had not quite jelled. This organization was in the process of raising money and planning a final television blitz. However, the Los Angeles County Tax Assessor, Alexander Pope, released—just three weeks before the election—the assessments for Los Angeles County. That's not usually done until September. When people saw how bad things were—I mean, you could feel it in the air—then, one by one, other counties began to release their data. The attitude of the people quickly became: We'll show them!

Brown, who had finally endorsed a bill late in the legislative session and opposed Proposition 13, began to waffle. And by the time Proposition 13 had passed, the voters who had supported him actually believed that he had supported Proposition 13 from the very beginning. In other words, with the right leadership from the governor, you wouldn't have had Proposition 13. People wanted the tax situation straightened out. They weren't against the schools. But Jerry failed to take a stand—and let everything unravel.

It's tragic! We're still feeling the effects of Proposition 13. The schools have suffered terribly. The passage of Proposition 13 was not only a savage blow to the kids, the schools, and the entire state, but our entire program was set back. At the time, we were moving forward, making great headway. Once Proposition 13 passed, we had to stop and devote our full energies to keeping the system from falling apart. Just imagine, the moment it passed, the schools lost more than one-third of their total financial support.

We met around the clock in order to develop various contingency plans for coping with the situation. Fortunately, the state treasury had a surplus at the time. I went to Leo McCarthy, the speaker of the assembly, and said, "We've got to have some bail-out money." And Leo said, "Wilson, I know you opposed Proposition 13, and I opposed it, but it won. I'm not in favor of a bail-out bill. The people voted for it; now they've got to suffer." And I said, "Leo, I know how you feel. At times I've felt the same way. But there are four million kids out there. I'm concerned about them. If they could have voted, it would never have passed. Some of us who feel strongly are going to have to stand up and hold this thing together." But McCarthy was unconvinced, although he did eventually support a bail-out.

JE: How would you assess the impact of Proposition 13 on the state's public school system?

WR: The real miracle—one which most people don't understand because the schools remained open—is that the system survived. Most people assume that because it survived everything was all right. They're wrong. The fact is, many needed programs have either been emasculated or eliminated. Today, people talk about year-round schools. One of the first casualties was the loss of summer school. Moreover, buildings have deteriorated—routine maintenance is next to impossible. Many fine teachers have left the system. It's becoming more and more difficult to attract good teachers. For the first time in this state's history, kids don't have enough textbooks.

However, the most important change is in the area of governance. Prior to the passage of Proposition 13, over 50 percent of school support came from the local districts. Approximately 40 percent came from the state. And about 6 or 7 percent came from federal sources. The moment Proposition 13 passed, the local funds were wiped out and the state was forced to contribute over 75 percent of the revenue. Now you have a situation in which the local boards are charged with running the schools but have little or no control over the resources.

The power has shifted to the state legislature. As a school superintendent, there is no way to know what your final budget will be until late June (with school starting in September), when the state legislature approves the budget. It's extremely difficult to operate a school district on this basis, as you have to delay many critical decisions, such as new hires, programs, and activities until the last minute. If a corporation were forced to operate in this manner, it would find it next to impossible. So today you have the state legislature serving as the superboard of education, with local officials simply going through the motions.

This is not a good way for a state as large as California to run its school system. All decisions cannot and should not be made in Sacramento. Many decisions should be made at the local level where the community is best able to assess its needs. The present system reduces community involvement to the extent that the kids and their parents are virtually eliminated from the decision-making process. It's a tragic thing!

JE: Did the passage of Proposition 13 contribute to your own defeat in 1982?

WR: Several factors contributed to my defeat, one of which, of course, was the passage of Proposition 13. I was—and still am, I suppose—a reformer. I want to see things improve. I had developed a course of action for the schools which, prior to the passage of Proposition 13, had succeeded in bringing about many needed changes.

From a strategic point of view, my goal was to start at the early childhood education level and work up—that is, to strengthen that area and then move to the next higher rung. Our efforts in the early childhood area, for example, won the plaudits of the state and were copied in many other states. For example, we succeeded in building a giant volunteer network, so that at one time there were more than 250,000 volunteers assisting in thousands of schools throughout the state.

From there my plan was to focus on the secondary schools—junior and senior high schools. We appointed a special commission to study the situation and recommend needed reforms. They came up with several good recommendations. We translated their ideas into legislation and muscled it through the state legislature. And Jerry Brown vetoed it. That proved to be a devastating setback. We did everything possible to convince him to sign the legislation, but he refused. Without even reading it, he vetoed the bill. We were then forced to spend the better part of a year trying to rescue many of our programs. We reformed the state's vocational programs. We developed a new textbook adoption process. We created a master plan for special education. Everything was moving again. Then came Proposition 13. At the time, we were just beginning to institute a series of much-needed reforms at the high school level. Once it passed, however, I had to devote my full efforts to keeping the schools afloat. Believe me, it was far from easy.

What did I fail to do? I did not recognize the changing political climate of the state. Actually, I was uncertain about whether I really wanted to run again. Twelve years as state superintendent is a long time. You get tired. But I felt that the system had been good to me. I owed it to the kids not to walk out simply because the schools were in trouble. I could see all of the programs that I had fought for go down the drain. That's what really motivated me to run. And I did so reluctantly.

I failed to realize that the state legislature had changed. The same people who were there at the beginning—who often crossed party lines to support our efforts—were no longer there. I woke up one morning to find a whole new cast of players. The new members had become increasingly partisan. Moreover, the parents—many of whom we had involved so directly in the schools—were also gone. Their children had grown up. The parents had dropped out of the picture. And their children, who were now parents, believed that the schools were always this way. They didn't remember what the schools had been like previously.

When the campaign started, I thought my strongest challenge would come from Richard Ferraro, a member of the Los Angeles Board of Education. He's a Max Rafferty type but not as smart. His educational views, however, mirrored those of Max. Another potential opponent, Bill Honig, indicated that he was not going to run if I did but then changed his mind. He proved to be my major nemesis.

The real problem, however, stemmed from the fact that I did not raise sufficient money. I didn't go out and raise a large enough war chest. Instead, I took it easy. The first polls showed me fluctuating between 44 and 48 percent of the vote. Honig, as late as early May—with the election in June—had only 3 percent in the polls. At the last minute, he spent a staggering $800,000 on a major television blitz. He could well afford it because he comes from an independently wealthy family. He ended up with 25 percent of the vote, which forced me into a runoff in the general election in November. I had hoped to win over 50 percent in the primary and thus avoid a runoff. Anyway, that proved not to be the case. In a nonpartisan race, if you're forced into the general, it's next to impossible to win.

Still, I felt very confident. I couldn't see him repeating such expenditures in the general. At the time, we were struggling. We were nearly broke. I spent night and day trying to raise money. Damn, if he didn't repeat it, except this time he spent over a million dollars in the general. He bought every time slot on television he could. It wiped us out.

You might ask, do I have any regrets? No one likes to lose an election. But I have to tell you, I did not realize the great pressure I was under until I was out of office. I should not have run. My heart wasn't in it. But it's very much like being a father or mother: These programs were my kids, and I wanted to see them grow up and develop. I couldn't stand to see them go down the drain. I don't regret having spent so much time trying to keep the system together, because win, lose, or draw I would have done that anyway. I also don't regret having opposed Proposition 13 and having worked hard against it.

JE: What issues proved most damaging to your candidacy? Could these have been overcome?

WR: Honig campaigned against the system. He used the same kind of strategy that Max had used. It was the old "Johnny can't read" theme. He buttressed his case by arguing that test scores had dropped significantly. These were completely phony issues. But that isn't why we lost. What did it was television. He had the money, which meant that he could buy unlimited time to reach the voters. There's no question that this proved to be the difference. This is especially true in the case of the schools where people don't really understand the system. They think the state superintendent runs the schools. That's not true. The state legislature and the local school boards run the schools. But it's easy to convince people that one man—in this case, me—was responsible for all of the ills of the system. They don't realize that the superintendent can't do anything unless it's authorized by law.

JE: What do you see as your proudest accomplishments?

WR: I would point to three things. First, the development of a first-rate early childhood education program; second, a massive citizen involvement program; and third, holding the system together after the passage of Proposition 13. We developed an early childhood program that was the envy of many other states. We involved hundreds of thousands of citizens in the schools. And we rescued the system from total collapse.

JE: What about major failings? Are there things that you wish you could have accomplished but didn't?

WR: I wish I had assumed a leadership role in the Proposition 13 battle. I opposed the measure, spoke out against it, and urged others to follow suit. But I should have done more. There were reasons, however, why I did not. I sensed that several organizations had felt left out—that they wished to assume that role. So, I made a decision to let them lead the fight. I would do whatever I could to help, but I would not spearhead the campaign. And so I stepped back and let them carry the ball.

Another failing was not being politically astute enough to deal with Jerry Brown. It's not enough to blame him. A person in a leadership position has to develop a way of dealing with people and circumstances. I found a way to deal with Reagan. But I didn't find a way to deal with Brown. Maybe I'm taking too much on myself. But, I think there should have been a way.

I wish I could have done more to develop a better relationship between teachers and administrators. We made some progress in this area, but not as much as I would have hoped. Many times there were deep differences of opinion which made it extremely difficult to bring them together.

JE: Finally, do you feel any bitterness toward the voters for your defeat?

WR: No, not at all. After all, I received 44 percent of the vote in the general election. And when you look at a state as large as California, that's a lot of people. Once the election was over, I was left with a rather large debt. Many people who were longtime supporters have contributed to erasing that debt. Moreover, I made many good friends during those twelve years. Whenever I walk through an airport or go to a restaurant, people come up to me and express their appreciation. So, no, I don't feel any bitterness.

I still have a strong commitment to education. I wish the new state superintendent well. I wish the school districts well. And most of all, I wish the kids well—because that's what it's all about. I feel privileged to have served. After all, who would have believed that a little black boy who lost his parents at the age of twelve, who was born in the rural South, would grow up to become superintendent of schools of the largest state in the nation? Hell, how could I be bitter? I just hope I can keep the same opportunities open for every boy and girl, black or white, as long as I live. After all, that's what the American dream is all about. I still believe in that dream. I believe that the future is ours to make. Sure, we have problems—big problems. But none of the problems are so big that we can't solve them. As long as we have the will, there is very little we can't do. The dream must not die.

Harvey B. Gantt

Politics at the Grass Roots

Harvey B. Gantt was born on January 14, 1943, in Charleston, South Carolina. He attended Iowa State University and Clemson University, from which he received a Bachelor of Architecture degree in 1965. From there he entered Massachusetts Institute of Technology and earned a Master of City Planning degree in 1970. He is a member of the American Institute of Architects (AIA), an associate member of the American Planning Association, a member of the AIA National Minority Affairs Committee, and secretary-treasurer of the North Carolina Board of Architecture.

Prior to his election as mayor of Charlotte, North Carolina, in 1983, Gantt served as mayor pro tempore from 1982 to 1983 and as a city councilman from 1974 to 1979. He has served on the Board of Directors of Sacred Heart College; as chairman of the Johnson C. Smith University United Negro College Fund Drive; as a board member of the Afro-American Cultural Center and the Charlotte Chamber of Commerce; and as co-chairman of the National Conference of Christians and Jews.

As a candidate for mayor, Gantt forged a board-based citizens' coalition that comprised businessmen and grass-roots organizers, poor people and middle class professionals, Democrats and Republicans, liberals and conservatives, and blacks and whites. In doing so, he bested his Republican opponent, Ed Peacock (a former Mecklenburg County commissioner, who had never before suffered political defeat), by a 4,033-vote margin, receiving 52.4 percent of the vote in a city where only 20 percent of the electorate is black. Gantt carried 41 percent of the vote in Charlotte's white-majority precincts, an unheard-of percentage for a black mayoral candidate, to become Charlotte's first black mayor.

A veteran campaigner, Gantt ran on his ten-year track record as a city councilman and mayor pro tempore, advocating district representation, strong zoning laws, tax exempt loans for downtown redevelopment, increased jobs for unemployed youth, and a citywide affirmative action program.

In winning the mayor's race, Gantt capitalized on Charlotte's changing political climate, which was more than twenty years in the making. Indeed, a series of developments—integration of public facilities, school desegregation and busing, the success of earlier black politicians, and the neighborhood movement—all contributed to his victory.

JE: When did you first develop an interest in politics? What issue or event provoked your interest?

HG: That's a difficult question to answer. My interest probably dates back to 1954, to the Supreme Court's historic decision in *Brown* v. *Board of Education*. I was eleven years old at the time. That entire period fascinated me. I can vividly recall the big, bold headlines in the *Charleston Evening Post*, which proclaimed "Segregation Unconstitutional!," although I really didn't understand what it meant.

From that time on, I developed a passionate interest in history, particularly southern history. In retrospect, I suspect that my interest dates back even further, to my boyhood years when my father was a card-carrying member of the National Association for the Advancement of Colored People (NAACP)—which was quite unpopular in those days—and to his suppertime discourses on the state of the world with regard to race and politics. I can clearly recall his terrible fear of Republicans and what might happen should they be elected.

As for my involvement in elective politics, I probably was the least likely person to have been a candidate, because I never aspired to public office nor was I actively involved in the political arena. From my perspective, I thought a good citizen should stay abreast of the issues, contribute to the candidates of his choice, and occasionally attend a local meeting of the city council or county commissioners.

I first became involved in grass-roots politics through my professional association with the American Institute of Architects when I chaired a task force on city planning in Charlotte. Our report attracted considerable press coverage, and, lo and behold, one year later I was appointed to fill a vacancy on the city council.

Many people contend that my involvement in politics dates back to 1963, when I became the first Black to enter Clemson University under a federal court order. And again, that occurred quite by chance. At the time, I was an undergraduate at Iowa State University. I decided, one cold February day—at 23 degrees below zero—that I disliked attending school in Iowa and that I should not delude myself into believing that I enjoyed it when I didn't. When I looked around and saw all of the other architecture students—most of whom had been born and reared in Iowa—talk about setting up practice in the state, it suddenly dawned on me why state schools existed. Iowa was their home, not mine. It made sense for them to attend school in Iowa; it didn't for me. At that moment, I decided to apply to Clemson University.

JE: Twenty years ago you made history as the first Black to enter Clemson after you had sued the state for admission. What do you recall of the experience? What effect did it have on you?

HG: When I applied to Clemson, I was extremely optimistic. However, when my friends at Iowa State discovered that I had applied for admission and had brought suit against the state for refusing my application, they thought I had gone crazy. Still, I had this uncanny feeling that if I appealed to the people of South Carolina's manners, rather than their morality, they would admit me, albeit with a stiff upper lip. My optimism was buoyed by the actions of Governor Ernest Hollings, who had been elected to the United States Senate when he proclaimed that the time had come to accept the reality of integration. This helped to set the tone for what would follow.

Still, I wondered, even if I was accepted, how the other students and faculty would view me. In my case, the experience proved peaceful. I knew that my success would depend upon maintaining a positive attitude. I wanted to be an architect and to set up practice in the South. There was a dire need for skilled architects, and the South appeared to be a good place, from a career point of view, to establish my practice.

JE: Although you've painted a very positive picture of your experience at Clemson, your admission was clouded by a bitter court battle. Can you trace the key events which led to your admission?

HG: Yes. On that February day to which I've just referred, I requested an application which I completed and promptly returned to Clemson. Soon thereafter, I received a letter from the university, stating that while I had attended high school in Charleston and had received satisfactory grades, I should reconsider my decision and attend school in Iowa.

I sent Clemson another letter. This time I stated that I wished to return to my native state of South Carolina and asked the university to reconsider my application. Again, they wrote back and restated their earlier position. At that point, I called my old friend Matthew Perry whom I had known in high school. Back then, he was a prominent civil rights attorney in South Carolina; today, he is a well-known judge in that state. I told Perry that I wanted to attend Clemson. He was extremely pleased. He asked me what steps I had taken to gain admission, and I told him about the two letters I had received. He said, in effect, I should keep writing, but, from then on, I should send him a copy of all correspondence. I followed his directive from February until mid-summer, at which point the university wrote to inform me that the registration period had closed.

Despite my good-faith efforts to provide Clemson with the information they requested, my application was rejected. So, in June 1962, we filed a motion in federal court to require the university to admit me for the September term. The case was assigned to Judge Wyche, a born and bred South Carolinian. He delayed the case as long as possible and refused to put it on the docket until November. We filed a motion, of course, to speed up the process so that I could attend school in September. Stating that the case had to be tried on its merits, the court denied our motion.

The university argued, in short, that I had failed to meet its admission requirements. These included: (1) a satisfactory grade point average: I clearly met this requirement; (2) a passing score on the Scholastic Aptitude Test: I definitely met this requirement; (3) a personal interview, in order to certify the applicant's moral character: I failed to meet this requirement because the university refused to schedule an interview; (4) a portfolio presentation: This requirement, we maintained, was irrelevant to the admissions process; it was simply used to determine class placement.

The trial occurred in November 1962. It lasted for roughly a week. We attempted to prove that my application was treated separately and differently from that of the other students. And the interrogatories confirmed that fact. In the end, Judge Wyche, following true to form, ruled that I had *not* been treated differently.

We then appealed the decision to the Fourth Circuit Court, which ruled in our favor. The state, in turn, appealed to the Supreme Court, filing a writ of certiorari, which the court refused to hear. At long last we had won. The university was ordered to admit me to the January 1963 term, two years after my initial application.

JE: Do you have a political role model? If so, whom?

HG: No, not really. I'd be lying if I said I did. I admire many people, but I admire each of them for different reasons. For example, I greatly admired Dr. Martin Luther King, Jr., but he wasn't really a politician, in that sense. He was a civil rights leader, which required very different skills and attributes. Some people don't understand that distinction, even today, which is why they find it so difficult to analyze

Reverend Jesse Jackson's candidacy. But I admired King for his personal integrity and courage, as well as for his lifelong commitment to nonviolence. I believe, quite strongly, that the future depends upon the nonviolent resolution of conflict. This is especially true in the case of minorities who lack the armed might necessary to effect a total revolution.

JE: Were you actively involved in the civil rights movement of the 1960s? If so, how?

HG: I was involved in two ways. First, as a seventeen-year-old student, I led a group in high school to integrate a lunch counter, for which I was arrested. Basically, that was the only kind of involvement activists could have at the time. Second, I was a member of the NAACP in the 1950s and took part in several of its activities. Considering my age and the times, I was quite active in the movement.

My interest in the Student Nonviolent Coordinating Committee (SNCC), the Congress of Racial Equality (CORE), and other civil rights groups was somewhat diminished in the early 1960s, because at the time I was living in Iowa, which was not exactly a hotbed of political activity. If you wanted to get involved, you had to do what I did—get involved when you went home for summer vacations. During those school breaks, I did voter registration with SNCC and various other civil rights groups.

As a student at Clemson, I helped to develop a plan to integrate public accommodations in Charleston. In 1963, similar efforts were taking place throughout the country in virtually every major southern city. So, I was involved in efforts of that kind. I did not take part, however, in any of the monumental demonstrations which occurred in the 1960s. For example, I did not participate in the March on Washington in 1963. At that time, I was working to catch up and complete my studies at Clemson. Nor did I attend the famous 1965 Selma to Montgomery march, but I did have an opportunity to meet virtually all of the major civil rights leaders.

JE: As you view America today, are Blacks better off than they were twenty-five years ago when you integrated Clemson?

HG: When people ask me that question, I answer, "Yes—some are." And when others ask, "Have Blacks made progress as a result of the elimination of segregation?," I also answer, "Yes—some have." And, still, when others ask, "Is racism less pronounced today than it was twenty-five years ago?," my answer is also, "Yes, in some cases."

Progress by black Americans can generally be defined as the positive movement of the black middle class up the economic and social ladder. Things have improved, in part, because the black middle class—a two-worker family—is highly motivated to succeed and to do whatever is necessary to achieve its fair share of the material wealth in our society. The elimination of the legal barriers of segregation clearly accelerated its upward mobility. However, I am firmly convinced that this class of Blacks would have overcome even in the face of legal barriers.

JE: Has the movement of the black middle class, from an economic point of view, tended to reduce the impact of discrimination?

HG: Yes. The only major dialogue between the races over the past twenty-five years has occurred between the black middle class and white America. For a large segment of black citizens, however, the progress has not been substantial. In fact, the evidence suggests that in this country, and indeed in my own city of Charlotte, there is developing an underclass of citizens who fall outside the norms of society—they are primarily black and often unemployed, generally lack an education beyond the eighth grade, and have likely had a negative encounter with the criminal justice system. For these citizens, life is not significantly different in a physical or psychic sense from 1960.

The civil rights movement was, by and large, middle class in orientation and benefitted, for the most part, persons such as myself. The America that accepted our advancement initially was comfortable as long as that black middle class was small enough in number and reasonably acculturated to the general values and mores of the majority society. Hence, tokenism at all levels of our society was fashionable in the late 1960s and early 1970s, when our chief goal was to eliminate the last vestiges of a racist legal structure.

Thus, in Charlotte, school integration in the 1960s meant the freedom of choice option. This placed the burden on black youngsters and produced only token enrollment of black students. Those black students who crossed the line were mainly middle class and highly motivated. Equal employment opportunity in the 1960s meant for most businesses and industries the promotion of one or two outstanding, or maybe even just loyal, Blacks to highly visible, but non-remunerative positions for the purpose of "window dressing." And, for a time, Charlotte made substantial efforts to insure the election or appointment of one or two token Blacks to governmental and civic boards, provided the leadership could influence their election or appointment. As a result, the era of tokenism produced a sense of false comfort.

JE: In your view, why are many whites reluctant to accept full and complete integration?

HG: Resistance surfaces when the government seeks to redress the legacy of discrimination for the *masses* of black citizens—middle and low income. A resultant fear and reaction is seen in the majority community directly proportional to the number of citizens seeking redress and inversely proportional to the degree of perceived difference in the values, culture, and mores of that group.

So, Charlotte, like most American cities, protested when Blacks sought to go beyond tokenism—toward the dream that Dr. King articulated. Busing for school integration replaced freedom of choice and caused considerable controversy. Affirmative action programs, with mandated hiring goals and quotas, caused many businesses and corporations to spend significant non-productive time seeking ways to circumvent or minimize the impact of this policy on traditional hiring practices. Fair housing was acceptable so long as only one black family moved onto the same neighborhood street. The presence of more than one black family triggered a chain reaction that is known today as "white flight." And token representation on boards and commissions has since given way to demands for "one-person, one-vote" district-type representation.

JE: Do you see signs that racial attitudes are changing—that discrimination is becoming less pronounced?

HG: Yes. I believe that racial attitudes have changed, due in part, to restrictions on behavior imposed by law, and also, in part, to the degree to which Blacks and whites have engaged in meaningful social interaction. The most encouraging attitudinal changes are found among our young people in the public school system. I don't mean to suggest that the schools are a utopia, but there are clear and positive signs that our young people are struggling to understand one another, to tolerate and appreciate the real differences between us, and not to let those differences serve as *the* barrier to real friendship and meaningful relationships.

But even with the success of our schools, predominant attitudes on race are still reflective of and influenced by adult prejudices. We rarely witness overt acts of racial prejudice and hatred. But all of us know about the private jokes we still hear in our parlors and living rooms—or the unspoken half-truths that often shape the perceptions of younger minds.

Let me cite several examples of stereotyped thinking that I have heard: (1) Black people are genetically inferior to whites; that's why they don't do well academically; (2) White folk think they're the smartest people in the world; they're always scheming to find a way to put black folk down; (3) Black people are the first to push for more social programs and handouts; they'd much rather collect welfare than work; (4) White folk have the best jobs not because they're better, but because they're white; (5) If black folk move next to you, the value of your property will go down, because Blacks have no respect for property; (6) White people are real funny; they're your friends as long as you don't get "uppity."

I could go on and on, but I think I've made my point. Attitudes manifest themselves in behavior. And behavior often results in the development of institutional, business, or governmental policy.

JE: As you assess the state of race relations today, how did we arrive at this point in history?

HG: In recent years, efforts to extend and enlarge freedom for black Americans have encountered public controversy, a faltering economy, and the establishment of conservative national leadership. This may have produced, as a result, sharpening attitudes of suspicion and mistrust between the races. For many whites, President Reagan's election signalled a policy of benign neglect; for many Blacks, it signalled the beginning of the Second Reconstruction. I'm sure that most Americans are frustrated by our inability to resolve our differences. I certainly am. Disillusionment exists on both sides. After all, the paternalistic but often ill-conceived social programs of the 1960s and 1970s held out great promise. Clearly, they succeeded to an extent but fell short of their goal. This was true of Johnson's "Great Society," Nixon's "Black Capitalism," and Carter's "Affirmative Action."

JE: Assuming your analysis is correct, what can and should be done to solve the race problem?

HG: We are discovering, more and more, that there is a steep price to pay to resolve racial conflict in our nation. And that price goes well beyond the tax dollars that we allocate. Too often the public, i.e., John Q. Citizen, has felt that government—or someone else—could solve our problems. Thus, the tendency on a personal level for non-involvement. As long as John Q. Citizen was not touched by social change, he benignly acquiesced to government programs.

We now know that real change exacts a price from all of us, be it in terms of attitude realignment, adaptation to new realities, or personal initiative and growth. For many, the price of busing their children, or sacrificing a promotion because of affirmative action, or accepting the scattered-site neighborhood housing project was too much. For others, the price of being a pioneer, of accepting new challenges in the face of hostility, of moving a family into a new and strange neighborhood was too high a price to pay.

So, we live today in a period, I believe, of temporary disillusionment; we have discovered that there is no inexpensive quick fix to our problems. Nor are there signs that our national leadership will rise to the occasion.

So, what should we do now? I wish I could offer an easy solution.

Unfortunately, I cannot. But I can offer some clues as to how we might address our predicament.

First, we must never lose sight of the fact that all human beings God made have the potential to lead productive, meaningful lives. If we believe that, we will have the foundation for all future actions we must take to improve our collective lot as sojourners on this planet.

Second, we must guard against the possibility that we may be developing a new underclass of citizens—which society has consigned to the junk heap. Most of these citizens feel they have little stake in our society. We must change that perception. As long as society gives up and makes the judgment that they are terminally poor and unredeemable, we shall live in close proximity to a potential powder keg. We must do more to address this segment of society and attempt to rekindle its hopes in its own future and that of its country. Third, we must strive to develop enlightened leadership—leadership that cuts across racial lines. If the will and the commitment exist at the top, then we will have solved a significant part of the battle to overcome prejudice and racism.

Finally, we must pay a price to correct the course of history. Often that price is money. Often it is fiscal resources and capital investment. More likely, it will be the expenditure of human energy, frustration, and even pain. Things often look worse before they look better.

JE: In 1950, the enemy was legal segregation. Who or what is the enemy today?

HG: Today, the enemy is harder to pinpoint, because there is no longer a clear distinction between villain and hero. There no longer exists the spectre of a Sheriff Bull Connor—armed with rabid dogs—being let loose upon non-violent demonstrators in Birmingham, Alabama. No longer do we have a George Wallace standing in the schoolhouse door denying entry to qualified black students. There is no longer the need for sit-in demonstrations to buy a cup of coffee or for freedom riders to ride a Greyhound Bus, or even for special registrars to register black voters in the black belt counties of Alabama, Mississippi, and South Carolina.

But, by the same token, there no longer exist the great movements of concerned citizens—black and white—led by dynamic and charismatic leaders like Dr. King. The kind of leadership that galvanized an entire nation to search its soul for a real solution is gone and may never be seen again in our generation. However, that era of non-violent protest served a positive purpose. It destroyed *legally*, and I stress "legally," a social system that sanctioned the oppression of an entire race of people and dealt a near-mortal blow to the soul of the nation. The legal victories of the 1960s served to reinforce the genius of our Declaration of Independence and to underscore the fact that "all men are created equal."

Although legal segregation is now dead, its destruction has not meant the realization of a fully integrated society in which equal opportunity is a fact of life for all Americans.

JE: Do you sense a pulling back from the idealism of the 1960s? If so, why?

HG: Yes, very much so. I sense a new tide of apathy and cynicism building in this country that seems to suggest that racism will always be a fact of life. I see numerous efforts on the part of government, industry, and private institutions to find new ways to *circumvent* the legal rights secured by black Americans over the past two or three decades. This has created a shift in the ideological pendulum from the idealism and liberalism of the left to the indifference and conservatism of the right.

JE: What specific developments best illustrate this shift?

HG: If you study the Supreme Court, once considered the last best hope for black people in securing equal rights and social justice, you will see what I mean. The court has become increasingly conservative in recent years. I don't hear people screaming about impeaching Chief Justice Burger as I did about Chief Justice Warren. Look at the *Bakke* decision, which, in a very real sense, dealt a death blow to affirmative action, or to other decisions of the court related to employment practices. There is ample evidence to suggest that the court no longer feels compelled to accelerate the push for justice and equality.

Moreover, the federal government—which is locked into expensive non-responsive social welfare programs—has shifted its priorities from equal justice to balanced budgets, reduction of inflation, and military preparedness. It is far less interested today in health care, unemployment, education, and equal rights. Increasingly, the federal government is returning power to the state and local governments, charging them with the responsibility of delivering social service programs. Sadly, many cities and states lack either the will or the resources or both to administer these programs in ways that will benefit the poor and the minorities. I submit that this trend, begun under President Nixon, was caused in large part by the failure of many ill-conceived and expensive programs of the late 1960s, such as the War on Poverty, and Model Cities. But the lesson is that Blacks and other minorities can ill afford to look to the federal government with certainty for relief from discriminatory practices. The battleground has shifted to the state and local levels.

JE: The present situation would seem to demand dynamic, aggressive new leadership. Do you see the rise of this leadership in the black community?

HG: Many Blacks who personally benefitted from the civil rights movement of the 1960s and early 1970s have, for whatever reasons, eschewed such a leadership position. As for me, I am turned off by those middle-class Blacks who have become comfortable with their two cars, suburban homes, and five-figure incomes; who place greater emphasis on material acquisition than they do on community involvement. I am turned off by those middle-class Blacks who express superficial concern about how badly the system discriminates but who fail to lift a finger to contribute to one of the civil rights organizations or to the survival of a black college. I am turned off by those middle-class Blacks who take personal advantage of the administrative jobs offered in government programs but who show no real interest in providing those services necessary to help their less fortunate brothers and sisters break the cycle of poverty. And I am most turned off by those so-called black politicians who value more their ability to be re-elected than they do their ability to serve the people they represent.

JE: How do you view the future of black America? What trends loom large on the horizon?

HG: I believe we can expect to see a more conservative federal government in the mid-1980s. There will be less money available for major new social programs. The problems of scarce energy resources, inflation, and the decline of the dollar could cause a shift in our concern for the social problems associated with minorities, urban decay, and regulatory programs such as equal employment opportunity and affirmative action. We will likely spend more on defense than we will on job training and housing. Also, in an effort to reduce the size of the federal bureaucracy, more responsibility will increasingly shift to state and local governments.

Certainly, I recognize the importance of solving these problems. Inflation hurts everybody—most severely the poor. It must be abated. Scarce energy supplies affect jobs—that hurts the poor as well as other Americans. But these problems should not be an excuse for discontinuing our commitment to equal opportunity and the elimination of racism and discrimination. Those who share this view must make it clear that the battle for freedom and justice does not necessarily require the vast expenditures of tax dollars. It is not nearly as necessary to increase the number of new programs as it is to replace, reform, and restructure many of the existing ones.

JE: What concrete political strategies would you recommend for solving the problems you've mentioned?

HG: In order to fight racism in the mid-1980s, we must organize *political* organizations, designed to deal with state and local governments, within the black community. Except in special cases, I believe the era of the protest march and the mass demonstration is over. On the local level, we must place increased emphasis on political organization for sustained power and less on national organizations led by charismatic leaders.

I don't mean to suggest that we should diminish the role of the Urban League and John Jacob, or the NAACP and Benjamin Hooks. Local organizations can and should maintain links with these powerful groups and support morally and financially the goals they espouse. But I *do suggest* that we resist movements that depend on *one* leader or personality, and develop organizations with concrete political goals, such as registering black voters, mobilizing the black vote, defining issues of concern, developing coalitions with sympathetic whites, and electing leaders who are sensitive to the need for grass-roots political organizations.

JE: Do you think it's possible to develop a political machine of the kind you propose?

HG: Yes. The task of organizing such a machine is neither easy, nor glamorous, nor exciting. But it is extremely necessary and will require a committed group of dedicated leaders—leaders who are more interested in social change than they are in personal aggrandizement. One of the best ways to eliminate racism is to have power—economic or political. Given our present circumstances, it is clear to me that, as a people, we can more quickly achieve political power than we can economic power. However, with political power will come economic power.

I am not advocating, however, an organization whose goal is to simply register black voters. It must also seek to educate Blacks to the issues and develop working coalitions with white and black politicians who share a common objective. Most important, it must motivate Blacks into believing that *they* can control their own destiny at the ballot box.

If you discuss this fact with black voters in Birmingham—or black voters in my own city of Charlotte—I think you will discover that they clearly understand this fact. For example, since city councils and mayors will increasingly divide up the tax dollar and set priorities, Blacks should work hard to elect councilpersons and mayors. Since governors and state legislators will increasingly decide the quality of public education and job training programs, Blacks should work hard to elect governors and state legislators. And we must do so consistently, not on a flash-in-the-pan, once-in-a-blue-moon basis. That's why I see politics as being so important in the mid-1980s, and why grass-roots political organizations offer our best hope of influencing the system.

JE: How do you propose to develop the kind of leadership that you envisage?

HG: I sincerely hope that the black middle class will play an increasingly active role in the struggle. After all, they benefitted most from the efforts of the 1960s and 1970s. Moreover, they have the resources, stamina, and potential know-how to make an important difference. This role can include such diverse contributions as tutoring disadvantaged youth, serving as spokesmen for a neighborhood organization, working as precinct chairmen, or encouraging their fraternities and sororities to contribute to worthy community causes.

More important, their positions as successful role models will surely be enhanced by their willingness to motivate and inspire young people to stay in school or to lend hope and encouragement to senior citizens who often served their community against great odds.

But *most important*, the black middle class can serve to strengthen the strong values and morals that we as a community have always held dear by their own actions and participation; for example, by returning to the old-fashioned notion of building strong families, enhancing the institution of the black church, and emphasizing the pursuit of excellence through hard work.

In short, I am suggesting that the key to the future—particularly at the local level—lies not in Washington, D.C., but in our cities and towns. We must tap the interests and talents of a growing, educated, and able black middle class—and not wait for some new messiah to burst on the scene.

I believe that we can accomplish these objectives. I saw it happen in Birmingham with the election of a black mayor. And I saw it happen in my own case when I was elected mayor of Charlotte. Our success was directly attributable to a sound political organization, the commitment of essentially young and middle-class leadership, the clear definition of issues, and the ability to forge a broad-based coalition of Blacks and whites.

JE: In winning the mayor's race, you not only swept the black precincts, but you garnered nearly 40 percent of the white vote. How do you explain your appeal to the white community?

HG: In my case, I've been involved in local politics for nearly a decade. In fact, many people view me as the "Dean" of Charlotte politics, having been in office since 1975 (with the exception of a two-year sabbatical, enforced).

Many factors made my victory possible. First, luck played a pivotal role: I was in the right place at the right time. Second, career training: I'm a professional urban planner and an architect. My training enabled me to play a major role in the city's managed growth campaign. Third, a changing political environment: In the decade or so prior to my election, I observed a growing sense of alienation, owing to the rapid growth of the city. I attempted to give voice to that concern.

I was able to appeal to the white community, I suspect, because elements of that community shared my concern about unplanned growth and the need for growth management. Had I run on a platform that simply spoke to the needs of the poor and the minorities, I doubt I would have received more than 25 or 30 percent of the vote—with only about 10 percent of the white vote. However, my goal from the beginning was to reach out to the entire community. I spoke to the concerns of all segments of the city. This struck a responsive chord in people of all backgrounds and political persuasions.

JE: As mayor of the state's largest city, what qualities do you think are most important in order to govern effectively?

HG: During the past decade, the population of Charlotte has become increasingly diverse. We won the mayor's race not only because we were able to address the legitimate concerns of the various segments of the community, but also because we sought to convey a genuine interest in the problems that are likely to face our city in the not-too-distant future. In my view, our success underscored the importance of coalition politics—which is sure to become increasingly important in cities with diverse populations.

I'd like to speak to this point more directly. I always tease my fellow black mayors who lead major urban cities—Chicago, Gary, Detroit—that they represent artificial entities. These are not natural cities, in the sense that they are the products of imaginary boundary lines and are surrounded by incorporated entities on all sides. These mayors preside, by and large, over large concentrations of black citizens. However, if you look closely at these metropolitan areas, most of them closely resemble Charlotte in many ways. It so happens that in North Carolina we annex anything that looks like a city. As a city, Charlotte closely mirrors the diversity of America. This requires that I govern in a manner that appeals to the broad cross section of the electorate—not simply to the black community or the poorer sections of the city. This, in my view, makes me a better mayor, because it forces me to be more circumspect.

JE: As you look at the issue of political access, are you satisfied with the gains that Blacks have made in the electoral arena?

HG: I'm satisfied in terms of where we've come, but not in terms of where we should be. That's a pat answer, but it accurately reflects my feelings. There are fewer than 7,000 black elected officials, nationwide; most of these are at the local level. As I see it, reapportionment will change this situation. I'm a great believer in district representation, for example, because I think that that will alter the composition of the general assembly (the lower house of the North Carolina legislature), which, incidentally, has fewer black elected officials than Alabama, Mississippi, or South Carolina at the state level.

In North Carolina, black political progress has been severely hampered by at-large elections. This method of electing representatives exists throughout the state. Under a district system, I am confident that we can significantly increase the number of black elected officials. For example, in Mecklenburg County we expect to increase black representation in the general assembly as a result of having filed suit to challenge the constitutionality of the existing district lines. District representation will, overnight, produce two additional black state representatives and one black state senator.

So, yes, I think we've made progress. We will make substantially more in the future. But it will require both increased black registration, as well as proof positive that Blacks have made a clear difference in the area of public policy. The black population must see that the election of Blacks means more than simply greater black representation, but also that it means public policy that speaks directly to the needs of the black community. Increased registration often produces a momentary euphoria that quickly subsides once voters realize that their lives have remained essentially unchanged. This tends to increase voter apathy and indifference. If Blacks can point to tangible changes, as a result of increased representation, then I think that black registration will continue to increase.

Unfortunately, it is extremely difficult for mayors of predominantly black cities or legislators who represent predominantly black districts to establish themselves as credible candidates at the state level. It requires that unique politician who is able to transcend the race issue and represent the diverse segments of the population. As a result, I don't expect to see governors elected in large numbers, because most states do not have a large enough black population to elect a governor. However, one day I do expect to see black governors, as I expect one day to see a black president.

In this regard, I think that Jesse Jackson's presidential candidacy has served an important purpose. An entire generation will forever remember his presidential campaign. My son, who is eight years old, will not think it unusual for a Black to run for president. He doesn't understand that fact now. He thinks his father is mayor because he was the most qualified candidate. He doesn't view my election in terms of race.

JE: If Jackson had been elected, do you think he would have been a good president?

HG: I think he would have grown into the office. I don't think he would have been a good president at the start. I do think, though, that he's a quick study. He's an extremely bright man. And he has enormous charisma. People either love him or hate him. I saw him grow tremendously during the campaign. Campaigns have a way of doing that to candidates. He is much more circumspect today than when he began. And he has a much more natural style. I expect that if he had been elected, the same kind of thing would happen to him that happened to John Kennedy. He would have grown enormously in office.

JE: Are there other black politicians whom you particularly admire—whom you think have made significant contributions?

HG: Yes. Atlanta Mayor Andrew Young stands out because of what he has done internationally in terms of linking America to the Third World. I don't think he has received nearly enough credit for his efforts. He's an outstanding diplomat, politician, and statesman. I also admire Detroit Mayor Coleman Young, because he understands the rough and tumble world of politics and has used the system to get Detroit moving again. The city is still plagued by many problems, but he has been able to bridge the gap between the automobile industry that dominates that town and the city's very feisty black population. I also admire California Assembly Speaker Willie Brown for his perseverance and tenacity. He's a superb politician. He has an extraordinary grasp of the nuts and bolts of grass-roots politics.

JE: Your list fails to include any black female politicians. Why? Do you see signs that Blacks are becoming increasingly willing to elect women to public office?

HG: Not in this part of the country. In our community, only one black woman holds elective office. She's a member of the school board. Barbara Jordan, the former congresswoman from Texas, was quite impressive and probably would have been more impressive had her health permitted her to remain in public office. I've been impressed by several of the female mayors I've met across the country, including San Francisco Mayor Dianne Feinstein, who is white. Unfortunately, there are very few black female politicians, particularly in this area of the country. I wish that were not the case, but it is.

JE: As you know, the cost of running for public office has risen dramatically in recent years. Has this deterred black candidates from seeking elective office?

HG: Yes, in some cases. This is especially true in several of the larger cities and states where the cost of running has become prohibitive. It's vital that we set limits on the amount of money a candidate can spend; otherwise, we will make it impossible for candidates of lesser means to seek public office. This poses significant implications for the future of American democracy.

Your question also raises another question—namely, can qualified people afford to run for office? It's important that we pay our officials better. For example, I would not be interested in the mayor's office today—given my circumstances in life—if I had to give up my architectural practice. That's because I'm an architect first and a public servant second. I wish to remain in my chosen profession, as opposed to becoming a full-time mayor. I also believe that, at the local level, it may be wise to have citizen-politicians. These individuals can make a unique contribution to government. However, if someone is capable of serving on a full-time basis, I think they ought to be paid accordingly. They should receive a decent salary, one on which they can live.

JE: What are your future political goals? Where do you see yourself in the next five or ten years?

HG: I don't really know. Many people are more worried about my future than I am. After all, I've only been in office a short time. I can say, however, that all things being equal, I intend to run for re-election, because I very much enjoy being mayor. On the other hand, I don't expect to set any records for being mayor. My goals are to be a good mayor, improve my architectural practice, and spend more time with my family. Moreover, there's nowhere for me to go in Charlotte politics. I have no interest in the general assembly. I think that would be a step down. I'm not particularly interested in the governor's office. And I'm certainly not interested in going to Congress. I don't want to move to Washington, D.C. I'm happy where I am.

JE: Finally, when you leave office, what would you like the public to say about your tenure as mayor?

HG: I certainly wouldn't want them to talk about the buildings I built or didn't build. That's a relatively low priority on my list of priorities. Rather, I would want them to say that I cared and that I tried to make this a better community in which to live. I would like them to say that I tried to serve all the people—black and white, young and old, rich and poor. Basically, I would like them to measure me by that famous line of President Reagan's, namely: Is this a better community than it was when I came into office? My hope is that they will be able to answer in the affirmative.

Melvin H. King

"The Rainbow Coalition"

Melvin H. (Mel) King was born on October 20, 1928, in Boston, Massachusetts. He was educated at Boston Technical High School and awarded a Bachelor of Science degree from Claflin College in Orangeburg, South Carolina. He went on to receive a Master of Education degree from Boston Teachers College. In addition, King has completed academic work at Northeastern University, Boston University, and the University of Massachusetts at Amherst.

A professional educator, King has held positions as a mathematics teacher in the Boston Public Schools and as an instructor at Northeastern University and Boston University's Metropolitan College. In 1971, he joined the Massachusetts Institute of Technology, as associate director of the Community Fellows Program (a program which he helped to create) and as a lecturer in the Department of Urban Studies. In 1975, he was promoted to adjunct professor and director of the Community Fellows Program.

King has been a vital force in community development for over thirty years. For fifteen years, he worked as a youth worker/organizer for United South End Settlements. In 1967, he became executive director of the Urban League of Greater Boston. During his term, King was instrumental in the development of the Joint Center for Community/University Training—a collaboration with Boston College. The Small Business Development Center resulted from that collaboration. He has also been chairman of the Bishop's Housing Action Group; chairman of Low-Cost Housing, Inc.; a contributor to the Presidential Committee on Transportation; and a board member of the Metropolitan Council for Educational Opportunity.

In 1973, King was elected to the Commonwealth of Massachusetts legislature, as a state representative for the communities of Jamaica Plain, South End, Roxbury, Mission Hill, and Fenway. During his tenure in the Massachusetts legislature (1973-1982), King successfully led the 1981 referendum campaign to establish district elections in Boston. He also sponsored and co-sponsored legislation to create the Community Development Finance Corporation, which received an appropriation of $10 million. As one result of this legislation, the Boston Bank of Commerce recently received over $800,000 in state funds. King's final legislative victory occurred in 1982, when he successfully spearheaded a drive to override then Governor Edward J. King's veto of legislation to withdraw public pension funds invested in South Africa.

In 1979, King ran for mayor of Boston, hoping to become that city's first black mayor. Race proved to be a decisive issue in the contest, because Boston had been wracked by a bitter, violent dispute over the continuation of court-ordered busing to achieve racial integration. A leader of the pro-busing forces, King lost the election, finishing third in a six-way race, with 15 percent of the vote.

In 1983, King waged a second bid to become mayor. In the eight-candidate primary field, King finished first, receiving 98 more votes (out of a record 165,688 cast) than his principal opponent, white City Councilman Raymond L. Flynn. The runoff, however, proved to be a different story. In the end, Flynn won the election by a 2-1 margin, with King receiving 95 percent of the black vote and 15 percent of the white vote and carrying half of the city's wards, including mostly white Allston and upscale Back Bay and Beacon Hill.

King had hoped that his "rainbow coalition"—composed largely of Blacks, poor people, the elderly, Hispanics, women, gays and lesbians, workers, and the unemployed—would prove sufficient. Running as a progressive, King called for a crackdown on drug pushers, improved city services, better schools, affordable housing, job training, and fiscal responsibility. To win, King had to pick up 30 percent of the city's white vote, which was 12 percent more than Harold Washington received when he won the mayoral race in Chicago. Although he fell short, King's campaign struck a responsive chord among Boston's minority population, white progressives, organized labor, feminists, and the gay and lesbian community. Clearly, race played a major factor in his defeat. Dormant during the first four weeks of the runoff, the race issue reasserted itself in the closing days of the campaign, with several violent incidents in what was otherwise a peaceful campaign. Although unspoken, the race issue loomed large, and despite King's efforts to defuse the issue, it proved insurmountable—at least in 1983. (King is presently contemplating another run at the mayor's office in 1987.)

JE: How would you describe your political philosophy?

MK: As I view it, government's primary function is to serve the needs of the neediest among us. It exists to protect those who most need protection. Its goal should be to empower those most in need of empowerment. As far as I am concerned, government has no other function. If it fails in these areas, it has lost its reason for being. Unfortunately, too many Americans view government as the protector of the rich and powerful. I do not. The rich and powerful do not need help. They can help themselves. It is the poor and powerless who need government. I think it's time that we returned to this notion. The process has long since been corrupted.

JE: Do you have political role models? If so, whom?

MK: Two names immediately spring to mind: Paul Robeson and Rosa Parks. Robeson was a giant. He could do everything. He was bright, articulate, artistic, athletic. He stood for the politics of inclusion. He embraced working class people and working class struggles. He would not back down for anyone.

Rosa Parks is in a league of her own. I think that she, more than anyone else, made it possible for the rest of us to be where we are today. She was the single most important catalyst for change in this country. She had a profound impact on my life, as well as on the lives of black people everywhere. I don't think she's received the credit she deserves. Her strength, courage, and determination set her apart from the rest of us. She's a very tall woman, in the most majestic sense—an inspiration and an example of sacrifice and service.

JE: Why did you run for mayor in 1983? What did you hope to accomplish?

MK: As a candidate for mayor, I campaigned on three major issues: (1) Boston Jobs for Boston People; (2) affordable housing; and (3) access to all parts of the city for all Bostonians.

As mayor, I wanted to enforce the policy of Boston Jobs for Boston People, a program designed to provide greater access to the city's jobs for Boston residents. I wanted to institute a measure whereby all construction work involving the expenditure of public funds would set aside 50 percent of all jobs for Boston residents, 25 percent for workers of color, and 10 percent for women. In addition, a fixed percentage of the jobs would have been set aside for training and recruitment. To bring this about, I wanted to convert the existing weak executive order to an ordinance; work with unions and contractors to place those requiring little training into jobs directly; and strengthen city compliance.

In addition, I felt—and feel—that the mayor must assume a leadership role to ensure that all of Boston's residents have access to safe, decent, and affordable housing. We must work with tenants to improve public housing. We must institute a strong arson prevention and vandalism control program. We must minimize housing deterioration by enforcing the housing code. We must reinstate rent control and hold the rate of condominium conversion until the vacancy rate on low and moderate housing is above 5 percent. And we must encourage the development of new housing in currently unused property.

I believe that Boston can be an open city: open government, open neighborhoods, and open access for all citizens. I would enforce existing anti-discrimination laws and advocate ordinances to protect all Bostonians, including people of color, the elderly, women, and gays and lesbians.

JE: When you announced your candidacy, did you think you could win?

MK: Yes. When I ran in 1979, I thought I could win. When I ran in 1983, I thought I could win. And I think I can win should I decide to run again in 1987. When I ran for mayor four years ago, many people said we won a moral victory. With just $60,000, I placed third, ahead of the fourth place finisher who spent $350,000. By building on the coalition developed then, I thought I could win in 1983. We went into the September primary with a solid and growing base of support throughout the city. With so many candidates in the race, I felt that a strong effort would guarantee us a place in November's runoff. And I was right. We won the primary but lost the runoff. We could have won that, too. But we didn't do the job. The numbers were there. We simply failed to do what we had to do.

I don't believe those who argue that a black person can't be elected mayor. I know from experience that people all over the city are more practical than that. They would rather build a responsible community that benefits them than participate in a divided and destructive city.

Having said that, there is no doubt in my mind that—given my background, experience, and credentials—I would be the mayor today if I were white. There's no question about it. But even recognizing the level of racism and its accompanying problems in Boston, I still believe we have the power to change things. Maybe the next time around we'll be able to prove the skeptics wrong. We can win. But to do so, we'll have to adopt a different strategy, particularly as it relates to the white community.

JE: Did you have hopes that you would be able to attract a larger white vote? What problems did you face in terms of reaching the white community?

MK: Obviously, our loss is largely attributable to our inability to persuade sufficient numbers of whites to vote for our candidacy. We thought that we could make deeper inroads into the white community.

Some experts thought that we had. Clearly, that was not the case. It's important to understand that it's difficult to persuade people to vote for what they *want*. They're usually influenced by what they're told they can *have*. Fortunately, a lot of people—both black and white—did vote for what they wanted.

We failed for several reasons, one of which was the polls. Many people believe that the polls are infallible—that they're an accurate barometer of voter sentiment. In the primary, it was obvious that we would be one of two candidates in the runoff. The polls reported that fact, giving rise to great public excitement. In the runoff, the polls reported that we were running well behind, which served to decrease voter turnout and persuade the voters that we couldn't win. This taught us an important lesson. Somehow, we must figure out how to escape that box and convince people to vote for what they *want*.

JE: Did you receive much support from Boston's political establishment? If so, whom?

MK: We received the endorsement of several black leaders, in both the primary and runoff. However, we did not receive any major white endorsements (from politicians) until the runoff. In the runoff, we received the support of several state representatives, both past and present. Our campaign also enjoyed considerable support in the Jewish community. We received several major Jewish endorsements in the primary and even more in the runoff. Jewish elected officials openly supported our effort and worked actively in our behalf. In the runoff, we received one endorsement from a white state representative—who represents Back Bay and Beacon Hill—but very few white, non-Jewish elected officials in this city have much courage.

JE: What role, if any, did the outgoing mayor, Kevin White, play in the campaign?

MK: He played *no* role. He did not endorse any candidate. His sole contribution was his decision not to seek re-election and to stay neutral in the campaign.

JE: During the campaign, you attempted to forge a "rainbow coalition." What were its chief elements?

MK: Our campaign attempted to reach out to those individuals and groups who have historically been excluded from the political process. We sought to represent the poor and the powerless—individuals who have been denied equal access to the city's goods and services. Their cause is our cause—and we will not be free until they are free.

The rainbow coalition encompasses virtually every minority group, as well as progressive white males who believe in social, political, and economic justice. It consists of people of color, women, the elderly, Jews, gays and lesbians, the disabled, environmentalists, consumer activists, anti-war dissidents, workers, and others. The rainbow coalition speaks to the special needs of these groups, but it also speaks to the broader needs of the community. It seeks to make real the ideals upon which this nation was founded.

JE: During the campaign, you took a strong stand in favor of gay and lesbian rights? Did this cost you significant voter support?

MK: Perhaps. But that doesn't matter. I support gay and lesbian rights. I not only support gay and lesbian rights, but I fought aggressively for protective legislation throughout my tenure in the state legislature. I think it's imperative that we expand the present city ordinance against discrimination in housing, as well as develop a mechanism for adequate enforcement of equal access to housing in this city. I also support a policy of non-discrimination in employment and would, if elected mayor, actively promote affirmative action in hiring in the private sector by employers utilizing city services.

JE: Did you receive widespread support from the gay and lesbian community?

MK: Yes. We received considerable support from the gay and lesbian community, because we had a strong record of commitment and action on which to build. The support of the gay and lesbian community proved extremely important in the campaign. If I should be elected mayor in the future, gays and lesbians will play an active part in my administration.

As for voter backlash, yes, there was some. In my first mayoral campaign, one man came up to me and said, "What is this, your involvement with gay people?" He said, "I like your policies, but I can't deal with *them*," to which I responded, "Well, you can't work on this campaign." He looked at me, a bit surprised, but understood that I would not back down.

Support, however, is a two-way street. I also made certain demands on the gay and lesbian community. They must join the struggle against the oppression of other people: people of color, women, the elderly. It's vital that *all* oppressed people join together to create an environment in which all people, regardless of race, color, creed, gender, or sexual preference, share in the benefits of the society. You cannot demand a right that you're not willing to extend. Gay and lesbian liberation is part and parcel of the broader struggle for liberation. Gays and lesbians, like Blacks, must fight for freedom and justice for all oppressed people.

JE: Given the composition of the rainbow coalition, were there sufficient numbers to elect you mayor?

MK: Absolutely. But the fact is, the turnout proved disappointing. For example, we received 95 percent of the black vote, but we were only able to generate a 65-70 percent black turnout. We needed to generate a 90 percent black turnout and win 95 percent of that vote. That would have made a tremendous difference in the runoff. Had we succeeded, we would have received an additional 20,000-25,000 votes from people of color.

JE: Was it difficult to raise the money necessary to wage an effective campaign? Would the results have been different had you been more successful in this area?

MK: That's difficult to say. Certainly, money was *a* problem, but I'm not sure it was a *major* problem. Early in the campaign, we made a conscious decision to put a cap on the amount of money we would raise and spend. That may have been a mistake. I don't know. We raised nearly $300,000, which was considerable compared to my first campaign, where we only raised about $65,000. Of course, my opponent (Raymond L. Flynn) did not set such a cap. He raised over $700,000. I suppose we could have raised more had we not instituted a cap.

JE: Did you organize an aggressive voter registration drive? If so, did it prove effective?

MK: Yes. We worked very hard in this area. We knew that victory depended upon our success in registering new voters. And it *did* make a difference in our showing. In addition, we were helped by Mayor Harold Washington's victory in Chicago, which was a major boost to the campaign. His decision to come to Boston and campaign on our behalf proved to be an even bigger boost. Mayor Wilson Goode's victory in Philadelphia was also a boost. So some of what made our efforts effective was beyond our control. The victories of these and other black officials had a tremendous impact on Boston. People realized that if they registered to vote and voted, they could make a major difference.

JE: Was there a turning point in the campaign? Did any particular event or development prove crucial in your defeat?

MK: I'm not sure. Many people contend that the turning point occurred when I made several widely publicized statements about Cuba and Fidel Castro. However, much of what was reported was inaccurate. The facts are quite simple. I was asked a question on a radio talk show, in which the person asked who I would vote for if given the choice: Reagan or Castro. I said, "Fidel." There was no opportunity for explanation or discussion.

Unlike many of Castro's critics, I have been to Cuba. I came back impressed by two things that I witnessed: First, people who had never before had decent housing were actually building their own housing—

learning construction skills, maintenance skills, organization skills. They were building a new community in which to live. Second, I observed a nationwide literacy program, in which people were teaching each other how to read. Young people were even helping to teach reading to their elders.

When I responded "Fidel," I was reminded of these two facts and what I have witnessed since Reagan took office—cuts in housing programs, welfare programs, school lunch programs, and student loan programs. I believe that President Reagan is working primarily in the interests of the privileged and not in the interests of those who have the greatest need.

The question was not whether Castro's government would work in Boston—the question was which person I thought was most worthy of my vote. I also saw many things in Cuba that I did *not* like. But I *did* see that Castro was assisting those people most in need. I view myself as a very honest person. I say what I think. When I made that statement, I did not consider the possible damage it would do to the campaign. And I intend to be honest about my thoughts in the future. But I'm also willing to listen to views different from my own.

JE: Did you attempt to change your image in the campaign, as the press reported? If so, why?

MK: I don't think so. Several reporters made a big to-do about the fact that I shed my dashiki for a suit and tie. To some people, clothes are important. They were disturbed when they saw me in African garb. I felt that such comments were quite silly. But since it mattered to some people, I decided to wear a suit and tie. As far as I'm concerned, what I wear is far less important than what I say. If I can get people to listen to me by wearing a suit and tie, then so be it. It's not that important to me. But no, I didn't make a conscious attempt to change my image. I shed my dashiki in the hopes that people would judge me by my words and deeds, not my attire.

JE: During the campaign, you championed a number of controversial issues, one of which was affirmative action. What specific steps would you take in this area?

MK: My approach to affirmative action is not simply to replace one group with another at the head of the line but to address the heart of the problem and work to increase those scarce resources, such as housing, which become the focus of fierce competition. As mayor, I would strongly enforce the Boston Jobs for Boston People program, which came about as a result of my 1979 drive for mayor. I would take steps to ensure that "checkerboarding" would not be used to meet the

10 percent goal for workers of color and women in the construction trade. We would work class by class through the trades to make sure that this goal is met at each skill level. I would also ensure that Boston's hiring practices reflect the racial, ethnic, and sexual composition of the city. We would begin by filling key staff roles in this manner and then ensure that all agencies follow similar guidelines. As civil service workers retire, we would employ similar goals to refill those positions. City hall should be a model for the rest of the city, both in the public and private sectors. In our citywide search for people, we would establish a skills bank which could be useful to other employers as well.

In the firefighters' department, for example—which is under court order to employ affirmative hiring—we would also look at other job descriptions, including support services and administrative roles. We should sponsor a series of frank discussions with the concerned parties—unions, executives, and others—to develop a clear rationale for affirmative action and to discuss ways in which to implement such a program. Clearly, we need to develop a more widespread understanding and acceptance of affirmative action.

In addition, I would probably establish a new position to monitor the compliance and implementation of affirmative action guidelines in all areas of employment and hiring. The existing compliance department is hopelessly and woefully understaffed. In addition to compliance, the agency should attempt to leverage as many new jobs as possible, clearly defining the term "lowest and most responsible" bidder in these terms. Other city programs should focus on increasing the housing stock and promoting access to other resources to redress the need for affirmative action in the first place.

JE: How would you ensure the implementation and enforcement of minority access to jobs?

MK: The Boston Jobs for Boston People program would be a major starting point for ensuring equal access to jobs. As mayor, I would guarantee that the existing policy is drafted as an ordinance and that the various categories of jobs go well beyond short-term construction jobs.

The mayor can promote equal access to employment in numerous other ways, including a set-aside policy similar to the state's for Boston businesses owned by people of color and women; defining "lowest and most responsible" bidders on city jobs in terms of equal hiring practices for all types of city contracts; and rewarding businesses with contracts for being able to demonstrate a progressive social profile.

It is extremely important that the city begin now to develop and prepare workers for those jobs which are likely to exist in the immediate future. Basic job development will reduce the competition for employment; we need to expand the pie while ensuring that Boston residents and particular groups among those residents receive their fair share. This job development effort should involve the unemployed, investors, and the community.

In addition, we must reexamine the organization and structure of the Occupational Resource Center and all other skill training resources in the city to ensure that there is synchronization between educational programs, students, and workers seeking training and employment. Skill building of Boston residents should be a major part of the city's approach to the employment issue.

JE: What strategy would you propose to support minority business development as a basis for neighborhood/commercial revitalization?

MK: The city should support businesses run and owned by people of color and women in a variety of ways: directing city contracts toward these businesses; working closely with city, state, and federal agencies to tap all available resources; and ensuring that all city funds made available by federal and state sources are actively directed toward supporting these businesses.

The city should also employ set-asides in all city contracts, similar to the state's system, for at least 5 percent of the total dollar amount for new businesses. Similarly, the city should target areas with a high proportion of businesses owned and managed by people of color and women for major improvements in maintenance, city services, police and security, and capital investments. We should also explore revolving loan funds and other mechanisms to assist small businesses.

JE: What enforcement measures would you advocate to promote fair housing opportunities?

MK: First and foremost, we must increase the stock of affordable housing in Boston. We can best accomplish this through a major housing reclamation program to recover abandoned and vacant units and through a streamlined city system which will allocate such units to nonprofit community developers. This housing should be targeted for low and moderate income occupants.

Second, we must recognize that one of the most serious aspects of Boston's housing emergency stems from the fact that many people who attempt to seek housing are met with racial violence. We must employ the full weight of the law to prevent such violence.

In addition, we must work with organizations such as Education/Instruction to develop a full-scale fair housing tracking and monitoring program and to develop a strong fair housing ordinance and bill, which I would personally take to the city council and the state legislature.

Third, we must support all efforts to integrate public housing units. Every effort should be made to treat public housing as a vital part of the community, not as a "second class" of housing. To that end, the city must assume its rightful role in providing basic services to free up the precious funds allocated to the Boston Housing Authority for physical improvements and tenant services. All city employees should be expected to contribute to this effort in their own neighborhoods and should be rewarded for their service.

JE: Beyond enforcement policies, what affirmative action stance would you take?

MK: My primary concerns would be to increase the stock of housing through major changes in city departments charged with handling abandoned housing and a variety of rehabilitation and construction programs. Those nonprofit developers who obtain housing through the city's program should agree to affirmative action efforts in locating tenants or new owners.

I strongly support rent control and a ban on condominium conversion and displacement to help reduce the pressures on the low and moderate income families, people of color, and households headed by women, all of whom suffer most from housing discrimination. We must look at a variety of ways of improving the utilization of existing housing stock, including congregate housing, mixed use developments, and possibly rooming house licenses for some units.

In addition, there are numerous parcels of land in the city which we should consider as sites for new housing construction. I would bring together all housing advocacy groups, communities, and institutions such as the Catholic Church which have a long history of concern about fair housing, and draw on the goodwill of these groups to draft a housing policy and agenda which could be put into action.

JE: Why are certain areas of Boston "off limits" to Blacks and other minorities? What would you do to guarantee safe access to all areas of the city?

MK: Certain areas are "off limits" because racial violence is both tolerated and condoned in this city. We should not use words like "incidents" when the disturbance involves assault or racial violence. Instead, we should employ both the correct descriptive phrase and the official response appropriate to the magnitude of the offense. We must view these attacks as civil rights violations and seek the appropriate penalties in such cases.

We should employ a wide variety of approaches to minimize racial violence, including police training, community work, and organizational efforts to help the population deal with the racial and sexual fears and insecurities that breed violence and encourage a climate of tolerance for such violence. We should also organize a group of Boston legislators and other notable citizens who would be willing to speak out in the event that racial violence does occur. We should also enforce affirmative action in police recruitment and hiring to ensure that the law enforcement teams more nearly reflect the composition of the particular neighborhood. A civilian review board should be established to monitor police behavior.

JE: Many Bostonians have become increasingly concerned about crime. As mayor, what would you do to combat crime in the city?

MK: I believe that every neighborhood requires adequate police protection. But I also believe that crime is a complicated problem, one which requires a comprehensive program, including: citizen participation (e.g., crime watches and police accountability); police retraining; stringent enforcement of laws against drug dealers and professional criminals; and major programs aimed at job development and youth street workers to encourage young people on their own blocks to become constructively involved in the city's development. We must work to increase police protection, as well as to increase police services. At the same time, we must develop programs which will encourage citizens to become more involved in making their neighborhoods safer.

JE: Like many major cities, Boston faces serious fiscal difficulties. What factors produced the present situation?

MK: There are several reasons for the present crisis, but two stand out. First, the White administration (Mayor Kevin White) permitted waste, mismanagement, and patronage to bloat the city's budget. Second, the city has felt the impact of several deep, chronic structural flaws in the way in which we finance city services.

JE: What are these structural flaws? Can they be corrected?

MK: Some problems are built into the system. You can weed out waste and dismiss corrupt employees, but the problem remains if it is endemic to the system. All knowledgeable public finance experts agree that Boston has several structural problems. For example, Boston is overdependent on the property tax. Most other major American cities have other, better tax sources. However, the state won't allow us to raise taxes in a more equitable way.

JE: If elected mayor, would you raise taxes?

MK: I would only ask for a tax increase as a last resort. The people of this city have been overtaxed for years. First, I would go to the state legislature and ask the state to shoulder a greater share of the city's tax burden. We've been subsidizing the shoppers, the commuters, the students, and the tourists for long enough. It's time to give Boston the revenue—and the respect—it deserves.

JE: What impact did the passage of Proposition 2½ have on the city?

MK: With the property tax capped by Proposition 2½, Boston lacks the ability to raise revenue to meet legitimate service needs. The city's tax base is fast eroding. Almost half of the city's property is tax exempt. However, the city must provide services—like police and fire protection—to these tax exempt institutions. Unfortunately, the Boston taxpayer must foot the bill. Federal aid to Boston has dropped sharply under Reaganomics. City residents have suffered deep cuts in housing programs and in direct welfare assistance. The city's federal contribution has, for a variety of programs, gone down by 46 percent since 1981.

JE: What role did race play in the mayoral runoff? Did your opponent make it an issue?

MK: Flynn's approach was to deny the existence of racism. To him, the real issue was poverty. Quite frankly, I think that's a very overt racial approach. Everyone knows that race is directly related to poverty. People of color are worse off than the majority community, not because they lack the incentive to work or the ability to perform but because of the stigma attached to race. To deny that race is an issue—when, in fact, it is—is to distort a basic reality.

After several unsuccessful attempts, we finally forced Flynn to address the issue. He *did* admit that people of color do have certain unique problems. I suppose that represents an accomplishment. But I am distressed that he refused to acknowledge that fact, until pressured to do so. In any event, every sensible person—both black and white—knows that race affects virtually every aspect of a person's life. His admission simply reconfirmed what everyone already knew.

JE: To what extent, if any, did the campaign contribute to healing the city's racial wounds?

MK: To answer that question, we have to examine several key issues. One reason for Boston's bad image is that the city has long been plagued by overt racism. As far as I am concerned, racism is, by definition, overt. But to most people, racism exists only when individuals are verbally or physically attacked or when they are denied access to basic institutions and services. It's that kind of racism for which Boston is known. To the extent that people can move freely from one area of the city to another, in ways that were unthinkable a year or two ago, I think the campaign made a difference. After all, we campaigned across this city, including many areas which were known for their hostility to people of color.

Having said that, we made far less of an impact on the manifestations of racism as evidenced in housing, employment, government, and private industry. For example, consider the question of housing. Housing discrimination has not changed significantly, despite the fact that some families have moved into public housing in some parts of the city where they had been the victims of racial violence. Clearly, the problem is less pronounced today—but it is far from solved. As for being able to find housing in the private market, I don't know that we made a difference. In terms of employment, we made a difference to the extent that we were able to obtain commitments from the construction industry to honor minority set-asides for people of color and women. However, beyond that, the question still remains as to whether people of color and women can find work. Major institutions in the downtown area, like the financial institutions, are still 100 percent white and almost exclusively male. Have we made a difference in that? No.

JE: As a result of the campaign, are whites more willing today to confront the issue of race?

MK: By and large, those white candidates who did confront the race issue were defeated. My principal opponent, Mr. Flynn, did not confront the issue head-on. He did, however, raise the issue of openness and access after he heard me address the issue. In fact, in the primary, he was called on the carpet by one white candidate, David I. Finnegan—who was then the front-runner—for issuing blatantly racist literature. In the black community, Flynn distributed literature which contained black faces, whereas in the white community, his literature was devoid of black faces. He pitched black to the black community and white to the white community. Finnegan's campaign was badly hurt by his attacks on Flynn's racist literature.

JE: Did Flynn campaign aggressively for the black vote? If so, how?

MK: He tried to cultivate the impression that he was interested in the black vote. For example, he had several Blacks on his staff. But every politician campaigns for every vote he or she can get. I don't think that a politician who argues that blacks and whites in South Boston face the same problems is really serious about winning the black vote. Everyone knows that the problems are significantly different—that race plays a major role in who gets what, when, where, and how.

JE: Did Flynn moderate his earlier stance on the race issue in order to win?

MK: The old style politics, which Flynn represented, has become less saleable. It was vital that he change his approach if he hoped to win. Frankly, I think that he and the other candidates hoped that they would receive a large enough share of the moderate vote so as to be guaranteed a spot in the runoff against me. They felt—and the results proved them correct—that the majority population would not support a black candidate. Many people, including one newspaper, supported a white candidate because they felt that a Black could not be elected. In Flynn's case, he recognized that he had to move in a moderate direction in order to win. And that's what he did. As a result, he has now been boxed into a position where he must behave as though he's a moderate.

JE: To what extent are Blacks well represented in Boston's political establishment? Are there signs of progress?

MK: No, not really. There are, however, a few Blacks in visible leadership positions. But if you're asking me whether that's true across the board, then, no, that's not the case. Still, I think there's reason for hope. If we stay on their cases and continue to apply pressure, the potential for such change exists. But remember, we're talking about a city with a $32–40 million deficit, which means that some people will have to go. We're talking about a city in which people filed suit to eliminate affirmative action—what they describe as "quota systems." That doesn't bode well for the future. Obviously, it's easy to appoint a Black to a position of prominence, but it only means something if that approach is applied to the masses.

JE: Have Blacks penetrated the city's private sector? Has significant progress been made in this area?

MK: It depends on how you define "progress." Yes, there are Blacks—one or two—in every business. But across the board, no, it's not happening. The numbers are insignificant. Real change will require a personal attack on the persons who head these corporations. Rather than attacking the First National Bank, we must attack the president personally. The other way, of course, to increase minority representation is to gain control of city hall. The new mayor could then exert pressure on these corporations to change their policies.

JE: In your concession speech, you stated: "The coalition did not win, but it can never be said that it was defeated." What did you mean?

MK: Although we lost the election, we won the war. We proved that we could put together a broad-based coalition—comprised of the poor and the powerless—and reshape the direction of city politics. Although the election is over, the struggle continues. We won't be satisfied until we solve those problems which formed the basis of our candidacy. The future is ours. Certainly, we would have liked to win. Who wouldn't? We faced enormous odds. We took on the political establishment of this city. We challenged injustice wherever it reared its head. And despite the fact that we lost the election, we created a dialogue that will continue long after the election. We proved that we could make a difference—that we could influence public policy in this city. And we demonstrated that we could unite this city's minorities into a potent political force. The results demonstrated that we struck a responsive chord in every section of this city.

JE: Will the rainbow coalition survive beyond the election? If so, how?

MK: Yes. We have forged an ongoing organization—one which will press the fight that we began in this campaign. To do so, we have created a permanent structure. We established by-laws, a steering committee, and neighborhood councils. The organization is composed of dues-paying individuals who believe in the ideals and policies which we advocated in the campaign. During the upcoming months, we intend to focus heavily on organization building. Special workshops will be held on block organizing, media relations, voter registration, policy research, political fund-raising, and many other subjects. No, we're here for the long haul. We have no intention of going away. We are a force to reckon with.

JE: Do you sense a new optimism in the black community? Has your campaign generated a new resolve?

MK: Yes, very much so. However, in the end, our success will ultimately depend on numbers. If people understand they have the numbers and thus the power, they will participate. That's a reality. In addition, our campaign demonstrated that it is possible to build a broad-based coalition. This, by itself, has generated renewed enthusiasm and commitment. We succeeded in bringing together a wide variety of groups. This diversity proved to be a strength, not a liability. We demonstrated that it is possible to create unity out of diversity. That in itself was a great accomplishment. And, of course, ours was only *one* campaign. As we flex our political muscle and prove instrumental in future political campaigns, we will strengthen that resolve and encourage even greater optimism.

JE: Finally, if asked, would you encourage Blacks to move to Boston? Does the future bode well for Blacks?

MK: That depends. Many Blacks who possess marketable skills tell me that Boston is a hospitable city—that it's fairly easy to find employment. However, the same cannot be said for Blacks without such skills. I would caution Blacks, however, that the future depends on their active participation. Regardless of skill level, Blacks have an obligation to contribute to the change process. That's the only way we can make this city a better place in which to live. It's a hell of an opportunity. We have an opportunity to create a city which reflects the ideals upon which this nation was built. It's time to get started.

Selected Bibliography

Aberbach, Joel D., and Jack L. Walker. *Race in the City: Political Trust and Public Policy in the New Urban System*. Boston: Little, Brown, 1973.

Aiken, Charles. *The Negro Votes*. San Francisco: Chandler, 1965.

Amoda, Moyibi. *Black Politics and Black Vision*. Philadelphia: Westminster Press, 1972.

Anderson, Jervis B. *A. Philip Randolph: A Biographical Portrait*. New York: Harcourt Brace Jovanovich, 1973.

Aptheker, Herbert, ed. *A Documentary History of the Negro in the United States*. New York: Citadel Press, 1951.

Bailey, Harry A., Jr., ed. *Negro Politics in America*. Columbus, Ohio: Charles Merrill, 1967.

Bailey, Ronald W., ed. *Black Business Enterprise: Historical and Contemporary Perspectives*. New York: Basic Books, 1971.

Barbour, Floyd B., ed. *The Black Power Revolt: A Collection of Essays*. Boston: P. Sargent, 1968.

————, ed. *The Black Seventies*. Boston: P. Sargent, 1970.

Bardolph, Richard. *The Civil Rights Record: Black Americans and the Law, 1849–1970*. New York: Thomas Y. Crowell, 1970.

Barker, Lucius J., and Jesse J. McCorry, Jr. *Black Americans and the Political System*. Cambridge, Mass.: Winthrop, 1980.

Barnett, Marguerite Ross, and James A. Hefner, eds. *Public Policy for the Black Community: Strategies and Perspectives*. Port Washington, N.Y.: Alfred, 1976.

Bates, Daisy. *The Long Shadow of Little Rock*. New York: David McKay, 1962.

Bell, Derrick A., Jr. *Race, Racism, and American Law*. Boston: Little, Brown, 1973.

Bell, Ingel P. *CORE and the Strategy of Non-Violence*. New York: Random House, 1968.

Bennett, Lerone, Jr. *Before the Mayflower: A History of Black America*. New York: Penguin Books, 1982.

————. *Black Power U.S.A.: The Human Side of Reconstruction, 1867–1877*. Chicago: Johnson, 1962.

———. *Confrontation: Black and White*. Chicago: Johnson, 1965.

———. *Pioneers in Protest*. Chicago: Johnson, 1968.

———. *The Shaping of Black America*. Chicago: Johnson, 1975.

———. *What Manner of Man: A Biography of Martin Luther King, Jr.* Chicago: Johnson, 1968.

Berger, Morroe. *Equality by Statute: The Revolution in Civil Rights*. Garden City, N.Y.: Doubleday, 1967.

Berry, Mary Frances. *Black Resistance, White Law: A History of Constitutional Racism in America*. New York: Appleton-Century-Crofts, 1971.

Blair, Walter D. *Retreat to the Ghetto: The End of a Dream?* New York: Hill and Wang, 1977.

Bland, Randall W. *Private Pressure on Public Law: The Legal Career of Justice Thurgood Marshall*. Port Washington, N.Y.: Kennikat Press, 1973.

Blaustein, Albert B., and Clarence C. Ferguson. *Desegregation and the Law: The Meaning and Effect of the School Desegregation Cases*. New York: Random House, 1962.

Bond, Julian. *A Time to Speak, A Time to Act: The Movement in Politics*. New York: Simon and Schuster, 1972.

Bracey, John H., Jr., August Meier, and Elliott Rudwick, eds. *Conflict and Competition: Studies in the Recent Black Protest Movement*. Belmont, Calif.: Wadsworth, 1971.

Brazier, Arthur M. *Black Self-Determination: The Story of the Woodlawn Organization*. Grand Rapids, Mich.: Eerdmans, 1969.

Brink, William J., and Louis Harris. *The Negro Revolution in America*. New York: Simon and Schuster, 1964.

Brown, H. Rap. *Die, Nigger, Die!* New York: Dial Press, 1969.

Brown, Norma, ed. *A Black Diplomat in Haiti: The Diplomatic Correspondence of U.S. Minister Frederick Douglass from Haiti, 1889–1891*. Salisbury, N.C.: Documentary Publications, 1977.

Bruner, Richard. *Black Politicians*. New York: David McKay, 1971.

Bryce, Herrington J., ed. *Urban Governance and Minorities*. New York: Praeger, 1976.

Bullock, Charles S., III, and Charles M. Lamb, eds. *Implementation of Civil Rights Policy*. Monterey, Calif.: Brooks/Cole, 1984.

Bullock, Charles S., III, and Harrell R. Rodgers, Jr., eds. *Black Political Attitudes: Implications for Political Support*. Chicago: Markham, 1972.

———, eds. *Racial Equality in America: In Search of an Unfulfilled Goal*. Palisades, Calif.: Goodyear, 1975.

———, eds. *Racism and Inequality: The Policy Alternatives*. San Francisco: W.H. Freeman, 1975.

Bunche, Ralph J. *A World View of Race*. Port Washington, N.Y.: Kennikat Press, 1968.

Bunche, Ralph J., and Dewey W. Grantham. *The Political Status of the Negro in the Age of FDR*. Chicago: University of Chicago Press, 1973.

Bush, Rod, ed. *The New Black Vote: Politics and Power in Four American Cities*. San Francisco: Synthesis Publications, 1984.

Carmichael, Stokely, and Charles V. Hamilton. *Black Power: The Politics of Liberation in America*. New York: Random House, 1967.

Carson, Clayborne. *In Struggle: SNCC and the Black Awakening of the 1960s*. Cambridge, Mass.: Harvard University Press, 1981.

Chavis, Benjamin F., Jr. *Psalms from Prison*. New York: Pilgrim Press, 1983.

Chisholm, Shirley. *The Good Fight*. New York: Harper & Row, 1973.

———. *Unbought and Unbossed*. Boston: Houghton Mifflin, 1970.

Christopher, Maurine. *America's Black Congressmen*. New York: Thomas Y. Crowell, 1971.

Clark, Kenneth B. *Dark Ghetto: Dilemmas of Social Power*. New York: Harper & Row, 1965.

———, ed. *The Negro Protest*. Boston: Beacon Press, 1963.

Clarke, John Henrik, ed. *Malcolm X: The Man and His Times*. New York: Macmillan, 1969.

———, ed. *Marcus Garvey and the Vision of Africa*. New York: Random House, 1974.

Clayton, Edward T. *Martin Luther King: The Peaceful Warrior*. Englewood Cliffs, N.J.: Prentice-Hall, 1964.

———. *The Negro Politician: His Success and Failure*. Chicago: Johnson, 1964.

Cleaver, Eldridge. *Soul on Fire*. Waco, Texas: Word Books, 1978.

———. *Soul on Ice*. New York: McGraw-Hill, 1968.

———, and Robert Scheer. *Post-Prison Writings and Speeches*. New York: Random House, 1969.

Clement, Lee, ed. *Andrew Young at the United Nations*. Salisbury, N.C.: Documentary Publications, 1978.

Cole, Leonard A. *Blacks in Power: A Comparative Study of Black and White Elected Officials*. Princeton: Princeton University Press, 1976.

Cone, James H. *Black Theology and Black Power*. New York: Seabury Press, 1969.

Conyers, James E., and Walter L. Wallace. *Black Elected Officials: A Study of Black Americans Holding Governmental Office*. New York: Russell Sage Foundation, 1976.

Cronin, E. David. *Black Moses: The Story of Marcus Garvey and the Universal Improvement Association*. Madison: University of Wisconsin Press, 1969.

Cross, Theodore L. *Black Capitalism*. New York: Atheneum, 1969.

Cutler, John Henry. *Ed Brooke: Biography of a Senator*. Indianapolis: Bobbs-Merrill, 1972.

Dalfiume, Richard M. *Desegregation of the U.S. Armed Forces: Fighting on Two Fronts, 1939–1953*. Columbia: University of Missouri Press, 1969.

Davis, Angela Y. *An Autobiography*. New York: Random House, 1974.

Dean, John. *The Making of a Black Mayor: A Study of Campaign Organization, Strategies, and Techniques in Prichard, Alabama*. Washington, D.C.: Joint Center for Political Studies, 1973.

Douglass, Frederick. *Life and Times of Frederick Douglass, Written by Himself*. Boston: De Wolfe, 1895.

Draper, Theodore. *The Rediscovery of Black Nationalism*. New York: Viking Press, 1970.

DuBois, W. E. B. *The Autobiography of W. E. B. DuBois: A Soliloquy on Viewing My Life from the Last Decade of Its First Century*. New York: International Publishers, 1971.

———. *Black Folk: Then and Now; An Essay in the History and Sociology of the Negro Race*. New York: Octagon Books, 1970.

———. *Dusk of Dawn: An Essay Toward an Autobiography of a Race Concept*. New York: Schocken Books, 1968.

———. *The Souls of Black Folk: Essays and Sketches*. Greenwich, Conn.: Fawcett, 1961.

Dye, Thomas R. *The Politics of Inequality*. Indianapolis: Bobbs-Merrill, 1971.

Dymally, Mervyn M., ed. *The Black Politician: His Struggle for Power*. Belmont, Calif.: Duxbury Press, 1971.

Eisinger, Peter K. *The Politics of Displacement: Racial and Ethnic Transition in Three American Cities*. New York: Academic Press, 1980.

Ellis, Arthur L. *The Black Power Brokers*. Saratoga, Calif.: Century Twenty One, 1980.

Ellis, William W. *White Ethnics and Black Power: The Emergence of the West Side Organization*. Chicago: Aldine, 1970.

Ermer, Virginia B., and John H. Strange, eds. *Blacks and Bureaucracy: Readings in the Problems and Prospects of Change*. New York: Thomas Y. Crowell, 1972.

Evers, Charles, and Grace Halsell. *Evers*. New York: World, 1971.

Evers, Myrlie, and William Peters. *For Us, The Living*. Garden City, N.Y.: Doubleday, 1967.

Farmer, James. *Freedom—When?* New York: Random House, 1965.

———. *Lay Bare the Heart: An Autobiography of the Civil Rights Movement*. New York: Arbor House, 1985.

Fenderson, Lewis H. *Thurgood Marshall: Fighter for Justice*. New York: McGraw-Hill, 1969.

Filler, Louis. *Wendell Phillips on Civil Rights and Freedom*. New York: Hill and Wang, 1965.

Foner, Jack D. *Blacks and the Military in American History: A New Perspective*. New York: Praeger, 1974.

Foner, Philip S. *Frederick Douglass: A Biography*. New York: Citadel Press, 1969.

———, ed. *The Black Panthers Speak*. New York: Lippincott, 1970.

———, ed. *The Life and Writings of Frederick Douglass*. New York: International Publishers, 1950.

———, ed. *Paul Robeson Speaks: Writings, Speeches, Interviews, 1918–1974*. Larchmont, N.Y.: Brunner/Mazel, 1978.

Forman, James. *The Making of Black Revolutionaries: A Personal Account*. New York: Macmillan, 1972.

———. *The Political Thought of James Forman*. Detroit: Black Star Press, 1970.

Franklin, John Hope. *From Slavery to Freedom: A History of Negro Americans*. New York: Alfred A. Knopf, 1980.

————. *Reconstruction: After the Civil War*. Chicago: University of Chicago Press, 1961.

————, and August Meier, eds. *Black Leaders of the Twentieth Century*. Urbana: University of Illinois Press, 1982.

————, and Isidore Starr, eds. *The Negro in Twentieth Century America: A Reader on the Struggle for Civil Rights*. New York: Vintage Books, 1967.

Frazier, E. Franklin. *The Black Bourgeoisie*. New York: Free Press, 1957.

————. *The Negro in the United States*. New York: Macmillan, 1957.

Frye, Hardy T. *Black Parties and Political Power: A Case Study*. Boston: G. K. Hall, 1980.

Gardner, Carl. *Andrew Young: A Biography*. New York: Drake, 1978.

Garvey, Amy Jacques, ed. *The Philosophy and Opinions of Marcus Garvey*. New York: Atheneum, 1965.

Gilliam, Reginald E., Jr. *Black Political Development: An Advocacy Analysis*. Port Washington, N.Y.: Kennikat Press, 1975.

Glazer, Nathan. *Affirmative Discrimination: Ethnic Inequality and Public Policy*. New York: Basic Books, 1975.

Goldman, Peter L. *The Death and Life of Malcolm X*. New York: Harper & Row, 1973.

Gosnell, Harold F. *Negro Politicians: The Rise of Negro Politics in Chicago*. Chicago: University of Chicago Press, 1967.

Grant, Joanne, ed. *Black Protest: History, Documents, and Analyses, 1619 to the Present*. New York: Fawcett, 1968.

Greer, Edward. *Big Steel: Black Politics and Corporate Power in Gary, Indiana*. New York: Monthly Review Press, 1979.

————, ed. *Black Liberation Politics: A Reader*. Boston: Allyn and Bacon, 1971.

Gregory, Dick, and Robert Lipsyte. *Nigger: An Autobiography*. New York: E. P. Dutton, 1964.

————, and James R. McGraw. *The Shadow That Scares Me*. New York: Stein and Day, 1976.

Grier, William H., and Price M. Cobbs. *Black Rage*. New York: Basic Books, 1968.

Hamilton, Charles V. *The Bench and the Ballot: Southern Federal Judges and Black Voters*. New York: Oxford University Press, 1973.

————. *The Black Preacher in America*. New York: Morrow, 1972.

————, ed. *The Black Experience in American Politics*. New York: Putnam, 1973.

Hare, Nathan. *The Black Anglo-Saxons*. New York: Macmillan, 1970.

Haskins, James. *Adam Clayton Powell: Portrait of a Marching Black*. New York: Dial Press, 1974.

————. *A Piece of the Power: Four Black Mayors*. New York: Dial Press, 1972.

————. *Fighting Shirley Chisholm*. New York: Dial Press, 1975.

————. *Profiles in Black Power*. Garden City, N.Y.: Doubleday, 1972.

Hawley, Willis D. *Blacks and Metropolitan Governance: The Stakes of Reform*. Berkeley, Calif.: Institute of Governmental Studies, 1972.

Henderson, Lenneal J., Jr. *Administrative Advocacy: Black Administrators in Urban Bureaucracy*. Palo Alto, Calif.: R & E Research Associates, 1979.

————, ed. *Black Political Life in the United States*. San Francisco: Chandler, 1972.

Hickey, Neil, and Ed Edwin. *Adam Clayton Powell and the Politics of Race*. New York: Fleet, 1965.

Hine, Darlene Clark. *Black Victory: The Rise and Fall of the White Primary in Texas*. New York: KTO Press, 1979.

Holden, Matthew, Jr. *Politics of the Black "Nation"*. New York: Chandler, 1973.

————. *The White Man's Burden*. New York: Chandler, 1973.

Holloway, Harry. *The Politics of the Southern Negro: From Exclusion to Big City Organization*. New York: Random House, 1969.

Hughes, Langston. *Fight for Freedom: The Story of the NAACP*. New York: W. W. Norton, 1962.

Huie, William Bradford. *Three Lives for Mississippi*. New York: WCC Books, 1965.

Jack, Robert L. *History of the National Association for the Advancement of Colored People*. Boston: Meador, 1943.

Jackson, George. *Blood in My Eye*. New York: Random House, 1972.

————. *Soledad Brother: The Prison Letters of George Jackson*. New York: Coward-McCann, 1970.

Jackson, Jesse, and Elaine Landau. *Blacks in America: A Fight for Freedom*. New York: J. Messner, 1973.

Jacobs, Andy. *The Powell Affair: Freedom Minus One*. Indianapolis: Bobbs-Merrill, 1973.

Jamal, Hakim A. *From the Dead Level: Malcolm X and Me*. New York: Random House, 1972.

Johnson, James Weldon. *Along This Way: The Autobiography of James Weldon Johnson*. New York: Viking Press, 1933.

Jones, Edward H. *Blacks in Business*. New York: Grosset & Dunlap, 1971.

Jordan, June. *Fannie Lou Hamer*. New York: Thomas Y. Crowell, 1972.

Karnig, Albert K., and Susan Welch. *Black Representation and Urban Policy*. Chicago: University of Chicago Press, 1980.

Keech, William R. *The Impact of Negro Voting: The Role of the Vote in the Quest for Equality*. Chicago: Rand-McNally, 1969.

Kellogg, Charles Flint. *A History of the NAACP, 1909–1920*. Baltimore: Johns Hopkins Press, 1967.

Key, V. O., Jr. *Southern Politics in State and Nation*. New York: Random House, 1949.

Killian, Lewis M. *The Impossible Revolution?: Black Power and the American Dream*. New York: Random House, 1968.

King, Coretta Scott. *My Life with Martin Luther King, Jr.*, New York: Holt, Rinehart and Winston, 1969.

King, Martin Luther, Jr. *Stride Toward Freedom: The Montgomery Story*. New York: Harper & Row, 1958.

————. *The Trumpet of Conscience*. New York: Harper & Row, 1967.

————. *Where Do We Go From Here: Chaos or Community?* New York: Harper & Row, 1967.

————. *Why We Can't Wait*. New York: Harper & Row, 1964.

King, Mel. *Chain of Change: Struggles for Black Community Development*. Boston: South End Press, 1981.

Kluger, Richard. *Simple Justice: The History of Brown v. Board of Education and Black America's Struggle for Equality*. New York: Alfred A. Knopf, 1976.

Knowles, Louis L., and Kenneth Prewitt, eds. *Institutional Racism in America*. Englewood Cliffs, N.J.: Prentice-Hall, 1969.

Kugelmass, J. Alvin. *Ralph J. Bunche: A Fighter for Peace*. New York: J. Messner, 1952.

Ladd, Everett C., Jr. *Negro Political Leadership in the South*. New York: Atheneum, 1969.

Lawson, Steven F. *Black Ballots: Voting Rights in the South, 1944–1969*. New York: Columbia University Press, 1976.

Levine, Charles H. *Racial Conflict and the American Mayor: Power, Polarization, and Performance*. Lexington, Mass.: Lexington Books, 1974.

Levinsohn, Florence Hamlish. *Harold Washington: A Political Biography*. Chicago: Chicago Review Press, 1983.

Levitan, Sar A., William B. Johnston, and Robert Taggart. *Still a Dream: The Changing Status of Blacks Since 1960*. Cambridge, Mass.: Harvard University Press, 1975.

Lewis, Claude. *Adam Clayton Powell*. Greenwich, Conn.: Fawcett, 1963.

Lewis, David L. *King: A Critical Biography*. New York: Praeger, 1970.

Lewison, Paul. *Race, Class, and Party*. New York: Oxford University Press, 1931.

Lincoln, C. Eric. *The Black Muslims in America*. Boston: Beacon Press, 1973.

————. *Race, Religion, and the Continuing American Dilemma*. New York: Hill and Wang, 1984.

————. *Sounds of the Struggle: Persons and Perspectives in Civil Rights*. New York: Morrow, 1967.

————, ed. *Is Anybody Listening to Black America?* New York: Seabury Press, 1968.

————, ed. *Martin Luther King, Jr.: A Profile*. New York: Hill and Wang, 1970.

Logan, Rayford W. *The Negro in the United States*. New York: D. Van Nostrand, 1970.

————, ed. *W.E.B. DuBois: A Profile*. New York: Hill and Wang, 1971.

Lokos, Lionel. *House Divided: The Life and Legacy of Martin Luther King*. New Rochelle, N.Y.: Arlington House, 1969.

————. *The New Racism: Reverse Discrimination in America*. New Rochelle, N.Y.: Arlington House, 1971.

Lomax, Louis E. *The Negro Revolt*. New York: Harper & Row, 1962.

Lubell, Samuel. *White and Black: Test of a Nation*. New York: Harper & Row, 1964.

Malcolm X and Alex Haley. *The Autobiography of Malcolm X*. New York: Grove Press, 1964.

Marine, Gene. *The Black Panthers*. New York: New American Library, 1969.

Matthews, Donald R., and James W. Prothro. *Negroes and the New Southern Politics*. New York: Harcourt Brace & World, 1966.

McAdam, Doug. *Political Process and the Development of Black Insurgency, 1930–1970*. Chicago: University of Chicago Press, 1982.

McEvoy, James, and Abraham Miller. *Black Power and Student Rebellion*. Belmont, Calif.: Wadsworth, 1969.

McGriggs, Lee A. *Black Legislative Politics in Illinois: A Theoretical and Structural Analysis*. Washington, D.C.: University Press of America, 1977.

McKissick, Floyd B. *Three-Fifths of a Man*. New York: Macmillan, 1969.

McNeil, Genna Rae. *Groundwork: Charles Hamilton Houston and the Struggle for Civil Rights*. Philadelphia: University of Pennsylvania Press, 1983.

Meier, August. *Black Experience: The Transformation of Activism*. New York: E. P. Dutton, 1973.

———, and Elliott Rudwick. *CORE: A Study in the Civil Rights Movement, 1942–1968*. Urbana: University of Illinois Press, 1975.

———, and Elliott Rudwick, eds. *Along the Color Line: Explorations in the Black Experience*. Urbana: University of Illinois Press, 1976.

Meredith, James H. *Three Years in Mississippi*. Bloomington: Indiana University Press, 1966.

Metcalf, George R. *Up From Within: Today's New Black Leaders*. New York: McGraw-Hill, 1971.

Miller, Loren. *The Petitioners: The Story of the Supreme Court of the United States and the Negro*. New York: Pantheon Books, 1966.

Moody, Anne. *Coming of Age in Mississippi: An Autobiography*. New York: Dell, 1968.

Moon, Henry Lee. *Balance of Power: The Negro Vote*. Garden City, N.Y.: Doubleday, 1948.

Moreland, Lois B. *White Racism and the Law*. Columbus, Ohio: Charles E. Merrill, 1970.

Morris, Milton D. *The Politics of Black America*. New York: Harper & Row, 1975.

Muhammad, Elijah. *Message to the Blackman in America*. Chicago: Muhammad Mosque of Islam, No. 2, 1965.

Myrdal, Gunnar. *An American Dilemma: The Negro Problem and Modern Democracy*. New York: Harper & Row, 1944.

Naison, Mark. *Communists in Harlem During the Depression*. Urbana: University of Illinois Press, 1983.

Neary, John. *Julian Bond: Black Rebel*. New York: Morrow, 1971.

Nelson, Jack, and Jack Bass. *The Orangeburg Massacre*. New York: World, 1970.

Nelson, William E., Jr. and Philip J. Meranto. *Electing Black Mayors: Political Action in the Black Community*. Columbus: Ohio State University Press, 1977.

Newby, Idus A., ed. *The Development of Segregationist Thought*. Homewood, Ill.: Dorsey, 1968.

Newman, Dorothy K., et al. *Protest, Politics, and Prosperity: Black Americans and White Institutions, 1940–1975*. New York: Pantheon Books, 1978.

Newton, Huey P. *Revolutionary Suicide*. New York: Harcourt Brace Jovanovich, 1973.

———. *To Die for the People: The Writings of Huey P. Newton*. New York: Random House, 1972.

Nowlin, William F. *The Negro in American National Politics*. New York: Russell & Russell, 1970.

Oates, Stephen B. *Let the Trumpet Sound: The Life of Martin Luther King, Jr.* New York: Harper & Row, 1982.

Parris, Guichard, and Lester Brooks. *Blacks in the City: A History of the National Urban League*. Boston: Little, Brown, 1971.

Peck, James. *Freedom Ride*. New York: Simon and Schuster, 1962.

Peeks, Edward. *The Long Struggle for Black Power*. New York: Scribner, 1971.

Peltason, Jack W. *Fifty-eight Lonely Men: Southern Federal Judges and School Desegregation*. Chicago: University of Illinois Press, 1961.

Poinsett, Alex. *Black Power Gary Style: The Making of Mayor Richard Gordon Hatcher*. Chicago: Johnson, 1970.

Powell, Adam Clayton, Jr. *Adam by Adam: The Autobiography of Adam Clayton Powell, Jr.* New York: Dial Press, 1971.

———. *Keep the Faith, Baby!* New York: Trident Press, 1967.

———. *Marching Blacks: An Interpretive History of the Rise of the Black Common Man*. New York: Dial Press, 1973.

Powledge, Fred. *Black Power, White Resistance: Notes on the New Civil War*. Cleveland: World, 1967.

Preston, Michael B., Lenneal J. Henderson, Jr., and Paul Puryear, eds. *The New Black Politics: The Search for Political Power*. New York: Longman, 1982.

Quarles, Benjamin. *Black Abolitionists*. New York: Oxford University Press, 1969.

———. *Frederick Douglass*. Englewood Cliffs, N.J.: Prentice-Hall, 1968.

Rabinowitz, Howard N., ed. *Southern Black Leaders of the Reconstruction Era*. Urbana: University of Illinois Press, 1982.

Reynolds, Barbara A. *Jesse Jackson: The Man, The Movement, The Myth*. Chicago: Nelson-Hall, 1975.

Riles, Wilson C. *United States Urban Education Task Force*. New York: Praeger, 1970.

Ross, B. Joyce. *J. E. Spingarn and the Rise of the NAACP, 1911–1939*. New York: Atheneum, 1972.

Rowan, Carl T. *Go South to Sorrow*. New York: Random House, 1957.

———. *Just Between Us Blacks*. New York: Random House, 1974.

———. *South of Freedom*. New York: Alfred A. Knopf, 1952.

Rozier, John. *Black Boss: Political Revolution in a Georgia County*. Athens: University of Georgia Press, 1982.

Ruchelman, Leonard I., ed. *Big City Mayors: The Crisis in Urban Politics*. Bloomington: Indiana University Press, 1969.

Rustin, Bayard. *Down the Line: The Collected Writings of Bayard Rustin*. Chicago: Quadrangle Books, 1971.

———. *Strategies for Freedom: The Changing Patterns of Black Protest*. New York: Columbia University Press, 1976.

Satcher, Buford. *Blacks in Mississippi Politics, 1865–1900*. Washington, D.C.: University Press of America, 1978.

Schyler, George S. *Black and Conservative*. New Rochelle, N.Y.: Arlington House, 1966.

Seale, Bobby. *A Lonely Rage: The Autobiography of Bobby Seale*. New York: Times Books, 1978.

———. *Seize the Time: The Story of the Black Panther Party and Huey P. Newton*. New York: Random House, 1970.

Shoemaker, Don, ed. *With All Deliberate Speed*. New York: Harper & Row, 1957.

Silberman, Charles E. *Crisis in Black and White*. New York: Random House, 1964.

Sowell, Thomas. *Civil Rights: Rhetoric or Reality?* New York: William Morrow, 1984.

Stokes, Carl B. *Promises of Power: A Political Autobiography*. New York: Simon and Schuster, 1973.

Stone, Chuck. *Black Political Power in America*. Indianapolis: Bobbs-Merrill, 1968.

Strong, Donald S. *Negroes, Ballots, and Judges*. University: University of Alabama Press, 1968.

Taper, Bernard. *Gomillion v. Lightfoot: The Tuskegee Gerrymander Case*. New York: McGraw-Hill, 1962.

Thornbrough, Emma Lou. *Black Reconstructionists*. Englewood Cliffs, N.J.: Prentice-Hall, 1972.

———. *Booker T. Washington*. Englewood Cliffs, N.J.: Prentice-Hall, 1969.

Tussman, Joseph, ed. *The Supreme Court on Racial Discrimination*. New York: Oxford University Press, 1963.

Uhlman, Thomas M. *Racial Justice: Black Judges and Defendants in an Urban Trial Court*. Lexington, Mass.: Lexington Books, 1979.

Vincent, Theodore G. *Black Power and the Garvey Movement*. Berkeley, Calif.: Ramparts Press, 1971.

Vose, Clement E. *Caucasians Only: The Supreme Court, the NAACP, and the Restrictive Covenant Cases*. Berkeley: University of California Press, 1959.

Walton, Hanes, Jr. *Black Political Parties: An Historical and Political Analysis*. New York: Free Press, 1972.

———. *Black Politics: A Theoretical and Structural Analysis*. Philadelphia: Lippincott, 1972.

———. *Black Republicans: The Politics of the Black and Tans*. Metuchen, N.J.: Scarecrow Press, 1975.

———. *Invisible Politics: Black Political Behavior*. Albany: State University of New York Press, 1985.

———. *The Negro in Third Party Politics*. Philadelphia: Dorrance, 1969.

———. *The Political Philosophy of Martin Luther King, Jr*. Westport, Conn.: Greenwood Press, 1971.

Warner, Mary R. *The Dilemma of Black Politics: A Report on Harassment of Black Elected Officials*. Sacramento, Calif.: Mary R. Warner, 1977.

Washington, Booker T. *My Larger Education: Being Chapters from My Experience*. Garden City, N.Y.: Doubleday, 1911.

———. *The Negro in Business*. Boston: Hertel, Jenkins, 1907.

———. *Up From Slavery: An Autobiography*. New York: Doubleday, 1948.

Weaver, Robert C. *Dilemmas of Urban America*. New York: Atheneum, 1967.

Weinberg, Kenneth G. *Black Victory: Carl Stokes and the Winning of Cleveland*. Chicago: Quadrangle Books, 1968.

Weiss, Nancy J. *The National Urban League, 1910–1949*. New York: Oxford University Press, 1974.

———. *Farewell to the Party of Lincoln: Black Politics in the Age of FDR*. Princeton: Princeton University Press, 1983.

Westin, Alan F., ed. *Freedom Now!: The Civil Rights Struggle in America*. New York: Basic Books, 1964.

Wilkins, Roy, and Tom Matthews. *Standing Fast: The Autobiography of Roy Wilkins*. New York: Viking Press, 1982.

Williams, Walter E. *The State Against Blacks*. New York: New Press, 1982.

Wilson, James Q. *Negro Politics: The Search for Leadership*. Glencoe, Ill.: Free Press, 1960.

Wilson, William J. *The Declining Significance of Race: Blacks and Changing American Institutions*. Chicago: University of Chicago Press, 1978.

Woodward, C. Vann. *The Strange Career of Jim Crow*. New York: Oxford University Press, 1974.

Woody, Bette. *Managing Crisis Cities: The New Black Leadership and the Politics of Resource Allocation*. Westport, Conn.: Greenwood Press, 1982.

Wright, Nathan. *Black Power and Urban Unrest: Creative Possibilities*. New York: Hawthorn Books, 1967.

Young, Margaret B. *Black American Leaders*. New York: Franklin Watts, 1969.

Young, Richard P., ed. *Roots of Rebellion: The Evolution of Black Politics and Protest Since World War II*. New York: Harper & Row, 1970.

Young, Whitney M., Jr. *Beyond Racism: Building an Open Society*. New York: McGraw-Hill, 1972.

———. *To Be Equal*. New York: McGraw-Hill, 1964.

Zinn, Howard. *SNCC: The New Abolitionists*. Boston: Beacon Press, 1964.